CHARMING SMA...

BR

CHARMING SMALL HOTEL GUIDES

BRITAIN

Including Ireland

EDITED BY

Fiona Duncan & Leonie Glass

HUNTER
PUBLISHING

This new expanded and redesigned 2001 edition
conceived, designed and produced by
Duncan Petersen Publishing Ltd,
31 Ceylon Road, London W14 0PY

14th edition

Editorial Director Andrew Duncan
Editors Fiona Duncan & Leonie Glass
Production Editor Nicola Davies
Art Director Mel Petersen
Designers Christopher Foley
Beverley Stewart
Maps Map Creation Ltd

This edition published 2001 by
Duncan Petersen Publishing Ltd,
31 Ceylon Road, London W14 0PY

Sales representation and distribution in the U.K. and Ireland by
Portfolio Books Limited
Unit 5, Perivale Industrial Park
Horsenden South Lane
Greenford, UB6 7RL
Tel: 0208 997 9000 Fax: 0208 997 9097
E-mail: sales@portfoliobooks.com

A CIP catalogue record for this book is available
from the British Library

ISBN 1-903301-10-6

Published in the USA by
Hunter Publishing Inc.,
130 Campus Drive, Edison, N.J. 08818.
Tel (732) 225 1900 Fax (732) 417 0482

For details on hundreds of other travel guides and language courses, visit
Hunter's Web site at http://www.hunterpublishing.com

ISBN 1-58843-110-X

DTP by Duncan Petersen Publishing Ltd
Printed by Delo-Tiskarna, Slovenia

CONTENTS

INTRODUCTION

IN THIS INTRODUCTORY SECTION

Welcome to this 2000 edition of *Charming Small Hotel Guides* **Britain**. Partly as a nod to the new Millennium, but above all to improve the guide, we've introduced some big changes – more than ever before to a single edition:

• *Every hotel now has a colour photograph and a full page of its own. No more half-page entries without a photograph.*

• *Hotels which we consider particularly special are now marked *Editors' Choice*.*

• *The maps have been upgraded.*

• *The layout has been changed in order to take you more quickly to essential booking information.*

We hope that you will think these real improvements, rather than change for its own sake. In all other respects, the guide remains true to the values and qualities that make it unique (see opposite), and which have won it so many devoted readers. This is its fourteenth consecutive update since it was first published in 1986. It has sold hundreds of thousands of copies in the U.K., U.S.A. and in five European languages.

WHY ARE WE UNIQUE?

This is the only independently-inspected (no hotel pays for an entry) UK-originated accommodation guide that:

- has colour photographs for every entry;

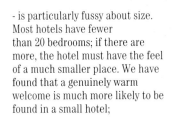

- concentrates on places that have real charm and character;

- is highly selective;

- is particularly fussy about size. Most hotels have fewer than 20 bedrooms; if there are more, the hotel must have the feel of a much smaller place. We have found that a genuinely warm welcome is much more likely to be found in a small hotel;

- gives proper emphasis to the description, and doesn't use irritating symbols;

- is produced by a small, non-bureauocratic company with a dedicated team of like-minded inspectors.

See also '*So what exactly do we look for?*', page 8.

So what exactly do we look for? – Our selection criteria

• A peaceful, attractive setting. Obviously, if the entry is in an urban area, we make allowances.

• A building that is handsome, interesting or historic; or at least with real character.

• Adequate space, but on a human scale. We don't go for places that rely too much on grandeur, or with pretensions that could be intimidating.

• Good taste and imagination in the interior decoration. We reject standardized, chain hotel fixtures, fittings and decorations.

• Bedrooms that look like real bedrooms, not hotel rooms, individually decorated.

• Furnishings and other facilities that are comfortable and well maintained. We like to see interesting antique furniture that is there to be used, not simply revered.

• Proprietors and staff who are dedicated and thoughtful, offering a personal welcome, but who aren't intrusive or overly effusive. *The guest needs to feel like an individual.*

• Interesting food. In Britain, it's increasingly the norm for food to be above average. There are few entries in this guide where the food is not of a high standard.

• A sympathetic atmosphere; an absence of loud people showing off their money; or the 'corporate feel'.

Dorset Square, London

A FATTER GUIDE, BUT JUST AS SELECTIVE

In order to accommodate every entry with a whole-page description and colour photograph, we've had to print more pages. *But we have maintained our integrity by keeping the selection to around 300 entries.*

Over the years, the number of charming small hotels in Britain has increased steadily – not dramatically. We don't believe that there are presently many more than about 300 truly charming small hotels in Britain, and that if we included more, we would undermine what we're trying to do: produce a guide which is all about places that are more than just a bed for the night. Every time we consider a new hotel, we ask ourselves whether it has that extra special something, regardless of category and facilities, that makes it worth seeking out.

TYPES OF ACCOMMODATION IN THIS GUIDE

Despite its title, this guide does not confine itself to places called hotels, or places that behave like hotels. On the contrary, we actively look for places that offer a home-from-home (see page 10). We include small and medium-sized hotels; pubs; inns; restaurants-with-rooms; guest-houses and bed-and-breakfasts. Some places, usually private homes which take guests, operate on house-party lines, where you are introduced to the other guests, and take meals at a communal table. If you don't like making small talk to strangers, or are part of a romantic twosome that wants to keep itself to itself, this type of establishment may not be for you. On the other hand, if you are interested in meeting people, perhaps as a foreign visitor wanting to get to know the locals, then you'll find it rewarding.

NO FEAR OR FAVOUR

To us, taking a payment for appearing in a guide seems to defeat the object of producing a guide. If money has changed hands, you can't write the whole truth about a hotel, and the selection cannot be nearly so interesting. This self-evident truth seems to us to be proved at least in part by the fact that pay guides are so keen to present the illusion of independence: few admit on the cover that they take payments for an entry, only doing so in small print on the inside.

Not many people realize that on the shelves of British book-

Priory Bay Hotel, Isle of Wight

shops there are many more hotel guides that accept payments for entries than there are independent guides. This guide is one of the few that do not accept any money for an entry.

HOME FROM HOME

Perhaps the most beguiling characteristic of the best places to stay in this guide is the feeling they give of being in a private home – but without the everyday cares and chores of running one. To get this formula right requires a special sort of professionalism: the proprietor has to strike the balance between being relaxed and giving attentive service. Those who experience this 'feel' often turn their backs on all other forms of accommodation – however luxurious.

OUR PET DISLIKES

Small hotels are not automatically wonderful hotels; and the very individuality of small, owner-run hotels makes them prone to peculiarities that the mass-produced hotel avoids. For the benefit of those who run the small hotels of Britain – and those contemplating the plunge – we repeat once more our list of pet hates.

The Hushed Dining-Room This commonly results when an establishment falls between the two stools of a really small place, where the owner makes sure that the ice is broken, and the not-so-small hotel, where there are enough people to create a bit of a hubbub.

The Ordinary Breakfast Even hotels that go to great lengths to prepare special dinners are capable of serving prefabricated orange juice and processed bread at breakfast.

The Schoolteacher Mentality People tempted to set up small hotels should perhaps undergo psychometric testing to determine whether they are sufficiently flexible and accommodating to deal with the whims of travellers; some of them certainly are not.

The Excess of Informality At one not-cheap London address (which did not find its way into the guide) we were shown around by a young man in jeans (which might be acceptable) and no socks (which is not). A recent reader's letter about an establishment (which has been dropped) recounted the owner greeting him in shabby gardening clothes, with a pack of unruly dogs at her heels. When she brought him tea, she was still in Wellington boots, and her hands were still encrusted with mud.

The Inexperienced Waiter Or waitress. Running a small operation does not excuse the imposition on the paying public of completely untrained (and sometimes ill-suited) staff who can spoil the most beautifully cooked meal.

The Imposing Name An unimportant one, this, but an irritant nonetheless. A charmingly cosy, whitewashed cottage in the Lake District does not, in our view, constitute a 'county house hotel'.

The Lumpy Old Bed Surely, every hotel proprietor knows that they should occasionally sleep in each of the beds in each of their rooms? Otherwise it's the easiest thing in the world to fail to spot the gradual decay of a mattress.

The Erratic Boiler There is nothing worse than arriving, chilled and tired, at your chosen destination, only to step into a tepid bath. Lashings of hot water (and generous towels, not drying-up cloths) are prerequisites.

CHECK THE PRICE FIRST

In this guide we have adopted the system of price bands, rather than giving actual prices as we did in previous editions. This is because prices were often subject to change after we went to press. The price bands refer to a standard double room (high season rates) with breakfast for two people. They are as follows:

£	under £70
££	£70 - £120
£££	£120 - £180
££££	over £180

To avoid unpleasant surprises, always check what is included in the price (for example, VAT and service, breakfast, afternoon tea) when making the booking.

HOW TO FIND AN ENTRY

In this guide, the entries are arranged in geographical groups. First, the whole of Britain and Ireland are divided into five major groups, starting with Southern England and working northwards to Scotland; Ireland comes last.

Within these major groups, the entries are grouped into smaller regional sub-sections such as the South-West, Wales, the Midlands, and the Highlands and Islands – for a full list, see page 5. Within each sub-section, entries are listed alphabetically by nearest town or village; if several occur in or near one town, entries are arranged in alpha order by name of hotel.

To find a hotel in a particular area, use the maps following this introduction to locate the appropriate pages.

To locate a specific hotel, whose name you know, or a hotel in a place you know, use the indexes at the back, which list entries both by name and by nearest place name. We have now included a third index which lists hotels by county; and the name of the county follows the town name in the heading for each entry.

HOW TO READ AN ENTRY

Name of hotel

Type of establishment

Description – never vetted by the hotel

Places of interest within reach of the hotel

This sets the hotel in its geographical context and should not be taken as precise instructions as to how to get there; always ask the hotel for directions.

Rooms described as having a bath may well also have a shower; rooms described as having a shower only have a shower.

Essential booking information.

This information is only an indication for wheelchair users and the infirm. Always check on suitability with the hotel.

THE SOUTH-WEST

EVERSHOT, DORSET

SUMMER LODGE
~ COUNTRY HOUSE HOTEL ~

Summer Lane, Evershot, Dorset DT2 0JR
TEL (01935) 83424 **FAX** (01935) 83005 **E-MAIL** sumlodge@sumlodge.demon.co.uk
WEBSITE www.relaischateaux.fr/summer

THE CORBETTS ARE the living evidence that not all 'professional' hoteliers are mediocre; we don't know what contribution they made to guests' happiness when they were at The Savoy, but the dedication they have applied to that cause since they escaped to Dorset is remarkable indeed. A recent inspection confirmed that their standards, and enthusiasm, remain unchanged. Our only quibble: the lack of a non-smoking sitting-room.

For many visitors, Summer Lodge is all that a country house hotel should be. The Georgian/Victorian building is on just the right scale to give a sense of slight extravagance without being intimidating, and the Corbetts and their staff are masters at making guests feel at home in it. French windows lead from the public rooms (William Morris fabrics, open fires) to the beautiful flowery garden. Charming bedrooms range from the merely delightful to the quite grand. Bathrooms are spacious and have large white fluffy towels.

The surrounding countryside has retained its rural beauty and there are many places of interest to visit, and some good pubs for lunch. The hotel's cream tea (included in half board rates) is a tempting reason to return there in the afternoon, and dinner remains a highlight.

~

NEARBY Minterne and Maperton Gardens; Parnham House; Montacute.
LOCATION 15 miles (24 km) NW of Dorchester, off A37 on edge of village; ample car parking
MEALS breakfast, lunch, dinner; room service
PRICE £££
ROOMS 17; 13 double, 3 single, 1 suite, all with bath; all rooms have phone, TV, hairdrier
FACILITIES dining-room, sitting-room, bar, reading-room, garden; croquet, heated swimming-pool, tennis court **CREDIT CARDS** AE, DC, MC, V
CHILDREN accepted **DISABLED** access good to ground-floor bedrooms
PETS accepted by arrangement (£5 per night) **CLOSED** never
PROPRIETORS Nigel and Margaret Corbett

Some or all the public rooms and bedrooms in an increasing number of hotels are now non-smoking. Smokers should check the hotel's policy when booking.

City, town or village, and county, in which the hotel is located.

Where children are welcome, there are often special facilities for them, such as high chairs, cots, baby-listening and high teas. Always check whether children are accepted in the dining-room.

Postal address and other key information.

Breakfast, either full English or continental, is normally included in the price of the room. We have not quoted prices for lunch and dinner. Other meals, such as afternoon tea, may also be available. 'Room service' refers to food and drink, either snacks or full meals, which can be served in the room.

We list the following credit cards:
AE   American Express
DC   Diners Club
MC   Mastercard
V   Visa

Always let the hotel know in advance if you want to bring a pet. Even where pets are accepted, certain restrictions may apply, and a small charge may be levied.

In this guide we have used price bands rather than quoting actual prices. They refer to a standard double room (high season rates, if applicable) with breakfast for two people. Other rates – for other room categories, times of the year, weekend breaks, long stays and so on – may well be available. In some hotels, usually out-of-the-way places or restaurants-with-rooms – half-board is obligatory. Always check when booking. The price bands are as follows:

£	under £70
££	£70 - £120
£££	£120 - £180
££££	over £180

REPORTING TO THE GUIDE

Please write and tell us about your experiences of small hotels, guest-houses and inns, whether good or bad, whether listed in this edition or not. As well as hotels in Britain and Ireland, we are interested in hotels in France, Italy, Spain, Austria, Germany, Switzerland and the U.S.A. We assume that reporters have no objections to our publishing their views unpaid.

Readers whose reports prove particularly helpful may be invited to join our Travellers' Panel. Members give us notice of their own travel plans; we suggest hotels that they might inspect, and help with the cost of accommodation.

The address to write to us is:

Editor, *Charming Small Hotel Guides*,
Duncan Petersen Publishing Limited,
31 Ceylon Road,
London W14 0PY.

Checklist
Please use a separate sheet of paper for each report; include your name, address and telephone number on each report.

Your reports will be received with particular pleasure if they are typed, and if they are organized under the following headings:

Name of establishment
Town or village it is in, or nearest
Full address, including postcode
Telephone number
Time and duration of visit
The building and setting
The public rooms
The bedrooms and bathrooms
Physical comfort (chairs, beds, heat, light, hot water)
Standards of maintenance and housekeeping
Atmosphere, welcome and service
Food
Value for money

We assume that in writing you have no objections to your views being published unpaid, either verbatim or in an edited version. Names of major outside contributors are acknowledged, at the editor's discretion, in the guide.

HOTEL LOCATION MAPS

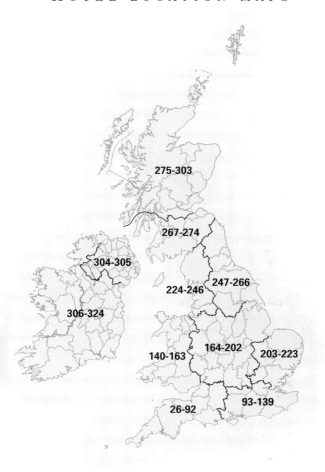

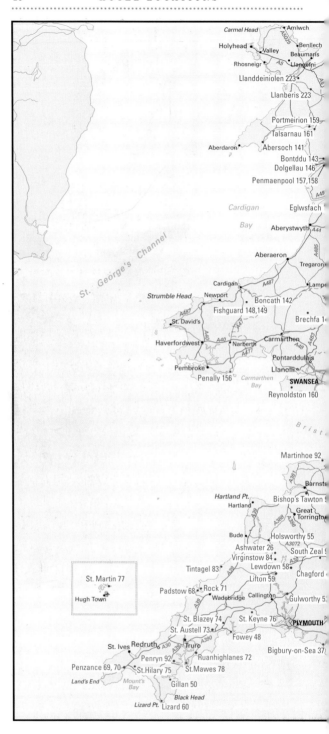

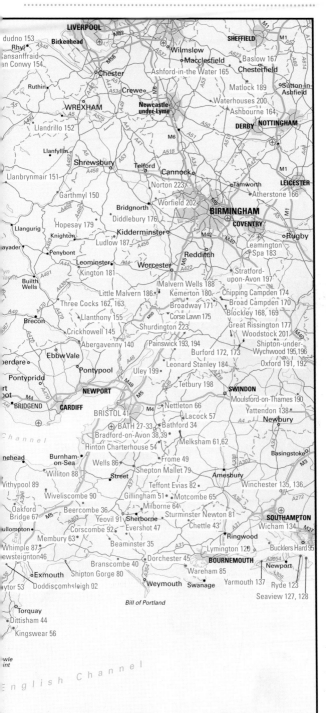

Bill of Portland

English Channel

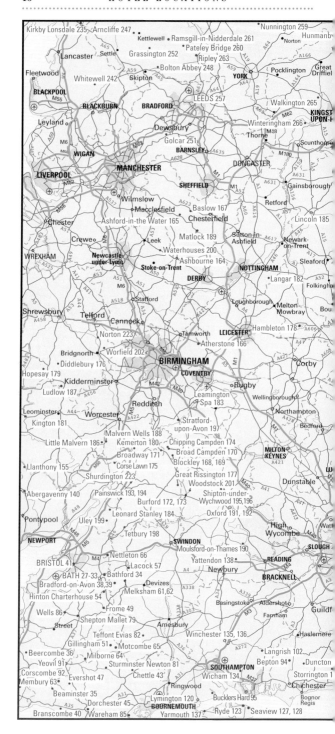

LONDON 104-119

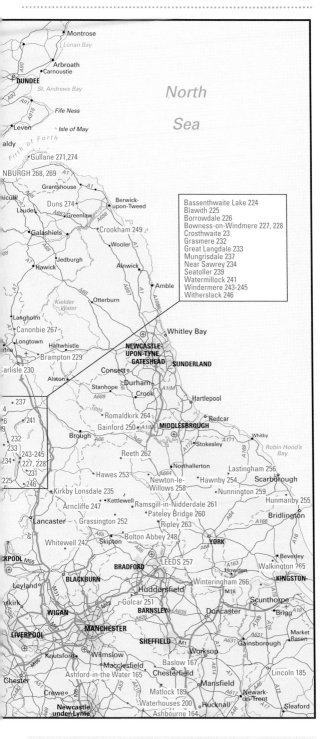

Bassenthwaite Lake 224
Blawith 225
Borrowdale 226
Bowness-on-Windmere 227, 228
Crosthwaite 23
Grasmere 232
Great Langdale 233
Mungrisdale 237
Near Sawrey 234
Seatoller 239
Watermillock 241
Windermere 243-245
Witherslack 246

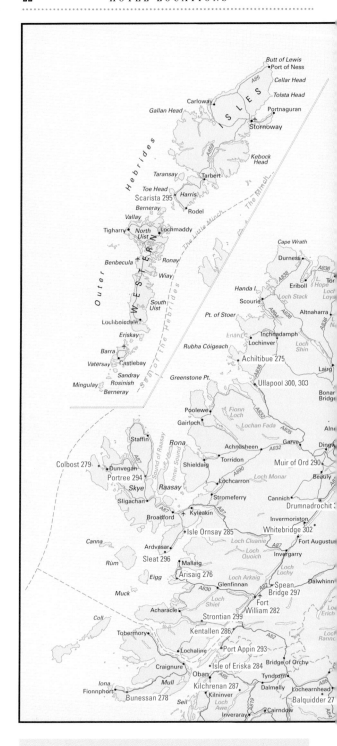

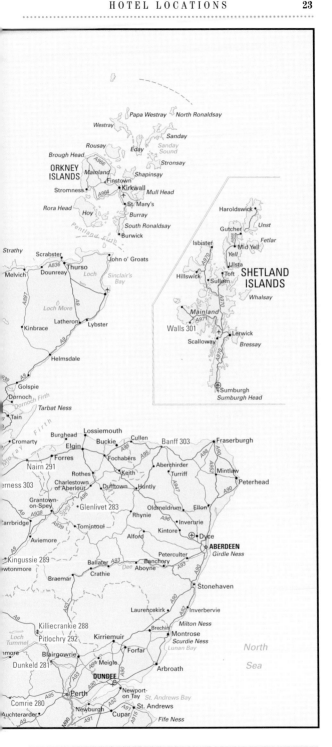

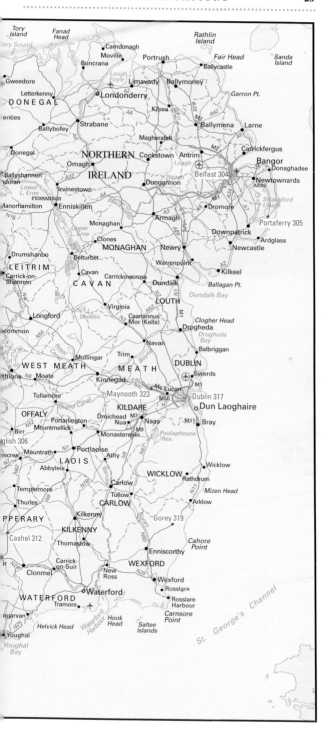

THE SOUTH-WEST

ASHWATER, DEVON

BLAGDON MANOR

~ COUNTRY HOUSE HOTEL ~

Ashwater, Beaworthy, Devon EX21 5DF
TEL (01409) 211224 **FAX** (01409) 211634 **E-MAIL** stay@blagdon.com
WEBSITE: www.blagdon.com

DON'T BE PUT OFF by Blagdon Manor's isolated situation: it lies plum in the middle of the West Country, so no place of interest is really very far away.

This Grade II-listed former farmhouse, surrounded by rolling country-side, was derelict when Tim and Gill Casey discovered it on their return, in 1991, from Hong Kong, where they had spent many years. Having brought the building back to life, they opened it as a hotel in 1994. Their determination to succeed and attention to detail are evident everywhere, from the home-made jams and bowls of fresh fruit to the shortbread in the bedrooms and Belgian chocolates with the coffee.

Bedrooms are deliciously pretty and comfortable, with fluffy towels and crisp linen and plenty of thoughtful extras in the bathrooms. The dramatic dining-room is dominated by a vast table and incredibly heavy matching chairs made specially in the Far East. The 'easy listening' music may not be to everyone's taste, but overall this is a relaxing small-scale hotel/guest-house, with near-faultless standards of service and delicious food: though entirely self-taught, Gill is a gifted cook of professional ability, and the food is beautifully presented. And some of her culinary products are available to take home as gifts.

~

NEARBY National Trust coast; golf courses.
LOCATION just off A388 Launceston-Holsworthy road, 4 miles (6.5 km) S of Holsworthy, in 20 acres; ample parking and helicopter pad
MEALS breakfast, dinner
PRICE ££
ROOMS 7; 5 double, 2 twin, all with bath; all rooms have phone, TV, hairdrier
FACILITIES sitting-room, library, dining-room, bar/snooker-room, terrace, garden; practice golf course, croquet **CREDIT CARDS** AE, MC, V **CHILDREN** welcome over 12
DISABLED access difficult **PETS** not accepted **CLOSED** Christmas
PROPRIETORS Tim and Gill Casey

THE SOUTH-WEST

BATH

APSLEY HOUSE

~ TOWN HOTEL ~

Newbridge Hill, Bath, Avon BA1 3PT
TEL (01225) 336966 **FAX** (01225) 425462 **E-MAIL** info@apsley-house.co.uk
WEBSITE www.apsley-house.co.uk

ONCE UPON A TIME this was a grand house with huge grounds leading down to the River Avon. It was built for the Duke of Wellington in 1830, thus missing the flourishing Georgian period for which Bath is famous. The grounds were sold off long ago to make way for the houses which now surround Apsley House, leaving enough garden to ensure privacy for the occupants.

There are, however, still remnants of its eminent past within, from the grand sweeping staircase to the high ceilings of the spacious rooms. There is a large, comfortable drawing-room for guests' use, as well as a licensed bar. Since taking over Apsley House four years ago, David and Annie Lanz have updated the bedrooms and bathrooms with the help of an interior designer, added a few antique pieces and hung large reproduction oils on the walls. Bedroom No. 9 is fashioned from the old kitchen, complete with bread oven and a splendid marble fireplace.

On the minus side, books from *Reader's Digest* and old back issues of *Hello* and *Country Life* in the bedrooms, and constant piped music in the public rooms, mar an otherwise stylish hotel. Even so, business is so brisk that the Lanzes no longer live on the premises and have invested in another hotel, Paradise House, on the other side of the city.

~

NEARBY Bath centre.
LOCATION on A431 to NW of city; ample car parking
MEALS breakfast
PRICE ££
ROOMS 9 double, 8 with bath, 1 with shower; all rooms have phone, TV, hairdrier
FACILITIES sitting-room, bar, breakfast-room, garden **CREDIT CARDS** AE, DC, MC, V
CHILDREN welcome
DISABLED access difficult **PETS** not accepted
CLOSED Christmas
PROPRIETORS David and Annie Lanz

THE SOUTH-WEST

BATH

BARROW CASTLE

~ TOWN GUEST-HOUSE ~

Rush Hill, Bath, Avon BA2 2QR
TEL (01225) 480725

BARROW CASTLE has been in Liz Hall's family for over 100 years. Built in 1850, the creeper-clad Victorian building is hidden up a winding drive on the southern outskirts of Bath, yet only five minutes by car from the centre. The interior is most pleasing. The spacious drawing-room is prettily painted in soft yellows, with polished antique furniture and a fine collection of modern pictures. The only ornaments in this guest-house are family silver, a refreshing change from the tortured dried flower arrangements and collections of dolls that decorate so many. With its warm red walls complementing the antique pine, the breakfast-room also serves as a dining-room for guests who have booked dinner in advance, while the bedrooms are soothingly painted in eau-de-nil, dusty pinks, soft blues. A confection of a brass bed, which looks as though it was made for a pharaoh, in fact came from France. Most of the rooms have sweeping views over the countryside to the Bristol Channel and beyond. The huge gardens are mostly laid to lawn, with some superb specimen trees dotted here and there. The conservatory is a riot of greenery and water, completing the picture of a Victorian estate aeons away from today's hustle. Mrs Hall talks of selling Barrow Castle, so check before you go.

~

NEARBY Bath.
LOCATION next to Culverhay School, 3 miles (5 km) SW of Bath centre; in 30 acres of grounds, with car parking
MEALS breakfast; dinner by arrangement
PRICE ££
ROOMS 3; 1 double with bath en suite, 1 double with bath adjacent, 1 twin with shower; all rooms have TV
FACILITIES sitting-room, breakfast-room, terrace, garden
CREDIT CARDS not accepted **CHILDREN** accepted
DISABLED access difficult **PETS** not accepted
CLOSED Christmas and New Year
PROPRIETOR Liz Hall

THE SOUTH-WEST

BATH

BATH PRIORY
◇ EDGE-OF-CITY HOTEL ◇

Weston Road, Bath, Avon BA1 2XT
TEL (01225) 331922 **FAX** (01225) 448276/480725
E-MAIL bathprioryhotel@compuserve.com **WEBSITE** www.slh.com/thepriory

UNLIKE MANY OF ITS BREED of manicured country house hotels with health spas, the Bath Priory has a feeling of small-scale intimacy – which makes it, we feel, appropriate for our guide, despite the high prices.

Within walking distance of the centre, the hotel is shielded from the suburbs of Bath by a large park-like garden, while inside, the atmosphere of a gracious country house has been artfully created. The 'superior' bedrooms are seriously comfortable and very pretty (particularly Carnation with a four-poster in palest green silk, and Orchid, with an oriental theme).

Chef Robert Clayton has gained a Michelin star for his cooking, inspired by Nico Ladenis, and dinner is served in an intimate, candlelit room hung with oil paintings. Sink side by side into the deliciously squashy, red velvet banquette, and don't miss the risotto – of lobster, perhaps, or wild mushroom. When you aren't exploring Bath, you can curl up in front of the drawing-room fire, attended by a discreet fleet of charming ladies and white-aproned French waiters, or slip downstairs to the health spa for a beauty treatment, a session in the well-equipped gym, and a swim in the inviting and elegant indoor pool.

◇

NEARBY Bath centre.
LOCATION 1 mile (1.5 km) W of centre; in grounds with parking
MEALS breakfast, lunch, dinner; room service
PRICE ££££
ROOMS 28; 22 double and twin, 5 suites, 1 single, all with bath; all rooms have phone, TV, fax/modem point, hairdrier
FACILITIES drawing-room, 2 dining-rooms, library, indoor swimming-pool, leisure centre, gym, lift, terrace, garden; croquet, outdoor swimming-pool
CREDIT CARDS AE, DC, MC, V **CHILDREN** accepted
DISABLED 1 bedroom on ground floor specially adapted **PETS** not accepted
CLOSED 1 week in early Jan
MANAGER Tim Pettifer

THE SOUTH-WEST

BLOOMFIELD HOUSE

~ TOWN GUEST-HOUSE ~

16 Bloomfield Road, Bath, Avon BA2 2AS
TEL (01225) 420105 **FAX** (01225) 481954 **E-MAIL** bloomfieldhouse@compuserve.com
WEBSITE www.bloomfield-house.co.uk

EVEN THE BLANK WINDOWS overlooking the car park have been painted with *trompe l'oeil* books and flowers, hinting at the visual treats in store for the visitor to Bloomfield House. The rounded hall, with hand-painted fresco of flowers and peacocks, positively confirms the initial impression that this is somewhere out of the ordinary.

Bridget and Malcolm Cox bought Bloomfield House seven years ago from a talented producer of opera and his architect partner who had poured money and artistry into the Georgian building. The Coxes have wisely kept the grand interior they inherited – decorative paint finishes, French crystal chandeliers, superb heavy silk curtains – but they continue to update and add their own touches.

There was a seductive smell of oranges when our inspector called as the Coxes were both busy making marmalade for their guests' breakfasts, served in the elegant dining-room overlooking the garden. The bedrooms are beautifully decorated and, although not all can be described as spacious, they are without exception comfortable. Furniture is antique and fine, but not so refined that guests feel intimidated. In the evening, you can help yourself to sherry and relax in one of the gold damask-covered armchairs in the drawing-room in front of the fire. In summer, a seat in the garden makes a peaceful alternative, with views across Bath.

~

NEARBY Bath centre.
LOCATION off A367 to S of city; limited private, ample street parking
MEALS breakfast
PRICE ££
ROOMS 8; 6 double, 3 with bath en suite, 3 with separate bath, 1 twin with bath, 1 single with bath; all rooms have phone, TV, hairdrier
FACILITIES sitting-room, dining-room, terrace, garden **CREDIT CARDS** MC, V
CHILDREN accepted over 8 **DISABLED** access difficult **PETS** not accepted **CLOSED** never
PROPRIETORS Bridget and Malcolm Cox

THE SOUTH-WEST

BATH

FOURTEEN RABY PLACE
∼ TOWN GUEST-HOUSE ∼

14 Raby Place, Bath, Avon BA2 4EH
TEL (01225) 465120 **FAX** (01225) 465283

BATH HAS MORE THAN ITS FAIR SHARE of hotels and guest-houses that exact a heavy toll from the many visitors who come to view the Roman Baths and splendid Georgian architecture. The few that manage to keep their prices reasonable are usually either far from the centre, or uninspiring, and we don't know of any that can match Muriel Guy's delightful Georgian house on the lower slopes of Bathwick Hill.

The house is in a typical Bath terrace, single-fronted, and not overly spacious. The railway runs close behind too, but offset these minor detractions against the price, comfort and richly decorated interior, and you will soon be persuaded by its advantages.

Mrs Guy is an inveterate traveller and collector, who has furnished her home with mementoes of her travels. Bedrooms are tastefully done in an interesting mix of colours and styles: white Portuguese bedcovers, crewel work curtains, embroidered peasant materials and handsome rugs are used to great effect throughout. Books on every conceivable subject fill the shelves, adding to the cosmopolitan feel of the place.

Breakfast (only organic produce is served) is taken around a large mahogany table in the kitchen/dining-room. Don't automatically expect bacon with your free-range eggs – it has to be specially requested. Smoking is not allowed.

∼

NEARBY Bath centre.
LOCATION on E side of city; street parking
MEALS breakfast
PRICE £
ROOMS 4; 2 double, both with shower, 1 twin with separate shower, 1 family room with bath; all rooms have TV
FACILITIES dining-room, garden **CREDIT CARDS** not accepted
CHILDREN accepted **DISABLED** not suitable **PETS** not accepted **CLOSED** never
PROPRIETOR Muriel Guy

THE SOUTH-WEST

BATH

LETTONIE

RESTAURANT-WITH-ROOMS

35 Kelston Road, Bath, Avon BA1 3QH
TEL (01225) 446676 **FAX** (01225) 447541
WEBSITE www.bath.co.uk/lettonie

SINCE MOVING from Bristol in 1997, Lettonie has established itself as a serious restaurant on the flourishing Bath scene. Siân Blunos has a somewhat stiff front-of-house manner, although it is probably due to a natural reserve, and the initial impression is not eased by the formally grouped leather chairs in the drawing-room.

There is plenty of humour in Martin's food, however: a tiny, succulent sirloin steak topped with a morsel of *foie gras*, accompanied by miniscule chips and an onion marmalade; 'boiled egg with soldiers' which are unmasked as eggshell filled with mango sorbet and vanilla cream, and 'soldiers' made of shortbread fingers. His cooking is theatrical in presentation and tastes sublime. The staff, mainly French, are charming. Although a local, Martin's origins are Latvian and so we find on the menu *blinis* and caviar, served with vodka, and *borscht*. Be sure to book: the restaurant is often full.

The house is Georgian, overlooking the Avon Valley, and a night spent in one of the four bedrooms is most welcome after one of Martin's special eight-course gourmet dinners. Decorated in soft colours, they are well furnished and have decent-sized bathrooms en suite. Continental breakfast, with home-made croissants, brioches and *pain raisin*, is served in the rooms.

NEARBY Bath centre.
LOCATION 2 miles (3 km) W of city centre on A431; ample car parking
MEALS breakfast, lunch, dinner
PRICE £££
ROOMS 4 double, all with bath; all rooms have phone, TV, hairdrier
FACILITIES sitting-room, restaurant, private dining-room, terrace, garden
CREDIT CARDS AE, DC, MC, V **CHILDREN** welcome **DISABLED** access difficult
PETS not accepted **CLOSED** 2 weeks in Jan and Aug; Sun and Mon
PROPRIETORS Siân and Martin Blunos

THE SOUTH-WEST

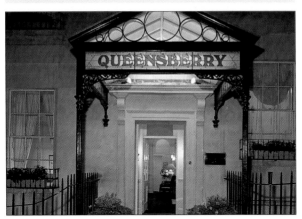

QUEENSBERRY
~ TOWNHOUSE HOTEL ~

Russel Street, Bath, Avon BA1 2QF
TEL (01225) 447928 **FAX** (01225) 446065
E-MAIL queensberry@dial.pipex.com

THIS BATH HOTEL is slightly large for our purposes, but cannot be allowed to escape the net. Its owners, Stephen and Penny Ross, opened it in 1988 and transformed three Georgian terraced houses into one of the most sophisticated and yet personal places to stay in the city. When we visited in early 2000, the hotel staff were on a high: the Queensberry had just been voted 'Hotel and Restaurant of the Millennium' by *The Times*.

The Queensberry is a discreet, quiet and beautifully decorated haven right in the centre of Bath. It has the advantage of a lift to all levels, which cuts down on confusion in the maze of stairwells and corridors which link the three buildings. Despite the small-scale appearance of the hotel, the majority of the bedrooms are surprisingly spacious, and are kitted out to the highest standards of comfort and elegance. Double beds generally mean king-size here, almost guaranteed to give you a good night's sleep, and made up with lovely cotton sheets. Rooms on the first floor are largest, with armchairs and breakfast tables; bathrooms are lavish, with quality toiletries and proper towels.

Downstairs, the principal sitting-room is beautifully furnished in muted colours. The hotel's relaxed basement restaurant, the Olive Tree, has a life of its own: it's one of the most popular places to eat in Bath.

~

NEARBY Assembly Rooms; Museum of Costume; The Circus.
LOCATION in middle of city, close to main shopping area; paved gardens behind; daytime car parking restricted
MEALS breakfast, lunch, dinner; room service
PRICE £££
ROOMS 22 double, all with bath; all rooms have phone, TV, hairdrier
FACILITIES sitting-room, bar, restaurant. lift, courtyard **CREDIT CARDS** MC, V
CHILDREN welcome **DISABLED** access possible
PETS not accepted **CLOSED** Christmas
PROPRIETORS Stephen and Penny Ross

THE SOUTH-WEST

BATHFORD, AVON

EAGLE HOUSE

~ VILLAGE GUEST-HOUSE ~

Church Street, Bathford, Bath, Avon BA1 7RS
TEL (01225) 859946 **FAX** (01225) 859430 **E-MAIL** jonap@eagleho.demon.co.uk
WEBSITE www.bath.co.uk/eaglehouse

A STALWART OF OUR GUIDE, Eagle House provides a tranquil alternative to the bustle of staying in nearby Bath. Despite its outwardly grand Georgian exterior – the house was designed by John Wood the Elder – this is above all a family home, where John and Ros Napier go out of their way to provide a relaxed welcome to their guests.

Aquila, the black Labrador, wanders about, and toys are readily available for the children, yet John's early training at The Ritz underpins informality with an innate professionalism. Personal service is the watchword here, but not in the nannying sense. As there is no licence to serve alcohol, the Napiers are quite happy for people to bring their own to drink in the large, elegant drawing-room hung with family heirloom portraits which include Mary Queen of Scots and Charles I and II.

The bedrooms are decorated in pretty wallpapers and comfortably furnished in country style. There is also the option of the Walled Garden Cottage for those who value complete privacy. Equipped with kitchen, sitting-room and two bedrooms each with bath, guests can still have breakfast in the main house. As ever at Eagle house, there is no pressure.

~

NEARBY Bath.
LOCATION 2.5 miles (4 km) E of Bath, off A363, in village; in 2-acre gardens, with ample car parking
MEALS breakfast
PRICE ££
ROOMS 8; 4 double with bath, 2 single with shower, 2 family with bath; all rooms have phone, TV, hairdrier
FACILITIES 2 sitting-rooms, breakfast-room, garden; lawn tennis, croquet
CREDIT CARDS MC, V
CHILDREN welcome
DISABLED access difficult **PETS** accepted **CLOSED** I0 days over Christmas
PROPRIETORS John and Rosamund Napier

The South-West

BEAMINSTER, DORSET

BRIDGE HOUSE
~ COUNTRY HOTEL ~

Beaminster, Dorset DT8 3AY
TEL (01308) 862200 **FAX** (01308) 863700

DATING FROM THE 13TH CENTURY, Bridge House is reputedly a former monastery or clergy house and the oldest building in Beaminster. Whatever its antecedents, it is certainly a venerable and charming building and has been run as a hotel by Peter Pinkser and his wife for the past 14 years. He is ex-Navy, very jovial, and says he looks on Bridge House as a hobby. All the signs, however, are of a professional operation.

The sitting-room and bar areas are cheerfully decorated in cherry and green tartans; daughter Ann Pinkser's paintings, some of which are for sale, hang on the cream walls. Lunch and dinner are served in the pretty pink-panelled dining-room or the conservatory which looks out on to the walled gardens. Linda Pagett has recently been promoted to chef, having been with the Pinkser's for over three years as *sous-chef*. Young and enthusiastic, her cooking is beginning to make waves in an area blessed with quality local produce: fish, meat and cheese all come from nearby. Bread, biscuits, ice-cream and chocolates are all made in the Bridge House kitchens; even the marmalade that accompanies the satisfying breakfasts is made on the premises.

Bedrooms are all different, as would be expected in a building so full of nooks and crannies, with a priest's hole to boot. Those in the converted coach house are more modern, but equally comfortable.

~

NEARBY Parnham House; Mapperton Gardens.
LOCATION on B3163 in centre of town; ample car parking
MEALS breakfast, dinner
PRICE ££
ROOMS 14; 12 double and twin, 1 family all with bath, 1 single with shower; all rooms have phone, TV
FACILITIES sitting-room, bar, restaurant, conservatory, walled garden
CREDIT CARDS AE, DC, MC, V **CHILDREN** accepted
DISABLED 4 bedrooms with easy access **PETS** accepted **CLOSED** never
PROPRIETOR Peter Pinkser

THE SOUTH-WEST

BEERCROCOMBE, SOMERSET

FROG STREET FARM

FARM GUEST-HOUSE

Beercrocombe, Taunton, Somerset TA3 6AF
TEL & FAX (01823) 480430

VERONICA COLE has been running her farmhouse retreat, a flower-bedecked 'longhouse' hidden deep in the Somerset countryside, for over 20 years now. Her husband has recently leased the farmland and is now able to give Veronica a helping hand.

The house has considerable character and warmth, with a handsome oak-beamed inglenook in the sitting-room and some very antique panelling. Guests walk through the front door straight in to the highly polished dining-room. Veronica, an accomplished cook, makes as much as she possibly can for her carefully-prepared set dinner menus, from soups to ice-creams. Eggs come from her own hens, vegetables from the organic garden, beef from the farm. The couple also own a successful National Hunt stable, and horse-racing features prominently in their lives. The stables at the back of the farm invariably hold a variety of brood mares, hunters and young horses, guarded by the farm collie.

Bedrooms look out on to farmland, cider apple orchards and the pretty garden. They are all spacious and comfortable, with floral duvets, and a mix of antique furniture. One is virtually self-contained, having its own staircase and sitting-room, separated from the shared sitting-room by superb Jacobean panelling. The atmosphere is friendly, restful and unpretentious.

NEARBY Barrington Court; Vale of Taunton.
LOCATION on SW side of village, 10 miles (16 km) SE of Taunton; in gardens, with ample parking
MEALS breakfast, dinner
PRICE £
ROOMS 3 double, 2 with bath, 1 with shower; all rooms have hairdrier
FACILITIES 3 sitting-rooms, dining-room, terrace, garden **CREDIT CARDS** not accepted
CHILDREN accepted over 11
DISABLED not suitable **PETS** not accepted **CLOSED** Nov to Mar
PROPRIETOR Veronica Cole

THE SOUTH-WEST

BIGBURY-ON-SEA, DEVON

BURGH ISLAND
~ ISLAND HOTEL ~

Bigbury-on-Sea, Devon TQ7 4BG
TEL (01548) 810514 **FAX** (01548) 810243 **E-MAIL** reception@burghisland.ndirect.co.uk
WEBSITE www.burghisland.ndirect.co.uk

FOR GUESTS ARRIVING AFTER SUNSET, tiny Burgh Island is dominated by what appears to be an illuminated cruise liner, topped by a Chinese pagoda. Guests are advised to alert staff of their imminent arrival; the sea tractor is then sent across the spit of sand which, when the tide is out, separates the hotel from the mainland.

Yes: staying at Burgh Island is an experience, best savoured by those of a theatrical bent and a love of Art Deco. Once the haunt of Edward and Mrs Simpson, Noel Coward and Earl Mountbatten, the hotel also provided the setting for two of Agatha Christie's novels. Some 15 years ago Beatrice and Tony Porter restored the building to its former pre-war glory with passion and authenticity. Now it serves honeymooning couples, holiday-makers and weekenders who soak up the raffish atmosphere of the Thirties as appreciatively as they do the cocktails. Cooking, although competent, makes less of an impact than the decoration, and even that can be a little frayed at the edges; but the staff try hard to please. The ballroom doubles as a grand dining-room, where, on Saturday nights, a band plays melodies of the period and guests play their part by donning black tie. It's not everyone's cup of tea, but it is romantic and out of the ordinary.

~

NEARBY Torquay; Buckfast Abbey; Polperro.
LOCATION on own 26-acre island off Bigbury-on-Sea, on B3392; parking in secure parking area; free transport by sea tractor or landrover to island
MEALS breakfast, lunch, dinner; room service
PRICE £££
ROOMS 14 suites, all with bath; all rooms have phone, TV, hairdrier
FACILITIES bar, sun lounge, dining-room, ballroom, lift, sauna, terrace, garden; tennis **CREDIT CARDS** AE, DC, MC, V **CHILDREN** welcome
DISABLED no special facilities **PETS** not accepted **CLOSED** weekdays Jan, Feb
PROPRIETORS Beatrice and Tony Porter

THE SOUTH-WEST

BRADFORD-ON-AVON, WILTSHIRE

BRADFORD OLD WINDMILL
~ TOWN GUEST-HOUSE ~

4 Masons Lane, Bradford-on-Avon, Wiltshire BA15 1QN
TEL (01225) 866842 **FAX** (01225) 866648

ALTHOUGH IT FUNCTIONED as a windmill only briefly, the Roberts's extraordinary home was built as one (in 1807). It now appears something of a folly, with its four-storey Cotswold stone tower, conical tiled roof, pointed Gothic windows and restored sail gallery.

The sitting-room (cosy, round, with a log fire and books) and the principal bedroom each occupy a whole floor of the old tower. Bedrooms are romantic. A suite with minstrel gallery has views across parkland to the White Horse at Westbury. One room has a round bed, another a waterbed. The Roberts travel far and wide, and the house is crammed with curiosities from around the globe.

There is a pretty terrace overlooking old Bradford, where breakfast and dinner are served, weather permitting. Breakfast is taken at a communal table, but special provision is made for honeymoon couples who wish to eat late and alone.

Priscilla will cook dinner if given notice – you will encounter Mexican, Thai, Nepalese and other exotic influences. A soup tray is provided if dinner is unavailable. This is a very different kind of guest-house, and one with great character. See also our other windmill B&B on page 207.

~

NEARBY Bath; Kennet and Avon Canal.
LOCATION just N of town centre; with cottage garden and parking for 3 cars
MEALS breakfast, dinner (Mon, Thur, Sat only)
PRICE ££
ROOMS 3; 2 double, 1 with bath, 1 with shower; 1 suite; all rooms have TV
FACILITIES sitting-room, dining-room
CREDIT CARDS AE, DC, MC, V
CHILDREN welcome over 6
DISABLED access difficult
PETS not accepted **CLOSED** Jan, Feb, Christmas
PROPRIETORS Peter and Priscilla Roberts

THE SOUTH-WEST

BRADFORD-ON-AVON, WILTSHIRE

PRIORY STEPS
~ TOWN GUEST-HOUSE ~

Newtown, Bradford-on-Avon, Wiltshire BA15 1NQ
TEL (01225) 862230 **FAX** (01225) 866248

HIGH ABOVE the lovely little wool town of Bradford-on-Avon, Carey and Diana Chapman's converted row of weavers' cottages look out over the predominantly Georgian houses interspersed with a smattering of Saxon and medieval buildings. Although only three minutes walk from the centre, Priory Steps is not easy to find. It is so discreetly signposted that it looks like a private home – which it is for the Chapmans and their children. As a result, the pictures and pieces that decorate the house have family connections and the atmosphere is informal and easy-going, especially in the book-lined sitting-room.

Each of the bedrooms has a theme – Indian, Chinese and so on. In spite of the cottage architecture, there is nothing cramped about them: they are light and airy, with wonderful views. Beautifully decorated by Diana's mother-in-law, each has its own character and is furnished mainly with antiques.

Diana is a keen cook and dinner is served either at a communal table in the elegant dining-room or, on fine days, out on the terrace of the garden looking down over the town. Dinners are three courses, with no choice, but special requirements are happily met, given notice. You will be made to feel like a house guest in a particularly well-run home. 'A really lovely place,' writes our reporter.

~

NEARBY Barton Tithe Barn; Bath.
LOCATION off A363 on N side of town; in 0.5-acre garden, with car parking
MEALS breakfast, dinner
PRICE ££
ROOMS 5 double and twin, all with bath; all rooms have TV
FACILITIES sitting-room, dining-room, terrace, garden
CREDIT CARDS MC, V
CHILDREN accepted **DISABLED** access difficult **PETS** not accepted
CLOSED occasionally **PROPRIETORS** Carey and Diana Chapman

THE SOUTH-WEST

BRANSCOMBE, DEVON

MASONS ARMS

~ SEASIDE VILLAGE INN ~

Branscombe, Devon EX12 3DJ
TEL (01297) 680300 **FAX** (01297) 680500

BRANSCOMBE IS A PICTURESQUE little Devon village, at the end of a winding lane, surrounded by steep, wooded hillsides and overlooking the sea. The National Trust owns most of the land around, and the South Devon Coastal Path passes through it. In other words, this village is a hive of activity, inspiring visits from walkers in winter and beachcomers in summer, many of whom pitch up at the Masons Arms. Welcoming, yes; popular, certainly. It's just what a village pub should be, although its success has meant that the owners have expanded to meet the demand. So what was a simple inn, converted from four cottages, now has two restaurants (one non-smoking), a large function room, four self-catering units, eight Garden Cottages, and 19 bedrooms in the main building.

The bedrooms have a cottagey feel, with pretty fabrics, beamed ceilings and sloping floors, Ones without bathrooms en suite can mean a trek down a dark corridor, carpeted in something left over from the Fifties, to a mean-looking set of plumbing contraptions, but, hey, it's all part of the atmosphere. The bathrooms in the Cottages are, conversely, slickly modern. Food is good pub grub, with the restaurants offering a more up-market, and, therefore, more costly, menu. As long as you aren't expecting a superabundance of silence or suavity, then the Masons Arms will do.

~

NEARBY South Devon Coastal Path; Sidmouth.
LOCATION in village 8 miles (12 km) S of Honiton, off A3052 between Sidmouth and Seaton; with ample car parking
MEALS breakfast, lunch, dinner
PRICE £-££
ROOMS 19; 16 double, twin and family with bath en suite, 3 with separate bath; self-catering cottages; all rooms have phone, TV; some have hairdrier
FACILITIES sitting-room, bar, restaurants, terrace, garden
CREDIT CARDS MC, V **CHILDREN** welcome
DISABLED access easy to self-catering cottages **PETS** accepted
CLOSED never **PROPRIETORS** Murray Ingles and Christopher Painter

THE SOUTH-WEST

BRISTOL

HOTEL DU VIN
~ TOWN HOTEL ~

The Sugar House, Narrow Lewins Mead, Bristol, Avon BS1 2NU
TEL (0117) 925 5577 **FAX** (0117) 925 1199 **E-MAIL** admin@bristol.hotelduvin.co.uk
WEBSITE www.hotelduvin.co.uk

AFTER ITS REJUVENATING appearances first in Winchester and then in Tunbridge Wells, the Hotel du Vin, concept of hotelier Robin Hutson and wine expert Gérard Basset, has most recently brought style and panache to the hotel scene in Bristol. Converted from a collection of derelict 18thC sugar warehouses, the hotel's gracious Queen Anne frontage belies the wizardry behind its façade. Open brickwork, black-painted girders and sweeping stairs with a curving steel bannister combine traditional industrial elements with contemporary glamour to great effect.

Sponsored by and named after different wine houses, the huge bedrooms contain custom-made, superbly comfortable beds, alongside equally huge bathrooms with dazzling showers and free-standing baths. Though it fronts on to Bristol's main thoroughfare, the hotel's double glazing effectively blocks any traffic noise. Many of the staff who serve in the hotel's Bistro have been imported from the sister hotels at Winchester and Tunbridge Wells, and are well versed in the Hotel du Vin's ethos of relaxed, unpretentious service of imaginative dishes cooked with a sure hand. The aptly-named Sugar Bar is dominated by a large mural of grapes on the vine, while whitewashed walls, big squashy sofas, wood flooring and rugs contribute to the unhurried, plantation house feel.

~

NEARBY city centre; docks; Christmas steps.
LOCATION in city centre, with car parking and garages
MEALS breakfast, lunch, dinner
PRICE ££
ROOMS 40 double and twin, all with bath; all rooms have phone, TV, CD player, minibar, hairdrier
FACILITIES sitting-room, billiards-room, dining-room, bar, humidor, lift, courtyard
CREDIT CARDS AE, DC, MC, V **CHILDREN** accepted
DISABLED access possible **PETS** accepted by arrangement
CLOSED never **PROPRIETORS** Robin Hutson, Gérard Basset and Peter Chittick

THE SOUTH-WEST

CHAGFORD, DEVON

GIDLEIGH PARK

~ COUNTRY HOUSE HOTEL ~

Chagford, Devon TQ13 8HH
TEL (01647) 432367 **FAX** (01647) 432574 **E-MAIL** gidleighpark@gidleigh.co.uk
WEBSITE www.gidleigh.com

THIS QUINTESSENTIAL COUNTRY HOUSE HOTEL, created 25 years ago by Americans Paul and Kay Henderson, has a low-key, very British appeal. It's all about ticking clocks and curled-up Siamese cats, and enveloping, understated luxury. Take your walking boots and your Labrador and prepare for the very rich, highly-praised cooking of Michael Caines (which merits two Michelin stars) and Paul Henderson's legendary wine cellar. For complete seclusion, take the Thatched Cottage that stands in the grounds.

On the edge of Dartmoor, lost in woods, the house is situated at the end of a long, bumpy, tree-lined lane which opens out to present an idyllic park setting. Behind the house are attractive terraced gardens, giving way to woods; in front, the rocky River Teign.

Inside, the oak-panelled sitting-room is large, with a log fire and comfortable furniture, and well stocked with current magazines and periodicals. Bedside books include volumes of Ted Hughes' poetry (he lived nearby and was a frequent visitor). All the bedrooms give an immediate feeling of comfort and friendliness. Two especially attractive ones are next to the main building in a converted chapel. If you are prepared to pay its heart-stoppingly high prices, you will find Gidleigh Park above all relaxing and friendly.

~

NEARBY Castle Drogo; Dartmoor; Rosemoor, Knighthayes Court Gardens.
LOCATION 2 miles (3 km) W of Chagford; in 45 acre-grounds with ample car parking
MEALS breakfast, lunch, dinner; room service
PRICE ££££
ROOMS 14 double, all with bath; 1 cottage in the grounds; all rooms have phone, TV, hairdrier **FACILITIES** sitting-room, bar, loggia, 2 dining-rooms, garden; croquet, fishing, tennis, bowls, putting **CREDIT CARDS** DC, MC, V
CHILDREN accepted **DISABLED** no special facilities **PETS** welcome
CLOSED never **PROPRIETORS** Paul and Kay Henderson

THE SOUTH-WEST

CASTLEMAN
~ COUNTRY HOUSE HOTEL ~

Chettle, near Blandford Forum, Dorset, DT11 8DB
TEL (01258) 830096 **FAX** (01258) 830051

CHETTLE IS ONE OF THOSE RARE estate villages that has hardly changed in the 150 years it has been in the benign ownership of one family – who live in the fine Queen Anne manor house, open to the public during summer months. Teddy Bourke, one of the family, took on the decrepit ex-dower house ("locals all thought it was haunted") in 1996, together with his partner, Barbara Garnsworthy, transforming it into a charmingly eccentric and very reasonably priced hotel and restaurant. Part of the building dates back 400 years, but it was much altered in Victorian times when it was tricked out with a galleried hall; a richly carved oak Jacobean fireplace was also installed in one of the reception rooms (the other is Regency style) with bookcases to match. Upstairs, the elegant proportions of the rooms have been left intact, and bedrooms are just right: comfortable and in good taste, but without room service or unnecessary frills so as to keep prices sensible; several of the bathrooms have Victorian roll-top baths. The 'large' rooms are enormous, one with a huge bay window overlooking the fields, while the smaller ones are still spacious. The garden could do with some love.

The Castleman's restaurant – a long, rather plain room at the rear – serves straightforward traditional and modern British dishes – and the bill is not indigestible, either. "Superb value", say regular guests.

~

NEARBY Kingston Lacy House; Cranborne Chase; Salisbury.
LOCATION in village, signposted off A354, 6 miles (9.5 km) NE of Blandford Forum; ample car parking
MEALS breakfast, Sunday lunch, dinner
PRICE ££
ROOMS 8 double, all with bath; all rooms have phone, TV, hairdrier
FACILITIES dining-room, 2 sitting-rooms, bar, garden **CREDIT CARDS** MC, V
CHILDREN welcome **DISABLED** access difficult
PETS not accepted in house; 2 stables available for guests' horses and dogs
CLOSED Feb **PROPRIETORS** Edward Bourke and Barbara Garnsworthy

THE SOUTH-WEST

DITTISHAM, DEVON

FINGALS

~ MANOR HOUSE HOTEL ~

Old Coombe Manor Farm, Dittisham, near Dartmouth, Devon TQ6 0JA
TEL (01803) 722398 **FAX** (01803) 722401 **E-MAIL** richard@fingals.co.uk
WEBSITE www.fingals.co.uk

FINGALS IS DIFFERENT, and those who love it will really love it – which sums up why we remain enthusiastic about this manor farmhouse in a secluded valley, close to the River Dart. Owner Richard Johnston, calls it a 'hotel and restaurant', but in practice, Fingals comes much closer to the 'country house party' type of guest-house, where it is normal (though not obligatory) for guests to share a table in the wood-panelled dining-room at mealtimes.

The house – 17thC with Queen Anne front additions – has plenty of charm, with a stylish blend of new and old furniture, pine and oak. An adjacent self-catering barn is ideal for a family or for those wanting extra space and privacy.

Fingals is an exceptionally relaxed place – you pour your own drinks, eat breakfast whenever you like, be it morning or afternoon – and those who insist on everything being just so are likely to be disappointed. The four-course dinners, chosen from a short menu, are modern in style, competent in execution, and ample in quantity. A laid-back place with a laid-back, yet thoroughly professional, proprietor. ~

NEARBY Dartmouth Castle.
LOCATION 4 miles (6.5 km) N of Dartmouth, 1 mile (1.5 km) from village; with garden and ample car parking
MEALS breakfast, snack lunch, dinner
PRICE ££
ROOMS 13; 11 double, 10 with bath, 1 with shower, 2 family rooms with bath; all rooms have phone; some have TV
FACILITIES dining-room, bar, library, TV room; swimming-pool, jacuzzi, sauna, snooker, croquet, tennis, table tennis, sailboat available
CREDIT CARDS AE, MC, V
CHILDREN accepted **DISABLED** access difficult **PETS** accepted, but not in public rooms
CLOSED New Year to Easter **PROPRIETOR** Richard Johnston

THE SOUTH-WEST

DORCHESTER, DORSET

CASTERBRIDGE

~ TOWN HOTEL ~

49 High East Street, Dorchester, Dorset DT1 1HU
TEL (01305) 264043 **FAX** (01305) 260884 **E-MAIL** reception@casterbridgehotel.co.uk
WEBSITE www.casterbridgehotel.co.uk/

YOU MIGHT EASILY drive straight past the Casterbridge, assuming it to be just another one of those dreary country town hotels which seem to dominate British high streets. However, when you learn that it is owned and run by the brother of John Turner of The Priory (see page 85) you might stop and wisely think again. The hotel has been in the Turner family since 1930, but in the 1980s family scion Stuart and wife Rita took it over and started on the monumental task of updating its moribund interior.

They succeeded in bringing life to an old Georgian building that remains faithful to its origins, but incorporates the modern touches we all crave; above all it is a very comfortable place in which to stay. A drawing-room has been decorated in soft blue-greys and pink, with several large, pleasing oil paintings and an abundance of reading matter. The Georgian furniture is all in keeping. A well-stocked bar next door leads into a delightful conservatory and to a little courtyard with fountain beyond.

Unlike The Priory at Wareham, the Casterbridge only offers bed and breakfast. The bedrooms are prettily decorated, with delightful wallpapers, quality fabrics and pleasant bathrooms. Bedrooms in the modern annexe beyond the courtyard are equally comfortable, but have less charm than those in the main building. The Turners are charming hosts and happy to help their guests.

~

NEARBY Hardy country; Dorset coast.
LOCATION on main road in NE side of town; limited street parking
MEALS breakfast
PRICE ££
ROOMS 18; 14 double, 4 single, all with bath or shower; all rooms have phone, TV, hairdrier
FACILITIES sitting-room, bar, conservatory/breakfast-room
CREDIT CARDS AE, DC, MC, V **CHILDREN** welcome
DISABLED 2 rooms on ground floor **PETS** not accepted
CLOSED Christmas Day and Boxing Day **PROPRIETORS** Stuart and Rita Turner

THE SOUTH-WEST

DREWSTEIGNTON, DEVON

HUNTS TOR

~ VILLAGE RESTAURANT-WITH-ROOMS ~

Drewsteignton, near Exeter, Devon EX6 6QW
TEL & **FAX** (01647) 281228

HUNTS TOR IS an interesting building off the main square of a small and peaceful village. Close to Lutyens' 19thC pile, Castle Drogo, the village is on the edge of Dartmoor, with superb walking from the door. Run in a low-key way by Chris and Sue Harrison, who quit the rat race back in 1985, it makes an excellent place in which to stay for a night or two, and to enjoy good food. When we last revisited, we noted again how well the Harrisons had restored the house, a compact 17thC building with Regency additions, and a glass-roofed porch stretching across the front. It is furnished in a distinctive style, indulging the Harrisons' affection for Art Deco and Art Nouveau, with a mixture of modern and Victorian furniture. There are two dining-rooms, one with a low beamed ceiling and plenty of house plants, the other a much more informal room with an original woodblock floor and huge open fireplace. Here guests eat communally around a large oak table. Bedrooms are simple and neat, and – especially for the price – huge, two with sitting-rooms and one a sitting area. One reader says they "could be more lively", another that they are "smart".

Sue's food has gained a red 'M' from Michelin, and is 'beautifully cooked and presented'. Dinner is four courses, with no choices, though you can discuss preferences when you book. Excellent local cheeses to finish.

~

NEARBY Castle Drogo; Dartmoor National Park.
LOCATION on village square, 12 miles (19 km) W of Exeter; with private parking for 2 cars and street parking on main square
MEALS breakfast, dinner
PRICE ££
ROOMS 3; 2 double, 1 twin, all with bath; all rooms have TV, hairdrier
FACILITIES 2 dining-rooms (1 with bar), sitting-room
CREDIT CARDS not accepted **CHILDREN** accepted over 10
DISABLED access difficult **PETS** accepted in bedrooms **CLOSED** Nov to Mar
PROPRIETORS Sue and Chris Harrison

THE SOUTH-WEST

EVERSHOT, DORSET

SUMMER LODGE
~ COUNTRY HOUSE HOTEL ~

Summer Lane, Evershot, Dorset DT2 0JR
TEL (01935) 83424 **FAX** (01935) 83005 **E-MAIL** sumlodge@sumlodge.demon.co.uk
WEBSITE www.relaischateaux.fr/summer

THE CORBETTS ARE the living evidence that not all 'professional' hoteliers are mediocre; we don't know what contribution they made to guests' happiness when they were at The Savoy, but the dedication they have applied to that cause since they escaped to Dorset is remarkable indeed. A recent inspection confirmed that their standards, and enthusiasm, remain unchanged. Our only quibble: the lack of a non-smoking sitting-room.

For many visitors, Summer Lodge is all that a country house hotel should be. The Georgian/Victorian building is on just the right scale to give a sense of slight extravagance without being intimidating, and the Corbetts and their staff are masters at making guests feel at home in it. French windows lead from the public rooms (William Morris fabrics, open fires) to the beautiful flowery garden. Charming bedrooms range from the merely delightful to the quite grand. Bathrooms are spacious and have large white fluffy towels.

The surrounding countryside has retained its rural beauty and there are many places of interest to visit, and some good pubs for lunch. The hotel's cream tea (included in half board rates) is a tempting reason to return there in the afternoon, and dinner remains a highlight.

~

NEARBY Minterne and Maperton Gardens; Parnham House; Montacute.
LOCATION 15 miles (24 km) NW of Dorchester, off A37 on edge of village; ample car parking
MEALS breakfast, lunch, dinner; room service
PRICE £££
ROOMS 17; 13 double, 3 single, 1 suite, all with bath; all rooms have phone, TV, hairdrier
FACILITIES dining-room, sitting-room, bar, reading-room, garden; croquet, heated swimming-pool, tennis court **CREDIT CARDS** AE, DC, MC, V
CHILDREN accepted **DISABLED** access good to ground-floor bedrooms
PETS accepted by arrangement (£5 per night) **CLOSED** never
PROPRIETORS Nigel and Margaret Corbett

THE SOUTH-WEST

FOWEY, CORNWALL

FOWEY HALL

~ SEASIDE FAMILY HOTEL ~

Hanson Drive, Fowey, Cornwall PL23 1ET
TEL (01726) 833866 **FAX** (01726) 834100

FOR A HOLIDAY HOTEL which caters to the whims of children and adults in equal measure, look no further than Fowey Hall. The owners are adept practitioners of the formula, with three similar establishments, Woolley Grange in Bradford-on-Avon, The Old Bell in Malmesbury, and Moonfleet Manor near Weymouth under their belts. The idea is to keep the children happy with a long list of activities, and adults likewise content with good food and luxurious accommodation.

On a hill overlooking Fowey Harbour, the imposing building was allegedly Kenneth Grahame's inspiration for Toad Hall in *The Wind in the Willows*. Built over 100 years ago by a former Lord Mayor of London, it is a turreted white mansion with the feel of a small French château and none of the oppressiveness associated with Victorian domestic architecture. Public rooms are warm and welcoming, some with log fires, and most with a view over the harbour. There are two dining-rooms, one in the style of a Palm Court, which serves a brasserie menu, the other an elegant adult-only affair. Bedrooms are impressively furnished with the needs of a family in mind; those with sitting areas in the turrets are great fun for children. During the day, parents can relax, while their offspring cavort in the Den and the Bear Pit, staffed by nannies.

~

NEARBY Fowey; Looe.
LOCATION at the top of the town; ample car parking
MEALS breakfast, lunch, dinner; room service
PRICE £££
ROOMS 25; 14 double and twin, 11 suites, all with bath; all rooms have phone, TV, hairdrier
FACILITIES 2 dining-rooms, sitting-room, TV-room, video games-room, indoor swimming-pool, crèche, games-room, terrace, garden; croquet, badminton
CREDIT CARDS AE, DC, MC, V **CHILDREN** accepted
DISABLED access possible **PETS** accepted **CLOSED** never
PROPRIETORS Nigel Chapman and Nicholas Dickinson

THE SOUTH-WEST

FROME, SOMERSET

BABINGTON HOUSE
~ COUNTRY HOUSE HOTEL ~

Babington, near Frome, Somerset BA11 3RW
TEL (01373) 812266 **FAX** (01373) 812112
E-MAIL babhouse@compuserve.com

BABINGTON WAS THE BRIGHT IDEA of Nick Jones, owner of the trendy Soho Club in London, and bought as a country retreat for club members. There is still talk about 'members' and 'non-members' but in practice anyone can stay here, although it might be better if you were young, or at least young at heart, street-wise, and preferably in the media business. Having said that, everyone is made to feel welcome, in an atmosphere which is so laid-back that it's almost horizontal, yet at the same time professional (much helped by the manager, Bodo, who has run some of London's finest hotels). If you are tired of stuffy country house hotels, with too many swags and drapes and no concessions to children, you will find Babington enormously refreshing: a contemporary hotel set in an elegant country house that offers metropolitan chic and unpretentious luxury. Bedrooms are wonderful, with huge bottles of complimentary lotions in the bathrooms (no mean sachets here) and 24-hour room service. You can have any number of beauty treatments in the Cow Shed, where there is also an indoor pool and a gym. Small children are kept occupied in the well-equipped crèche. We would particularly welcome feedback on Babington: how does it feel staying here if your face doesn't fit?; how did you cope with life in the bar/sitting-room?
~

NEARBY Bath; Bradford-on-Avon.
LOCATION in countryside, 15 miles (24 km) S of Bath; ample parking
MEALS breakfast, lunch, dinner; room service
PRICE ££££
ROOMS 22 double and twin, all with bath; all rooms have phone, TV, DVD player, CD player, fax/modem point, minibar, hairdrier
FACILITIES sitting-room/bar, snooker-room, dining-room, bistro, computers, indoor swimming-pool, health club, crèche, cinema, terrace, garden; tennis court
CREDIT CARDS AE, DC, MC, V **CHILDREN** welcome
DISABLED bedrooms on ground floor and adapted WC **PETS** accepted
CLOSED never **PROPRIETOR** Nick Jones

THE SOUTH-WEST

GILLAN, CORNWALL

TREGILDRY

~ SEASIDE HOTEL ~

Gillan, Manaccan, Helston, Cornwall TR12 6IIG
TEL (01326) 231378 **FAX** (01326) 231561

GETTING TO TREGILDRY through twisting country lanes is something of a challenge; it's well off the beaten track and you should be sure to ask the hotel for directions before you set out. What's special about it? Certainly not the pebble-dashed building itself, which owners Lynne and Huw Phillips readily agree is unexciting. The view, on the other hand, is unforgettable. On a high point above The Lizard Peninsula, Tregildry commands a magical panorama over the Helford River and Falmouth Bay.

Lynne and Huw could do little to change the exterior, beyond painting it, but they have transformed the interior, which could never be called unexciting. It's all very sunny, using bright, bold colours such as apricots and yellows, with rattan and Indonesian furniture lending a vaguely colonial look. The bedrooms are attractive and well equipped, and they all have views of the sea, though No 3, with its double aspect, is the favourite. Behind the hotel, a footpath leads down to what is effectively a private beach – a great bonus.

Our inspector, visiting for the first time (the hotel is new to the guide this year), commented on the helpfulness and professionalism of its owners, and also enjoyed Huw's (Modern British) cooking.

~

NEARBY National Trust coast; golf courses.
LOCATION just off A388 Launceston–Holsworthy road, 4 miles (6.5 km)
S of Holsworthy, in 20 acres; ample parking and helicopter pad
MEALS full breakfast, dinner; full licence
PRICES ££
ROOMS 5 double, 2 twin, all with bath; all rooms have central heating, phone, TV, radio, tea/coffee kit, hairdrier
FACILITIES sitting-room, library, dining-room, bar/snooker-room, terrace; practice golf course, croquet
CREDIT CARDS AE, MC, V **CHILDREN** welcome over 12
DISABLED access difficult **PETS** not accepted **CLOSED** Christmas
PROPRIETORS Huw and Lynne Phillips

THE SOUTH-WEST

GILLINGHAM, DORSET

STOCK HILL HOUSE
~ COUNTRY HOUSE HOTEL ~

Gillingham, Dorset SP8 5NR
TEL (01747) 823626 **FAX** (01747) 825628 **E-MAIL** reception@stockhill.net
WEBSITE www.stockhill.net

THIS RESTORED VICTORIAN MANOR HOUSE, reached up a long drive through wooded grounds, has been immaculately furnished and decorated in individual, opulent and somewhat heavy turn-of-the-century style by its hands-on owners, the Hausers, who have been at the helm for the past 15 years. Bedrooms are luxurious, and although the atmosphere is definitely formal (ties must be worn at dinner) one is relieved to discover that it is also genuinely warm and friendly. Three of the bedrooms are in a separate coach house, and are more contemporary in style.

Peter Hauser does all the cooking and produces superb results. His Austrian roots are reflected in the varied, generous menu, which changes daily. Fruit and vegetables come from his impressive walled kitchen garden. While he works away in the kitchen, guests are apt to pop in for a chat or to see what he is planning for dinner that evening. Many of the hotel's staff are recruited from Germany and they are attentive and friendly.

The extensive grounds include formal gardens and a tennis court. More reports would be appreciated.

NEARBY Shaftesbury; Stourhead House and Gardens.
LOCATION 5 miles (8 km) NW of Shaftesbury on B3081; in 10-acre grounds with ample car parking
MEALS breakfast, lunch, dinner
PRICE ££££
ROOMS 10; 9 double, 8 with bath, 1 with shower, 1 single, with bath; all rooms have TV, phone, hairdrier
FACILITIES sitting-room, dining-room, breakfast-room, garden; tennis court, croquet, trout fishing, putting green **CREDIT CARDS** AE, DC, MC, V
CHILDREN welcome over 7 **DISABLED** 1 suite on ground floor
PETS not accepted **CLOSED** never; restaurant closed Sat and Mon lunch
PROPRIETORS Peter and Nita Hauser

The South-West

Gulworthy, Devon

Horn of Plenty
~ Country restaurant-with-rooms ~

Gulworthy, Tavistock, Devon PL19 8JD
Tel & Fax (01822) 832528

The Horn of Plenty has long featured in the pages of this guide, despite the several changes of ownership which it has undergone in recent years. Readers' letters told us that the standard of the bedrooms was not high enough during the last regime, but a recent inspection reassured us that the enthusiastic new owners, Paul and Andie Roston, had largely put things right.

Built in 1830 by the Marquess of Tavistock, the secluded, creeper-covered house is approached down a short avenue of tall trees and has a splendid location overlooking the Tamar Valley, a view shared by the bedrooms, some of which have small terraces. The majority are in a converted coach house 50 yards from the main house; they are comfortable and well equipped, decorated in modern style, with light floral fabrics and pine furniture and a host of minor luxuries. Best, however, are the two rooms above the restaurant in the main house which the Rostons have recently refurbished.

The Horn of Plenty is primarily a restaurant, and dinner is the main event, skilfully prepared by chef Peter Gorton (well-known now, thanks to a recent television series) and served in front of picture windows in the two-part dining-room.

Nearby Cotehele House; Dartmoor; Plymouth.
Location 3 miles (5 km) W of Tavistock on A390; wtih ample car parking
Meals breakfast, lunch, dinner
Price £££
Rooms 8; 6 double and twin, 4 with bath, 2 with shower, 2 suites with bath; all rooms have phone, TV, video, minibar, hairdrier
Facilities sitting-room, bar, restaurant, terrace, garden
Credit Cards AE, MC, V **Children** accepted **Disabled** 2 suitable bedrooms
Pets accepted **Closed** Christmas
Proprietors Paul and Andie Roston

THE SOUTH-WEST

HAYTOR, DEVON

BEL ALP HOUSE
～ COUNTRY HOTEL ～

Haytor, near Bovey Tracey, Devon TQ13 9XX
TEL (01364) 661217 **FAX** (01364) 661292

PEACEFULLY SET IN eight lush acres, this is a fine, white-painted Edwardian house high above Haytor, enjoying magnificent views over a patchwork of fields and woodland, and the rolling foothills of Dartmoor.

Bel Alp House was once owned by the tobacco millionairess Dame Violet Wills; with its present owners, Jack and Mary Twist, who came here three years ago, it has fallen into very caring hands. We are delighted that they have fulfilled the much needed promise they made when they took to upgrading the bedrooms and improving all the facilities. Consequently, the guest rooms, which are furnished and decorated with an emphasis on quiet, restful colours, are now among the largest and most comfortable that you are likely to come across. "Our smallest room", according to Jack, has an area double the size of many hotel bedrooms. Bathrooms are equally spacious, with modern fittings, except for the two which feature original Edwardian basins and baths mounted on marble plinths.

Public rooms are light and airy, with large bay windows looking south over the moor. Dinner comprises a set menu, with a few daily changing choices. A quiet, steady place. A recent visitor enthuses about the food and the warm welcome.

～

NEARBY Haytor Rocks; Lustleigh; Dartmoor National Park; Castle Drogo; Torquay.
LOCATION in countryside, E of Haytor, 2.5 miles (4 km) W of Bovey Tracey off B3387; ample car parking
MEALS breakfast, lunch by arrangement, dinner
PRICE ££
ROOMS 8 double and twin, all with bath; all rooms have phone, TV, hairdrier
FACILITIES 2 sitting-rooms, dining-room, garden
CREDIT CARDS AE, DC, MC, V
CHILDREN accepted **DISABLED** access possible
PETS accepted **CLOSED** Christmas and New Year
PROPRIETORS Jack and Mary Twist

THE SOUTH-WEST

HINTON CHARTERHOUSE, AVON

HOMEWOOD PARK

~ COUNTRY HOUSE HOTEL ~

Hinton Charterhouse, Bath, Avon BA3 6BB
TEL (01225) 723731 **FAX** (01225) 723820 **E-MAIL** enquiries@homewoodpark.com
WEBSITE www.homewoodpark.com

HOMEWOOD PARK has been in these pages for over a decade and has
undergone several changes of ownership in this time, most recently,
in 1998. It used to be in the hands of Stephen and Penny Ross (now at the
Queensberry – see page 33). Frank Gueuning continues to manage
Homewood Park using the same formula of mixing the informal with the
solicitous in supremely elegant surroundings.

The large Georgian building is surrounded by award-winning gardens
and parkland. Flowers from the garden and the restored greenhouses are
used to decorate the hotel. Bedrooms are individually decorated in country house style – matching curtains, bedcovers and canopied bedheads in
soft prints – while in the bathrooms Italian tiles and stencilling give a
slightly exotic air.

In the Michelin-starred restaurant, chef, Nigel Godwin, offers pan fried
scallops and langoustines, seasonal game and mouthwatering desserts, or
a selection of cheeses with homemade fig and walnut bread.

Some recent comments from visitors imply that the hotel has 'lost its
spark', with bedrooms which are beginning to look tired. We would welcome further reports.

~

NEARBY American Museum; Bath.
LOCATION 5 miles (8 km) S of Bath, close to A36; in 10-acre grounds with ample
car parking
MEALS breakfast, lunch, dinner; room service
PRICE £££
ROOMS 17 double, 2 suites, all with bath; all rooms have phone, TV, hairdrier
FACILITIES sitting-room, bar, 3 dining-rooms, garden; tennis, croquet, outdoor
heated swimming-pool
CREDIT CARDS AE, DC, MC, V **CHILDREN** welcome
DISABLED access easy; 2 ground-floor bedrooms **PETS** not accepted **CLOSED** never
PROPRIETOR A. Moxon

THE SOUTH-WEST

HOLSWORTHY, DEVON

◆ EDITORS' CHOICE ◆

COURT BARN

~ COUNTRY HOUSE HOTEL ~

Clawton, Holsworthy, Devon EX22 6PS
TEL (01409) 271219 **FAX** (01409) 271309
E-MAIL ctbarn@bestloved.com

COURT BARN LACKS any trace of stuffiness or pretentiousness; and it has an abundance of easy-going warmth. It is a four-square house, dating from the 16th century but partly rebuilt in 1853, where antiques, souvenirs, books and games jostle with sometimes unusual furnishings in a carefree medley of patterns. The result is reassuring: this home-like environment spells comfort far beyond the meretricious harmony of hotels colour-matched by designers. And its owners, Susan and Robert Wood, spare no effort to make you feel at home and welcome.

Downstairs, there is a drawing-room with open log fire and views over the garden, a breakfast-room which looks out on to the croquet lawn, and an elegant dining-room which is candlelit in the evenings. The food, on our most recent visit, was satisfying, accompanied by an extensive wine list, annotated by Robert ('Norwegian wines are terrible and may account for the country's lowest wine consumption in Europe').

Beautifully kept park-like grounds surround the house; croquet hoops, putting holes, badminton and lawn tennis suggest plenty to do outside. Beyond are gently rolling hills; and Court Barn is perfectly placed for exploring both Devon and Cornwall.

~

NEARBY Bude; Boscastle; Tintagel; Hartland Abbey; Dartmoor.
LOCATION on A388 from Launceston to Holsworthy, at Clawton; ample car parking
MEALS breakfast, lunch, dinner
PRICE ££
ROOMS 8; 7 double and twin, 1 suite, all with bath; all rooms have phone, TV, hairdrier
FACILITIES dining-room, breakfast-room, drawing-room, TV-room, garden; croquet, badminton, lawn tennis, 4-hole pitch and putt
CREDIT CARDS DC, MC, V **CHILDREN** accepted
DISABLED access difficult **PETS** accepted by arrangement **CLOSED** never
PROPRIETORS Robert and Susan Wood

THE SOUTH-WEST

KINGSWEAR, DEVON

NONSUCH HOUSE
~ RIVERSIDE VILLAGE GUEST-HOUSE ~

Church Hill, Kingswear, Dartmouth, Devon TQ6 0BX
TEL (01803) 752829 **FAX** (01803) 752357

THE NOBLE FAMILY are old friends of this guide, having for many years run Langshott Manor near Horley in Surrey with great warmth and professionalism. A recent inspection made us decide to drop Langshott, a lovely brick-and-timber Elizabethan manor, from the guide, as we detected that, without the Nobles at the helm, it smacked too much of corporate anonymity (reports, please). However, we are delighted to follow its owners, originally from New Zealand, away from the suburban sprawl of Horley and Gatwick to their new venture in Devon, which is primarily run by their son, Christopher.

Nonsuch House in fact combines two tall, slim houses which stand, rather unprepossessingly, on a hairpin bend in a one-way system high above the Dartmouth ferry at Kingswear. The views, looking across the river towards Dartmouth, are superb, and can be had from all the windows. Bedrooms are named after shipping forecasts, but there is more of Langshott Manor about them than anything to do with the sea: they are smart, comfortable and well equipped – certainly a cut above the normal guest-house. The public rooms have been boldly decorated: apricot and burgundy, yellow and blue, and a deep-green dining-room that gives on to a conservatory. Dinner consists of a daily-changing set menu, simple but satisfying.

~

NEARBY Dartmouth; Dartmoor; Torquay.
LOCATION from Dartmouth ferry to Kingswear, take Fore Street, then turn right into Church Road; street parking
MEALS breakfast, dinner
PRICE ££
ROOMS 3 double, 2 with bath, 1 with shower; all rooms have TV
FACILITIES sitting-room, dining-room, conservatory, terrace
CREDIT CARDS not accepted **CHILDREN** accepted over 12
DISABLED not suitable **PETS** not accepted **CLOSED** never
PROPRIETORS Noble family

THE SOUTH-WEST

LACOCK, WILTSHIRE

AT THE SIGN OF THE ANGEL
~ VILLAGE INN ~

6 Church Street, Lacock, near Chippenham, Wiltshire SN15 2LA
TEL (01249) 730230 **FAX** (01249) 730527

LACOCK AND THE SIGN OF THE ANGEL go hand-in-hand: the 'perfect' English village (almost entirely in the preserving hands of the National Trust) and the epitome of the medieval English inn – half-timbered without, great log fires, oak panelling, beamed ceilings, splendid old beds and polished antique tables within.

There are many such inns sprinkled around middle England, but most are better enjoyed over a beer or two, or a meal, than overnight. Even here, the rooms vary in comfort and none could be called spacious. But they are all cosy and charming nonetheless, and full of character. The Angel is emphatically run as a small hotel rather than a pub – tellingly, there are no bars, and the residents' oak-panelled sitting-room on the first floor is quiet. It has belonged to the Levis family for over 40 years, and is now jointly run by daughter-in-law Lorna Levis and George Hardy with the help of village ladies. Lorna and George also share the traditional cooking (best for Sunday lunch). Breakfast offers old-timers such as junket and prunes, as well as a huge cooked meal if you want it.

If the rooms in the inn itself are booked, don't turn down the cottage annexe, which is equally attractive and pleasantly secluded. The Angel's gardens are somewhat scruffy – probably due to the ducks.

~

NEARBY Lacock Abbey; Bowood House; Corsham Court; Sheldon Manor
LOCATION 3 miles (5 km) S of Chippenham off A350, in middle of village; with gardens, and some car parking
MEALS breakfast, lunch, dinner
PRICE ££
ROOMS 10 double and twin, all with bath; all rooms have phone, TV
FACILITIES 3 dining-rooms, sitting-room, terrace, garden
CREDIT CARDS not accepted **CHILDREN** accepted
DISABLED 1 bedroom on ground floor
PETS accepted **CLOSED** Christmas and New Year, restaurant Mon lunch
PROPRIETORS George Hardy and Lorna Levis

THE SOUTH-WEST

LEWDOWN, DEVON

LEWTRENCHARD MANOR

~ MANOR HOUSE HOTEL ~

Lewdown, near Oakhampton, Devon EX20 4PN
TEL (01566) 783256 **FAX** (01566) 783332

DRIVING EAST DOWN the narrow road from Lewdown, on the edge of Dartmoor, nothing quite prepares you for the first sight of Lewtrenchard Manor, a magnificent 16thC stone manor house, with some Victorian additions, approached by an avenue of beech trees and set in stunningly beautiful grounds which lead down to a lake studded with swans.

The interior is equally impressive. The massive reception rooms are rich in ornate ceilings, oak panelling, carvings and large open fireplaces. Despite its size, however, the hotel has the warm and hospitable atmosphere of a much humbler building, engendered in great part by its hostess, Sue Murray. Peek into the drawing-room on your arrival, and you'll be hopping to get in there and curl up with a good book.

On the first floor, a splendid long gallery, full of family paintings and portraits, leads to the spacious bedrooms, all of which have extensive views through leaded windows and over the Devon countryside.

A former owner of Lewtrenchard Manor was the Reverend Sabine Baring Gould (who wrote, amongst others, the rousing hymn *Onward, Christian Soldiers*). Mercifully, he largely resisted the Victorian habit of embellishing an already beautiful building.

~

NEARBY Dartmoor; Tintagel; Exeter; Boscastle.
LOCATION from old A30 at Lewdown, take road signposted Lewtrenchard; in 11-acre grounds with ample car parking
MEALS breakfast, light weekday lunch, Sun lunch, dinner
PRICE ££-£££
ROOMS 9; 8 double and twin, 1 suite, all with bath; all rooms have phone, TV, hairdrier
FACILITIES sitting-room, bar lounge, restaurant, breakfast-room, ballroom, garden; croquet, fishing lake **CREDIT CARDS** AE, DC, MC, V **CHILDREN** under 5s by arrangement **DISABLED** access difficult **PETS** accepted **CLOSED** never
PROPRIETORS Sue and James Murray

THE SOUTH-WEST

LIFTON, DEVON

ARUNDELL ARMS
~ FISHING INN ~

Lifton, Devon PL16 0AA
TEL (01566) 784666 **FAX** (01566) 784494
E-MAIL ArundellArms@btinternet.com

A 200-YEAR-OLD COACHING INN, on a site that dates back to Saxon times, which is famous for fishing and food. Traditional country pursuits are taken seriously here: the hotel runs a series of courses on fly fishing for both beginners and the experienced, but people also come to the Arundell Arms for riding, golf, birdwatching and to enjoy some of the loveliest country in England. Anglers have a 20-mile stretch of private fishing at their disposal.

Then there is the food, for which resident chef Philip Burgess has established a fine reputation. You might start with a home-made soup, followed by pan-fried salmon with a ginger and chilli salsa, and end with basil ice-cream with poached pears and raspberries. Almost all the staff are local people and tend to stay for a long time, following the example of the proprietor Anne Voss-Bark who has managed the hotel since 1961.

From the sitting-room you can see the garden and the 250-year-old former cockpit, now a tackle room. There are two rather grand interconnecting dining-rooms and, of course, a bar. Bedrooms are homely rather than sophisticated, and those in the old part of the building are preferable to those in the annexe. A friendly, welcoming, traditional country inn.

~

NEARBY Dartmoor; Tintagel; Boscastle; Port Isaac; Exeter.
LOCATION 3 miles (5 km) E of Launceston, just off A30 in Lifton; with ample car parking
MEALS breakfast, lunch, dinner
PRICE ££
ROOMS 28; 20 double and twin, 8 single, all with bath; all rooms have phone, TV, hairdrier
FACILITIES 2 restaurants, 2 bars, games-room, drying-room, garden; fishing (20 miles of private rights) **CREDIT CARDS** AE, DC, MC, V
CHILDREN accepted **DISABLED** access possible **PETS** accepted
CLOSED Christmas **PROPRIETOR** Anne Voss-Bark

THE SOUTH-WEST

THE LIZARD, CORNWALL

LANDEWEDNACK HOUSE

~ COUNTRY HOUSE BED-AND-BREAKFAST ~

Church Cove, The Lizard, Cornwall TR12 7PQ
TEL (01326) 290909 **FAX** (01326) 290192

A BEAUTIFUL 17THC former rectory, which has been skilfully and sympathetically restored by owners Peter and Marion Stanley to become a warm and elegant private home to which they welcome paying guests. The parish of Landewednack, at the end of The Lizard Peninsula, is the most southerly in England and is fortunate enough to have a climate mild enough for most of the year to encourage a wide variety of trees, plants and shrubs to flourish. Marion has made the most of this opportunity and her gardens are a delight.

Inside, the house is equally enchanting. Leading off the flagstoned hall is the dining-room with a beamed ceiling and massive granite fireplace where guests can dine by candlelight (by prior arrangement with Marion) in front of a crackling log fire. Breakfast is taken in a separate, smaller room. House guests can relax in the elegant drawing-room at any time of the day, or in the evening for pre-dinner drinks. The three bedrooms are all different, and all charming. The best view is from the Yellow Room, with a mahogany half-tester. Through its large bay window you can see across the garden to the church and the sea beyond – a wonderful sight at sunset.

~

NEARBY The Lizard Peninsula; St Ives; Penzance.
LOCATION from Helston take A3083 to Lizard; before entering village turn left to Church Cove, then left towards lifeboat station
MEALS breakfast; other meals by arrangement
PRICE ££
ROOMS 3 double and twin, 1 with bath, 2 with shower; all rooms have phone, TV, hairdrier
FACILITIES dining-room, drawing-room, breakfast-room, garden; swimming-pool
CREDIT CARDS MC, V **CHILDREN** not accepted
DISABLED access difficult **PETS** accepted by arrangement **CLOSED** Christmas
PROPRIETORS Peter and Marion Stanley

THE SOUTH-WEST

MELKSHAM, WILTSHIRE

SHURNHOLD HOUSE
~ MANOR HOUSE GUEST-HOUSE ~

Shurnhold, Melksham, Wiltshire SN12 8DG
TEL (01225) 790555 **FAX** (01225) 793147

YET ANOTHER GRAND old house rescued from decay in the late 1980s and put to new use – in this case, a bed-and-breakfast guest-house. The house is a beautifully proportioned stone-built Jacobean affair dating from 1640. It sits quite close to a busy main road on the out-skirts of an unremarkable town, but is well shielded by trees (look for the signs, because you will not spot the house) and well placed for touring in several directions.

Inside, all is as you would wish. A flagstone floor in the bar/sitting-room, oak beams, log fires and pretty floral fabrics here and in the break-fast-room and sitting-room, which is full of books. Period furnishings are used wherever the opportunity arises and the budget allows. The beamed bedrooms are spacious, with restrained decoration – perhaps rich floral drapes against plain white walls – and several different styles of bed; sev-eral have fireplaces. There is a proliferation of cute teddy bears.

Prices have been set at just the right level – higher than your typical B&B, but at half the rate of many 'country house hotels' occupying similarly splendid buildings. The licensed bar is an unusual feature for a B&B establishment.

~

NEARBY Lacock; Bradford-on-Avon.
LOCATION in countryside, 1 mile (1.5 km) NW of Melksham on A365 to Bath; in large garden with ample car parking
MEALS breakfast
PRICE ££
ROOMS 6 double, 1 family room, all with bath or shower; all rooms have TV
FACILITIES dining-room, sitting-room, bar/sitting-room
CREDIT CARDS AE, MC, V
CHILDREN welcome **DISABLED** no special facilities **PETS** accepted by arrangement
CLOSED never
PROPRIETOR Sue Tanir

THE SOUTH-WEST

TOXIQUE

~ RESTAURANT-WITH-ROOMS ~

187 Woodrow Road, Melksham, Wiltshire SN12 7AY
TEL (01225) 742773 **FAX** (01225) 742773

O**UR ORIGINAL REPORTERS** were attracted to Toxique by a Michelin recommendation for its excellent stone farmhouse restaurant, but their curiosity was aroused by the pictures of its four bedrooms, and they decided to return for a night of decided luxury.

Melksham itself is not a pretty place, but the house is on the road towards the National Trust village of Lacock and stands in a stone-walled garden. There are two dining-rooms, both candlelit, one with a pastoral mural across one wall, the other dark blue. They are separated by a cocoon-like sitting-room, its dark walls eccentrically studded with fir cones. Chairs are draped in deep purple and piled high with gold cushions which only adds to the general impression of a cosy and intimate cottage swept away by contemporary style. This finds its freest expression in the extremely comfortable bedrooms and en suite bathrooms, each one appropriately named: Desert, in summer lemon and blue, with sand around the bath; Oriental in black and white, with seagrass matting, low bed and spa bath with perfumed oils; Rococo with deep-red walls, black velvet and gold brocade; and Colonial – basketwork furniture and mosquito netting. All very surprising in such a suburban setting; some may find it excessive, others great fun.

~

NEARBY Lacock; Bath; Bradford-on-Avon.
LOCATION turn left off Melksham High Street signposted Calne for 0.5 mile, then take left-hand exit, Forest Road, for 1 mile; ample car parking
MEALS breakfast, dinner; room service
PRICE ££
ROOMS 4 double with bath; all rooms have hairdrier, 1 has TV
FACILITIES 2 dining-rooms, sitting-room, garden **CREDIT CARDS** AE, MC, V
CHILDREN accepted **DISABLED** access difficult **PETS** not accepted
CLOSED restaurant only, Sun to Wed
PROPRIETOR Peter Jewkes

THE SOUTH-WEST

MEMBURY, DEVON

◆ EDITOR'S CHOICE ◆

LEA HILL
~ COUNTRY HOTEL ~

Membury, near Axminster, Devon EX13 7AQ
TEL (01404) 881881 **FAX** (01404) 881388

OF THE LARGE CROP of hotels new to our guide in this edition, this is one of those that we are most delighted to recommend. Its setting, to begin with, is enchanting: on a prominent hilltop with bucolic views over woodland and meadows. Then the building itself: a prime example of a thatched Devon longhouse, with parts dating from the 14th century when it did service as a medieval farmhouse. The nearby village of Membury is quiet and picturesque.

Lea Hill's interior is equally charming, with a wealth of polished flag-stones, beams and inglenook fireplaces creating the archetypal image·of the perfect English country house. The pretty split-level dining-room has exposed stone walls and a large fireplace, and leading off is a comfortable sitting area and a residents' study with a collection of books which are worth poring over. The bar has an unusual assortment of antique furniture.

Each of the eleven bedrooms is differently furnished; most of them are in two adjacent converted barns. The two suites are well worth the extra cost; one has a Jacuzzi, the other its own private garden.

Owners Chris and Sue Hubbard, who took over at Lea Hill in early 1998, are delightful hosts, and their son James, responsible for the food, is a good cook.

~

NEARBY Lyme Regis; Axminster; Sidmouth.
LOCATION in 8-acre grounds, 1 mile (1.5 km) S of Membury; ample car parking
MEALS breakfast, snack lunch, dinner
PRICE ££
ROOMS 11; 9 double and twin, 2 suites, all with bath; all rooms have phone, TV, hairdrier
FACILITIES 2 sitting-rooms, bar, study, restaurant, terrace, garden; 6-hole par 3 golf course **CREDIT CARDS** AE, MC, V
CHILDREN not accepted **DISABLED** access difficult
PETS accepted **CLOSED** Feb **PROPRIETORS** Chris and Sue Hubbard

THE SOUTH-WEST

MILBORNE PORT, DORSET

OLD VICARAGE
~ TOWN HOTEL ~

Sherborne Road, Milborne Port, Dorset DT9 5AT
TEL (01963) 251117 **FAX** (01963) 251515
WEBSITE www.milborneport.freeserve.co.uk

THE SOMEWHAT FORBIDDING Gothic frontage belies the colourful interior of this interesting venture on the Somerset/Dorset borders. Jörgen Kunath and Anthony Ma (German and Vietnamese in that order) ran a successful restaurant in West London for 13 years, moving here only two years ago. Thus the Old Vicarage is essentially a weekend house-party place, particularly for fans who knew the couple in London, rather than a typical roadside hotel.

Displayed to great effect in the mango-coloured hall, the delightful drawing-room and the bedrooms upstairs, Anthony's skill as a painter/decorator is exemplary. The drawing-room is stuffed with an eclectic mix of comfortable sofas, gold-painted Russian icons, polished pewter plates, a Vietnamese coffer and a Broadwood baby grand piano. Large mullioned windows look over the park-like gardens and fields beyond.

The south-facing dining-room is more simple, with solid bamboo chairs and boat-shaped pine sideboard. It's Anthony's cooking that takes centre-stage here, blending exotic and traditional local flavours. Dinner is only served on Fridays and Saturdays, but both pubs in the village are recommended for their food.

The bedrooms in the coach house are smaller and less interesting than those in the main house.

~

NEARBY Yeovil; Glastonbury; Dorchester.
LOCATION in town on A30; in 3-acre garden with ample car parking
MEALS breakfast, dinner (Fri, Sat, only)
PRICE ££
ROOMS 7; 5 double and twin, 1 single, 1 family room, all with bath; all rooms have phone, TV, hairdrier **FACILITIES** sitting-room, restaurant, terrace, garden; croquet
CREDIT CARDS AE, MC, V **CHILDREN** accepted **DISABLED** access difficult
PETS accepted in coach house (£5 per night) **CLOSED** early Jan to early Feb
PROPRIETORS Jörgen Kunath and Anthony Ma

THE SOUTH-WEST

COPPLERIDGE INN

~ COUNTRY INN ~

Motcombe, Shaftesbury, Dorset SP7 9HW
TEL (01747) 851980 **FAX** (01747) 851858

AN INVITING 18THC FARMHOUSE standing in an elevated position above the Blackmore Vale, and surrounded by its own meadows and woodland. Ranged around a large central courtyard are the former farm buildings, now skilfully converted into the hotel's ten spacious bedrooms. They are unpretentiously furnished with pine, bright fabrics and comfortable armchairs.

Guests wander across to the farmhouse for dinner where proprietor Chris Goodinge has created a homely atmosphere – flagstones, log fire, candlelight – and an eclectic menu. The bar is noted for its traditional beers and wines by the bottle or glass, and bistro-style meals can be eaten here or in the charming dining-room where a more elaborate *à la carte* menu is also served. Children are well catered for and breakfasts are imaginative.

Those keen on exercise will do well here: apart from the tennis courts, cricket pitch and skittles available on site, an equestrian centre, leisure centre, clay pigeon shooting and trout fishing are all on hand in the village.

The hotel has a wedding licence and wedding parties are often in progess at weekends.

~

NEARBY Shaftesbury; Stourhead House and Gardens.
LOCATION 2 miles (3 km) NW of Shaftesbury at the N end of Motcombe on the minor road to Mere; 15-acre grounds with ample car parking
MEALS breakfast, lunch, dinner
PRICE ££
ROOMS 10 double, all with bath; all rooms have phone, TV, minibar
FACILITIES sitting-room, bar, garden-room, dining-room, 2 tennis courts, cricket pitch, skittle alley (party bookings), children's play area
CREDIT CARDS AE, DC, MC, V **CHILDREN** welcome **DISABLED** access easy **PETS** welcome
CLOSED never **PROPRIETOR** Christopher Goodinge

THE SOUTH-WEST

NETTLETON, WILTSHIRE

FOSSE FARMHOUSE
~ COUNTRY HOTEL ~

Nettleton Shrub, Nettleton, near Chippenham, Wiltshsire NS14 7NJ
TEL (01249) 782286 **FAX** (01249) 783066 **E-MAIL** CaronCooper@compuserve.com
WEBSITE www.fossefarmhouse.8m.com

OWNER CARON COOPER RESEARCHED and presented her own television pro-gramme on BBC2 in 1997 entitled *Cooking with Confidence*, and con-fidence underpins her every endeavour, whether as cook, journalist, inte-rior decorator, antique dealer or, as here at Fosse Farmhouse, hotelier. She has decorated it with some style, mostly *à la française*: the family-room has a wonderful French pine bed, the sitting-room could be in provincial Normandy, while the dining-room has checked tablecloths, a plastercast frieze decorated with wine-coloured grapes and a definitely Gallic atmosphere.

When it comes to cooking, though, Caron leaves behind French influ-ences. There is no choice at mealtimes, but guests can let her know beforehand of any particular requirements. What they will get is an inter-esting slant on classical English cuisine: perhaps smoked salmon on a bed of roasted peppers, or parsnip and apple soup to start, duck breast with elderberry wine sauce as a main course. Puddings are traditional.

Across a courtyard are three pleasantly decorated bedrooms in a con-verted stable block, still with original cobbled flooring in the downstairs sitting-room. In sharp contrast to the neatness of the house and stables, the garden could do with attention, especially the ropey garden furniture.

~

NEARBY Castle Combe; Cotswolds.
LOCATION in countryside off B4039, 6 miles (9.5 km) NW of Chippenham; in 1.5 acres of garden with car parking
MEALS breakfast, lunch, dinner
PRICE ££
ROOMS 6; 4 double and twin with bath or shower, 1 single with shower, 1 family room with bath; all rooms have TV, hairdrier
FACILITIES sitting-room, dining-room, tea-room, terrace, garden
CREDIT CARDS AE, MC, V **CHILDREN** accepted **DISABLED** access difficult **PETS** accepted by arrangement **CLOSED** never **PROPRIETOR** Caron Cooper

THE SOUTH-WEST

OAKFORDBRIDGE, DEVON

BARK HOUSE
~ COUNTRY HOTEL ~

Oakfordbridge, near Tiverton, Devon EX16 9HZ
TEL (01398) 351236

WE WERE ALERTED TO THIS CHARMING and picturesque small hotel, new to the guide this year, by one of our readers. Tucked away in the tiny hamlet of Oakfordbridge in the beautiful Exe Valley, it's a delightful discovery. It has been owned and run for the last three years by Alastair Kameen, whose training includes a prestigious Relais et Châteaux establishment; his aim is to create the perfect spot for a short break in the countryside.

The building is about 200 years old and was originally used to store bark for use in tanning. It's everyone's idea of a Devon cottage, particularly in spring when the façade is smothered by a magnificent old wistaria. Around the hotel there are woodland paths and small gardens, with seats, a stream and goldfish pond. A croquet lawn is planned, and a sitting area opposite the building.

Inside, there is an intimate and cosy sitting-room with an open fire, and a particularly welcoming dining-room, candlelit at night. Alastair is the cook, and his food, when we visited, was both innovative and carefully presented. The bedrooms reflect the essential simplicity of Bark House, but they are also comfortable. Above all, the atmosphere, created by Alastair and his assistant, Justine, is gentle and relaxed.

~

NEARBY Exmoor; Lynton; Lynmouth; Saunton Sands.
LOCATION in own grounds, on A396 near Bampton; car parking
MEALS breakfast, lunch by arrangement, dinner
PRICE ££
ROOMS 5; 2 double with bath, 3 double with shower; all rooms have phone, TV
FACILITIES sitting-room, dining-room, garden; croquet
CREDIT CARDS not accepted
CHILDREN accepted **DISABLED** access difficult **PETS** accepted
CLOSED for a short period during winter
PROPRIETOR Alastair Kameen

THE SOUTH-WEST

PADSTOW, CORNWALL

SEAFOOD RESTAURANT & ST PETROC'S HOTEL

~ RESTAURANT-WITH-ROOMS ~

Riverside, Padstow, Cornwall PL28 8BY
TEL (01841) 532700 **FAX** (01841) 532942

RICK STEIN'S PADSTOW EMPIRE now extends to three different places to stay, at varying prices, and three places to eat: his flagship Seafood Restaurant, the Bistro in St Petroc's Hotel, and the Café in Middle Street.

If you are intent on eating at the quayside Seafood Restaurant (superb seafood, straight from the fishing boats, served by friendly staff in a lively dining-room) then the bedrooms above make the best choice for a night's stay. They are spacious and more than comfortable in an understated way, with superb estuary views from Nos 5 and 6. What the place lacks in public rooms, it makes up for in laid-back atmosphere and its prime position on the quay. Less expensive, but no less tasteful, are the rooms in St Petroc's Hotel just up the hill, a little removed from the bustle of the quayside. This is an attractive white-painted building with views across the older parts of town as well as of the estuary. Some rooms are on the small side. The place exudes a friendly ambience, not least in the Bistro, where a short, very reasonably priced menu features meat and vegetable dishes as well as seafood. There are also three attractive, inexpensive rooms above the Café in Middle Street.

~

NEARBY surfing beaches; Trevose Head.
LOCATION in village centre, 4 miles (6.5 km) NW off A39 between Wadebridge and St Columb; car parking
MEALS breakfast, lunch, dinner
PRICE ££
ROOMS 29 single, double and twin in 3 different buildings, most with bath, some with shower; all rooms have phone, TV, hairdrier; some have minibar
FACILITIES 3 restaurants, bar, sitting-room, conservatory
CREDIT CARDS MC, V
CHILDREN welcome **DISABLED** access difficult **PETS** accepted
CLOSED Christmas and New Year
PROPRIETORS Rick and Jill Stein

THE SOUTH-WEST

PENZANCE, CORNWALL

THE ABBEY
~ TOWN HOTEL ~

Abbey Street, Penzance, Cornwall TR18 4AR
TEL (01736) 366906 **FAX** (01736) 351163

WHEN WE LAST VISITED The Abbey, one of our overriding impressions was of consistent good management. We don't often get reports about it, but this doesn't change our continuing belief that it is one of the most exceptional places to stay in the West Country. Jean and Michael Cox have taken a house with character in the heart of old Penzance (it was built in the mid-17th century and given a Gothic façade in Regency times); they have decorated and furnished it with unstinting care, great flair and a considerable budget; and they have called it a hotel. But they run it much more as a private house, and visitors who expect to find hosts eager to satisfy their every whim may be disappointed.

For its fans, the absence of hovering flunkies is, of course, a key part of the appeal of The Abbey. But there are other attractions – the confident and original decoration, with abundant antiques and bric-a-brac, the spacious, individual bedrooms (one with an enormous pine-panelled bathroom); the welcoming, flowery drawing-room and elegant dining-room (both with log fires burning 'year-round'); the delightful walled garden behind the house; and not least, the satisfying dinners. Front rooms overlook the harbour and the dry dock.

~

NEARBY Tregwainton Garden; St Michael's Mount; Land's End.
LOCATION in middle of town, overlooking harbour; with private parking for 6 cars in courtyard
MEALS breakfast, dinner; room service
PRICE ££-£££
ROOMS 7; 4 double and twin, 1 suite, 2 single, 4 with bath, 3 with shower; all rooms have TV, hairdrier
FACILITIES sitting-room, dining-room, walled garden
CREDIT CARDS AE, MC , V **CHILDREN** accepted
DISABLED access difficult **PETS** accepted in bedrooms only **CLOSED** Christmas
PROPRIETORS Jean and Michael Cox

THE SOUTH-WEST

SUMMER HOUSE

~ TOWN RESTAURANT-WITH-ROOMS ~

Cornwall Terrace, Penzance, Cornwall TR18 4HL
TEL (01736) 363744 **FAX** (01736) 360959 **E-MAIL** summerhouse@dial.pipex.com
WEBSITE www.cornwall-online.co.uk

LINDA AND CIRO ZAINO moved to the tip of Cornwall from London, where Ciro had managed some of the capital's top restaurants, to open this restaurant-with-rooms in a Grade II-listed Georgian house close to the sea-front. They run it with great panache, reports our inspector, who considers it a 'great find'. He describes it as Mediterranean in colour and feel, quirky in style and breezy in atmosphere. Brighton meets the Neapolitan Riviera.

The former home of one of Cornwall's leading naïve artists, the house is still full of paintings, idiosyncratic furniture and lush pot plants. Downstairs there is a little cosy sitting-room as well as the most important room in the building, the restaurant. Here blues and yellows predominate in a room that spills out in to a small walled garden burgeoning with terracotta pots and palm trees. Ciro's sunny cooking, using fresh local ingredients, has become a great draw.

Upstairs, the five simple bedrooms are highly individual with a diverse mix of family pieces and collectables. Fresh flowers are everywhere. Linda is charming and her front-of-house presence is just right: enthusiastic, friendly and welcoming.

More reports please.

~

NEARBY Tregwainton Garden; St Michael's Mount; Land's End; St Ives; Newlyn School art colony.
LOCATION close to the harbour; drive alongside the harbour and turn right immediately after the Queen's Hotel; car parking
MEALS breakfast, dinner
PRICE £
ROOMS 5 double and twin, all with bath
FACILITIES sitting-room, dining-room, small walled garden
CREDIT CARDS MC, V **CHILDREN** not accepted **DISABLED** access difficult
PETS not accepted **CLOSED** Jan
PROPRIETORS Ciro and Linda Zaino

THE SOUTH-WEST

ROCK, CORNWALL

ST ENODOC
~ SEASIDE HOTEL ~

Rock, Cornwall PL27 6LA
TEL (01208) 863394 **FAX** (01208) 863970 **E-MAIL** enodoc@aol.com
WEBSITE www.enodoc-hotel.co.uk

WELL-HEELED BRITISH FAMILIES have flocked to Rock for their bucket-and-spade holidays for generations, but hotels which are both stylish and child-friendly have been thin on the ground hereabouts – until, that is, the emergence in 1998 of the old-established St Enodoc Hotel from a change of ownership and total makeover.

The imposing building is typical of the area: no beauty, but solid and purposeful, with pebble-dashed walls and slate roof. Emily Todhunter's interior decoration suits its seaside location, with its bright colours (paint, fabrics, painted furniture, modern art), clean lines, and easy-going comfort. The Californian-style Porthilly Bar and split-level Grill is popular with non-residents, although reports indicate that the Pacific Rim food could improve. It has panoramic views, with a wide terrace for outdoor dining. Bedrooms feel like bedrooms rather than hotel rooms, with marvellous views across the Camel Estuary.

With its child-friendly facilities, the hotel is particularly popular during holidays and half-terms. Last year the Marlers put it on market, but it has since been taken off. More reports please.

NEARBY Polzeath; Padstow (by ferry).
LOCATION overlooking the Camel Estuary, bordering St Enodoc golf course in Rock, 2 miles (3 km) off B3314 from Wadebridge; car park (expensive)
MEALS breakfast, lunch, dinner; room service
PRICE £££
ROOMS 15 double, 3 suites, all with bath; all rooms have phone, TV, radio, hairdrier, fan
FACILITIES sitting-room, library, dining-room, bar, billiard-room, gym, sauna; squash court, swimming-pool
CREDIT CARDS AE, DC, MC, V
CHILDREN welcome **DISABLED** ramp at side entrance; adapted WC on ground floor
PETS not accepted **CLOSED** never **MANAGER** Mark Gregory

THE SOUTH-WEST

RUANHIGHLANES, CORNWALL

CRUGSILLICK MANOR

~ MANOR GUEST-HOUSE ~

Ruanhighlanes, Truro, Cornwall TR2 5LJ
TEL (01872) 501214 **FAX** (01872) 501214/501228
E-MAIL barstow@adtel.co.uk

SITUATED ON THE LOVELY Roseland Peninsula, with its many coves and harbours, Crugsillick is a beautiful listed Grade II* Queen Anne manor house. Lying in a sheltered hollow twenty minutes' walk from the Coastal Path and Pendower beach, it has a truly peaceful atmosphere, with views across the attractive gardens to a wooded valley beyond.

The antique-filled house is the home of the Barstows, who are superb hosts, treating their visitors as house guests while at the same time recognizing their desire for privacy. Their elegant drawing-room, with its log fire and its highly unusual ceiling and scalloped friezes – reputedly moulded by French prisoners during the Napoleonic wars – is for the use of guests, and a four-course dinner is served by candlelight at a communal table in the 17thC dining-room with beautiful flagstone floor. Ingredients often include fruit and vegetables from the garden. Communal dining seems to work well here, with animated conversations reported by our impressed inspector. Bedrooms are extremely comfortable, with cosy beds, prettily decorated and furnished with antiques. One satisfied reader writes of his enchantment with 'this wonderful old house', of 'the high standards' and 'the warmth and hospitality of his hosts'. A cottage sleeping four (suitable for disabled) is available to rent.

~

NEARBY St Mawes; Gardens of Heligan; Trelissick and Trewithin.
LOCATION on road to Veryan off A3078; in extensive garden with ample car parking
MEALS breakfast, picnic lunch on request, dinner
PRICE ££
ROOMS 3 double, 2 with bath, 1 en suite, 1 adjacent, 1 with shower; all rooms have hairdrier
FACILITIES drawing-room, dining-room, large hall
CREDIT CARDS MC, V **CHILDREN** accepted over 12
DISABLED access difficult **PETS** accepted **CLOSED** never
PROPRIETORS Oliver and Rosemary Barstow

THE SOUTH-WEST

ST AUSTELL, CORNWALL

BOSCUNDLE MANOR
∾ COUNTRY HOUSE HOTEL ∾

Tregrehan, St Austell, Cornwall PL25 3RL
TEL (01726) 813557 **FAX** (01726) 814997

A VISIT BY ONE OF OUR most experienced reporters confirms that Boscundle Manor continues to deserve its place in this guide. She was especially impressed by the attractive breakfast-room, the high standard of the bedrooms and the easy-going atmosphere, despite upmarket trappings such as spa baths, minibars and fridges in the bedrooms, and a helicopter landing pad. The house itself was originally built in 1740 as a private home and is a listed building. The Flints continue to exude enthusiasm, still attend as carefully as ever to the needs of guests, and still find time to look after the large terraced garden themselves. The daily changing menu of simple but imaginative dishes is an important ingredient of this success story.

The delight of the place is its happy informality – the house is the Flints' home, with assorted furniture (some luxurious modern, some stripped pine, while some are elegant antiques). There are pictures, flowers, books and postcards everywhere. A snooker table, table tennis and darts are available in a beautifully converted barn.

∾

NEARBY Fowey; Restormel Castle; The Eden Project.
LOCATION 2.5 miles (4 km) E of St Austell, close to A390; in 14- acre woodland gardens; ample car parking
MEALS breakfast, light lunches, dinner
PRICE £££
ROOMS 10; 6 double, 2 suites, all with bath, 2 single with shower; all rooms have phone, TV, minibar, safe, fridge
FACILITIES 2 sitting-rooms, bar, 2 dining-rooms, conservatory/breakfast-room, exercise-room, heated indoor and outdoor pool, garden; croquet, 2 practice golf holes, snooker, table tennis, darts
CREDIT CARDS AE, MC, V **CHILDREN** welcome
DISABLED access difficult to house; easy access to bungalow in grounds
PETS accepted by arrangement, but not in public rooms
CLOSED Nov to Easter **PROPRIETORS** Andrew and Mary Flint

THE SOUTH-WEST

NANSCAWEN MANOR HOUSE
∼ COUNTRY GUEST-HOUSE ∼

Prideaux Road, Luxulyan Valley, near St Blazey, Cornwall PL24 2SR
TEL & FAX (01726) 814488 **E-MAIL** KeithMartin@compuserve.com
WEBSITE www.nanscawen.currantbun.com

DATING FROM THE 16TH CENTURY, Nanscawen Manor has been carefully extended in recent years and sits amidst five acres of mature and very pretty gardens and grounds, with a 'wonderfully located' outdoor swimming-pool. Its seclusion is enviable: approached by a fairly steep uphill track from the road, you can't see the house until you are almost upon it. As well as the pool, you can also sink into the whirlpool spa, and there is a terrace on which to sit in the sunshine amongst palm trees and hydrangeas. A recent inspection confirmed readers' reports that the Martins' family home is an excellent bed-and-breakfast guest-house.

The entrance hall, with polished parquet floor, leads to a large, attractive sitting-room with an honesty bar. Breakfast is taken in a sunny, cane-furnished conservatory; it's very good, and includes dishes such as locally smoked salmon with scrambled eggs. A semi-spiral staircase takes you up to the three bedrooms, described by one reader as 'charming, but perhaps a touch too feminine for some tastes.' Rashleigh, in the newer part of the house, is vast, while the two in the original wing have large beds, one a four-poster, and views of the garden to the south.

∼

NEARBY Fowey; Lanhydrock House; The Eden Project; Polperro; Looe.
LOCATION in countryside, 0.5 mile (1 km) off A390, NW of St Blazey, 3 miles (5 km) NE of St Austell; in 5-acre grounds, with car parking
MEALS breakfast
PRICE ££
ROOMS 3 double and twin, all with bath; all rooms have phone, TV, hairdrier; video on request
FACILITIES drawing-room, conservatory, breakfast-room, terrace, garden; heated outdoor swimming-pool, whirlpool spa
CREDIT CARDS MC, V **CHILDREN** accepted over 12 **DISABLED** access difficult
PETS not accepted **CLOSED** Christmas
PROPRIETORS Keith and Fiona Martin

THE SOUTH-WEST

ST HILARY, CORNWALL

ENNYS

~ COUNTRY HOUSE BED-AND-BREAKFAST ~

St Hilary, Penzance, Cornwall TR20 9BZ
TEL (01736) 740262 **FAX** (01736) 740055 **E-MAIL** ennys@zetnet.co.uk
WEBSITE www.ipl.co.uk/ennys.html

TRAVEL JOURNALISTS don't often move over into the hospitality business themselves, but Gill Charlton is one who has, and she has brought her considerable knowledge of what makes an interesting place to stay to this excellent country guest-house.

Ennys is a beautiful, creeper-clad 17thC Cornish manor house situated at the end of a long tree-lined drive in little St Hilary, a few miles from Penzance. The sheltered gardens are full of shrubs and flowers and include a swimming-pool and grass tennis court. The fields stretch down to the River Hayle, along which you can walk and picnic.

Bedrooms in the main house are prettily decorated, furnished in country house style, and all have window seats with garden or country views. Two family suites are in an adjacent converted stone barn near which self-catering accommodation is also available. Breakfasts, as well as proper cream teas, are served in the rustic farmhouse-style kitchen, around a large wooden table which is big enough for guests to chat to one another – or not – as they wish. Afterwards, you can curl up in the large comfortable sitting-room with open log fire.

Gill is the perfect hostess, and a mine of information on the surrounding area.

~

NEARBY Land's End; Penzance; The Lizard Peninsula.
LOCATION in gardens with parking; from B3280 from Marazion turn left into Trewhella Lane, just before Relubbus
MEALS breakfast
PRICE £
ROOMS 5; 3 double, 2 suites, all with bath; all rooms have TV, hairdrier
FACILITIES breakfast-room, sitting-room, garden; grass tennis court, heated outdoor swimming-pool **CREDIT CARDS** MC, V
CHILDREN welcome **DISABLED** access difficult **PETS** accepted
CLOSED mid-Nov to mid-Feb **PROPRIETOR** Gill Charlton

THE SOUTH-WEST

ST KEYNE, CORNWALL

WELL HOUSE

~ COUNTRY HOTEL ~

St Keyne, Liskeard, Cornwall PL14 4RN
TEL (01579) 342001 **FAX** (01579) 343891 **E-MAIL** wellhse@aol.com
WEBSITE ww.wellhouse.co.uk

WE'VE HAD CONSISTENTLY satisfied feedback on this hotel in recent years. Attention to detail is part of Nicholas Wainford's policy of providing a comfortable and restful background at this Victorian hilltop house with an outdoor heated swimming-pool. Everything here has been carefully chosen to create an atmosphere of calm and stylish luxury – up to country house standard, but on a smaller scale (and at lower cost).

The house itself was built by a tea-planter in 1894, obviously with no expense spared. The beautifully tiled entrance hall, the staircase and all the woodwork are as new. The dining-room, terrace and most of the richly decorated bedrooms look out over wooded grounds to the Looe valley. The sitting-room, with its roaring log fire, is a haven of warmth and peace on a cold night.

The contemporary decoration and paintings on the walls are in no way at odds with the atmosphere of the old stone house. Nor is the modern style of the dishes on the imaginative menu. This is one of the best places to eat at in Cornwall. It is also one of the most attractive, with its soft yellow colour scheme. The wine list is extensive and largely French, with a heavy slant towards prestigious clarets. The lunch and dinner menus change daily. "Mouthwatering, inventive and great value for money", says our most recent inspector.

~

NEARBY Looe; Plymouth; Bodmin Moor; The Eden Project.
LOCATION in countryside just outside village of St Keyne, 2 miles (3 km) S of Liskeard, off B3254; in 3.5-acre gardens with ample car parking
MEALS breakfast, lunch, dinner; room service
PRICE £££
ROOMS 9; 8 double, 1 family room, all with bath; all rooms have phone, TV, hairdrier **FACILITIES** sitting-room, dining-room, bar, garden; tennis, heated swimming-pool, croquet **CREDIT CARDS** AE, DC, MC, V **CHILDREN** welcome
DISABLED no special facilities **PETS** accepted by arrangement **CLOSED** never
PROPRIETORS Nicholas Wainford and Ioné Nurdin

THE SOUTH-WEST

ST MARTIN, ISLES OF SCILLY

ST MARTIN'S ON THE ISLE

~ ISLAND HOTEL ~

St Martin, Isles of Scilly, Cornwall TR25 0QW
TEL (01720) 422092 **FAX** (01720) 422298
WEBSITE www.stmartinshotel.co.uk

AFICIONADOS RETURN to this upmarket island hotel time and again, either for family holidays, or as a peaceful getaway in superb surroundings. In the sunshine, the Scillies can vie with many a 'paradise' archipelago: there are lovely colourings, fabulous beaches and endless uninhabited islands scattered across a deep blue sea. St Martin's, near Tresco, is car-free, and the hotel is the only one on the island. The relaxed and friendly manager, Keith Bradford, usually meets guests at the quay.

The hotel is modern, built in the 1980s under the supervision of the Prince of Wales (also the Duke of Cornwall), and of local stone with slate roofs to resemble a string of traditional fishermen's cottages. Scattered on the expansive lawn in front, which runs down to the private beach, are deck-chairs and tables and chairs shaded by parasols. Boat trips, with picnics, can be arranged to uninhabited islands, as well as to Tresco, and a Cornish Crabber is available for fishing trips.

Bedrooms, in modern style, with pine fittings and white bathrooms, are practical and comfortable; the best have sea views. The food, served in the first-floor dining-room, is surprisingly rich and sophisticated; lighter meals are served in the bar.

NEARBY boat trips to Tresco and other Scilly Isles.
LOCATION on car free island, at N end, close to beach in own grounds; helicopter or boat from St Mary's; free transport from quay to hotel
MEALS breakfast, lunch, dinner; room service
PRICE £££
ROOMS 30; 28 double, twin and family, 2 suites; all rooms have phone, TV, hairdrier
FACILITIES sitting-room, bar, dining-room, games-room, TV-room, indoor swimming-pool, garden, private beach; sailing, fishing, clay pigeon shooting
CREDIT CARDS AE, DC, MC, V **CHILDREN** welcome
DISABLED access difficult **PETS** accepted **CLOSED** Nov to Feb
MANAGER Keith Bradford

THE SOUTH-WEST

ST MAWES, CORNWALL

TRESANTON
~ SEASIDE TOWN HOTEL ~

St Mawes, Cornwall TR2 5DR
TEL (01326) 270055 **FAX** (01326) 270053 **E-MAIL** info@tresanton.com
WEBSITE www.tresanton.com

IT'S EASY TO DRIVE PAST Tresanton, as it has no obvious entrance, particularly for cars. Look closer and you will see a discreet sign and some steps next to a pair of white-painted garages. Stop, and within seconds someone will appear to welcome you, take your luggage and park your car. This is not any old seaside hotel.

Tresanton was opened in the summer of 1998 by Olga Polizzi, daughter of Lord Forte, and it is now well established as the West Country hotel for chic townies who prefer not to forego sophistication when by the seaside. Yet St Mawes is a happy-go-lucky holiday village, full in summer of chirpy families, bucket and spade in hand, and the two must rub along together. A whitewashed former sailing club and a cluster of cottages on the seafront make up the hotel, which was well known back in the 1960s, but had long lost its glamour before Olga Polizzi came across it. She set about redesigning it in minimalist, elegant style, using restful, muted tones of oatmeal and flax, accentuated by blues, greens, browns or yellows. Bedrooms are a study in understated luxury and have stunning sea views. The warm and comfortable sitting-room and bar are more traditional.

After initial hiccups with food and service, it appears that Tresanton has now slipped into gear; the food, in particular, is gaining many plaudits.

NEARBY Trelissick, Glendurgan and Trebah Gardens; Truro.
LOCATION in town, just below castle, 14 miles (22 km) S of Truro; car parking
MEALS breakfast, lunch, dinner; room service
PRICE ££££
ROOMS 26; 22 double and twin, 4 suites, all with bath; all rooms have phone, TV, video, fax/modem point, hairdrier
FACILITIES sitting-room, dining-room, bar, cinema, terraces; boats, 8-metre yacht
CREDIT CARDS AE, MC, V **CHILDREN** welcome **DISABLED** 3 rooms on ground floor
PETS not accepted **CLOSED** Jan
PROPRIETOR Olga Polizzi

THE SOUTH-WEST

SHEPTON MALLET, SOMERSET

BOWLISH HOUSE
~ RESTAURANT-WITH-ROOMS ~

Wells Road, Shepton Mallet, Somerset BA4 5JD
TEL (01749) 342022 **FAX** (01749) 342022

THE FORMAL APPEARANCE of this fine Palladian house seems to suggest that new arrivals should perhaps knock before barging in, but the regime behind the elegant façade is anything but pompous. John and Deirdrè Forde have recently taken over from the Morleys who ran it for many years and, while some much-needed changes have taken place, the atmosphere remains relaxed and home-like rather than august – in fact the welcome is altogether warmer, say recent guests. Things had become decidedly tired and down-at-heel by the time the Fordes took over, and they have spruced up the decoration and improved the bathrooms, putting in showers as well as baths. Much of the country house furniture has remained, although they have changed many of the pictures on the walls.

The restaurant and its food remains the main focus of interest, and is popular with locals as well as residents. You can sink into armchairs for pre-dinner drinks in the panelled bar, before moving into a pale yellow dining-room, one wall hung with prints and paintings on an Egyptian theme, to sample Deirdrè Forde's polished culinary efforts.

Up the fine wood-panelled staircase (an imported but appropriate feature), there are just three bedrooms – all of them comfortably furnished, with large en suite bathrooms. Reports please.

~

NEARBY Wells; Glastonbury; Mendip Hills.
LOCATION just W of Shepton Mallet on A371; with walled garden and parking for 15 cars
MEALS breakfast, dinner
PRICE £
ROOMS 3 double, all with bath; all rooms have TV
FACILITIES dining-room, bar, sitting-room, conservatory **CREDIT CARDS** MC, V
CHILDREN welcome **DISABLED** access difficult **PETS** accepted, but not in public rooms
CLOSED 1 week in spring and autumn
PROPRIETORS John and Deirdrè Forde

THE SOUTH-WEST

INNSACRE FARMHOUSE

~ FARM GUEST-HOUSE ~

Shipton Gorge, Bridport, Dorset DT6 4LJ
TEL & **FAX** (01308) 456137

SET ON THE SIDE of a steeply rising, hill, this 17thC farmhouse is surrounded by ten acres of its own land, conveniently placed three miles from the sea and National Trust Coastal Path. The Davies's own flock of Jacob sheep graze the hillside, contributing to the atmosphere of peace and rural charm.

The farmhouse itself is quite dark inside, with only one main room serving the triple purpose of sitting-room, bar and dining-room. Warmed by a wood-burning stove in winter, the beamed room is divided by screens to separate diners and drinkers. It is decorated in an eclectic mix of objects, including colourful Provençal fabrics and strikingly large arrangements of flowers.

Jayne Davies is responsible for cooking the excellent suppers. There is no choice, although she takes into account the various likes and dislikes of guests and the three courses are all freshly prepared using local ingredients. Jayne will also make up picnic lunches for the many walkers that come to stay. Sydney (previously a hairdresser) has painted the bedrooms in strong heritage colours and furnished them with provincial French furniture in keeping with the rustic appeal of the place. Informality is the keyword here.

~

NEARBY National Trust Coastal Path; Lyme Regis; Chesil Beach; Dorchester.
LOCATION in quiet countryside, 2 miles (3 km) E of Bridport, S of A35; with ample car parking
MEALS breakfast, dinner
PRICE ££
ROOMS 4; 3 double, 1 twin, all with bath; all rooms have TV
FACILITIES bar, sitting-room
CREDIT CARDS MC, V **CHILDREN** accepted over 9 **DISABLED** no special facilities
PETS accepted (small charge) **CLOSED** Christmas Day to New Year
PROPRIETORS Sydney and Jayne Davies

THE SOUTH-WEST

STURMINSTER NEWTON, DORSET

PLUMBER MANOR

~ MANOR HOUSE HOTEL ~

Hazelbury Bryan Road, Sturminster Newton, Dorset DT10 2AF
TEL (01258) 472507 **FAX** (01258) 473370
E-MAIL book@plumbermanor.com

THIS IS A HANDSOME Jacobean manor house, 'modernized' in the early 20th century, that has been in the Prideaux-Brune family for well over 300 years. Since 1973, brothers Richard, Tim and Brian have been running it as an elegant but relaxed restaurant with comfortable bedrooms. Richard Prideaux-Brune is much in evidence front-of-house, as is his brother Tim. Together with Brian, who is responsible for the highly-regarded food, they draw in restaurant customers from far and wide – expect plenty of bustle on Friday and Saturday evenings, and non-residents in the dining-room.

The brothers make charming hosts, and have created a very relaxed and welcoming atmosphere. Old family portraits hang in the house; Labradors lounge in the bar; the decoration is homely and comfortable rather than smart. The large bar area might detract from the feeling of a family home, but it helps the Prideaux-Brunes' operation in a practical way (shooting parties are a feature in winter).

Bedrooms are divided between those in the main house (which lead off a gallery hung with portraits) and those in a converted stone barn and courtyard building which overlook the extensive gardens and stream. They are all spacious and comfortable.

~

NEARBY Purse Caundle Manor; Shaftesbury; Sherborne.
LOCATION 2 miles (3 km) SW of Sturminster Newton; private car parking
MEALS breakfast, Sun lunch, dinner
PRICE ££
ROOMS 16; 14 double, all with bath, 2 small doubles with bath; all rooms have phone, TV
FACILITIES dining-room, sitting-room, bar, garden; croquet, tennis court **CREDIT CARDS** AE, DC, MC, V **CHILDREN** welcome
DISABLED easy access to barn bedrooms and dining-room
PETS accepted by arrangement **CLOSED** Feb
PROPRIETOR Richard Prideaux-Brune

THE SOUTH-WEST

TEFFONT EVIAS, WILTSHIRE

HOWARD'S HOUSE

~ VILLAGE RESTAURANT-WITH-ROOMS ~

Teffont Evias, Salisbury, Wiltshire SP3 5RJ
TEL (01722) 716392 **FAX** (01722) 716820 **E-MAIL** paul.firmin@virgin.net
WEBSITE www.howardhousehotel.co.uk

TEFFONT EVIAS, IN THE NADDER VALLEY, has been owned by the same family, father to son, since 1692. It is picturesque and has great charm without being twee. In the grounds stands Howard's House, opposite a marvellously knotty topiary hedge, and embellished by a Swiss gabled roof in the early 19th century – its then owner had fallen for all things Swiss on the Grand Tour. It is surrounded by two acres of pretty garden.

Its *raison d'être* is the food, created by chef/patron Paul Firmin. A recent, very good, meal consisted of seared scallops with a saffron dressing, and steamed fillet of sea bass artfully piled on a lemon and garlic mash, and topped by a ravioli of salmon. The smallish dining-room, mint green with white tablecloths, is soothing but predictable, as is the decoration in the cosy sitting-room and the bedrooms: pastel-coloured walls, floral fabrics, pine furnishings. The four-poster room is the prettiest; rooms 1 and 2 look out over the garden.

Breakfast here is above reproach: excellent coffee, warm croissants and toast wrapped in a white napkin, and the frothiest, creamiest fresh orange juice you can imagine. You might choose a boiled egg, or something more sophisticated, such as poached egg tartlet with hollandaise sauce. The staff are friendly, practical and accommodating.

~

NEARBY Salisbury Cathedral; Wilton House; Stonehenge; Old Sarum.
LOCATION in village, off B3089 (signposted from Teffont Magna), 10 miles (16 km) W of Salisbury; car parking
MEALS breakfast, lunch, dinner
PRICE ££
ROOMS 9; 8 double and twin, 1 family, all with bath; all rooms have phone, TV, hairdrier
FACILITIES dining-room, sitting-room, terrace, garden **CREDIT CARDS** AE, DC, MC, V
CHILDREN welcome **DISABLED** access difficult **PETS** accepted **CLOSED** New Year
PROPRIETOR Paul Firmin

THE SOUTH-WEST

TINTAGEL, CORNWALL

TREBEA LODGE
~ MANOR HOUSE HOTEL ~

Trenale, Tintagel, Cornwall PL34 0HR
TEL (01840) 770410 **FAX** (01840) 770092

WARM ENDORSEMENTS from readers have brought this gracious and extremely hospitable hotel, run along the lines of a private house, to our attention. Though it dates back to the 14th century, the Grade II-listed house has a decorated grey stone Georgian façade, and, being only one room thick, all its windows enjoy the same sea views westwards across hedges and fields which run down to the Atlantic. It's a lovely sight at sunset.

Inside, all is calm, civilized, welcoming and rather grand without being in the least bit stuffy, with flagstone floors, panelled walls and deep, comfortable sofas. You can choose to relax either in the formal drawing- room on the first floor, furnished with antiques, or in the cosy ground-floor smoking-room where there is an honesty bar for guests to help themselves to drinks. Bedrooms are all different sizes and shapes, decorated with traditional and antique furniture. One is in the old wash house, with separate entrance; another has a fantastic carved four-poster.

Dinner at Trebea is an elegant, quite romantic occasion in the candlelit oak-panelled dining-room. One of the hotel's three friendly and helpful owners, Seán Devlin, is responsible for the cooking, and it's excellent, enjoyed by non-residents as well. Breakfast, too, is outstanding.

~

NEARBY Tintagel; Boscastle; Bodmin Moor; Lanhydrock House.
LOCATION in 4.5-acre grounds, 0.5 mile (1 km) SE of Tintagel; ample car parking
MEALS breakfast, dinner
PRICE £££
ROOMS 7 double and twin, 4 with bath, 3 with shower; all rooms have phone, TV, hairdrier
FACILITIES 2 sitting-rooms, dining-room, garden
CREDIT CARDS AE, MC, V **CHILDREN** accepted over 12
DISABLED access difficult **PETS** accepted by arrangement **CLOSED** Dec to mid-Feb
PROPRIETORS Seán Devlin, John Charlick and Fergus Cochrane

THE SOUTH-WEST

VIRGINSTOW, DEVON

PERCY'S AT COOMBESHEAD
~ COUNTRY RESTAURANT-WITH-ROOMS ~

Virginstow, Devon EX21 5EA
TEL (01409) 211236 **FAX** (01409) 211275 **E-MAIL** info@percys.co.uk
WEBSITE www.percys.co.uk

A WELCOME NEW ADDITION to the guide, this charming place was originally bought as their retirement home by the Bricknell-Webbs, who ran a restaurant in North London called Percy's. Fortunately for us, they decided to open the 16thC farmhouse in rural Devon as a restaurant-with-rooms, as well as running the 40-acre farm.

The bedrooms, in an adjacent converted barn, are spacious, understated and simple in the best way: there are no frills, but everything is of a high standard: the showers are power showers, the beds are king-size, and the real coffee comes in cafetières.

Two rooms, with stripped wood floors, pale wooden furniture, fresh flowers, candles on each table and a wood-burning stove make up the intimate and calming restaurant. Tina cooks in the modern English style, using fresh local ingredients in simple yet unexpected ways. Fish features strongly, and it is very good, not surprisingly as Tony has a licence to bid directly at the Looe fish auction. The scallops are superb, or you might opt for squid sautéed and served on a bed of mixed leaves. The wine list is equally good, with bottles listed in ascending order of price regardless of country of origin, and almost all available by the glass.

~

NEARBY Dartmoor; Tintagel; Clovelly; Tamar Otter Sanctuary.
LOCATION from the A30, travelling W, turn off after Okehampton to Broadwoodwidger, then follow signs to Virginstow
MEALS breakfast, dinner
PRICE ££
ROOMS 8; 7 double and twin, 1 family, all with shower; all rooms have TV, hairdrier
FACILITIES restaurant, bar, garden **CREDIT CARDS** AE, MC, V
CHILDREN welcome; over 10s only in restaurant
DISABLED 4 ground-floor rooms, 1 specially adapted
PETS accepted in bedrooms only **CLOSED** Nov
PROPRIETORS Tony and Tina Bricknell-Webb

THE SOUTH-WEST

WAREHAM, DORSET

THE PRIORY
COUNTRY TOWN HOTEL

Church Green, Wareham, Dorset BH20 4ND
TEL (01929) 551666 **FAX** (01929) 554519 **E-MAIL** reception@theprioryhotel.co.uk
WEBSITE www.theprioryhotel.co.uk

HIDDEN BEHIND THE CHURCH, this 16thC priory is the perfect retreat for anyone who appreciates a sense of history, as well as peace, comfort and good food. It has been run for the last 23 years by ex-accountant John Turner, born and bred in Wareham, who never dreamt that he would one day be the proud owner of this lovely building. He has seen to it that everything, from the excellent antiques to the pretty fabrics in the bedrooms, has been done with taste and in keeping.

The bedrooms are all that should be expected from a 16thC priory: beams, sloping ceilings and floors, as well as being supremely comfortable and well equipped with books (no *Reader's Digest* here) and attractive toiletries in the bathrooms. To keep up with the demand for rooms, Mr Turner has converted the boathouse to provide four extra bedrooms, or rather suites, equipped with luxury baths and French windows opening on to the River Frome. Indeed, by boat is the best way to arrive at The Priory: moorings are available and, after a quick walk through the stunning gardens (from which Mrs Turner gathers flowers for the arrangements) you can relax with a pre-dinner drink on the terrace. The food is richly satisfying, with a mainland European flavour emanating both from the menu and the French staff.

NEARBY Poole Harbour; Swanage; Lulworth Cove.
LOCATION in town near market square; in 4.5-acre gardens with ample car parking
MEALS breakfast, lunch, dinner
PRICE £££
ROOMS 19; 14 double, 3 single, 2 suites, all with bath; all rooms have phone, TV, hairdrier
FACILITIES sitting-room, bar, restaurant, terrace, garden; croquet
CREDIT CARDS AE, DC, MC, V
CHILDREN accepted over 8 **DISABLED** access difficult **PETS** guide dogs only
CLOSED never **PROPRIETORS** Turner family

The South-West

Wells, Somerset

The Market Place

~ Town hotel ~

Market Place, Wells, Somerset BA5 2RW
Tel (01749) 672616 **Fax** (01749) 679670 **E-mail** marketplace@heritagehotels.co.uk
Website www.heritagehotels.co.uk

DESPITE ITS LARGE NUMBER of rooms and despite being under the Best Western umbrella, this hotel has a very cosy feel. The gabled, cream-coloured exterior with grey-painted windows fronts the busy marketplace. A stone-clad archway leads to the courtyard entrance, and large palms in terracotta pots alert the visitor to the visual treats that await within.

The Chapman family have owned this 15thC building for over 40 years. Four years ago they decided to update and upgrade the hotel and the result is a stylish, colourful triumph. The restaurant adjacent to the reception and semi-circular bar at the entrance is a mix of soft green country checks teamed with Gustavian furniture, cream flagstones and rather dubious prints. Upstairs, a comfortable sitting-room runs the length of the building which, although peaceful, only provides Tourist Board literature as reading matter. Bedrooms are delightful, in a mix of style: from *toile de Jouy* wallpaper with fancy bedhangings to shocking pinks mixed with modern pine. Bathrooms are pristine with little painted chests adding a touch of quirkiness. Ten further bedrooms have been cleverly fashioned out of an old squash court.

~

Nearby Cathedral; Bishop's Palace; Glastonbury; Bath.
Location in town overlooking market square; public parking, limited on market days
Meals breakfast, lunch, dinner
Price ££
Rooms 29; 28 double and twin, 1 single, all with bath; all rooms have phone, TV, hairdrier
Facilities sitting-room, bar, restaurant, terrace
Credit Cards AE, DC, MC, V
Children accepted **Disabled** 1 ground-floor bedroom specially adapted
Pets accepted **Closed** never
Proprietors Chapman family

THE SOUTH-WEST

WHIMPLE, DEVON

WOODHAYES
~ COUNTRY HOUSE HOTEL ~

Whimple, near Exeter, Devon EX5 2TD
TEL & FAX (01404) 822237 **E-MAIL** info@woodhayes-hotel.co.uk
WEBSITE www.woodhayes-hotel.co.uk

WOODHAYES, LONG FEATURED in our guide, is the archetypal English country house hotel – comfortable, spacious and quiet. The gravel on the drive scrunches satisfyingly, the lawns are perfectly mown, nothing disturbs the peace of the countryside.

However, major changes are afoot. Having bought Woodhayes in 1998, Zimbabwean Eddie Katz and his English wife Lynda have begun to alter the interior, replacing the inoffensive pastels with more zingy colours, updating bathrooms and generally giving the place a facelift. They are, however, retaining the many architectural delights of the Georgian house, including the flagstone flooring in the bar and the wonderful white-painted Strawberry Gothic doors that are much in evidence throughout. Behind the main house, the Cottage has been completely revamped to provide a comfortable self-contained unit, perfect for four adults and a couple of children.

The greatest change, however, is on the culinary side: Lynda only cooks for parties of six or more, so our inspector was directed to a local pub for dinner. A sample menu of what might be offered appears to be acceptable dinner-party fare. If breakfast is anything to go by, it will be carefully and freshly prepared. More reports please.

~

NEARBY Cadhay House; Exe Valley.
LOCATION in village, 5 miles (8 km) NW of Exeter; ample car parking
MEALS breakfast, dinner by arrangement
PRICE ££
ROOMS 8; 3 double, 2 twin with bath en suite, 1 double with separate bath, 1 double, 1 twin with bath in Cottage; all rooms have phone, TV, hairdrier
FACILITIES sitting-room, library, bar, dining-room, gardens
CREDIT CARDS AE, DC, MC, V
CHILDREN accepted over 5 **DISABLED** access difficult **PETS** not accepted **CLOSED** never
PROPRIETORS Eddie and Lynda Katz

THE SOUTH-WEST

WILLITON, SOMERSET

WHITE HOUSE
~ RESTAURANT-WITH-ROOMS ~

Williton, Somerset TA4 4QW
TEL (01984) 632777

DESPITE BEING in the same little country town for over 30 years, Dick and Kay Smith continue to gather up awards for outstanding food, demonstrating their unwavering commitment to quality, sheer skill and changing fashion in the kitchen. They both cook, are both self-effacing about what they do so well, and deserve every accolade that comes their way. When we revisited the White House recently, we were again struck by their affability and easy-going manner.

What can you expect to find on the daily-changing menu? Starters might be dressed seared scallops with diced tomato, grilled marinated breast of wood pigeon on hot beetroot; main courses: a boned-out saddle of venison or a grilled sea bass fillet with aubergine and tomato *coulis*; puddings are just as tempting. Dick Smith's wine list is equally fine, and to add to the vinous atmosphere, posters in the bar advertise auctions of historical wine cellars. Both bar and sitting-room are informally furnished, large potted plants and ceramics made by the couple's potter son adding a jauntily artistic feel to the place. Soft colours, patchwork quilts and plain linens decorate the bedrooms. Those in the main house are the most spacious, while those in the converted stables and coach house are less exposed to traffic noise. Mediterranean plants in the garden include figs and palms in large pots.

NEARBY Cleeve Abbey; Quantock Hills.
LOCATION on A39 in centre of town; with ample parking
MEALS breakfast, lunch, dinner
PRICE ££
ROOMS 10 double and twin, all with bath; all rooms have phone, TV
FACILITIES sitting-room, bar, dining-room
CREDIT CARDS not accepted
CHILDREN accepted **DISABLED** access difficult **PETS** not accepted **CLOSED** Nov to May
PROPRIETORS Dick and Kay Smith

THE SOUTH-WEST

WITHYPOOL, SOMERSET

ROYAL OAK
~ VILLAGE INN ~

Withypool, Somerset TA24 7QP
TEL (01643) 831506 **FAX** (01643) 831659

WITHYPOOL IS A CENTRE for hunting, shooting and fishing, hidden away in the middle of Exmoor in a highly photogenic landscape. It is perhaps understandable to find that a former producer of TV commercials has recently taken over the village pub, and created a vision straight from the pages of *Country Living* magazine.

Don't worry that history and charm have been lost: Gail Sloggett is very aware of what she has inherited (this is where R.D. Blackmore wrote his classic tale *Lorna Doone* in 1866, and also where Eisenhower stayed in 1944), and the Royal Oak remains first and foremost a country pub, with bars suitably kitted out in antlers and hunting scenes. However, changes are afoot. Gail has painted the walls in the dining-room blue and yellow to match the new blue carpeting throughout – blue is very much in, pink of any hue very much out. The bedrooms upstairs are comfortable, some beamed, but as the programme of refurbishment gathers pace, the obviously traditional is being replaced by something much more striking. Two cottages at the rear are used as overflow accommodation or for self-catering. Don't turn them down – they are delightful.

Food looks set to remain in the good pub grub category, using excellent local produce, especially meat and game.

~

NEARBY Exmoor; Minehead.
LOCATION in middle of village, just off B3223, 15 miles (24 km) SW of Minehead; ample car parking
MEALS breakfast, lunch, dinner
PRICE ££
ROOMS 8 double and twin, all with bath; all rooms have phone, TV, hairdrier
FACILITIES sitting-room, 2 bars, restaurant, terrace
CREDIT CARDS AE, DC, MC, V
CHILDREN welcome **DISABLED** not suitable **PETS** accepted **CLOSED** never
PROPRIETOR Gail Sloggett

THE SOUTH-WEST

WIVELISCOMBE, SOMERSET

LANGLEY HOUSE

~ COUNTRY HOUSE HOTEL ~

Langley Marsh, near Wiveliscombe, Somerset TA4 2UF
TEL (01984) 623318 **FAX** (01984) 624573
E-MAIL user@langley.in2home.co.uk

IT HAS BEEN FIFTEEN YEARS NOW since Peter and Anne Wilson opened Langley House, and everything still appears to be running along well-ordered lines. Peter, who cooks, comes from a background in hotel-keeping, while Anne, who fronts, used to run the British Tourist Authority's Commendation Scheme – gamekeeper turned poacher, as it were. Between them, they know what they are about.

The house is a modest building with a rambling garden in delectable, rolling Somerset countryside which is neglected by most visitors to the West Country. (Anne Wilson is happy to advise guests on where to go touring during the day and provides them with maps.) It feels like a family home rather than a hotel, although it is not ideally furnished – less elegance, more informality would be our prescription, both for the sitting-rooms and some of the bedrooms – but the Wilsons' warmth of welcome overcomes such reservations. Peter's four-course dinners help too. They are entirely fixed until the dessert, when there is an explosion of choice 'icky sticky pudding', strawberry galette, syllabub). His food is light and unconventional, lovingly presented, in the best modern British manner, and elicits plenty of praise from his guests – 'the Wilsons are exemplary in their care'.

~

NEARBY Gaulden Manor; Exmoor; Quantock Hills.
LOCATION 1 mile (1.5 km) NW of Wiveliscombe, off B3227; in 4-acre gardens with ample car parking
MEALS breakfast, dinner
PRICE ££
ROOMS 9; 7 double, 6 with bath, 1 with shower, 2 single, both with bath, 1 family room, with bath; all rooms have TV, phone, hairdrier
FACILITIES bar, 2 sitting-rooms, restaurant, garden; croquet **CREDIT CARDS** AE, MC, V
CHILDREN welcome **DISABLED** access to ground floor easy
PETS accepted **CLOSED** never
PROPRIETORS Peter and Anne Wilson

THE SOUTH-WEST

YEOVIL, SOMERSET

LITTLE BARWICK HOUSE
~ RESTAURANT-WITH-ROOMS ~

Barwick, near Yeovil, Somerset BA22 9TD
TEL (01935) 423902 **FAX** (01935) 420908

VERONICA AND CHRISTOPHER COLLEY built up Little Barwick's reputation for
fine food over many years, so their many devotees will be reassured to
know that their successors come armed with impeccable culinary pedi-
grees. Tim Ford is one of Britain's finest young chefs: he trained at
Sharrow Bay and spent time in several top hotels refining his art. Latterly
he has been head chef at Summer Lodge in Evershot (see page 47), and
now he and his wife Emma, who was front-of-house there, have taken on
their own place.

They should have no problems in attracting custom, old and new.
Locally-sourced meat, game and fish provide the cornerstone of Tim's
cooking (our inspector enjoyed pink roasted rump of Dorset lamb with
aubergine caviar and black olive sauce), while the newly-introduced lunch
menu is a simpler variation of the dinner menu – a snip at only £12.50 for
three courses.

Little Barwick has featured in these pages for years, recommended for
its friendly informality, and this looks set to remain. However, the Fords
have embarked on a programme of redecoration to freshen up both the
interior and exterior of this lovely listed Georgian dower house. The dining
-room is now a creamy yellow; bathrooms are gradually being updated.
Bedrooms remain cheerful.

~

NEARBY Brympton d'Evercy; Montacute House.
LOCATION 2 miles (3 km) S of Yeovil off A37; car parking
MEALS breakfast, lunch, dinner
PRICE ££
ROOMS 5 double and twin, all with bath; all rooms have TV
FACILITIES sitting-room, dining-room, bar/private dining-room, garden
CREDIT CARDS AE, MC, V
CHILDREN welcome **DISABLED** access difficult **PETS** accepted **CLOSED** 2 weeks in Jan
PROPRIETORS Emma and Tim Ford

THE SOUTH-WEST

BISHOPS TAWTON, DEVON

Halmpstone Manor

Bishop's Tawton, near Barnstaple, Devon EX32 0EA
TEL (01271) 830321 **FAX** (01271) 830826 **PRICE** ££

Family home of the owners, Jane and Charles Stanbury, set in lovely
North Devon countryside. Excellent five-course dinners; plush bedrooms.

CORSCOMBE, DORSET

Fox Inn

Corscombe, Dorchester, Dorset DT2 0NS
TEL & FAX (01935) 891330 **PRICE** ££

Charming, atmospheric pub in a Dorset village with a good reputation
for inventive food, especially seafood, and three pretty bedrooms.

DODDISCOMBSLEIGH, DEVON

Nobody Inn

Doddiscombsleigh, near Exeter, Devon EX6 7PS
TEL (01647) 252394 **FAX** (01647) 252978 **PRICE** £

Archetypical country pub with loads of character, plus 200 whiskies
and 700 wines. A recent report, however, complained of poor quality
bedrooms.

MARTINHOE, DEVON

Old Rectory

Martinhoe, Parracombe, Devon EX31 4QT
TEL (01598) 763368 **FAX** (01598) 763567 **PRICE** ££

Quiet, homely hotel on the edge of Dartmoor, close to the north coast,
run with attention to detail by Jayne and Dennis Bennett.

PENRYN, CORNWALL

Clare House

Broad Street, Penryn, Cornwall TR10 8JH
TEL (01326) 373294 **PRICE** £

We haven't had a chance yet to inspect this gracious 17thC Grade
II-listed guest-house in the heart of Penryn, but early reports are very
positive.

SOUTH ZEAL, DEVON

Oxenham Arms

South Zeal, near Okehampton, Devon EX20 2JT
TEL (01837) 840244 **FAX** (01837) 840791 **PRICE** ££

Characterful, creeper-covered granite inn constructed uniquely around
a standing stone. Cosy bar, sitting-room; simple bedrooms.

THE SOUTH-EAST

BATTLE, EAST SUSSEX

LITTLE HEMINGFOLD FARMHOUSE
~ COUNTRY HOTEL ~

Telham, Battle, East Sussex, TN33 0TT
TEL (01424) 774338 **FAX** (01424) 77535

DON'T BE MISLED BY the word 'farmhouse': apart from the setting there is not much that is agricultural about this substantial, rambling building, part 17thC, part early Victorian. The house has a peaceful setting in 40 acres of farm and woodland; it is surrounded by gardens, and overlooks a pretty 2-acre trout lake (the Slaters are happy to lend fishing rods). Inside, intriguing nooks and crannies give the house a special charm. The two sitting-rooms and the cosy dining-room all have log fires. So do four of the nine bedrooms, all individually furnished, and accommodated in the converted coach house and stables, grouped around a flowery courtyard.

Allison and Paul emphasize fresh ingredients in their traditional cooking, though we have received mixed reports from visitors about the food. One reader writes: 'the beef we ordered for dinner was quite the best ever and the puddings most unusual and delicious...on Sunday, after a walk through their lovely grounds we indulged in a huge breakfast, which was again superb'. Another was less happy with the choice of bread at breakfast time, and was irritated by the slow service and having to share a table. We welcome further reports.

~

NEARBY Bodiam Castle; Great Dixter; Rye; Sissinghurst.
LOCATION 1.5 miles (3 km) SE of Battle, off A2100; in 40-acre garden, with trout lake, fields and woods; ample car parking
MEALS breakfast, light lunch, dinner
PRICE ££
ROOMS 13 double, 1 family room, 10 with bath; all rooms have phone, TV, electric blankets; 4 rooms have log-burning stoves
FACILITIES 2 sitting-rooms, dining-room, bar, garden; boating, trout fishing, tennis, croquet **CREDIT CARDS** AE, DC, MC, V **CHILDREN** welcome
DISABLED access difficult
PETS accepted **CLOSED** 6 Jan to12 Feb
PROPRIETORS Paul and Allison Slater

THE SOUTH-EAST

PARK HOUSE
~ COUNTRY HOTEL ~

Bepton, near Midhurst, West Sussex GU29 0JB
TEL (01730) 812880 **FAX** (01730) 815643 **E-MAIL** reservations@parkhouse.com
WEBSITE www.parkhouse.com

PARK HOUSE HAS BEEN in the O'Brien family for over 50 years, and has always retained the atmosphere of a private country house – thanks first to the careful attention of Ioné O'Brien, and now to her son, Michael.

A 16thC farmhouse with Victorian additions, the hotel, with its cream-painted roughcast walls, at first looks rather suburban. Inside, however, the elegant public rooms strike a very different note. The honesty bar, festooned with mementoes and photographs of polo players (Cowdray Park is close at hand) is admirably well stocked, while the drawing-room, particularly appealing at night, gleams with polished parquet floor, velvet-backed alcoves filled with books and china, yellow walls, and table lamps which cast a golden glow. Bedrooms are traditional; best are the two in the annexe, one of which has a private patio. The dinner menu is amazingly limited for these days. It might feature mushroom or tomato soup, melon and parma ham or prawn cocktail, roast beef or lamb or a plainly served fish. It is symptomatic of this idiosyncratic, endearing time-warp, and none the worse for that. The new gallery space (for local artists) in an ancient adjoining barn comes as a bit of a jolt.

NEARBY Petworth; Goodwood; Cowdray Park; Chichester.
LOCATION in countryside, on the B2226 just N of Bepton village, 3 miles (5 km) SW of Midhurst; ample car parking
MEALS breakfast, lunch, dinner; room service
PRICE £££
ROOMS 12 double, 1 single, 1 family room, all with bath; all rooms have phone, TV, hairdrier
FACILITIES dining-room, sitting-room, bar, garden; swimming-pool, tennis, croquet, putting green, 9-hole pitch and putt course, art gallery
CREDIT CARDS AE, DC, MC, V **CHILDREN** welcome
DISABLED specially adapted ground-floor bedroom **PETS** accepted **CLOSED** never
PROPRIETOR Michael O'Brien

THE SOUTH-EAST

BUCKLERS HARD, HAMPSHIRE

MASTER BUILDER'S HOUSE
~ RIVERSIDE HOTEL ~

Bucklers Hard, Beaulieu, Hampshire SO42 7XB
TEL (01590) 616253 **FAX** (01590) 616297

A NEW ENTRY TO THE GUIDE, the superbly sited Master Builder's House has long been ripe for a carefully judged overhaul, and when its lease from Lord Montagu of Beaulieu came up for renewal, Jeremy Willcock and John Illsley, proprietors of The George in Yarmouth, Isle of Wight (see page 137) were just the right pair to step in. Lord Montagu's daughter, interior designer Mary Montagu, undertook the redecoration, creating a straightforward traditional style with a maritime theme (plenty of old prints on the walls) in keeping with the spirit of Bucklers Hard, where some of Nelson's ships were built in the 18th century. Today it is a picturesque and popular marina, with a street of shipwrights' dwellings, a popular bar for visiting yachtsmen, and a maritime museum.

The 18thC Master Builder's House was lumbered some years back with an unsympathetic modern annexe, the Henry Adams Wing. Even the designer's best efforts cannot give the bedrooms here the character they lack, and although they are now comfortable and attractive, given their size, we feel they are somewhat ambitiously priced. Bedrooms in the main building have much more character. The sophisticated new reception area is a vast improvement on the old, and in the smart dining-room, with absorbing views down to the river, 'modern classical' dishes are served.

~

NEARBY New Forest; Beaulieu; Lymington.
LOCATION overlooking Beaulieu river at Bucklers Hard, 2 miles (3 km) SE of Beaulieu, 9 miles (14 km) SE of Lyndhurst; ample car parking.
MEALS breakfast, lunch, dinner
PRICE £££
ROOMS 25 double, all with bath; all rooms have phone, TV, hairdrier; 2 self-catering cottages
FACILITIES sitting-room, dining-room, yachtsman's bar, terrace, garden; private pontoon **CREDIT CARDS** AE, MC, V **CHILDREN** welcome
DISABLED access difficult **PETS** not accepted **CLOSED** never
PROPRIETORS Jeremy Willcock and John Illsley

THE SOUTH-EAST

CRANBROOK, KENT

KENNEL HOLT

~ MANOR HOUSE HOTEL ~

Goudhurst Road, Cranbrook, Kent TN17 2PT
TEL (01580) 712032 **FAX** (01580) 715495

HAVING BEEN DROPPED from our guide some years back after a crop of complaints, we now frequently hear excellent things from readers about the new regime at this Elizabethan manor of soft red brick and white wooden boards, set in 5 acres of secluded and flowery gardens, notable for its impressive yew hedging. Certainly no one complained about the building – which has Edwardian additions – or its setting; indeed you would be hard pressed to find a better-placed base for an exploration of south-east England than Cranbrook, and you certainly will not find a hotel which feels more at one with its Kentish surroundings.

It is a homely manor rather than a grand one, with capacious sofas before the open fires of its beamed sitting-rooms, and honest antiques dotted about. The Chalmers have been at the helm since 1992, and, judging from recent reports, have maintained the high standards they first set when they took over, 'achieving what so many aspire to achieve, but never do; leaving was a wrench'.

Neil Chalmers taught himself to cook when he took over, and now serves accomplished set menus of seasonal food, each course with six or seven choices, to both residents and locals. More reports please.

~

NEARBY Sissinghurst Castle Gardens; Hole Park; Weald of Kent; Rye.
LOCATION 1.5 miles (2.5 km) NW of Cranbrook, close to A262; in gardens, with ample car parking
MEALS breakfast, lunch, dinner; room service
PRICE £££
ROOMS 10; 8 double, 2 single, 7 with bath, 3 with shower; all rooms have phone, TV, hairdrier
FACILITIES 2 sitting-rooms, dining-room, gardens; croquet and putting lawns
CREDIT CARDS AE, MC, V
CHILDREN welcome, but no children under 6 in restaurant for dinner
DISABLED access difficult **PETS** not accepted **CLOSED** 3 weeks in Jan
PROPRIETORS Neil and Sally Chalmers

THE SOUTH-EAST

CRANBROOK, KENT

OLD CLOTH HALL
~ MANOR HOUSE GUEST-HOUSE ~

Cranbrook, Kent TN17 3NR
TEL (01580) 712220 **FAX** (01580) 712220

MRS MORGAN'S WARMTH OF WELCOME has made her many friends among
the guests who negotiate the sweeping gravelled drive to this splendid 15thC half-timbered manor, which can count Queen Elizabeth I as one
of its visitors.

Diamond-paned windows look out on to 13 acres of glorious Kentish
gardens – rhododendrons and azaleas, a sunken rose garden, swimming-
pool, tennis court, and a superb croquet lawn to complete the picture.

The interior, as you would expect, is also rather special. There are log
fires in the inglenooks; oak floors and panelling gleam; and the antiques,
fine chintz fabrics, porcelain and flower arrangements are all evidence of
Mrs Morgan's appreciation of how to make her home look its best. The
bedrooms, furnished with antiques, are exceptionally pretty, and offer a
very high standard of comfort.

A couple who spent their autumnal wedding night at the Old Cloth Hall
report in glowing terms on everything from the tranquil setting to the fruit
fresh from the garden; and a recent inspection confirms that it thoroughly
deserves its place in this guide. Mrs Morgan is currently converting her
adjacent barn and oast houses and with a view to moving there, where she
will carry on as before.

~

NEARBY Sissinghurst; Scotney Castle Gardens.
LOCATION in countryside, 1 mile (1.5 km) E of Cranbrook on road to Tenterden,
before cemetery; in grounds of 13 acres; ample car parking
MEALS breakfast, dinner by arrangement
PRICE ££
ROOMS 3 double, all with bath; all rooms have TV and hairdrier
FACILITIES sitting-room, dining-room, terrace, garden; swimming-pool, tennis
court, croquet **CREDIT CARDS** not accepted
CHILDREN accepted by arrangement **DISABLED** access difficult **PETS** not accepted
CLOSED Christmas **PROPRIETOR** Katherine Morgan

THE SOUTH-EAST

CUCKFIELD, WEST SUSSEX

OCKENDEN MANOR

~ MANOR HOUSE HOTEL ~

Ockenden Lane, Cuckfield, West Sussex RH17 5LD
TEL (01444) 416111 **FAX** (01444) 415549 **E-MAIL** ockenden@hshotels.co.uk
WEBSITE www.hshotels.co.uk

A TELLING COMMENT FROM the inspector we sent recently: "Anne Goodman oversees the decoration herself, so gives it the personal touch, rather than simply splashing out on the finest." She has made many changes for the better here since taking over this attractive 16th/17thC manor house.

Bedrooms are spacious and individual (and crammed with giveaways); a superb master suite with sombre panelling relies on reds and greens to give a feeling of brightness. Several of the bathrooms are notably spacious, and they are equipped with Molton Brown toiletries. The main sitting-room, though lavishly furnished, has a personal feel. Staff are friendly and obliging. (A notice in the hotel states that whatever a hotel's character and charm, it is only as good as its staff.)

Dinner, which is served in the oak-panelled restaurant with painted ceiling and stained glass windows, is another highlight. Food is based on local produce, with vegetables and herbs from the garden.

Although Ockenden Manor is popular with business people, it is a human, comfortable hotel, with a very pleasant young manager in Kerry Turner. "Hidden away behind trees and a high wall; quiet; good value", says our inspector.

~

NEARBY Nyman's Gardens; Sissinghurst; Wakehurst Place; Gatwick; Brighton.
LOCATION 2 miles (3 km) W of Hayward's Heath close to
middle of village, off A272; in 9-acre grounds, with ample car parking
MEALS breakfast, lunch, dinner
PRICE £££
ROOMS 21 double, 1 single, all with bath; all rooms have phone, TV, hairdrier
FACILITIES sitting-room, bar, dining-room, terrace, garden
CREDIT CARDS AE, DC, MC, V
CHILDREN welcome **DISABLED** no special facilities
PETS not accepted **CLOSED** never
PROPRIETORS Sandy and Anne Goodman

THE SOUTH-EAST

EAST GRINSTEAD, WEST SUSSEX

GRAVETYE MANOR

~ MANOR HOUSE HOTEL ~

Vowels Lane, near East Grinstead, West Sussex RH19 4LJ
TEL (01342) 810567 **FAX** (01342) 810080 **E-MAIL** gravetye@relaischateaux.fr
WEBSITE www.relaischateaux.fr/gravetye

THE COUNTRY HOUSE HOTEL, now so much a part of the tourist scene in Britain, scarcely existed when Peter Herbert opened the doors of this serene Elizabethan house over 40 years ago. It is scarcely surprising that in that time he and his team have got their act thoroughly polished; but it is remarkable that Gravetye is not in the least eclipsed by younger competitors. Standards in every department are unflaggingly high. Service consistently achieves the elusive aim of attentiveness without intrusion, while the ambitious food is about the best in the county. A recent visitor, who has known the hotel for 30 years, remained as impressed as ever: "A sleek operation that doesn't compromise." However, another commented on "lots of wealthy-looking people in sunglasses and strange-looking jogging suits".

The pioneering gardener William Robinson lived in the house for half a century until his death in 1935. Great care is taken to maintain the various gardens he created; Robinson was also responsible for many features of the house as it is seen today – the mellow oak panelling and grand fireplaces in the calm, gracious sitting rooms, for example. Bedrooms – all immaculate – vary in size from the adequate to the enormous, and prices range accordingly.

~

NEARBY Wakehurst; Nyman's Gardens.
LOCATION 4.5 miles (7 km) SW of East Grinstead by B2110 at Gravetye; in 30-acre grounds with ample car parking
MEALS breakfast, lunch, dinner; room service
PRICE ££££
ROOMS 16 double, 2 single, all with bath; all rooms have phone, TV, fax/modem points, hairdrier; 2 rooms have air-conditioning
FACILITIES 2 sitting-rooms, bar, dining-room; croquet, trout fishing
CREDIT CARDS MC, V **CHILDREN** welcome over 7 **DISABLED** access possible
PETS dogs accepted in kennel **CLOSED** never **PROPRIETORS** Herbert family

THE SOUTH-EAST

FLETCHING, EAST SUSSEX

GRIFFIN INN
~ VILLAGE INN ~

Fletching, near Uckfield, East Sussex TN22 3SS
TEL (01825) 722890 **FAX** (01825) 722800
WEBSITE www.thegriffininn.co.uk

THIS COSY, WELCOMING, lively 16thC village inn, owned by the Pullan family for 20 years (Nigel Pullan is a director of Ebury Wine Bars) has a winning combination of good food and four-posters in pretty bedrooms with beams and low ceilings. It's popular for Glyndebourne and romantic weekends. Everything is a bit uneven, quaint, on a small scale, but endearing rather than cramped. What is called the Coach House – behind the pub – was converted in 1998 to provide four new bedrooms with hand-painted murals and attractive small Victorian-style bathrooms, tiled in black and white, and with oak floors. The original bedrooms in the main building are soon to be upgraded to the same standard, though these overlook the main street and are not as quiet as those to the rear. 'Homely and civilized' is the desciption of one regular guest. The pub, with more beams, panelling, open fires and hunting prints, has a bustling atmosphere, with people coming and going; the old public bar is being turned into a kind of sitting-room, with sofas, armchairs and a backgammon board. Good food is always at hand, either in the pub, or in the restaurant, which uses fresh seasonal ingredients and local organic vegetables. The back garden looks over the parkland of Sheffield Park.

~

NEARBY Sheffield Park; Glyndebourne; Ashdown Forest.
LOCATION in village off A22 and A275 between East Grinstead and Uckfield; with car parking
MEALS breakfast, lunch, dinner
PRICE ££
ROOMS 8 double and twin, 3 with bath, 5 with shower; all rooms have TV, hairdrier
FACILITIES bars, restaurant, bar billiards, terrace, patio, garden
CREDIT CARDS AE, DC, MC, V
CHILDREN welcome **DISABLED** 2 bedrooms on ground floor
PETS accepted, but not in bedrooms **CLOSED** Christmas Day
MANAGERS James Pullan and John Gatti

THE SOUTH-EAST

FRANT, KENT

THE OLD PARSONAGE

~ COUNTRY GUEST HOUSE ~

Frant, Tunbridge Wells, Kent TN3 9DX
TEL & **FAX** (01892) 750773

AT THE HEART OF the charming village of Frant, The Old Parsonage is set in 3 acres of gardens. This is a fine Georgian country house beautifully renovated by Tony and Mary Dakin. The tall and spacious reception rooms are filled with plants and decorated with lithographs and watercolours as well as Mary's unusual tapestries and Tony's evocative photographs of village scenes.

The centrepiece is the exceptionally large and airy atrium, which floods light on to the main staircase, landing and hall, and shows off the black-and-white photographic portraits in the picture gallery. The drawing-room is delightful, too, gracious in style, with Persian rugs, crystal chandeliers and antiques – impressive without being overpowering. The freshly decorated bedrooms (two with four-posters) have large bathrooms (one, with sunken bath, is almost a sitting-room). Their decoration and furnishing are constantly under review.

The Dakins are evidently enthusiastic and dedicated: "This is our home, so we want it to look its best," says Mary. Tony is responsible for breakfast, and for maintaining the pleasant garden. (Free sherry on the terrace.) An excellent base for visiting the several famous National Trust properties in the area – see below.

~

NEARBY Bodiam, Leeds, Hever and Scotney Castles; Sissinghurst and Sheffield Park Gardens; Bateman's; Penshurst Place; Knole.
LOCATION near church in village 2 miles (3 km) S of Tunbridge Wells; in large gardens with ample car parking
MEALS breakfast
PRICE ££
ROOMS 3 double (1 twin), all with bath; all rooms have TV, hairdrier
FACILITIES sitting-room, breakfast-room, conservatory
CREDIT CARDS MC, V **CHILDREN** welcome **DISABLED** access difficult **PETS** accepted in bedrooms **CLOSED** never **PROPRIETORS** Tony and Mary Dakin

THE SOUTH-EAST

LANGRISH HOUSE
~ MANOR HOUSE HOTEL ~

Langrish, Petersfield, Hampshire GU32 1RN
TEL (01730) 266941 **FAX** (01730) 260543

THERE IS A GREAT DEAL yet to do at Langrish House, as its charming owners are the first to admit, but we include it because we sense their
commitment, enthusiasm, and determination to succeed. And the story of
how the Talbot-Ponsonbys came to run this hotel is a touching one.

Nigel was brought up in this 17thC, much extended manor house set in
16 acres of grounds amidst lovely countryside, and always hoped it would
be his one day. But circumstances meant that it was sold by his father,
and turned into a hotel. Up for sale again in 1997, they came for a last look
before it went to a housing association – and decided to buy. "Nigel was in
love with the place," says Robina, "and I was happy to help him live here
again, even if it meant becoming a hotelier instead of a housewife." And,
despite her inexperience, she runs the hotel with the humour, friendliness
and management skills of a professional. Gradually, as money permits,
they are upgrading the bedrooms; the ones she has completed are charming and (those in the attic) fun; those still to be done, however, are perfectly acceptable, comfortable if dated. Their plan is to reinstate the drawing-room (at present two bedrooms) as an elegant public room, and to say
goodbye to the swirly patterned carpet. The food is already excellent, as is
the polite and willing service and the relaxed and informal ambience. We
wish them well.

~

NEARBY Winchester; Chawton; Selborne; Portsmouth; Chichester.
LOCATION signposted off the A272 at Langrish; ample car parking
MEALS breakfast, lunch, dinner; room service
PRICE ££
ROOMS 13; 11 double and twin, 1 single, 1 family, all with bath; all rooms have
phone, TV
FACILITIES sitting-room, dining-room, bar, terrace, garden
CREDIT CARDS AE, DC, MC, V **CHILDREN** welcome
DISABLED 1 bedroom on ground floor **PETS** accepted **CLOSED** never
PROPRIETORS Nigel and Robina Talbot-Ponsonby

THE SOUTH-EAST

ROMNEY BAY HOUSE

~ SEASIDE HOTEL ~

Coast Road, Littlestone, New Romney, Kent TN28 8QY
TEL (01797) 364747 **FAX** (01797) 367156
WEBSITE www.uk-travelguide.co.uk/rombayho.htl

THE APPROACH THROUGH sprawling Littlestone is unpromising, particularly in the dark when you don't know where you're heading. But this dignified 1920s house, built by Clough Williams Ellis for American columnist Hedda Hopper, has a superb position between the sea and Romney Marsh. There's a smell of wood smoke and fresh flowers as you enter, and Jennifer Gorlich's interiors are reminiscent of a small hotel in Provence, with plenty of French furniture and fabrics. She is usually in the kitchen, whipping up her famous cream teas (they can be had at any time, from breakfast onwards) and delicious four-course dinners. This is a thoroughly relaxed place: the cosy bar; the warm, firelit sitting-room packed with groups of comfortable, inviting chairs; late breakfasts in the pretty conservatory; drinks on the terrace; and entertaining Helmut happily attending to everyone's needs. It was his idea not to have phones in the house and mobile addicts are asked to use them.

Bedrooms have creamy cottons, fresh white bedlinen, bright checks, and antiques; an upstairs 'look-out' room has the feel of a beach house, with piles of towels for swimming, faded blue denim cushions on wicker chairs, and an assortment of sea shells. An entry in the Visitor's Book records that the Gorlichs are great practitioners of the art of good living; all this, and the beach too.

~

NEARBY Rye; Dungeness Lighthouse; Sandwich.
LOCATION in New Romney, take Station Road to seafront, turn left, and follow hotel signs for 1 mile (1.5 km); car parking
MEALS breakfast, weekend sandwich lunch, dinner
PRICE ££
ROOMS 10 double and twin, all with bath or shower; all rooms have TV, hairdrier
FACILITIES sitting-room, dining-room, look-out room, terrace, garden; croquet, boules, beach **CREDIT CARDS** DC, MC, V **CHILDREN** accepted over 14
DISABLED access difficult **PETS** not accepted **CLOSED** Christmas
PROPRIETORS Jennifer and Helmut Gorlich

THE SOUTH-EAST

LONDON

THE BEAUFORT

~ TOWN BED-AND-BREAKFAST ~

33 Beaufort Gardens, London SW3 1PP
TEL (020) 7584 5252 **FAX** (020) 7589 2834 **E-MAIL** thebeaufort@nol.co.uk
WEBSITE www.thebeaufort.co.uk/index.htm

THREE HARRODS DOORMEN in a row gave our inspector unerring directions for the hundred-yard walk to The Beaufort, part of a Victorian terrace overlooking a quiet Knightsbridge cul-de-sac. Owned by Sir Michael Wilmot and his wife, Diana Wallis (but presided over by Harry the cat), this must be one of the few hotels in the world which surprises you with what doesn't appear later on your bill. Feel like a glass of champagne? No charge. Cream tea? Limo to or from the airport? Light meal in your room? The answer's still no charge. And, just when you have been made to feel so good that you want to give a tip, you fall victim to a no-tipping policy.

All the rooms are different, some decorated in muted pastels, others following in the cheerful footsteps of the public areas. Each room has a CD player, video and portable stereo and, for those who need added protection from the English weather, there are also chocolates, shortbread, brandy and umbrellas. And then there are the flowers. Plenty of them. Many are real, but most are hanging on the walls as part of the Wilmots' enormous collection of English floral watercolours. Noted for the friendliness of its predominantly female staff, The Beaufort has many faithful regulars.

~

NEARBY Harrods; Victoria and Albert Museum.
LOCATION off Brompton Road, just W of Harrods; pay and display parking in street
MEALS breakfast; room service
PRICE ££££
ROOMS 28 double, twin, single and suites, all with bath or shower; all rooms have phone, TV, video, CD player, air-conditioning, hairdrier; fax/answering machines on request
FACILITIES sitting-room, bar **CREDIT CARDS** AE, DC, MC, V
CHILDREN accepted
DISABLED some bedrooms on ground floor
PETS not accepted **CLOSED** never **PROPRIETORS** Sir Michael Wilmot and Diana Wallis

THE SOUTH-EAST

LONDON

COVENT GARDEN
~ TOWN HOTEL ~

10 Monmouth Street, London WC2H 9HB
TEL (020) 7806 1000 **FAX** (020) 7806 1100 **E-MAIL** covent@firmdale.com
WEBSITE www.firmdale.com

THE BURGEONING GROUP OF SEDUCTIVE London hotels owned by Tim and Kit Kemp will increase to half-a-dozen with the opening of their latest, Charlotte Street Hotel. They began with Dorset Square (see page 106) and then opened several more similar townhouse hotels, before becoming more expansive here in Covent Garden, but without losing any of their previous assurance.

Monmouth Street is an attractive, fairly quiet street ideally placed for theatre and media-land. The building was formerly a French hospital, which Tim and Kit (she is responsible for all the interior decoration), have transformed into a hotel which at once feels glamorous, yet at the same time welcoming and not in the least intimidating. A stunning drawing-room stretches across the first floor, with a really well-stocked drinks-and-snack bar at one end where guests can help themselves at any time. On the ground floor is the small bar/bistro, Max's, serving tasty, simply cooked dishes *à la mode*; or you can order from the well-balanced room service menu at any hour.

Bedrooms all look different, although each possesses a matching fabric-covered mannequin (the hotel is a favourite with models), and they all have superb granite bathrooms with double basins and excellent mirrors. One bedroom has a musical theme, another is split-level, another has a memorable four-poster bed; the cosy attic rooms are also delightful.

~

NEARBY Covent Garden; Royal Opera House; West End theatres.
LOCATION in fairly quiet street between Shaftesbury Avenue and St Martin's Lane; metered parking or public car park nearby
MEALS breakfast, lunch, dinner; room service
PRICE ££££ **ROOMS** 50; 38 double and twin, 4 suites, 8 single, all with bath; all rooms have phone, TV, video, CD player, fax/modem point, air-conditioning, minibar, hairdrier **FACILITIES** drawing-room, restaurant, bar, library, work-out room, lift **CREDIT CARDS** AE, DC, MC, V **CHILDREN** accepted **DISABLED** access possible
PETS not accepted **CLOSED** never **PROPRIETORS** Tim and Kit Kemp

THE SOUTH-EAST

LONDON

DORSET SQUARE
∽ TOWNHOUSE HOTEL ∽

39 Dorset Square, London NW1 6QN
Tel (020) 7723 7874 **Fax** (020) 7724 3328 **E-mail** dorset@firmdale.com
Website www.firmdale.com

LOOKING OUT OVER the original site of Lord's cricket ground, this perfectly restored Regency house is like one of those impossible geometric shapes that are bigger on the inside than on the outside. Yet it is still cosy, and, although it offers the services and technology of a new, purpose-built hotel, there is always a real person to welcome you home at any time of the day or night. Kit Kemp and her husband Tim (who also own the Covent Garden, page 105, among other hotels) have thought of just about everything in this, their original venture into hotel-keeping: fabrics and furniture of the style and age to complement the building, bathrooms of such marble splendour that even the most fanatical of critics would look forward to them, fresh flowers everywhere, and last but not least real radios in all the (good-sized) rooms.

If you need more than a drink from the honesty bar in the sitting-room there is the Potting Shed Restaurant and Bar in the basement, so-called because it was here that the Lord's groundsmen kept their pots. Today the restaurant is decorated with cricketing and ballooning scenes and serves modern English food. During the summer you can even ask the hotel to bring your drinks out to you in the square's gardens.

∽

Nearby Regent's Park; Madame Tussaud's; Oxford Street.
Location close to Marylebone and Baker Street station, in square with access to 2-acre private gardens; with garaged car parking nearby
Meals breakfast; room service
Price £££
Rooms 38; 32 double and twin, 6 single, all with bath or shower; all rooms have phone, TV, air-conditioning, minibar, hairdrier, safe; some have fax/modem point
Facilities sitting-room, restaurant, bar
Credit Cards AE, MC, V
Children welcome **Disabled** not suitable **Pets** not accepted **Closed** never
Manager Sharon Dolan

THE SOUTH-EAST

DUKES
~ TOWN HOTEL ~

35 St James's Place London SW1A 1NY
TEL (020) 7491 4840 **FAX** (020) 7493 1264 **E-MAIL** enquiries@dukeshotel.co.uk
WEBSITE: www.dukeshotel.co.uk

DISCREETLY SET BACK in its own gaslit courtyard, this civilized Edwardian hotel makes an excellent address in a prestigious West End area, and is run with efficiency and a marked thoughtfulness for its guests by manager Andrew Phillips and his young, friendly team. The place was in a creaky, frayed state by the time hotelier David Naylor-Leyland (who also owns The Franklin, page 109) bought it and gave it a new lease of life a few years ago. One asset he sensibly did hang on to was master barman Gilberto Preti, said to concoct the best dry martini in London, which he does with great aplomb each evening in the clubby, animated bar.

The feel of Dukes is of an English country house, mercifully decorated without resorting to excess. This is particularly evident in the restrained but charming bedrooms, which feel more like guest rooms in a private house than hotel rooms, with the bonus of excellent king-size beds. The penthouse, with superb views, would make a perfect romantic hideaway in which to hole up for a few days – finances permitting.

The hotel has recently added fitness and beauty treatment facilities, putting it on a par with much larger luxury establishments. Public rooms are small, but that's what gives the place its cosy feel. Staff are smiling and willing; we would welcome comments on the food.

~

NEARBY St James's; Piccadilly Circus; Royal Academy; Green Park.
LOCATION in West End, tucked off St James's Street; valet parking in nearby public car park
MEALS breakfast, lunch, dinner; room service
PRICE ££££ **ROOMS** 81; 74 double and twin, 7 suites, all with bath; all rooms have phone, TV, fax/modem point, minibar, air-conditioning, hairdrier
FACILITIES sitting-room, restaurant, bar, lift, gym, sauna, beauty treatment rooms
CREDIT CARDS AE, DC, MC, V
CHILDREN accepted **DISABLED** access possible **PETS** not accepted **CLOSED** never
MANAGER Andrew Phillips

THE SOUTH-EAST

LONDON

FIVE SUMNER PLACE

~ TOWN BED-AND-BREAKFAST ~

5 Sumner Place, London SW7 3EE
TEL (020) 7584 7586 **FAX** (020) 7823 9962 **E-MAIL** no.5@dial.pipex.com
WEBSITE www.sumnerplace.com

IF YOU HAVE SERIOUS SHOPPING in mind, or want to attend a Christie's auction at their salerooms round the corner, and you are looking for a place to stay which is less hard on the purse than some of the neighbouring 'house hotels', consider Five Sumner Place. The rooms in this townhouse are freshly decorated, furnished in traditional style, and reasonably priced for the area. Despite its central location (a few yards from the hurly-burly of South Kensington), it is quiet and unpretentious, there are no signs outside, and you come and go as you please with your own key to the permanently locked front door. South Kensington is the place for buses and tubes to just about anywhere (including Heathrow airport) and boasts one of the few London cab-ranks that actually has taxis waiting on it. Inside, the lift is quite snug (as are the rooms), but in early Victorian houses like this, it is a fairly rare amenity.

Breakfast is a pan-European buffet with cold cuts and cheese as well as the more expected toast, cereal, fruit and yogurt. It is served in a quiet and (sometimes) sunny conservatory which takes up half the small garden. Manager Tom Tyranowicz runs the hotel with quiet efficiency from a minute office and will cheerfully bring you anything from a cup of tea to an ironing board.

~

NEARBY Science Museum; Natural History Museum; Knightsbridge.
LOCATION in residential street off Old Brompton Road; with public car park and meters nearby
MEALS breakfast
PRICE £££
ROOMS 13; 10 double and twin, 3 single, all with bath or shower; all rooms have phone, TV, hairdrier
FACILITIES conservatory, lift, patio **CREDIT CARDS** AE, MC, V
CHILDREN accepted over 6
DISABLED bedrooms on ground floor **PETS** not accepted **CLOSED** never
MANAGER Tom Tyranowicz

THE SOUTH-EAST

LONDON

THE FRANKLIN

↝ TOWNHOUSE HOTEL ↝

28 Egerton Gardens, London SW3 2DB
TEL (020) 7584 5533 **FAX** (020) 7584 5449 **E-MAIL** booking@thefranklin.co.uk
WEBSITE www.franklinhotel.co.uk

LONDON HAS MORE THAN a smattering of *bijoux* townhouse hotels, and it can be bewildering trying to decide which one to plump for, since they are all centrally located, all abound in acres of expensive fabric in their luxurious bedrooms and smart, rather formal public rooms, and all specialize in friendly yet professional service. The ones we least prefer are almost claustrophobic in their preciousness; the best have an easy-going lack of self-consciousness, while at the same time feeling protective and relaxing, and that's what we like about The Franklin, sister hotel to Dukes (see page 107).

However, what really sets The Franklin apart are the bedrooms. Some are enormous, some have original features such as plasterwork and panelling, some are split-level, with the bed above and a sitting area below. Best of all are the ground-floor Garden Rooms, which open directly on to private communal gardens, full of white roses in summer, and in which guests are allowed to wander. All the bedrooms are decorated in florals and stripes, flounces and swags, and have king size beds, some canopied. The elegant, richly decorated public rooms also have garden views, with floor-length windows. Service is prompt and willing, and the young staff are charming. There is now a small 'internet-room' which acts as a one-guest-at-a-time business centre.

↝

NEARBY Victoria and Albert Museum; Natural History Museum; Science Museum; Knightsbridge; Hyde Park.
LOCATION in side street off Brompton Road, opposite Brompton Oratory; valet parking in public car park
MEALS breakfast; room service
PRICE £££ **ROOMS** 50; 41 double and twin, 9 single, all with bath; all rooms have phone, TV, fax/modem point, minibar, air-conditioning, hairdrier
FACILITIES sitting-room, breakfast-room, bar, internet-room, lift
CREDIT CARDS AE, DC, MC, V **CHILDREN** accepted **DISABLED** access possible
PETS not accepted **CLOSED** Christmas **MANAGER** Karen Marshall

THE SOUTH-EAST

LONDON

THE GORE
~ TOWNHOUSE HOTEL ~

189 Queen's Gate, London SW7 5EX
TEL (020) 7584 6601 **FAX** (020) 7589 8127
E-MAIL reservations@gorehotel.co.uk

I N 1990 THE TEAM who opened Hazlitt's (see page 111) bought this Victorian townhouse (long established as a hotel) set in a wide tree-lined street near Kensington Gardens, and since then have given it the Hazlitt treatment: the bedrooms are furnished with period antiques, the walls are enlivened with pictures, and they have recruited a young and friendly staff, trained to give efficient but informal service.

It has character by the bucketload; walls whose every square inch is covered with prints and oil paintings; bedrooms furnished with antiques, each with its own style – a gallery in one room, Judy Garland's bed in another. There is also an impressive dossier in each room describing what to do locally – 'put together with verve and a feel for what the guest might really want'. The panelled bar on the ground floor is a popular rendezvous for non-residents as well as guests. Across the hallway is Bistrot 190 (same owners, same style, different business) which opens from 7.30 am to 11.30 pm and, as well as breakfast, offers light-hearted modern dishes with an international spin.

Restaurant 190, which is famous for its ways with fish, is stylish with rosewood panels and deep-red velvet chairs.

~

NEARBY Kensington Gardens; Hyde Park; Albert Hall; Harrods.
LOCATION just S of Kensington Gardens; metered parking and public car park nearby
MEALS breakfast, lunch, dinner
PRICE £££
ROOMS 54; 31 double, 23 single (32 baths and 22 showers); all rooms have phone, TV, minibar, hairdrier, safe
FACILITIES sitting-room, bar, restaurant, bistro, lift
CREDIT CARDS AE, DC, MC, V **CHILDREN** welcome
DISABLED access possible **PETS** accepted by arrangement **CLOSED** Christmas
PROPRIETORS Peter McKay and Douglas Blaine

THE SOUTH-EAST

HAZLITT'S
~ TOWNHOUSE HOTEL ~

6 Frith Street, Soho, London W1V 5TZ
TEL (020) 7434 1771 **FAX** (020) 7439 1524 **E-MAIL** reservations@hazlitts.co.uk
WEBSITE: www.hazlitts.com

THERE IS NO QUARTER of central London with more character than Soho; and there are few places to stay with more character than Hazlitt's, formed from three Georgian terraced houses off Soho Square. The sloping, creaking floorboards have been retained (it can be an uphill walk to your bed), and the rooms decorated with suitable antiques, busts and prints. The bedrooms, named after some of the people who visited or stayed in the house where the eponymous essayist himself lived, are delightfully different from most London hotel rooms, some with intricately carved wood headboards, one with a delightful four-poster, all with free-standing bathtubs and Victorian fittings in the bathrooms.

As befits an establishment with such literary connections, Hazlitt's is particularly popular with visiting authors, who leave signed copies of their works when they depart. Sadly, the dresser in the little sitting-room in which they are kept is now locked to protect the books, which had a habit of going missing.

Continental breakfast is served in the bedrooms, as well as light dishes such as *blinis* and filled baguettes. A hotel for people who like their comforts authentic, yet stylish.

~

NEARBY Oxford Street; Piccadilly Circus; Covent Garden; theatres.
LOCATION in Soho, between Oxford Street and Shaftesbury Avenue; public car parks nearby
MEALS breakfast; room service
PRICE £££
ROOMS 17 double (1 twin) all with bath; all rooms have phone, TV, fax/modem point, hairdrier, safe
FACILITIES sitting-room **CREDIT CARDS** AE, DC, MC, V
CHILDREN welcome
DISABLED not suitable **PETS** accepted by arrangement **CLOSED** Christmas
PROPRIETORS Peter McKay and Douglas Blaine

THE SOUTH-EAST

LONDON

L'HOTEL

~ TOWN GUEST-HOUSE ~

28 Basil Street, London SW3 1AS
TEL (020) 7589 6286 **FAX** (020) 7823 7826

A RECENT REVISIT CONFIRMED L'Hotel as a delightfully tranquil haven in busy Knightsbridge, especially considering that its chic little Metro restaurant in the basement has long made this a popular address with local residents and shoppers. The entrance is pleasantly understated, which gives it the look of a private house. Inside, hand-stencilled motifs embellish the striped colour-washed walls and wooden floor. The small but well-equipped bedrooms, designed by Margaret Levin, have padded fabrics on the walls, in soft creams and beiges, wooden shutters and antique pine furniture, as well as double glazing and cooling fans. Some rooms can be interconnected to form a suite, which is popular with families.

The restaurant has a bright, continental brasserie look and it is also where the hotel guests have breakfast. Plain walls set off black-and-white photographs; the seating combines banquettes, mint green and chrome chairs at wooden-topped tables, and bar stools at the black marble bar. The food is modern British, the menus now devised by Eric Chavot, the Michelin-starred head chef, who also presides at L'Hotel's sister establishment and neighbour, the Capital Hotel, where there is a smart, formal dining-room.

~

NEARBY Knightsbridge; Hyde Park; Buckingham Palace.
LOCATION between Sloane Street and Harrods; public car park opposite
MEALS breakfast, lunch, dinner
PRICE £££
ROOMS 12; 11 double, 1 suite, all with bath; all rooms have phone, TV, minibar, safe
FACILITIES restaurant/bar **CREDIT CARDS** AE, DC, MC, V
CHILDREN welcome **DISABLED** not suitable **PETS** accepted by arrangement
CLOSED restaurant only, Sun lunch and dinner
PROPRIETOR David Levin

THE SOUTH-EAST

LONDON

LONDON BRIDGE
~ TOWN HOTEL ~

8-18 London Bridge Street, London SE1 9SG
TEL (020) 7855 2200 **FAX** (020) 7855 2233 **E-MAIL** sales@london-bridge-hotel.co.uk
WEBSITE www.london-bridge-hotel.co.uk

WHERE DO THEY PUT all those rooms? This large, comfortable, independently-owned hotel, opened in late 1998 and tucked away in a small street beside London Bridge station, manages to feel small, cosy and intimate. The enticing lobby sets the scene, with tartan sofas, pretty lamps, ornamental pillars, silver French chairs, Matisse prints and a smart little concierge's stand; the shiny, chrome luggage trolley gets parked behind some *faux* box trees. Extra executive rooms and a health club were added in 1999 and on the ground floor is a Simply Nico restaurant, so this is a perfect base for business people, who walk across London Bridge to the City. Right on the doorstep are all the attractions of Bankside, including the new Tate Gallery and Millennium Bridge to St Paul's, and the weekend rates are good value for central London. Standard bedrooms are smallish and double-glazed; those to the rear of the hotel have views over rooftops, church spires and trees. Neat black-and-white bathrooms have power showers and granite-topped washbasin units; rooms have checked fabrics, painted wood furniture and navy blue blankets on the beds. Stowed away in cupboards are special safes for laptops. On the way down to breakfast in the basement you can see Roman remains discovered under the building.

~

NEARBY The City; Tower of London; Globe Theatre; Bankside; Tate Gallery.
LOCATION beside London Bridge station; public car park
MEALS breakfast, lunch, dinner; room service
PRICE £££
ROOMS 138; 134 double and twin, all with bath, 4 single with shower; all rooms have phone, fax/modem point, TV, air-conditioning, minibar, hairdrier, safe
FACILITIES lobby, dining-room, restaurant, 2 lifts, health club
CREDIT CARDS AE, DC, MC, V **CHILDREN** welcome
DISABLED 6 bedrooms specially adapted
PETS accepted by arrangement **CLOSED** never
MANAGER Nicholas Cowell

THE SOUTH-EAST

LONDON

MILLERS

~ TOWN BED-AND-BREAKFAST ~

111a Westbourne Grove, London W2 4UW
TEL (020) 7243 1024 **FAX** (020) 7243 1064 **E-MAIL** enquiries@millersuk.com
WEBSITE www.millersuk.com

IF YOU ARE AN ANTIQUE LOVER who thinks your house is as full as it can be, a stay at Martin Miller's hotel (he is the author of the much respected *Millers Antiques Guide*) will be an educational as well as a comfortable experience. Only local knowledge or skilful map-reading will bring you to the hotel's maroon door in Hereford Road. The sedan chair in the hall and the oriental rugs and prints on the stairs do a poor job of preparing you for the eclectic (and some might say eccentric) splendour of the large first-floor drawing-room. It is not so much full of antiques as stacked with them, and you can't help feeling that the addition of just one more snuff-box might cause a perilous situation. Lit in the evening by dozens of candles (helped here and there by a little electricity), a stay at Millers is an entirely unique experience.

Your welcome from manageress Anthea Pouli and her staff couldn't be warmer, and the bedrooms (all named after poets and up more stairs on the second floor) are elegantly if less dangerously furnished, each in a style appropriate to its poet. Breakfast, taken at one large table, is a do-it-yourself affair and there is a tremendous choice of restaurants within easy walking distance – but don't forget your key as the front door is always locked.

~

NEARBY Portobello Road Market; Notting Hill Gate; Kensington Gardens; Kensington High Street.
LOCATION on first floor above restaurant on corner of Westbourne Grove and Hereford Road (entrance in Hereford Road); car parking on meters
MEALS breakfast
PRICE £££
ROOMS 8 double and twin, all with bath; all rooms have phone, TV
FACILITIES sitting-room, library **CREDIT CARDS** AE, MC, V
CHILDREN accepted **DISABLED** not suitable **PETS** not accepted **CLOSED** Christmas
PROPRIETORS Martin Miller and Carey Ravden

THE SOUTH-EAST

LONDON

NUMBER SIXTEEN

~ TOWN GUEST-HOUSE ~

16 Sumner Place, London SW7 3EG
TEL (020) 7589 5232 **FAX** (020) 7584 8615 **E-MAIL** reservations@
numbersixteenhotel.co.uk **WEBSITE** www.numbersixteenhotel.co.uk

NUMBER SIXTEEN IS one of London's most characterful luxury bed-and-breakfast establishments. The original building has spread along its early Victorian South Kensington terrace, to encompass four adjoining houses – all extensively refurbished in the last few years.

Public rooms and bedrooms alike are brimful of pictures, including a huge eye-catching abstract in the reception-room. Downstairs there are always big bowls of fresh flowers – sweet peas or roses perhaps – and the large rear patio garden is well kept and full of colour. Inside, the decoration is richly traditional and harmonious. A series of small sitting-rooms with Victorian moulded ceilings, polished antiques and luxurious drapes, lead to an award-winning conservatory, from where, on summer days, you can sit and admire the profusion of flowers outside.

Bedrooms are generously proportioned, comfortable and stylish, largely furnished with period pieces or reproductions; some have French windows opening on to the garden. The tiled bathrooms have recently been upgraded. Breakfast Is served in your room. The hotel has no dining-room but there are plenty of restaurants on the Old Brompton Road nearby.

NEARBY South Kensington museums; Knightsbridge; King's Road.
LOCATION off Old Brompton Road; no private car parking
MEALS breakfast; room service
PRICE £££
ROOMS 36; 27 double, 23 with bath 4 with shower, 9 single with shower; all rooms have phone, TV, minibar, hairdrier, safe
FACILITIES sitting-room, bar, conservatory, lift, small garden
CREDIT CARDS AE, DC, MC, V
CHILDREN accepted over 12
DISABLED access difficult
PETS not accepted **CLOSED** never
MANAGER Jean Branham

THE SOUTH-EAST

PEMBRIDGE COURT

~ TOWN HOTEL ~

34 Pembridge Gardens, London W2 4DX
TEL (020) 7229 9977 **FAX** (020) 7727 4982 **E-MAIL** reservations@pemct.co.uk
WEBSITE www.pemct.co.uk

MANAGED BY VIVACIOUS Valerie Gilliat, but supervised by Spencer and Churchill (a pair of vast and presidential ginger cats), Pembridge Court is a 19thC townhouse guarded by bay trees and just far enough removed from the bustle, buses and tubes of Notting Hill Gate to be quiet. Long-established and much loved by its regular guests – many from the worlds of music, motor racing and antiques – the hotel is very much treated as a home from home. One faithful guest actually went so far as to buy it. Rooms vary in size and cost, but, unusually for a small hotel, those advertised as large are exactly that: substantial enough for a business meeting or a small party if you feel like it, and certainly smart enough and well equipped enough for either. The smallest room is also honestly described: it is called The Last Resort.

On the ground floor is a comfortably furnished sitting-room dressed in yellow and blue, and which can also be borrowed for private meetings. Hung everywhere in frames are Victorian lace gloves, fans, beadwork and other fascinating, but less instantly recognizable, items of millinery. Downstairs is the bare brick-walled Darling Bar and next to it, Caps restaurant (its varied and Eastern-influenced menu is also available via room service).

~

NEARBY Kensington Gardens; Kensington High Street; Portobello Road.
LOCATION in residential street just N of Notting Hill Gate; with garage for 2 cars
MEALS breakfast, lunch, dinner; room service
PRICE £££
ROOMS 20; 17 double and twin, 3 single, all with bath; all rooms have phone, TV, hairdrier; some have air-conditioning
FACILITIES sitting-room, bar **CREDIT CARDS** AE, DC, MC, V
CHILDREN welcome
DISABLED access difficult **PETS** accepted by arrangement **CLOSED** never
MANAGER Valerie Gilliat

THE SOUTH-EAST

LONDON

PORTOBELLO
~ TOWNHOUSE HOTEL ~

22 Stanley Gardens, London W11 2NG
TEL (020) 7727 2777 **FAX** (020) 7792 9641 **E-MAIL** reception@portobello-hotel.demon.co.uk **WEBSITE** www.portobello-hotel.demon.co.uk

OWNED BY TIM HERRING, who also owns the popular Julie's Bar in Clarendon Road, the Portobello has long been the darling of the film, fashion and music industries. You get the feeling that life no longer holds many surprises for the laid-back management. With so many night owls and international time travellers as regulars, its reception, bar and restaurant are open right round the clock. Pastel decoration with antique armchairs in the bar and cane chairs in the tiled dining-room (the preserve of chef/manager Johnny Ekperigin) give a fresh, light air. The back of the hotel looks out over quiet private gardens framed by a large mimosa tree. The sitting-room is a mixture of styles, with Victorian sofas, a large leather-topped desk, parlour palms and stripped French doors draped with brilliant red livery. Military prints and mirrors in gilded frames deck the walls.

Bedrooms vary in size from the spacious (the Round Room has a large round bed and an Edwardian bathing machine in it) to the microscopic 'cabins' on the top floor that, nevertheless, have refrigerators and colour televisions with a bewildering selection of channels. There are two brand new rooms in the basement, one in Japanese style, the other colonial.

~

NEARBY Kensington Gardens; Kensington High Street; Portobello Road.
LOCATION in residential area of Notting Hill Gate, off Kensington Park Road; with pay and display and metered parking
MEALS breakfast, lunch, dinner; room service
PRICE £££
ROOMS 22; 17 double and twin, 5 single, all with bath or shower; all rooms have phone, TV, fax/modem point, minibar, hairdrier; some have air-conditioning
FACILITIES sitting-room, dining-room, bar **CREDIT CARDS** AE, MC, V
CHILDREN accepted if well-behaved
DISABLED not suitable **PETS** accepted by arrangement **CLOSED** late Dec to early Jan
PROPRIETOR Tim Herring

THE SOUTH-EAST

LONDON

THE ROOKERY

~ TOWN HOTEL ~

Peter's Lane, Cowcross Street, London EC1M 6DS
TEL (020) 7336 0931 **FAX** (020) 7336 0932
E-MAIL reservations@rookery.co.uk

RECENTLY OPENED BY the owners of The Gore and the imaginative Hazlitt's (see pages 110 and 111), this homely little hotel full of old curiosities and flights of fancy is in a traffic-free alleyway among the restaurants of fashionable Clerkenwell. Created from a row of converted listed Georgian cottages, it is packed with character and 'time-warp' detail: wood panelling; period shutters; open fires; flagged floors; even a special creaky sound put into the treads of the new stairs to make them seem old. Pretty bedrooms have little half-shutters, fresh Egyptian cotton sheets, summer and winter duvets. Minibars and 'workstations' are discreetly hidden behind antique doors. Bathrooms are delightful, with Victorian fittings, exposed copper pipes and wainscotting. The suite – on two floors – pushes the general style further. The rococo French bed, attendant blackamoor, and Edwardian bathing machine behind lace curtains, are in the same room, and an electronically controlled ceiling panel shuts off the upper floor for business meetings, so no rumpled sheets are visible.

A conservatory, with open fire, leather chairs and rustic pictures, serves as a day room, opening on to a tiny terrace garden. Breakfast, continental, is on trays: fresh orange juice, coffee and croissants prepared and baked in the kitchen early every morning by the hotel's own *pâtissier*.

~

NEARBY The City; St Paul's; Smithfield; Farringdon Road tube station.
LOCATION in pedestrian street in Clerkenwell, near Smithfield and City; parking in nearby public car park
MEALS breakfast, light meals; rooms service
PRICE £££
ROOMS 31; 24 double, 6 single, 1 suite, all with bath; all rooms have phone, fax/modem points, TV, minibar, hairdrier, safe
FACILITIES conservatory, terrace **CREDIT CARDS** AE, DC, MC, V
CHILDREN accepted **DISABLED** 1 bedroom on ground floor **PETS** accepted by arrangement **CLOSED** Christmas
PROPRIETORS Peter McKay and Douglas Blaine

THE SOUTH-EAST

LONDON

SYDNEY HOUSE

~ TOWNHOUSE HOTEL ~

9-11 Sydney Street, London SW3 6PU
TEL (020) 7376 7711 **FAX** (020) 7376 4233
E-MAIL sydneyhousehotel@see-london.com **WEBSITE** www.sydneyhousehotel.com

THE HOTEL SPREADS ACROSS a terrace of mid-19thC townhouses in busy Sydney Street. Owned by a Swiss company, it was restored, designed and is managed by Swiss designer and hotelier Jean-Luc Aeby, who has created a comfortable, welcoming and whimsical residence. A maze of stairways and dark but intimate passages lead to much lighter, fair-sized bedrooms, each of which has its own delightful character, enhanced by rich fabrics, artefacts, prints and paintings from around the world. The penthouse has a large terrace overlooking Chelsea's rooftops, another room opens on to a sunny balcony, another has a gilded four-poster tented in silk and brocade, another leopard print fabrics and a Chinese theme. All have crisp white sheets and thick towels in the pristine bathrooms.

Public rooms are richly decorated and filled with interesting mirrors, carpets, marbles and furniture, including a screen from Matisse's Moroccan home. Staff are unobtrusive, but efficient and friendly. Breakfast is excellent, the fruit plate a work of art.

Since our last visit, the room service menu has perked up. Take-outs can also be ordered from two good local restaurants and, if you ask nicely, the staff will serve them in your room.

~

NEARBY King's Road; Michelin Building; South Kensington museums.
LOCATION in a street running between the King's and Fulham Roads, near the Fulham Road end
MEALS breakfast, light meals; room service
PRICE ££££
ROOMS 21; 13 double, 8 single, all with bath; all rooms have phone, TV, fax/modem plug, minibar, hairdrier
FACILITIES sitting-room, breakfast-room, restaurant/bar
CREDIT CARDS AE, DC, MC, V **CHILDREN** welcome
DISABLED access difficult **PETS** not accepted **CLOSED** never
MANAGER Jean-Luc Aeby

THE SOUTH-EAST

STANWELL HOUSE
∼ TOWN HOTEL ∼

High Street, Lymington, Hampshire, SO41 9AA
TEL (01590) 677123 **FAX** (01590) 677756
E-MAIL stanwellhouse@virgin.net

UNTIL ITS RECENT REINCARNATION, Stanwell House Hotel was a fading Georgian landmark in the prettiest part of Lymington's attractive High Street. When Jane McIntyre took over in 1995 the place was transformed: an Italianate stone-flagged courtyard now stretches the length of the building, affording inviting views from the street of a glass-roofed sitting-room strewn with velvet cushions; on one side of the entrance is a smart country clothing shop, Stanwells, on the other a bar and a cosy bistro in simple 17thC style – dark walls, oak settles, pewter plates and a *trompe l'oeil* fireplace complete with shaggy dog. Our meal here was delicious, in the modern English manner, and inexpensive.

In contrast to the bistro, the candlelit restaurant – steel chairs upholstered in purple, cerise, pink and deep-red velvet, swathes of silk curtains – and the bedrooms in the main house are theatrical, not to say over the top. The latter share a predeliction for dramatic walls, rich hangings in silk, velvet and brocade, piles of white cushions and baths, some of them roll-top, swathed in yet more fabric. The bedrooms in the extension are a lesson in how to make undistinguished rooms look pretty and welcoming. This hotel attracts a laid-back youngish clientèle, especially for weekends away from the city.

∼

NEARBY New Forest; Beaulieu; Isle of Wight.
LOCATION on High Street, close to the quay and marina; no private parking; public car parks nearby
MEALS breakfast, lunch, dinner
PRICE ££
ROOMS 31; 26 double, 3 luxury suites, 2-bedroomed cottage, all with bath, 1 with shower; all rooms have phone, TV, minibar, hairdrier
FACILITIES conservatory, bar, dining-room, bistro, garden; 50-ft yacht for charter
CREDIT CARDS AE, DC, MC, V **CHILDREN** welcome **DISABLED** access difficult
PETS accepted **CLOSED** never **PROPRIETOR** Jane MacIntyre

THE SOUTH-EAST

RINGLESTONE, KENT

RINGLESTONE INN

~ COUNTRY INN ~

Ringlestone, near Harrietsham, Maidstone, Kent ME17 1NX
TEL (01622) 859900 **FAX** (01622) 859966 **E-MAIL** bookings@ringlestone.com
WEBSITE www.ringlestone.com

AFFABLE MIKE MILLINGTON-BUCK (he used to run Leeds Castle) has this secluded little hamlet – up on the downs and well away from the diggers and excavators of the Channel rail link – buzzing with projects. The centrepiece is a 16thC inn, once used as a hospice for monks, with warm, traditional, oak-beamed bars offering good food, home-made pies, 32 English fruit wines, and French house and châteaux wines imported by Mike and his daughter, Michele Stanley.

Quiet, very comfortable lodgings are over the road in a converted tile-hung Kentish farmhouse, where one entry in the Visitor's Book remarks 'You've thought of everything'. Indeed, these are delightful rooms, with cream natural fabrics, French rustic furniture, pretty white embroidered sheets and pillowcases, and spotless bathrooms with power showers, but it is the thoughtfulness here that impresses. Summer and winter duvets, a whole tea set in your room so you can invite friends in, a washing machine and ironing board on the landing, *three* kinds of breakfast, including a tray in your room, and a housekeeper, Jane, to look after any other needs. The farmhouse suite is a new addition, and Mike now has his sights on converting a Norman flint barn for more rooms. Can Ringlestone go on growing and still retain its charm? Great walking country.

~

NEARBY Leeds Castle; Sissinghurst; Canterbury; Rochester; Rye.
LOCATION in hamlet; off A20, between Harrietsham and Wormshill; car parking
MEALS breakfast, lunch, dinner
PRICE ££
ROOMS 4 double and twin, all with bath; all rooms have phone, TV, CD player, hairdrier, minibar
FACILITIES dining-room, sitting-room, garden, terrace
CREDIT CARDS AE, DC, MC, V **CHILDREN** accepted
DISABLED access difficult **PETS** not accepted **CLOSED** Christmas Day, New Year's Eve
PROPRIETORS Mike Millington-Buck and Michele Stanley

THE SOUTH-EAST

RUSHLAKE GREEN, EAST SUSSEX

STONE HOUSE
~ COUNTRY HOUSE HOTEL ~

Rushlake Green, Heathfield, East Sussex TN21 9QJ
TEL (01435) 830553 **FAX** (01435) 830726
WEBSITE www.stonehousesussexco.uk

OUR LATEST REPORTER enthusiastically agrees with everything we have said about Stone House in the past. It is Peter and Jane Dunn's ancestral family home, a glorious 16thC manor house. The delightful Jane ('old world and lovely manners') does what she enjoys most – cooking, and looking after her guests individually. Her relaxed and friendly demeanour belies a very sure touch, and Stone House is run with great competence – which means it is much in demand for house parties, Glyndebourne visitors (luxury wicker picnic hampers can be prepared), shooting weekends and even small executive conferences. They have recently created a Victorian walled vegetable garden and an 18thC-style rose garden. Wine has become a hobby for Peter and Jane, and they are justly proud of their wine list.

Bedrooms are beautifully decorated; two have fine antique four-posters and are particularly spacious (the bathrooms can double as sitting-rooms). Televisions are hidden so as not to spoil the period charm. An excellent place in which to sample authentic English country living at its most gracious – log fires and billiards, woodland walks and croquet – together with the atmosphere of a home.

~

NEARBY Battle; Glyndebourne.
LOCATION just off village green 8 miles (13 km) NW of Battle; in large grounds with ample car parking
MEALS breakfast, lunch by arrangement, dinner
PRICE £££
ROOMS 7; 6 double and twin, 1 single, all with bath; all rooms have phone, TV, hairdrier
FACILITIES sitting-room, library, dining-room; billiards/snooker, gardens; croquet, fishing, shooting **CREDIT CARDS** not accepted
CHILDREN welcome over 9 **DISABLED** access difficult **PETS** accepted in bedrooms only
CLOSED Christmas to 6 Jan **PROPRIETORS** Peter and Jane Dunn

THE SOUTH-EAST

RYDE, ISLE OF WIGHT

BISKRA BEACH
~ SEASIDE HOTEL ~

17 Thomas's Street, Ryde PO33 2DL
TEL (01983) 567913 **FAX** (01983) 616976 **E-MAIL** info@biskra-hotel.com
WEBSITE www.biskra-hotel.com

OUR INSPECTOR REPORTED 'absolute delight' when she came across Biskra Beach 'on a vague tip-off that changes had happened of late'. And what changes. The charming and elegant proprietor, Barbara Newman, produced photographs of the hotel as it had been in its last incarnation: a riot of flock wallpaper and plastic flowers. Its transformation is immediately revealed by walking through the suburban road-front entrance and into the laid-back bar/restaurant, done in attractive colonial-chic style, but the real joy lies at the rear. French windows and steps lead down to a breezy, instantly inviting raised terrace directly above the Solent. The waters seem to lap the hotel, and the views across to the mainland are spectacular. It's a great spot for a drink before lunch or dinner; or you can sink in to the bubbling hot tub which is set into one corner of the terrace.

'Simple but good value' sums up Biskra Beach, where prices are kept deliberately reasonable. Bedrooms are without frills, but comfortable, painted in jolly colours, with pine furniture and matting on the floors. The food, on our visit, was excellent, and in keeping with the general 'modern British' ambience. Though it's not perhaps the place for a long summer holiday, this is an excellent base for exploring the island, despite the tackiness of Ryde itself (which only serves to make it feel like more of a haven).

~

NEARBY Ryde Pier; Seaview; Bembridge; Cowes.
LOCATION on the edge of central Ryde, with garden leading to seafront; limited car parking; public car park nearby
MEALS breakfast, lunch, dinner; room service
PRICE ££
ROOMS 14 double and twin, 8 with bath, 6 with shower; all rooms have phone, TV, minibar, hairdrier **FACILITIES** sitting-room, bar, 2 dining-rooms, terrace, garden; hot tub, beach **CREDIT CARDS** AE, MC, V **CHILDREN** welcome **DISABLED** not suitable **PETS** accepted by arrangement **CLOSED** never **PROPRIETOR** Barbara Newman

THE SOUTH-EAST

RYE, EAST SUSSEX

JEAKE'S HOUSE
~ TOWNHOUSE GUEST-HOUSE ~

Mermaid Street, Rye, East Sussex TN31 7ET
TEL (01797) 222828 **FAX** (01797) 222623 **E-MAIL** jeakeshouse@btinternet.com
WEBSITE www.s-h-systems.co.uk/hotels/jeakes.html

THIS SPLENDID 17TH C HOUSE – or rather three houses turned into one – has been lovingly restored to make a delightful small hotel: a verdict confirmed by many readers, who return time after time. It is the domain of Jenny Hadfield, who used to be an operatic soprano, and although the place is essentially a charming small hotel, she has lent it a certain theatrical quality. Originally built as a wool store in 1689, it later became a Baptist school and, earlier this century, the home of American writer Conrad Potter Aiken, when it played host to many of the leading artistic and literary figures of the time.

The beamed bedrooms, which come in various shapes and sizes, overlook either the old rooftops of Rye or Romney Marsh. Bedsteads are either brass or mahogany, bedspreads lace, furniture antique. There are plenty of thoughtful extras in the rooms. Downstairs, a galleried ex-chapel makes the grandest of breakfast-rooms. A roaring fire greets guests on cold mornings, and Jenny will serve you either a traditional breakfast or a vegetarian alternative. There is a comfortable parlour with a piano and a bar, with books and pictures lining the walls. "Situated on *the* street in Rye (the cobbled Mermaid Street) within walking distance of all the sights," says our inspector. "In all, a lovely place, and Jenny is bright, bonny and amusing."

~

NEARBY Great Dixter; Ellen Terry Museum.
LOCATION in centre of Rye; private car parking nearby
MEALS breakfast
PRICE ££
ROOMS 12; 8 double and twin, 1 single, 2 family rooms, 1 suite; 9 rooms with bath, 3 sharing
FACILITIES dining-room, 2 sitting-rooms, bar **CREDIT CARDS** MC, V
CHILDREN accepted over 12 **DISABLED** access difficult **PETS** by arrangement
CLOSED never **PROPRIETOR** Jenny Hadfield

THE SOUTH-EAST

RYE, EAST SUSSEX

THE OLD VICARAGE

∿ TOWN GUEST-HOUSE ∿

66 Church Square, Rye, East Sussex TN31 7HF
TEL (01797) 222119 **FAX** (01797) 227466
WEBSITE http:/homepages.tesco.net/-OldVicarageRye/html/

THIS CHARMING, SUGAR PINK, listed Georgian house with a fenced front garden filled with roses is on a footpath leading to the churchyard of St
Mary-the-Virgin. The church stands on top of the hill on which Rye is built,
so it is quiet and secluded, away from the noise and traffic. It's a warm
and welcoming house, and the experienced Masters have built up a faithful following; not surprisingly, their self-imposed high standards of hospitality have been rightly recognized. Paul, a former hotelier, cooks and
recently carried off a Best Breakfast in Britain competition with his hot
scones, home-made jam, home-made yogurt, local sausages and Romney
Marsh mushroom morning spreads. Julia, who used to work for a tea
importer, was recently a Landlady of the Year finalist. Her personal touches are everywhere: newspapers chosen for each guest (she's rarely wrong
about who reads what); maps and guidebooks in every room for those who
like exploring; home-made fudge and biscuits on the hot drinks tray. Her
most popular room is the first-floor front, overlooking the churchyard,
with four-poster bed. She uses Laura Ashley prints and fabrics for a pretty
effect and disguises shower-rooms as cupboards. Regulars return again
and again, giving a comforting sense of continuity. "A gem for those who
like small, family-run places," says our reporter.

∿

NEARBY Great Dixter; Ellen Terry Museum; Romney Marsh.
LOCATION on footpath in centre of Rye (on A259); private parking £2.50 a day
MEALS breakfast
PRICE ££
ROOMS 5; 4 double and twin, 1 family room, 4 with shower, 1 with bath; all rooms
have TV, hairdrier
FACILITIES sitting-room, library, TV-room, dining-room
CREDIT CARDS not accepted **CHILDREN** accepted over 8
DISABLED access difficult **PETS** not accepted **CLOSED** Christmas
PROPRIETORS Julia and Paul Masters

THE SOUTH-EAST

St Margaret's at Cliffe, Kent

WALLETT'S COURT

∽ MANOR HOUSE HOTEL ∽

Westcliffe, St Margaret's at Cliffe, Dover, Kent CT15 6EW
Tel (01304) 852424 **Fax** (01304) 853430 **E-mail** wallettscourt@compuserve.com
Website www.wallettscourt.com

"AMPLY PLUGS A GAP in an area where there is a dearth of decent hotels, other than the standard and predictable ones that serve the Dover ferry traffic," says an inspector, who adds that "it feels like Kent ."

The Oakleys started doing bed-and-breakfast in their handsome old manor house in 1979, rescuing it from a poor state of repair. They developed in steps into a hotel with a restaurant that now has a reputation locally as well as with guests. The number of compact pine-furnished rooms in a converted barn, each with their own individual character and 'a delightfully rustic feel', has increased to eight now; there are three grander ones in the main house, with abundant beams and brickwork in the best Kent tradition, and robust antique furniture. The public areas include a panelled sitting-room with period furniture and a grandfather clock ticking calmly away. The breakfast-room is pleasantly in keeping and there is an impressive old staircase.

Children enjoy seeking out the tree house in the orchard; there is also an indoor swimming-pool, steam-room and hydro-spa.

∽

Nearby Walmer Castle; ferries and Eurotunnel.
Location 3 miles (5 km) NE of Dover on B2058, off A258; ample car parking
Meals breakfast, lunch, dinner
Price £££
Rooms 13 double, twin and family, all with bath; all rooms have phone, TV
Facilities sitting-room, 2 dining-rooms, children's playground, table tennis, indoor swimming-pool, sauna, solarium, gym, garden; tennis court
Credit Cards AE, DC, MC, V
Children welcome
Disabled 6 ground-floor bedrooms
Pets in some bedrooms only
Closed Christmas
Proprietors Chris and Lea Oakley

THE SOUTH-EAST

SEAVIEW, ISLE OF WIGHT

PRIORY BAY HOTEL

~ SEASIDE HOTEL ~

Priory Drive, Seaview, Isle of Wight PO34 5BU
TEL (01983) 613146 **FAX** (01983) 616539 **E-MAIL** reservations@priorybay.co.uk
WEBSITE www.priorybay.co.uk

WHEN ANDREW PALMER'S motor boat broke down on the sweeping private beach of Priory Bay, he stumbled on an old-fashioned hotel with extensive grounds that he never knew existed, despite a lifetime of holidaying in the area. He bought it, and with the help of a talented friend, Annabel Claridge, effected a stunning transformation, opening in summer 1998. Bedrooms are decorated with charm and freshness, each different, some seaside simple, others more dramatic. The house itself has a colourful history and a quirky hotch-potch of styles with a Tudor farmhouse at its core and a Norman tithe barn in the grounds. Memorable details include the Gothic church porch brought from France in the 1930s, the Tudor fireplace depicting the *Sacrifice of Isaac*, and the delightful Georgian murals of pastoral island scenes in the dining-room. Less lovely are the grounds – at present – and the scattered outbuildings, some barrack-like. The highlight is the wonderful sweep of beach where children can be kept happy for hours (this is an extremely child-friendly hotel), with a beach bar, serving grills and salads, cutting out the need to retreat to the hotel for lunch.

Dinner, on our visit, was very good. Andrew Palmer is new to the hotel business (he founded the New Covent Garden Soup Company) and we wish him well.

~

NEARBY Osborne House; Bembridge Maritime Museum; Cowes.
LOCATION in own grounds with private beach, on B3330 S of Seaview between Nettlestone and St Helens; ample car parking
MEALS breakfast, lunch, dinner
PRICE £££ **ROOMS** 20 double and twin, all with bath; all rooms have phone, TV, hairdrier; also 17 self-catering cottages and family suites
FACILITIES drawing-room, sitting-room, bar, 2 dining-rooms, garden; 9-hole golf course, tennis, swimming-pool, private beach, sailing, fishing, windsurfing, beach bar **CREDIT CARDS** AE, MC, V **CHILDREN** welcome **DISABLED** access possible **PETS** not accepted **CLOSED** never **PROPRIETORS** Andrew and James Palmer

THE SOUTH-EAST

SEAVIEW, ISLE OF WIGHT

SEAVIEW HOTEL

~ SEASIDE HOTEL ~

High Street, Seaview, Isle of Wight PO34 5EX
TEL (01983) 612711 **FAX** (01983) 613729 **E-MAIL** seaviewhotel@virgin.net
WEBSITE www.seaviewhotel.co.uk

IF YOU HAVE A PENCHANT FOR breezy, old-fashioned English seaside resorts, you will love sailing-mad Seaview, and probably this hotel, which also acts as the central pub of the village. The Haywards have been at the helm for 20 years, but there seems to be no let-up in their enthusiasm for keeping up high standards and for providing a really personal service. Their dedication has paid off: amongst the raft of awards they have won over the years, a great source of pride must be last year's for UK Quality in Business Excellence; and indeed, when we last called, Nick was carrying out staff appraisal. It certainly appears to be a happy team, if the staff's willingness is anything to go by, and extra touches, such as turning down the beds at night and serving freshly squeezed orange juice with the early morning tea are appreciated by guests, many of whom return each year.

There is a public bar, towards the rear of the building, and two restaurants, one smoking and one non-smoking, but serving the same menu. One, called the Sunshine Room, but actually painted blue, is an airy room with a contemporary feel, a showcase for Nick's collection of model ships. The other is more formal, with a nautical bar. The food is unadventurous but satisfying.

~

NEARBY Osborne House; Flamingo Park; Bembridge.
LOCATION near the beach in seaside village 3 miles (5 km) E of Ryde; with car parking
MEALS breakfast, lunch, dinner; room service
PRICE ££
ROOMS 16; 14 double and twin, 12 with bath, 2 with shower, 2 suites both with bath; all rooms have phone, TV, hairdrier
FACILITIES 2 sitting-rooms, 2 dining-rooms, 2 bars
CREDIT CARDS AE, DC, MC, V **CHILDREN** welcome **DISABLED** 3 ground-floor bedrooms, but doors narrow **PETS** accepted but not in public rooms
CLOSED Christmas; restaurant closed Sun eve
PROPRIETORS Nick and Nicola Hayward

THE SOUTH-EAST

STORRINGTON, WEST SUSSEX

LITTLE THAKEHAM
~ COUNTRY HOUSE HOTEL ~

Merrywood Lane, Storrington, West Sussex RH20 3HE
TEL (01903) 744416 **FAX** (01903) 745022

WITH ITS HUGE SIGN at the gate and long wide drive, this is a somewhat daunting hotel at which to arrive. There tends to be a preponderance of large cars in the car park, and businessmen in suits getting in and out of them, but once at the front door, you will be escorted inside by two Jack Russells, Bertie and Poppy.

This Tudor-style manor house was built in 1902-3 by Sir Edwin Lutyens and is considered one of his finest. Although imposing, it has a human scale and rare character. The centrepiece is a double-height sitting-room with a vast fireplace and minstrel's gallery, and the furnishings – some by Lutyens himself – are of a high standard throughout. The Ratcliffs collect antiques, and these are in evidence all about. The bedrooms, as you would expect, are in keeping with the rest, and very comfortable; a master suite is virtually a small guest-house with two bathrooms.

The part-paved, part-grassy gardens, beautifully laid out and kept up, are lined with walnut trees and were created in the style of Gertrude Jekyll. Our latest reporter noted the serene, secluded setting, with views over the South Downs, but felt that, despite the genuinely relaxed atmosphere, it was in danger of becoming a little too corporate for our purposes. Is this fair? In the restaurant, the traditional menu changes on a daily basis.

NEARBY Parham House; Arundel; Petworth; Goodwood; Sussex Downs.
LOCATION in countryside, off A24 N of Worthing; off B2139 between Storrington and Thakeham; ample car parking
MEALS breakfast, lunch, dinner
PRICE £££
ROOMS 9 double, all with bath; all rooms have phone, TV, hairdrier
FACILITIES sitting-room, bar, restaurant; swimming-pool, tennis court, helipad
CREDIT CARDS AE, DC, MC, V **CHILDREN** welcome
DISABLED 1 bedroom on ground floor **PETS** not accepted **CLOSED** Christmas, New Year; restaurant closed Sun eve, Mon lunch **PROPRIETORS** Tim and Pauline Ratcliff

THE SOUTH-EAST

TUNBRIDGE WELLS, KENT

HOTEL DU VIN

~ TOWN HOTEL ~

Crescent Road, Tunbridge Wells, Kent TN1 2LY
TEL (01892) 526455 **FAX** (01892) 512044
E-MAIL reception@tunbridgewells.hotelduvin.co.uk **WEBSITE** www.hotelduvin.co.uk

THE MUCH-PRAISED Hotel du Vin & Bistro in Winchester (see page 135) has replicated itself twice over, first here in Tunbridge Wells, and more recently in Bristol (see page 41). They could now, therefore, be described as a group of chain hotels (more are planned), a species which this guide goes out of its way to ignore. However, such is the panache with which Robin Hutson, Gérard Basset and Peter Chittick have carried out their vision of an easy-going yet chic mid-price town hotel that we have no hesitation in including any of them: they are all great.

As in Winchester, once again the owners set their sights on a faded old hotel, ripe for conversion, in this case one with an elevated position, an abundance of space, and many period features such as the billiard-room (its walls now charmingly decorated with hand-painted cigar designs), the staircase, fireplaces in the bedrooms and the delightful terrace overlooking Calverley Park. Bedrooms are stylishly restrained and extremely comfortable, with huge bathrooms and deliciously deep tubs and spacious showers. The Bistro is a faithful copy of Winchester's, right down to the garland of hops and the world-class *sommelier*. This one – Henri Chapon – came from Le Manoir aux Quat' Saisons. We asked him why. "At Le Manoir, it was a case of keeping everything the same; here, with a new venture, we can move forward." The food has a sunny Mediterranean bias.

~

NEARBY Sissinghurst Castle Gardens; Rye.
LOCATION in centre of town; with car parking
MEALS breakfast, lunch, dinner
PRICE ££
ROOMS 32 double, all with bath; all rooms have phone, TV, CD player, minibar, hairdrier **FACILITIES** sitting-room, billiard-room, bar, bistro, lift, terrace
CREDIT CARDS AE, DC, MC, V **CHILDREN** welcome
DISABLED access possible **PETS** not accepted **CLOSED** never
PROPRIETORS Robin Hutson, Gérard Basset and Peter Chittick

THE SOUTH-EAST

UCKFIELD, EAST SUSSEX

HOOKE HALL

~ TOWN BED-AND-BREAKFAST ~

High Street, Uckfield, East Sussex TN22 1EN
TEL (01825) 761578 **FAX** (01825) 768025

HOOKE HALL HAS FEATURED in these pages for years now, and a recent inspection has confirmed that it continues its policy of providing comfortable bed-and-breakfast accommodation in gracious surroundings, although we have heard one dissenting voice which talked of things being stuck in a rut.

Hooke Hall is an elegant Queen Anne townhouse (built in the early 18th century), situated in the centre of Uckfield. Owner Juliet Percy runs her own interior design business and knows all about good taste in the traditional manner: designer fabrics, family portraits, panelled rooms, log fires, gentle lighting, her own charming botanical paintings, mementoes from foreign travels and plenty of flowers all contribute to the effect. The combination of home and guest-house is cleverly achieved; there is a domesticated, lived-in air about the place despite the presence of such chain hotel standbys as minibars and trouser-presses in the rooms. The upmarket Italian restaurant which she and her husband opened on the premises has now closed, and the Percys have gone back to concentrating on their bed-and-breakfast trade.

The nine bedrooms vary in size, some richly decorated with four-poster beds, others with sloping ceilings.

~

NEARBY Sheffield Park; Brighton; Glyndebourne.
LOCATION on the A22, 10 miles (16 km) SW of Tunbridge Wells, in the centre of town; car parking
MEALS breakfast
PRICE ££
ROOMS 9 double and twin, 7 with bath, 2 with shower; all rooms have TV, minibar hairdrier
FACILITIES sitting-room, garden **CREDIT CARDS** AE, MC, V
CHILDREN welcome over 12 **DISABLED** access difficult **PETS** not accepted
CLOSED Christmas **PROPRIETORS** Alister and Juliet Percy

THE SOUTH-EAST

WEST DEAN, EAST SUSSEX

THE OLD PARSONAGE

⟳ COUNTRY BED-AND-BREAKFAST ⟳

West Dean, Alfriston, near Seaford, East Sussex BN25 4AL
TEL & FAX (01323) 870432

IT'S A LONG WAY FROM EAST AFRICA – from where the owners came – to the exquisitely beautiful early Saxon hamlet of West Dean. Next to the 12thC church is this little 13thC priest's house (with Victorian additions), reputed to be the oldest small medieval house still to be lived in. The Woodhams have generously given over this tiny place – with stone spiral staircase (built to allow plenty of leeway to anyone wearing a sword) and pocket-sized Great Hall upstairs – to their guests so that others could enjoy this historic treat. "It's too special to keep to ourselves," they say. Furnished with antiques, the bedrooms are charming, with Angela's thoughtful, personal touches such as Alka Seltzer, shoe cleaner and sewing basket. Bathrooms are not attached, but private, and dressing gowns are provided for the journey. In the morning, Angela expertly moves about a few small tables and the sitting-room becomes a breakfast-room where guests can enjoy Raymond's home-made jam with their toast, and rhubarb from the garden.

Although there is quite enough history in this little house to keep anyone amused for a while – and it would be easy to get quite lost in time here – the rest of West Dean is also fascinating. Nearby there are walks through the forest and the lovely Cuckmere Estuary is only a mile away. A charming spot, with a friendly welcome.

⟳

NEARBY Charleston Farmhouse; Cuckmere Valley; Glyndebourne.
LOCATION off the A259 Brighton to Hastings coast road E of Seaford; car parking
MEALS breakfast
PRICE ££
ROOMS 3; 2 double with bath, 1 twin with shower; all rooms have hairdrier
FACILITIES sitting-room/breakfast-room, garden **CREDIT CARDS** not accepted
CHILDREN welcome over 12
DISABLED access difficult **PETS** not accepted **CLOSED** Christmas and New Year
PROPRIETORS Raymond and Angela Woodhams

THE SOUTH-EAST

WHITSTABLE, KENT

HOTEL CONTINENTAL
~ SEASIDE HOTEL ~

29 Beach Walk, Whitstable, Kent CT5 2BP
TEL (01227) 280280 **FAX** (01227) 280257

WHITSTABLE, WITH ITS ROWS of cottages and beach huts strung along the shore, has recently achieved cult status. For trendy thirty-somethings, this inspired small 1920s hotel, restored in Art Deco style and opened in the summer of 1998, is *the* place to be beside the seaside. With bright colours, simple decoration and excellent brasserie food, James Green of the Whitstable Oyster Fishery Company family – a thirty- something marine biologist – has brought light, life and fun back to what was, for years, a sad, squalid building. Right on the beach, it is perfect for families, and the large mustard yellow and red bar-room downstairs (kept cosy with a wood-burning stove) has tall windows overlooking the sea – ten of the bedrooms have sea views, too (four with balcony). Bedrooms are a bit too basic, with no pictures and a minimum of furniture – you hang your clothes on a brass peg on the wall. Bathrooms are small, white-tiled with a smart blue stripe. At night, you can lie in bed, pull back the blue curtains to see the lights of the ships in the distance and listen to the sound of the sea. You can get even closer to the sea in one of the simply converted fishermen's huts (especially fun for children) which stand on the beach. The vegetarian breakfast – egg, mushroom and tomatoes – is a big hit; the bar serves food all day long, with cream teas at £2.50, half a dozen oysters at £5.50 and house champagne at £19 a bottle; and there's the restaurant for dinner.

~

NEARBY Canterbury; Margate; North Downs.
LOCATION on seafront; with ample parking
MEALS breakfast, lunch, dinner
PRICE ££
ROOMS 23; 21 double and twin, 1 suite, 1 family room, all with bath; all rooms have phone, TV, hairdrier
FACILITIES bar, brasserie/restaurant **CREDIT CARDS** AE, DC, MC, V
CHILDREN welcome **DISABLED** no special facilities **PETS** not accepted
CLOSED never **MANAGER** James Green

THE SOUTH-EAST

WICKHAM, HAMPSHIRE

OLD HOUSE
~ TOWN HOTEL ~

The Square, Wickham, Hampshire PO17 5JG
TEL (01329) 833049 **FAX** (01329) 833672

THE OLD HOUSE, A STALWART of our guide for many years, possesses much that we look for: an interesting setting – at a corner of the main square of one of the finest villages in Hampshire; a superb building – Grade II-listed early Georgian; a delightful secluded garden; an immaculately kept and welcoming interior, with antiques and *objets* arranged to the best possible effect; and an attractive restaurant, created from the original timber-framed outhouse and stables.

Nothing is overstated – except perhaps the generous arrangements of fresh flowers which adorn all the public rooms. Bedrooms vary considerably – some palatial, others with magnificent beams, one or two rather cramped – but again a mood of civilized comfort prevails. Our reporter remarked on the imposing carved bar and the attractive beamed dining-room. However, times are changing for the Old House. The Skipwiths, who had been here for nearly 30 years, 'declared their innings closed' a couple of years ago, and since then the hotel has changed hands twice. Although the decorations, the ambience and even the French regional menu have happily stayed largely the same, it remains to be seen if the old heart can be put back into the operation; we would welcome further reports.

~

NEARBY Portsmouth (ferries); South Downs; Winchester; Chichester.
LOCATION 2.5 miles (4 km) N of Fareham, on square in middle of village; car parking
MEALS breakfast, lunch, dinner
PRICE ££
ROOMS 9; 7 double and twin, 2 single, all with bath; all rooms have TV, phone, hairdrier
FACILITIES 2 sitting-rooms, dining-room, bar **CREDIT CARDS** AE, DC, MC, V
CHILDREN accepted
DISABLED access difficult **PETS** not accepted **CLOSED** Christmas
PROPRIETORS John and Gloria Goodacre

THE SOUTH-EAST

WINCHESTER, HAMPSHIRE

HOTEL DU VIN

~ TOWNHOUSE HOTEL ~

14 Southgate Street, Winchester, Hampshire S023 9EF
TEL (01962) 841414 **FAX** (01962) 842458
E-MAIL admin@winchester.hotelduvin.co.uk **WEBSITE** www.hotelduvin.co.uk

THERE IS AN ALLURING BUZZ in the air at this stylish, affordable Georgian townhouse, flagship hotel in the now burgeoning Hotel du Vin group (see pages 41 and 130). It's got panache, and the wood-floored, hop-garlanded Bistro sets the tone: staffed by a charming bunch of mainly French youngsters, it has the intimate, slightly chaotic yet professional air of the genuine article. Start with a bucket of champagne in the voluptuous mirrored and muralled bar, then choose a bottle from the inventive, kindly priced wine list to go with the inventive, sunny, Modern English food.

The bedrooms and bathrooms are every bit as appealing, with fresh Egyptian cotton bedlinen, CD players, capacious baths and huge showers. For maximum quiet, ask for a Garden Room, or splash out on the sensuous Durney Vineyards suite with a four-poster draped in maroon velvet, a black slate double shower and murals depicting famous paintings of nudes. 'Breakfast in Bed' has recently been introduced, but otherwise there is no room service, helping to keep prices remarkably reasonable. There is also a loftily proportioned sitting-room, its walls decorated with *trompe l'oeil* panelling in delicious shades of caramel and pale green.

~

NEARBY Cathedral; Venta Roman Museum; Winchester College.
LOCATION in the town centre, a minute's walk from the cathedral; ample car parking
MEALS breakfast, lunch, dinner
PRICE ££
ROOMS 23; 22 double and twin, 21 with bath, 1 with shower; 1 suite with bath; all rooms have phone, TV, CD player, minibar, hairdrier
FACILITIES sitting-room, dining-room/breakfast-room, private dining-room, bar, wine-tasting cellar, garden; boules **CREDIT CARDS** AE, DC, MC, V
CHILDREN welcome
DISABLED several bedrooms on ground floor; 1 specially adapted
PETS accepted by arrangement **CLOSED** never
PROPRIETORS Robin Hutson, Gérard Basset and Peter Chittick

THE SOUTH-EAST

WYKEHAM ARMS
~ TOWN INN ~

75 Kingsgate Street, Winchester, Hampshire SO23 9PE
TEL (01962) 853834 **FAX** (01962) 854411

'ENORMOUSLY CHARMING; tons of personality,' confirms our latest reporter. Tucked away in the quietest, oldest part of the city, with Winchester College only yards away and the Cathedral also close by, this is primarily a well-frequented local pub, and a first-rate one: 250 years old with four cosy bars furnished with old school desks, one engraved with the Winchester motto, *Manners Makyth Man*. Interesting objects – old squash rackets, peculiar walking sticks – line the warm brick-red walls. This quirky character runs to the bedrooms, which are small in proportion and low-ceilinged, but each furnished in its own style with a personal feel, and adapted to accommodate all the usual facilities.

Breakfast is served upstairs, over the pub, in a pleasant straightforward English country breakfast-room with Windsor chairs and a fine collection of silver tankards. Hearty pub food at lunchtime and in the evenings; real ales and an impressive list of 40 wines, changed regularly, 22 served by the glass. Outside is a cobbled courtyard. Over the road is the 'Saint George' annexe with five pleasant bedrooms, a suite with a 'folly' bedroom in the old College Bakehouse, and the post office and general store, also belonging to the pub.

~

NEARBY Cathedral; Venta Roman Museum; Winchester College.
LOCATION in middle of city, between college and cathedral, on corner of Canon Street; small courtyard garden with some car parking
MEALS breakfast, lunch (not Sun), dinner
PRICE ££
ROOMS 13; 11 double with bath, 1 single with shower, 1 cottage suite; all rooms have phone, TV
FACILITIES sitting-room, 3 bars, sauna, patio
CREDIT CARDS AE, DC, MC, V
CHILDREN welcome over 14 **DISABLED** access difficult **PETS** welcome
CLOSED Christmas Day **MANAGERS** Tim Manktelow-Grey and Nigel Atkinson

THE SOUTH-EAST

YARMOUTH, ISLE OF WIGHT

GEORGE HOTEL

~ SEASIDE TOWN HOTEL ~

Yarmouth, Isle of Wight, Hampshire PO41 0PE
TEL (01983) 760331 **FAX** (01983) 760425
E-MAIL res@thegeorge.co.uk

IN MANY WAYS THE GEORGE is a perfect hotel: an atmospheric building in the centre of a breezy and historic harbour town, with welcoming rooms, a buzzing brasserie with tables spilling across the waterfront garden, and a quieter, more formal restaurant where good, inventive food is served. When they took over the peeling and faded 17thC former governor's residence, owners John Illsley (former bass guitarist of Dire Straits) and Jeremy and Amy Willcock took great care to restore and renovate with sympathy. A panelled and elegantly proportioned hall sets the scene, leading to a cosy wood-panelled sitting-room with thick velvet drapes at the windows, an amusing mid-Victorian evocation of the George above the fireplace and a roaring log fire in winter. Across the hall is the dark-red dining-room, and beyond the central stairs, the Brasserie and garden.

Upstairs, the bedrooms are all inviting and all different: one has a four-poster draped in tartan; another is a light and pretty corner room; two have wonderful teak-decked balconies with views across the Solent. (The hotel has its own motor yacht for outings.) 'It's a sheer pleasure,' writes a satisfied reader, 'to hop on the ferry at Lymington, alight at Yarmouth, and settle in to the George for two or three days.'

~

NEARBY Yarmouth Castle; Newport.
LOCATION in town, close to ferry port overlooking Solent; no car park
MEALS breakfast, lunch, dinner; room service
PRICE £££
ROOMS 16; 13 double and twin, 2 suites, 1 single, all with bath; all rooms have phone, TV, hairdrier
FACILITIES sitting-room, dining-room, brasserie, garden; private beach, 36-ft motor yacht available for charter **CREDIT CARDS** AE, MC, V
CHILDREN welcome over 8
DISABLED access difficult **PETS** accepted by arrangement **CLOSED** never
PROPRIETORS Jeremy and Amy Willcock, and John Illsley

THE SOUTH-EAST

YATTENDON, BERKSHIRE

ROYAL OAK

~ VILLAGE INN ~

The Square, Yattendon, near Newbury, Berkshire RG18 0UG
TEL (01635) 201325 **FAX** (01635) 201926

THIS INN HAS HAD A new lease of life in the past few years – attractive refurbishment of rooms, and food by Robbie Macrae which wins a steady stream of praise. It's not difficult to believe that the food is more stylish than when Oliver Cromwell dined there, as the hotel claims he did.

Lest you mistake it for a mere pub, the sign on the front of this cottagey, mellow red-brick inn announces 'Hotel and Restaurant'. Certainly, the Royal Oak is no longer a common-or-garden local. Its two restaurants have a style and elegance not usually associated with ale and darts. But there is still a small bar where residents and non-residents alike can enjoy a choice of real ales without having a meal.

Next to the smart/rustic informal dining area, with large open fireplace, is the light, relaxed and comfortable sitting-room (with newspapers and books within easy reach of its sofas) and beyond that the formal restaurant with its elegant reproduction furniture. Bedrooms are prettily decorated and equipped with every conceivable extra. Another attraction is the walled garden, full of colour and a delight, especially during the summer months.

~

NEARBY Basildon Park; Donnington Castle; Snelsmore Common.
LOCATION 7 miles (11 km) NE of Newbury, in middle of village; ample car parking
MEALS breakfast, lunch, dinner
PRICE ££
ROOMS 5; 4 double and twin, 1 suite, all with bath; all rooms have phone, TV, hairdrier
FACILITIES restaurant, sitting-room, dining-room, bar, walled garden
CREDIT CARDS AE, DC, MC, V
CHILDREN welcome
DISABLED access easy to restaurant and bar, but otherwise difficult
PETS accepted by arrangement **CLOSED** Christmas night; restaurant closed Sun eve
MANAGERS Corinne and Robbie Macrae

THE SOUTH-EAST

ALSO RECOMMENDED

DUNCTON, WEST SUSSEX

Duncton Mill

Duncton, near Petworth, West Sussex GU28 0LF
TEL (01798) 342294 **FAX** (01798) 344122
E-MAIL dunctonmill@compuserve.com **WEBSITE** www.dunctonmill.com **PRICE** ££

Small estate with plenty to do, including fishing in private trout lakes, and offering both bed-and-breakfast and self-catering accommodation.

WARTLING, EAST SUSSEX

Wartling Place

Wartling, Herstmonceux, East Sussex BN27 1RY
TEL & FAX (01323) 832590 **E-MAIL** accom@wartlingplace.prestel.co.uk
WEBSITE www.best-hotel.com/wartlingplace **PRICE** ££

Georgian house owned and run as a sophisticated guest-house by Rowena and Barry Gittoes. Spacious rooms; excellent breakfasts.

READERS' REPORTS

Please write and tell us about your experiences of small hotels, guest-houses and inns, whether good or bad, whether listed in this edition or not. As well as hotels in Spain, we are interested in hotels in Britain and Ireland, Italy, France, Portugal, Austria, Switzerland, Germany and other European countries, and those in the eastern United States.

The address to write to is:

The Editor,
Charming Small Hotel Guides,
c/o Duncan Petersen Publishing Ltd,
31 Ceylon Road,
London W14 OPY.

To the hundreds of readers who have written with comments on hotels in all the *Charming Small Hotel Guides*, a sincere 'thank-you'. We attach great importance to your comments and absorb them into the text each year. Please keep writing: for further information see page 14.

WALES

ABERGAVENNY, MONMOUTHSHIRE

LLANWENARTH HOUSE

~ COUNTRY GUEST-HOUSE ~

Govilon, Abergavenny, Monmouthshire NP7 9SF
TEL (01873) 830289 **FAX** (01873) 832199

AMANDA WEATHERILL HAS PUT tremendous efforts into rescuing this dignified, mainly late 16thC house set in large grounds and has, at the same
time, taken great care to keep the personal touches. Llanwenarth House is
still very much a family home, where guests gather for drinks in the handsome drawing-room (in front of a blazing log fire on chilly nights), dine as
if at a dinner-party in the splendid candlelit dining-room, and must at all
costs avoid tripping over the dog. Amanda, who is Cordon Bleu-trained,
supervises the kitchen, where the emphasis is on fresh home-grown and
local ingredients: home-produced meat and poultry, as well as vegetables
from the garden. Wines are from the exceedingly well-stocked cellar.

The bedrooms and public rooms (heavy on hunting memorabilia) are
notably bright, spacious and comfortable with period furniture, chintz fabrics and floor-to-ceiling windows, many of which reveal spectacular views
of the peaceful Usk Valley. The area attracts outdoors types, with trout
and salmon fishing on the River Usk and riding, pony-trekking and golf all
within easy reach. For the less sporty, there's croquet on the lawn and
Abergavenny, a delightful market town.

~

NEARBY Brecon Beacons; Offa's Dyke; Raglan Castle; Chepstow Castle.
LOCATION 4 miles (6.5 km) SW of Abergavenny, off A465; with ample car parking
MEALS breakfast, dinner
PRICE ££
ROOMS 5 double with bath or shower; all rooms have TV
FACILITIES sitting-room, dining-room, garden
CREDIT CARDS not accepted
CHILDREN welcome over 10
DISABLED 1 ground-floor bedroom
PETS accepted by arrangement
CLOSED Feb
PROPRIETOR Amanda Weatherill

WALES

ABERSOCH, GWYNEDD

PORTH TOCYN
~ SEASIDE HOTEL ~

Bwlchtocyn, Abersoch, Pwllheli, Gwynedd LL53 7BU
TEL (01758) 713303 **FAX** (01758) 713538 **E-MAIL** porthtocyn.hotel@virgin.net
WEBSITE www.porth-tocyn-hotel.co.uk

THIS WHITEWASHED, SLATE-ROOFED establishment, looking out over the sea from the Lleyn Peninsula towards Snowdonia, is a rare animal. The Fletcher-Brewers, who have owned it for over 50 years, call it a country house hotel; but it is not what most people would understand by the term. Porth Tocyn certainly contains as many antiques as the typical country house hotel and is run with as much skill and enthusiasm as the best of them. But the building – an amalgam of several old lead-miners' cottages, which has been much extended over the years – makes for a cosy, home-like atmosphere, emphasized by the chintzy decoration. And the seaside position has naturally encouraged the Fletcher-Brewers to cater for children as well as parents keen to enjoy the hotel's civilized attractions. Chief among these is the excellent dinner-party-style food; with seafood and temptingly sticky puddings as particular specialities, so don't go expecting to lose weight.

Bedrooms have been kept low-key and simply furnished, but are excellent value. There are splendid all-round views towards the sea and to the peaks of Snowdonia.

~

NEARBY Plas Yn Rhiw; Criccieth Castle; Snowdonia.
LOCATION 2.5 miles (4 km) S of Abersoch; in 25 acres of farmland with ample car parking
MEALS breakfast, lunch, dinner, picnics
PRICE ££
ROOMS 17; 13 double, 3 single, 1 family room, all with bath; all rooms have phone, TV
FACILITIES 6 sitting-rooms, TV-room, dining-room, bar, garden; swimming-pool, tennis **CREDIT CARDS** MC, V **CHILDREN** welcome
DISABLED 3 ground-floor bedrooms
PETS accepted by arrangement **CLOSED** early Nov to week before Easter
PROPRIETORS Fletcher-Brewer family

WALES

BONCATH, PEMBROKESHIRE

LLANCYCH

~ COUNTRY GUEST-HOUSE ~

Boncath, Pembrokeshire SA37 0LJ
TEL (01239) 698378 **FAX** (01239) 698686

IF YOU REACH LLANCYCH, you are either a dab hand with a map or your pronunciation of Welsh place names has met with a sympathetic hearing from someone you recently asked for directions. Tucked away up a small wooded valley named in Welsh legend and witness to centuries of Welsh history, Llancych is a white-painted manor house set in lawns on the narrow valley floor. It seems from the outside that each new tenant for several generations has added a wing (or at least a new gable, if times were hard), so that, like Cerberus, it looks all ways at once. Inside, however, as well as friendly owners Sarah and Tony Jones-Lloyd, you will find calm and well-furnished order.

The drawing-room, which occupies a large corner of the ground floor, has its grand piano and open hearth, and the mahogany table in the dining-room seats up to fourteen. Upstairs, five comfortable double bedrooms take in the views around the house. You can arrange to fish for the Cych trout a few moments' walk from the front door, and, if you are prepared to go a little further, this is also salmon and sea trout country: each August the coracle fishermen gather not far away at Cenarth for their annual races – a great sight.

~

NEARBY Cenarth; Pembrokeshire coast; Newcastle Emlyn; Cilgerran Castle.
LOCATION 6.5 miles (10.5 km) SE of Cardigan off B4332; with ample car parking
MEALS breakfast
PRICE ££
ROOMS 5 double and twin, 3 with bath
FACILITIES 2 sitting-rooms, dining-room, breakfast-room, garden
CREDIT CARDS MC, V **CHILDREN** by arrangement
DISABLED not suitable
PETS by arrangement
CLOSED early Nov to early Mar
PROPRIETORS Sarah and Tony Jones-Lloyd

WALES

BONTDDU, GWYNEDD

BORTHWNOG HALL

~ COUNTRY HOUSE HOTEL ~

Bontddu, Dolgellau, Gwynedd LL40 2TT
TEL (01341) 430271 **FAX** (01341) 430682 **E-MAIL** borthwnoghall@enterprise.net
WEBSITE www.homepages.enterprise.net/borthwnoghall

FACING SOUTH, on the very edge of the beautiful Mawddach Estuary (spring tides just lap the retaining wall of the small car park) and surrounded by mature gardens, this elegant little Regency house, built late in the 17th century, enjoys a glorious and absolutely unique position. The view stretches from the distant mouth of the river in the west, across to the Cader Idris range in the south and east as far as Barmouth Bridge. Tides and light create constant change, and the amazing variety of bird life explains the powerful telescope put at the disposal of the guests by owners Derek and Vicki Hawes.

Theirs is an unusual hotel in more ways than one: although there are only three bedrooms which (like the rest of the house) are superbly furnished as only a home can be, it is run on hotel lines. There is a civilized sitting-room for guests with an open fire, polished silver and ancestors gazing down from the walls. There is also a proper dining-room with a number of choices for dinner and an award-winning wine list. The Hawes have also founded an art gallery: housed in the library, and with great emphasis on matters Welsh, it is filled with paintings, sculpture and pottery. For those who want to look at the real thing there are splendid walks from the door.

~

NEARBY Cymer Abbey; Snowdonia; Lake Vyrnwy.
LOCATION beside estuary, outside village, 2 miles (3 km) from junction of A470 and A496; with car parking
MEALS breakfast, dinner
PRICE ££
ROOMS 3 double and twin with bath or shower; all rooms have phone, TV
FACILITIES sitting-room, dining-room, bar, garden
CREDIT CARDS AE, MC, V **CHILDREN** welcome
DISABLED not suitable **PETS** by arrangement **CLOSED** Christmas
PROPRIETORS Derek and Vicki Hawes

WALES

BRECHFA, CARMARTHENSHIRE

TY MAWR
~ COUNTRY HOTEL ~

Brechfa, Carmarthenshire SA32 7RA
TEL (01267) 202332/202330 **FAX** (01267) 202437
E-MAIL tymawr@tymawrcountryhotel.co.uk **WEBSITE** www.tymawrcountryhotel.co.uk

FIRMLY AT RIGHT ANGLES to the main street of this tiny village on the fringe of Brechfa Forest, and by the River Marlais, Ty Mawr has a pretty garden and fine views of the surrounding wooded hillsides. A warm welcome from Colin and Veronica Weston is guaranteed, and, once inside, the oak beams, stone walls and tiled floors proclaim the building's three and a bit centuries' tenure of this glorious spot. The public rooms are cosy and cheerful, and include an immaculate bar with smart pine fittings, and a comfy, chintzy sitting-room with an open log fire. The long slate-floored restaurant looks out on to the garden and, candlelit in the evenings, is where Veronica Weston's skill in the kitchen shows in earnest: fresh, usually Welsh, ingredients are assembled without undue fuss, but with plenty of imagination. A mouthwatering selection of fresh breads is explained when you discover that Roger Weston used to be a baker. The wines are well chosen and offered at eminently reasonable prices. Upstairs, the bedrooms are bright, comfortable and pleasantly rustic, and breakfast in the morning answers to appetites ranging from the merely peckish to the downright ravenous. The flowers in the garden tubs are quite impressive, but it's worth remembering that in spring 2000 the National Botanical Gardens of Wales opened a few miles away.

~

NEARBY Dinas Nature Reserve; Kidwelly Castle; Llansteffan Castle; Brecon Beacons.
LOCATION 10 miles (16 km) NE of Carmarthen, on B4310, in village; with ample car parking
MEALS breakfast, light lunch, dinner
PRICE ££
ROOMS 5; 3 double, 1 twin, 1 family, all with bath; all rooms have TV, hairdrier
FACILITIES sitting-room, dining-room, bar, garden
CREDIT CARDS MC, V **CHILDREN** welcome **DISABLED** not suitable **PETS** by arrangement
CLOSED never **PROPRIETORS** Roger and Veronica Weston

WALES

CRICKHOWELL, POWYS

THE BEAR

~ TOWN INN ~

Crickhowell, Powys NP8 1BW
TEL (01873) 810408 **FAX** (01873) 811696
E-MAIL bearhotel@aol.com

IT REALLY DOESN'T MATTER what route you take into Crickhowell as, like most other travellers for the last 500 years or so, you're bound to end up at The Bear. Owned and very much run by Judith Hindmarsh and her son Steve, it's one of those versatile places that can turn itself into whatever you want: if you feel like a drink, it's an excellent bustling pub shining with polished brass and pewter. If you feel like an informal meal, you'll be given an excellent one in either bar or in the oak-beamed and flag-floored kitchen restaurant. If you want something more upmarket, all you need do is move to the smaller, smarter *à la carte* restaurant that looks out into the courtyard (flower-filled in summer). Here, provided you are more than eight years old, you will find flowers on the table and food open to international influences, prepared with an imagination and a lightness of touch that belies the traditional trappings outside.

If you need a hotel, The Bear can comfortably surpass your expectations as well: the bedrooms are a mixture of sizes and of styles – old and new – but all are furnished and equipped to uncompromisingly high standards. Finally, if you need to escape the hurly-burly, there is a quiet, beamed sitting-room.

~

NEARBY Brecon Beacons; Offa's Dyke; Hay-on-Wye.
LOCATION in town centre, on A40 between Abergavenny and Brecon; with ample car parking
MEALS breakfast, lunch, dinner, bar snacks
PRICE ££
ROOMS 35 double and twin with bath or shower; all rooms have phone, TV, hairdrier
FACILITIES sitting-room, 2 dining-rooms, bar, garden
CREDIT CARDS AE, MC, V **CHILDREN** accepted **DISABLED** 2 ground-floor bedrooms
PETS accepted **CLOSED** Christmas Day; restaurant Sun
PROPRIETORS Judith and Steve Hindmarsh

WALES

DOLGELLAU, GWYNEDD

PLAS DOLMELYNLLYN

~ COUNTRY HOUSE HOTEL ~

Ganllwyd, Dolgellau, Gwynedd LL40 2HP
TEL (01341) 440273 **FAX** (01341) 440640 **E-MAIL** info@dolly-hotel.co.uk
WEBSITE www.dolly-hotel.co.uk

FOR LONGER THAN A DECADE the father-and-daughter team of Jon Barkwith and Jo Reddicliffe have been running 'Dolly' with considerable style. Parts of it are more than half a millennium old, but there was still work going on when we visited. It sits in a very comfortable way on its own bench above Ganllwyd, taking in the beautiful views across the valley, and, in the principally Victorian interior, antiques mingle equally comfortably with more modern furnishings to create a warm, friendly atmosphere. China and crystal twinkle on all sides. The drawing-room is elegant, but the dining-room is obviously where the team gets down to real business. Jo's award-winning *cuisine*, best described as 'imaginative modern British', has a widespread fan club and we could well understand people, even vegetarians, who might beg for an extension to their booking. There is an extensive wine cellar which is unlikely to lack the perfect complement to her food, and minor diners get an early sitting to themselves. Bedrooms are named after local rivers and individually furnished and decorated; most have splendid views. There is excellent walking from the front door and all guests have access to that essential Welsh facility, the drying-room. This a passionately non-smoking hotel.

~

NEARBY Cymer Abbey; Snowdonia; Lake Vyrnwy.
LOCATION in countryside, on A470 5 miles (8 km) N of Dolgellau; with ample car parking
MEALS breakfast, lunch by arrangement, dinner
PRICE ££
ROOMS 10; 9 double, 1 single, all with bath; all rooms have phone, TV, hairdrier
FACILITIES sitting-room, dining-room, conservatory bar, garden; fishing
CREDIT CARDS AE, DC, MC, V **CHILDREN** welcome over 8
DISABLED not suitable **PETS** accepted in 2 bedrooms
CLOSED Nov-Mar
PROPRIETORS Jon Barkwith and Jo Reddicliffe

WALES

EGLWYSFACH, POWYS

YNYSHIR HALL
~ COUNTRY HOUSE HOTEL ~

Eglwysfach, Machynlleth, Powys SY20 8TA
TEL (01654) 781209 **FAX** (01654) 781366 **E-MAIL** info@ynyshir-hall.co.uk
WEBSITE www.ynyshir-hall.co.uk

THE REENS HAVE BEEN at Ynyshir Hall for some years now and, happily, seem to know what they are about. In that time they have upgraded the interior rooms and bedrooms considerably. Both are ex-teachers, Joan of geography, Rob of design and art – and his paintings now decorate the walls of the whole house. Given Rob's background, you might well expect the decoration of the hotel to be rather special, too – and you would not be disappointed. The colour schemes are adventurous, the patterns bold, the use of fabrics opulent, the attention to detail striking. The bedrooms – including two brand new ones – are named after famous artists, and they are furnished accordingly.

The white-painted house dates from the 16th century, but is predominantly Georgian and Victorian. It stands in 12 glorious acres of landscaped gardens next to the Dovey Estuary.

The award-winning food is adventurous but not over-complex – modern British – based on fresh local ingredients, especially fish, game, shellfish and Welsh lamb.

~

NEARBY Llyfnant Valley; Aberystwyth.
LOCATION 11 miles (18 km) NE of Aberystwyth, just off A487; with ample car parking
MEALS breakfast, lunch, dinner
PRICE ££
ROOMS 10, 6 double, 4 suites, all with bath; all rooms have phone, TV
FACILITIES sitting-room, dining-room, bar, conservatory
CREDIT CARDS AE, DC, MC, V
CHILDREN accepted over 9
DISABLED 1 ground-floor room
PETS accepted in 1 bedroom
CLOSED never
PROPRIETORS Rob and Joan Reen

WALES

FISHGUARD, PEMBROKESHIRE

THREE MAIN STREET
~ RESTAURANT-WITH-ROOMS ~

3 Main Street, Fishguard, Pembrokeshire SA65 9HG
TEL (01348) 874275 **FAX** (01348) 874017

THE COLOURFUL OLD HARBOUR and this irresistible restaurant above it are the two best things about Fishguard. If you find that you're kicking your heels, waiting, say, for an early-morning ferry to Rosslare, then this three-storey Georgian townhouse with its stone-dressed façade and pretty hanging baskets is the place both to stay in and eat in. It's a two-woman show: Inez Ford and Marion Evans have teamed up to try 'to create the sort of restaurant we'd like to go to', and we admire their taste. Inez usually greets the guests and settles them into the small bar, where they can have pre-dinner drinks and peruse the menu, while Marion and a small, well-trained team slave at the stove.

The food is so imaginative and beautifully presented, without falling into the trap of being pretentious or over-complicated, that it has established the restaurant as one of the foremost in South Wales. As you'd expect, local fish and seafood are the specialities. During the day, coffee, tea, delicious home-baked cakes and light lunches are served in the two simply but stylishly furnished dining-rooms. Upstairs, there are three equally stylish, well-equipped bedrooms, that recall the Art Deco era.

~

NEARBY Pembrokeshire coast; Preseli Hills.
LOCATION in town centre; with limited car parking
MEALS breakfast, lunch, dinner
PRICE £
ROOMS 3; 2 double, 1 twin, all with shower; all rooms have TV, hairdrier
FACILITIES dining-room, bar, garden
CREDIT CARDS not accepted
CHILDREN welcome
DISABLED no special facilities
PETS not accepted
CLOSED late Jan to early Feb; restaurant Sun eve, Mon eve
PROPRIETORS Marion Evans and Inez Ford

WALES

TREGYNON
~ FARMHOUSE HOTEL ~

Gwaun Valley, Fishguard, Pembrokeshire SA65 9TU
TEL (01239) 820531 **FAX** (01239) 820808 **E-MAIL** tregynon@online-holidays.net
WEBSITE www.online-holidays.net/tregynon

IN THE 6TH CENTURY, Saint Brynach was supposed to have communed with angels at the summit of nearby Carn Ingli, but you don't have to climb quite so high to reach the Heards' blissfully isolated retreat which has matured nicely since its doors were opened in 1980. Set in unspoiled 'blue-stone' country (where the raw material for Stonehenge was quarried), it actually has an Iron Age fort on the property by a 200-foot waterfall. In the house the beams and stone walls keep the new millennium at bay and in winter the huge inglenook fireplace must exercise a magnetic attraction for guests just in from the hill; furnishing throughout is suitably cosy-rustic.

Only the smallest of the bedrooms is in the main 16thC stone farm-house, with the other larger ones in nearby cottages. Jane learned to cook at her French grandmother's knee, and it is around her skills that Tregynon's small, divided dining-room revolves. Her food is a highlight: traditionally based, wholesome and imaginative, with proper care taken of vegetarians, and there is a well-rounded wine list. The Heards even have their own smokehouse where they cure their bacon and gammon. Children eat at teatime, preserving adult peace at the dinner table. There is no smoking in the dining-room or bedrooms.

~

NEARBY Pembrokeshire coast; Pen-Lan-Uchaf; Pentre Ifan (Burial Chamber); Carnhuan Farm Park.
LOCATION isolated in countryside 7 miles (11 km) SE of Fishguard, 3 miles (5 km) S of Newport (get directions); with car parking
MEALS breakfast, packed lunch, dinner
PRICE ££
ROOMS 6; 4 double and twin, 2 family, all with bath; all rooms have phone, TV, hairdrier **FACILITIES** sitting-room, 2 dining-rooms, bar, garden **CREDIT CARDS** MC, V
CHILDREN welcome over 8 **DISABLED** not suitable **PETS** not accepted
CLOSED 2 weeks in winter **PROPRIETORS** Peter and Jane Heard

WALES

GARTHMYL, POWYS

GARTHMYL HALL

~ COUNTRY HOTEL ~

Garthmyl, near Montgomery, Powys SY15 6RS
TEL (01686) 640550 **FAX** (01686) 640609

IF YOU LEAVE THE HISTORIC TOWN of Montgomery behind you, and head directly towards Snowdonia, in a short space of time you will cross the upper reaches of the River Severn which perversely flows north at this point. Just beyond it is Garthmyl Hall, a Georgian gem flanked by cedars, backed by a walled garden and woods, and with enough height to look back across gently cultivated countryside towards the river. The open stone-flagged hall and light stone staircase give you an idea of the architectural merits of the rest of the building, and you will not be disappointed. As well as restoring the original features, Nancy and Tim Morrow have carefully added sympathetic furnishings and decoration. The vast drawing-room with its gilded ceiling is balanced by the smaller, more intimate library.

Dinner (pan-European, long on fresh produce and deliberately short on choice) and breakfast are both taken in the green dining-room. The bedrooms show just as much thought and attention to comfort: a spectacular array of antique bedsteads, crisp sheets, bouncy towels, flowers, chocolates – even the bathrooms are fit to sleep in. This is a friendly, informal hotel which does more than tolerate children and where quality seems to be beating price pretty handsomely.

~

NEARBY Powys Castle; Welshpool and Llanfair Light Railway.
LOCATION 5.5 miles (9 km) S of Welshpool, on A483; with ample car parking
MEALS breakfast, dinner
PRICE ££
ROOMS 9; 8 double and twin, 1 single, all with bath or shower; all rooms have phone; TV, fax/modem lead on request
FACILITIES sitting-rooms, bar, dining-room, garden
CREDIT CARDS MC, V
CHILDREN accepted **DISABLED** not suitable **PETS** not accepted **CLOSED** never
PROPRIETORS Tim and Nancy Morrow

WALES

LLANBRYNMAIR, POWYS

BARLINGS BARN
~ COUNTRY GUEST-HOUSE ~

Llanbrynmair, Powys SY19 7DY
TEL (01650) 521479 **FAX** (01650) 521520 **E-MAIL** barlbarn@zetnet.co.uk
WEBSITE www.telecentres.com/business/newtownbiz/barlingsbarn

THE ONLY SOUNDS TO DISTURB the peace come from the sheep on the surrounding hillsides, and from the nearby brook. It is a rural idyll, with a garden full of roses and honeysuckle – a picturesque setting for the outdoor activities, such as walking, birdwatching, fishing and golf which you can enjoy in the surrounding countryside.

It is, in fact, the perfect peace of the place that keeps it in these pages despite the Margolis's move a few years ago towards a self-catering set-up. Home-made biscuits await your arrival in the two secluded 'Barnlets' adjacent to Felicity and Terry's Welsh farmhouse – one with an oak-beamed stone fireplace and wood-burning stove. Their latest project has been to enclose the spring-fed, heated swimming-pool in a stunning new building, so guests can now make use of it, as well as the sauna, sunbed and squash court, all through the year.

Both 'Barnlets' are well equipped with fridge/freezers, microwaves and barbecues – Brookside even has a dishwasher. Though it's basically self-catering, Felicity will produce frozen home-made dishes on request, and the local baker will deliver delicious warm bread to the door. There's a colourful market every Wednesday in Machynlleth.

~

NEARBY Snowdonia; Aberdovey beach.
LOCATION 2 miles (3 km) NE of Llanbrynmair at end of private lane off road to Pandy; with ample car parking
MEALS home-cooked frozen meals
PRICE £-££
ROOMS 2 'Barnlets', Sunnyside sleeps 2-6; Brookside sleeps 8-12; both have TV
FACILITIES garden, swimming-pool, squash, sauna, sunbed
CREDIT CARDS not accepted **CHILDREN** welcome
DISABLED Brookside has 1 ground-floor bedroom and special facilities
PETS accepted by arrangement **CLOSED** never
PROPRIETORS Terry and Felicity Margolis

WALES

LLANDRILLO, DENBIGHSHIRE

TYDDYN LLAN
~ COUNTRY HOTEL ~

Llandrillo, near Corwen, Denbighshire LL21 0ST
TEL (01490) 440264 **FAX** (01490) 440414
E-MAIL tyddynllanhotel@compuserve.com

A FIRM FAVOURITE WITH READERS since our first edition, this Georgian stone house has been decorated by the Kindreds with elegant flair, period antiques and fine paintings, creating a serene ambience. It is very much a home, despite the number of guests it can accommodate – there is a major extension to the building, cleverly complementary to the original, using slate, stone and cast-iron.

Our latest report of Tyddyn Llan glowed: 'No intrusive reception desk; spacious sitting-rooms furnished with style; dining-room shows great flair; bedrooms well equipped with original pieces of furniture; small but modern and very pleasing bathrooms; peaceful, comfortable stay, warm atmosphere provided by attentive hosts; great charm.'

Chef Sean Ballington is continuing in the footsteps of his talented predecessor, Jason Hornbuckle, producing a new angle on Welsh country house food with inventive and well-planned small menus using quality local ingredients, and keeping the kitchen's high reputation secure.

The place is surrounded by large grounds; the lawn is large enough to practise fly-casting; and the hotel has four miles of fishing on the Dee.

NEARBY Bala Lake and Railway; Snowdonia.
LOCATION 5 miles (8 km) SW of Corwen off B4401; with ample car parking
MEALS breakfast, lunch, dinner
PRICE £££
ROOMS 10 double, 8 with bath, 2 with shower; all rooms have phone, TV
FACILITIES sitting-room, bar, restaurant; croquet, fishing
CREDIT CARDS AE, DC, MC, V
CHILDREN welcome
DISABLED not suitable
PETS accepted in bedrooms by arrangement
CLOSED never
PROPRIETORS Bridget and Peter Kindred

WALES

LLANDUDNO, CONWY

ST TUDNO
~ SEASIDE HOTEL ~

Promenade, Llandudno, Conwy LL30 2LP
TEL (01492) 874411 **FAX** (01492) 860407 **E-MAIL** sttudnohotel@btinternet.com
WEBSITE www.st-tudno.co.uk

THE BLANDS ARE METICULOUS in attending to every detail of this award-winning seafront hotel, which they have been improving for almost 30 years now. They could not, however, improve on its location: right on Llandudno's dignified promenade, opposite the carefully restored Victorian pier and sheltered from inclement weather by the Great Orme headland. The pretty rooms are each decorated differently in designer wallpapers and matching fabrics, and have found the balance between Victorian charm and modern facilities. A long list of thoughtful extras add to the sense of comfort, including complimentary wine. We continue to get favourable reports from readers.

The air-conditioned Garden Room Restaurant is light and inviting, and suits its name with a profusion of plants and cane-backed chairs. The seasonal menu with daily-changing *carte*, based on the best local ingredients, deserves serious study in the comfortable bar, and – though it's not cheap – the cooking is right on target. If you overindulge, you can try to recover your figure by pounding up and down the lovely covered pool, decorated with murals. All of this would be difficult to resist even without the bonus of the hotel's young and helpful staff.

~

NEARBY dry-ski slope; Conwy Castle; Bodnant Gardens; Snowdonia.
LOCATION on seafront opposite pier and promenade gardens; with
parking for 12 cars and unrestricted street parking
MEALS breakfast, lunch, dinner
PRICE ££-£££
ROOMS 22; 15 double and twin, 2 single, 1 suite, 4 family, all with bath or shower;
all rooms have phone, TV, fridge, hairdrier
FACILITIES 3 sitting-rooms, dining-room, bar, lift, garden; indoor swimming-pool
CREDIT CARDS AE, DC, MC, V **CHILDREN** welcome
DISABLED not suitable **PETS** accepted by arrangement **CLOSED** never
PROPRIETORS Martin and Janette Bland

WALES

LLANSANFFRAID GLAN CONWY, CONWY

THE OLD RECTORY

~ COUNTRY RECTORY ~

Llansanffraid Glan Conwy, Colwyn Bay, Conwy LL28 5LF
TEL (01492) 580611 **FAX** (01492) 584555 **E-MAIL** OldRect@aol.com
WEBSITE www.wales.com/oldrectory/

THIS PRETTY, FORMER Georgian rectory, home of the owners, enjoys an exceptional elevated position, standing in two-and-a-half acres of flowery gardens with lovely sweeping views across the Conwy Estuary to Conwy Castle and Snowdonia beyond. Most of the bedrooms, two of which are in a separate building, share this view. The rooms have an old-fashioned feel about them, with ponderous beds, mostly either half-tester or four-poster, in walnut, mahogany and oak. Downstairs, is an elegant panelled drawing-room with the Vaughans' collection of Victorian watercolours on the walls.

The couple's progression as hoteliers and particularly Wendy's as a chef has been remarkable. An ex-nurse with no culinary training whatsoever, she began by cooking for parties of visiting American tourists. As they started to take in bed-and-breakfast guests and then graduated to fully fledged hotel, so Wendy's culinary skills improved and they are now – since January 2000 – the proud possessors of a Michelin star, as well as several other awards for food. Wendy still produces a delicious and imaginative three-course dinner each night unaided, except for help with the washing-up and the vegetable chopping (done by Michael, who also oversees the wine list to complement her food). Guests eat at separate mahogany, candlelit tables dotted round the room. No smoking, except in the coach house.

~

NEARBY Bodnant Gardens; Betws-y-Coed; Llandudno.
LOCATION on A470 half a mile (1 km) S of junction with A55; with ample car parking
MEALS breakfast, dinner
PRICE £££
ROOMS 6 double, 5 with bath, 1 with shower; all rooms have phone, TV, hairdrier
FACILITIES sitting-room, dining-room, garden **CREDIT CARDS** MC, V **CHILDREN** accepted over 6 **DISABLED** 2 ground-floor rooms **PETS** accepted in coach house only
CLOSED Dec-Feb **PROPRIETORS** Michael and Wendy Vaughan

WALES

LLANTHONY, GWENT

ABBEY HOTEL

~ COUNTRY INN ~

Llanthony, Abergavenny, Gwent NP7 7NN
TEL (01873) 890487 **FAX** (01873) 890844

FAR INTO THE BLACK MOUNTAINS, on the west bank of the Afon Honddu and overlooked by Offa's Dyke to the east, Llanthony Priory lies high and remote in the Vale of Ewyas. The most spectacular approach is southwards from the sloping streets and busy bookshops of Hay-on-Wye. One of the earliest Augustinian houses in Britain, it was endowed by the de Lacy family, but, by the time of Henry VIII's dissolution of the monasteries, had fallen into disuse. The Prior's quarters survived amongst the ruins and are now used as the hotel. Gothic horror enthusiasts will be delighted not only by the setting, but also when they learn that the highest of the bedrooms can only be reached by climbing more than 60 spiral steps up into the south tower. This is not a hotel for the fastidious or the faint-hearted: it is a long way from anywhere and much used by walkers attracted to the stunning country that surrounds it. Unless you plan to arrive on foot yourself, you should remember that your fellow guests may have had their appetites sharpened by fresh air and their critical faculties dulled by fatigue. However, the chance to sleep in this unique piece of history (with a four-poster and half-tester available) and to wake up to the view from the tower also comes with a very modest price tag.

~

NEARBY Offa's Dyke; Brecon Beacons; Hay-on-Wye.
LOCATION off A465 from Abergavenny to Hereford, take mountain road heading N at Llanfihangel Crucorney; with ample car parking
MEALS breakfast, lunch, dinner
PRICE £
ROOMS 5 double and twin
FACILITIES sitting-room, dining-room, bar, garden
CREDIT CARDS not accepted **CHILDREN** accepted over 10
DISABLED access not possible **PETS** not accepted
CLOSED Sun-Thurs Nov to Easter; restaurant Mon eve
PROPRIETOR Ivor Prentice

WALES

PENALLY, PEMBROKESHIRE

PENALLY ABBEY
~ COUNTRY HOUSE HOTEL ~

Penally, near Tenby, South Pembrokeshire SA70 7PY
TEL (01834) 843033 **FAX** (01834) 844714
E-MAIL penally.abbey@btinternet.com

EVER SINCE THE MIDDLE AGES this has been recognized as one of the spots from which to appreciate the broad sweep of the Pembrokeshire coast from Tenby to Giltar Point. The links golf course which parallels the beach wasn't there, but the ruins of the medieval chapel which gave this Gothic country house its name are still in the secluded and well-tended gardens. The windows and doors (including the doors to the rooms) all have the characteristic double curve arches and Bela Lugosi himself would have been quite at home in the corridors and on the stairs. There is a comfortable and well-furnished drawing-room with an open fire, a welcoming bar far from the world's woes and weather, and a tall, candle-lit dining-room for the well-planned and prepared dinners, which include a wide choice of fresh Welsh game and produce. All the bedrooms are freshly decorated and well equipped: some you could play cricket in and are furnished on an appropriately grand scale. Steve Warren and his family have made a smart but easy and informal hotel which is child friendly (babysitting *and* baby listening on tap). Children are welcome in the dining-room for the (excellent) breakfasts, but an early supper sensibly makes this a child-free zone in the evening.

~

NEARBY Tenby; Colby Woodland Garden; Upton Castle.
LOCATION in village 1.5 miles (2.5 km) SW of Tenby; with ample car parking
MEALS breakfast, dinner
PRICE ££
ROOMS 12 double and twin with bath; all rooms have phone, TV, fax/modem point, hairdrier
FACILITIES sitting-room, billiards-room, dining-room, bar, indoor swimming-pool, garden **CREDIT CARDS** AE, MC, V **CHILDREN** accepted
DISABLED access possible to 2 ground-floor bedrooms
PETS not accepted **CLOSED** never
PROPRIETORS Steve and Elleen Warren

WALES

PENMAENPOOL, GWYNEDD

GEORGE III

~ COUNTRY INN ~

Penmaenpool, Dolgellau, Gwynedd LL40 1YD
TEL (01341) 422525 **FAX** (01341) 423565

PENMAENPOOL CLINGS to the south bank of the Mawddach Estuary; looking north across the water, crowded with enough birdlife to have persuaded the RSPB to establish a centre next door; you can see the Diffwys Mountains in the distance. There was once a flourishing boat-building industry here (half the hotel was originally a chandlery), and until the 1960s there was a railway station. The line, which used to separate the hotel from the shore, was closed and its waiting-room, ticket office and stationmaster's house were later bought and turned into additional bedrooms. Still very much a busy pub, there is excellent bar food from a long and varied menu. If you've come from the north side of the estuary and just popped in for a drink, do remember that the long wooden toll bridge which shortens your journey back by several miles closes at 7 pm. More 'serious' food is served in the restaurant which has French windows opening on to a long balcony overlooking the estuary. Residents have a separate sitting-room to themselves, complete with beams and an inglenook fireplace. Upstairs, most of the light, beamed bedrooms have the same view (some avid birdwatchers have been known to miss breakfast). Guests have free access to more than 12 miles of river and lake fishing, and there are wonderful walks from the door.

~

NEARBY Fairbourne Railway; Snowdonia; Lake Vyrnwy.
LOCATION 2 miles (3 km) W of Dolgellau on A493, on edge of Mawddach Estuary; with ample car parking
MEALS breakfast, lunch, dinner
PRICE ££
ROOMS 12 double and twin with bath or shower; all rooms have phone, TV, hairdrier **FACILITIES** sitting-room, dining-room, 3 bars; fishing, mountain bikes for hire **CREDIT CARDS** MC, V **CHILDREN** welcome **DISABLED** access possible to Lodge bedrooms **PETS** accepted by arrangement **CLOSED** never
PROPRIETORS Julia and John Cartwright

WALES

PENMAENPOOL, GWYNEDD

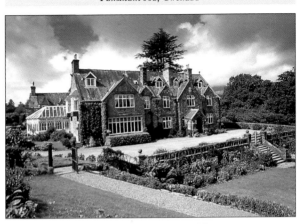

EDITORS' CHOICE

PENMAENUCHAF HALL

~ COUNTRY HOUSE HOTEL ~

Penmaenpool, Dolgellau, Gwynedd LL40 1YB
TEL (01341) 422129 **FAX** (01341) 422787
E-MAIL relax@penhall.co.uk

NOT FAR FROM THE MARKET town of Dolgellau, Penmaenuchaf Hall's drive winds steeply up a wooded hillside from the south bank of the Mawddach Estuary to this sturdy, grey stone Victorian manor house. Set on terraces in 21 acres of grounds, the views across Snowdonia must have been top of the list of reasons that brought the original builder – a Lancashire mill owner – to this peaceful spot at the foot of Cader Idris. A rose garden and a water garden add a charm of their own to the beautiful setting.

Indoors, Mark Watson and Lorraine Fielding have saved, but also softened, the Victorian character of the house so that, from the imposing main hall you are drawn to the warmth and light of the ivory morning- room, the sitting-rooms and the library. The same sympathetic treatment carries through to the bedrooms – fine fabrics are married with fine furniture and only the beds are baronial. If you are not tempted by the excellent walking in the surrounding hills, you can revive the skills of a misspent youth in the billiards-room or simply doze in the sunny conservatory. Dinner, a stylish modern British event, is served in the panelled dining-room.

~

NEARBY Mawddach Estuary; Snowdonia; Lake Vyrnwy.
LOCATION off A493 Dolgellau-Tywyn road; with ample car parking
MEALS breakfast, lunch, dinner
PRICE ££
ROOMS 14 double and twin with bath; all rooms have phone, TV, hairdrier; superior rooms have minibar
FACILITIES sitting-rooms, library, billiards-room, 2 dining-rooms, bar, garden; helipad; fishing **CREDIT CARDS** AE, DC, MC, V **CHILDREN** babes-in-arms and children over 6 accepted
DISABLED access possible to restaurant **PETS** accepted in 1 room by arrangement
CLOSED 10 days in Jun
PROPRIETORS Mark Watson and Lorraine Fielding

WALES

PORTMEIRION, GWYNEDD

PORTMEIRION HOTEL

SEASIDE HOTEL

Portmeirion, Gwynedd LL48 6ET
TEL (01766) 770228 **FAX** (01766) 771331 **E-MAIL** hotel@portmeirion-village.com
WEBSITE www.portmeirion-village.com

AT THE HEART OF Clough Williams-Ellis's delightful Italianate fantasy village is the Portmeirion Hotel, a magical white villa standing on a headland close to the seashore and surrounded by the 'Gwyllt', 70 acres of subtropical woodland gardens where camellias, rhododendrons and magnolias flourish. After it opened in 1926, the hotel became a magnet for the literati, attracting the likes of George Bernard Shaw, H. G. Wells and Noel Coward, who wrote *Blithe Spirit* while staying here in 1941.

Guests have the choice of staying in the hotel or in one of the paintbox-coloured cottages which are dotted around the village, but enjoy all the facilities of the hotel. These include the pretty, circular outdoor swimming-pool (heated from May to September) and the glorious 'ocean liner' dining-room, a 1930s addition, which at high tide really seems to be afloat, and whose reputation for modern Welsh cuisine is growing.

The interior of the hotel is decorated in vibrant colours: from the dramatic black-and-white marble floor in the hall to the icy-blue Mirror Room and exotic Jaipur Bar, a small slice of Rajasthan. The bedrooms in the main building are equally stylish, and more expensive than the less flamboyant cottage rooms.

NEARBY Ffestiniog Railway; Harlech Castle.
LOCATION in Portmeirion village; with ample car parking
MEALS breakfast, lunch, dinner
PRICE ££-£££
ROOMS 26 double and twin, 14 suites, all with bath; all rooms have phone, TV, hairdrier; some have minibar; self-catering cottages available
FACILITIES 2 sitting-rooms, library, conservatory, dining-room, garden; swimming-pool, tennis **CREDIT CARDS** AE, D, MC, V **CHILDREN** welcome
DISABLED no special facilities **PETS** accepted in 4 cottages
CLOSED last 3 weeks in Jan
PROPRIETOR Robin Llywelyn

WALES

REYNOLDSTON, WEST GLAMORGAN

FAIRYHILL
~ COUNTRY HOUSE HOTEL ~

Reynoldston, Gower, near Swansea, West Glamorgan SA3 1BS
TEL (01792) 390139 **FAX** (01792) 391358 **E-MAIL** postbox@fairyhill.net
WEBSITE www.fairyhill.net

OUR LATEST INSPECTION confirmed that standards were being well maintained in this quiet and utterly civilized retreat, situated in the heart of the Gower Peninsula and only about 25 minutes from the M4, since the current owners took over in late 1993.

Set in 24 acres of grounds – with walled garden, orchard, trout stream and lake, and much of it still semi-wild – the three-storey Georgian building has a series of spacious, attractively furnished public rooms on the ground floor, leading to the dining-room.

Paul Davies, one of the proprietors, is the chef, who has recently been joined by Adrian Coulthard. They enjoy producing seasonal menus and make excellent use of traditional local specialities such as Gower lobster and crab, Penclawdd cockles, Welsh lamb and laver bread. The extensive wine list, cellared in the old vaults of the house, includes five wines from Wales. Most bedrooms overlook the large park and woodland, and are comfortable and well-equipped – they even have CD players, on which to play your choices from the hotel's large and catholic collection of disks.

More reports please.

~

NEARBY Weobley Castle; Gower Peninsula; Long Cairn Water Mill; Swansea.
LOCATION 12 miles (19 km) W of Swansea, 1 mile (1.5 km) NW of village; in 24-acre park and woodland, with ample car parking
MEALS breakfast, lunch, dinner
PRICE £££
ROOMS 8 double with bath; all rooms have phone, TV, CD player
FACILITIES sitting-room, bar, 2 dining-rooms, conference-room; croquet
CREDIT CARDS AE, MC, V **CHILDREN** accepted over 8
DISABLED access possible to restaurant only
PETS not accepted
CLOSED 24-27 Dec
PROPRIETORS P. and J. Camm, P. Davies and A. Hetherington

WALES

TALSARNAU, GWYNEDD

MAES-Y-NEUADD
~ COUNTRY HOTEL ~

Talsarnau, Gwynedd LL47 6YA
TEL (01766) 780200 **FAX** (01766) 780211 **E-MAIL** maes@neuadd.com
WEBSITE www.neuadd.com

IF YOU HAVEN'T BEEN to Maes-y-Neuadd before, you run the risk of running out of confidence in your own map-reading skills as the little road from the coast winds up and up through woods. Fear not and press on, for the journey will be worth it. You will arrive outside a stone-built slate-roofed manor that is only a century or so younger than Harlech Castle, creeper-clad in parts, and if the time is right you can look back across the water to see the sun set behind the Lleyn Peninsula. It may be Snowdonia outside, but inside it is definitely deep-pile all the way. Chintzes in the drawing-room, leather in the bar and, in the pale and elegant dining-room, master-pieces from the kitchen of Peter Jackson (chef and co-owner) all combine to make this a seriously comfortable hotel.

Much of the fresh produce comes from Maes-y-Neuadd's own garden (the gardeners get a credit). Menus are set, with choices for each of the possible five courses until pudding when you reach 'Diweddglo Mawreddog' (the grand finale), which means you get them all. When you are shown to your room, take note of how you got there as the upstairs corridors are all similar. The reverse is true of the smart, variously-sized bedrooms which are individually decorated and furnished.

~

NEARBY Portmeirion; Ffestiniog Railway; Harlech Castle.
LOCATION 3 miles (5 km) NE of Harlech, up small road off B4573; with ample car parking
MEALS breakfast, dinner; room service
PRICE £££
ROOMS 16; 15 double and twin, 1 single, all with bath or shower; all rooms have phone, TV, fax/modem point, air-conditioning, hairdrier
FACILITIES sitting-room, conservatory, dining-room, bar, terrace, lift, garden; helipad **CREDIT CARDS** AE, DC, MC, V **CHILDREN** accepted
DISABLED 3 ground-floor rooms **PETS** accepted in bedrooms **CLOSED** never
PROPRIETORS Lynn and Peter Jackson

WALES

THREE COCKS, POWYS

OLD GWERNYFED

∽ MANOR HOUSE HOTEL ∽

Felindre, Three Cocks, Brecon, Powys LD3 0SG
TEL & FAX (01497) 847376

ROGER AND DAWN BEETHAM ran this splendid Elizabethan manor house 'very quietly' after taking over the lease from Roger's parents in 1979; but in 1986 the opportunity arose to buy Old Gwernyfed outright, and the two of them have since set about making it 'the best personal small hotel around'.

Happily, the improvements so far have not interfered with the historic character of the place. Decoration is kept to a minimum and the slightly haphazard collection of grand old furniture goes on growing. The four newest bedrooms, created where the kitchens used to be, have the same high ceilings and sense of space of the larger of the old rooms (which range in size from very small to positively enormous). The public rooms are especially impressive – the oak-panelled sitting-room is overlooked by a minstrel's gallery, the dining-room has a vast fireplace with a wood-burning stove. Period music is played as a background to Dawn's original and satisfying dinners ("designed for people who have just walked half of Offa's Dyke," says our inspector), with some choice at beginning and end. ∽

NEARBY Brecon Beacons; Hay-on-Wye.
LOCATION 11 miles (18 km) NE of Brecon, off A438, in open countryside; with ample car parking
MEALS breakfast, packed lunch by arrangement, dinner
PRICE ££
ROOMS 10; 9 double and family, 7 with bath, 1 with shower, 1 single with bath
FACILITIES sitting-room, games-room, dining-room, bar, garden; croquet
CREDIT CARDS not accepted
CHILDREN accepted if well-behaved
DISABLED access difficult
PETS accepted in bedrooms by arrangement
CLOSED Jan-Feb
PROPRIETORS Dawn and Roger Beetham

WALES

THREE COCKS, POWYS

THREE COCKS
~ VILLAGE INN ~

Three Cocks, near Brecon, Powys LD3 0SL
TEL (01497) 847215 **FAX** (01497) 847339
WEBSITE www.hay-on-wye.co.uk/3cocks

THE BUILDING IS A CHARMING, ivy-covered, 15thC coaching inn in the Welsh hills, constructed around a tree (still in evidence in the kitchen) and with its cobbled forecourt on the most direct route from Hereford to Brecon. Inside, carved wood and stone walls continue the natural look of the exterior, with beams and eccentrically angled doorways serving as proof positive of antiquity. The kitchen, presided over by Michael Winstone, is now its primary business, and draws people great distances to the warm welcome and roomy restaurant with its lace-covered tables. There are plenty of places where you can sit in peace, and residents now have a drawing-room of their own, in keeping with its public oak-panelled counterpart but with more light, stone and fabric in evidence.

Bedrooms are modest but comfortable and well equipped, with dark oak furniture and pale fabrics. But what makes the Three Cocks stand out is the Belgian influence on both the food and atmosphere – Marie-Jeanne is from Belgium, and she and Michael used to live and work there. The cuisine is deceptively simple, with great attention paid to the freshness and quality of its elements. Game and shellfish regularly feature on the menu, local lamb is given a continental spin, and a large selection of Belgian beers complements a well-balanced and keenly priced wine-list.

~

NEARBY Brecon Beacons; Hay-on-Wye; Hereford Cathedral; Black Mountains.
LOCATION in village, 11 miles (18 km) NE of Brecon on A438; with ample car parking
MEALS breakfast, lunch, dinner
PRICE ££
ROOMS 7 double and twin, 6 with bath, 1 with shower
FACILITIES 2 sitting-rooms, TV-room, dining-room, breakfast-room, garden
CREDIT CARDS MC, V **CHILDREN** welcome **DISABLED** access difficult **PETS** not accepted
CLOSED Dec to mid-Feb; restaurant Sun lunch, Tue
PROPRIETORS Michael and Marie-Jeanne Winstone

MIDLANDS

CALLOW HALL

~ COUNTRY HOUSE HOTEL ~

Mappleton, Ashbourne, Derbyshire DE6 2AA
TEL (01335) 300900 **FAX** (01335) 343624

THE SPENCERS HAVE been 'foodies' for generations. They have been master bakers in Ashbourne since 1724, and one of the highlights of staying at this fine Victorian country house hotel is its excellent dining-room. As well as growing many of their own ingredients, the Spencers also smoke and cure meat and fish themselves – arts that have been passed down through the family.

Set in extensive grounds at the entrance to the Peak District National Park, the hotel overlooks the stunning landscape of the Dove Valley. Public rooms and bedrooms are done out in an appropriate and not too flamboyant country house style. The walls of the entrance are guarded by stags' heads and the flagstoned floor is scattered with Persian rugs. In winter an open fire crackles, while guests dine in the glow of the deep-red dining-room, and in the drawing-room, comfy sofas and chairs provide plenty of space for relaxing. Carved antiques and family heirlooms mingle with period repro furniture. Ask for a decent-sized room when you book: one or two are on the small side for the price. Staff are helpful yet unobtrusive, and the Spencers are hands-on owners, with Dorothy front- of of-house and David and Anthony in charge of the kitchen.

~

NEARBY Chatsworth House; Haddon Hall; Hardwick Hall.
LOCATION 0.75 mile (1 km) N of Ashbourne on A515; with ample car parking
MEALS breakfast, lunch Sun or on request, dinner
PRICE £££
ROOMS 16; 15 double and twin, 1 suite, all with bath or shower; all rooms have phone, TV, hairdrier
FACILITIES sitting-room, dining-rooms, bar, garden; fishing
CREDIT CARDS AE, D, MC, V **CHILDREN** welcome **DISABLED** 1 specially adapted room
PETS accepted by arrangement
CLOSED Christmas Day, Boxing Day, New Year's Day
PROPRIETORS David, Dorothy and Anthony Spencer

MIDLANDS

ASHFORD-IN-THE-WATER, DERBYSHIRE

RIVERSIDE HOUSE
～ COUNTRY HOTEL ～

Fennel Street, Ashford-in-the-Water, Bakewell, Derbyshire, DE4 1QF
TEL (01629) 814275 **FAX** (01629) 812873
E-MAIL riversidehouse@enta.net **WEBSITE** info@riversidehousehotel.co.uk

NESTLING IN ONE of the Peak District's prettiest villages, this stone-built, ivy-clad house has an idyllic setting in its own secluded grounds, bordered by the River Wye. The village is aptly named – on our inspector's visit during a spate of heavy rain, the river was threatening to encroach, and manager was coping admirably, with sandbags at the ready, with the possibility of a flood alert.

Penelope Thornton (of the Thornton chocolate family), who took over the hotel in 1997, has instituted a refreshingly plain style, entirely in keeping with the house's Georgian origins. A large plant-filled conservatory leads into a cosy snug with an impressive recessed carved-oak mantelpiece and open fire. There is an elegant, comfortable sitting-room and a variety of well-equipped bedrooms of different sizes. Rooms in the newer Garden wing overlook the river.

Crucial to Riverside is its reputation for fine food, which is served in two intimate dining-rooms. Chef John Whelan creates imaginative dishes, such as *mille-feuille* of marinated salmon with beetroot *confit*, and celery and wild mushroom *strüdel*; he also offers an intriguing selection of cheeses – Lincolnshire Poacher, Belineigh Blue and Gubbeen. Coffee is accompanied by a little box of locally made Thorntons chocolates.

～

NEARBY Chatsworth; Haddon Hall; Bakewell.
LOCATION 2 miles (3 km) NW of Bakewell on A6, at top of village, next to Sheepwash Bridge; with ample car parking
MEALS breakfast, lunch, dinner
PRICE £££
ROOMS 15 double and twin, 13 with bath, 2 with shower; all rooms have phone, TV, hairdrier **FACILITIES** 2 sitting-rooms, conservatory, bar, 2 dining-rooms, garden
CREDIT CARDS AE, DC, MC, V **CHILDREN** welcome over 10
DISABLED access possible to 4 rooms **PETS** not accepted **CLOSED** never
PROPRIETOR Penelope Thornton

MIDLANDS

ATHERSTONE, WARWICKSHIRE

CHAPEL HOUSE
~ TOWN HOTEL ~

Friar's Gate, Atherstone, Warwickshire CV9 1EY
TEL (01827) 718949 **FAX** (01827) 717702

FROM ATHERSTONE'S MARKET SQUARE, you get a tantalizing glimpse of trees and flowers in the glorious, mature walled garden that envelops this handsome 18thC townhouse, and once beyond the walls, it feels so secluded that, if it weren't for the church bells next door that ring hourly, you might be in the depths of the country. Built as Atherstone Hall's dower house, it shows some signs of its 18thC roots, especially in the fine porticoed entrance and flagstoned hallway beyond. Both decoration and furnishings reinforce the style: pale rooms are filled with period furniture, gilt mirrors, swagged pelmets and antimacassar-draped chairs. Owner, David Arnold, has the knack of making his guests feel as though they are staying, not in a hotel, but with friends.

All the pretty, homely bedrooms are different. Some are small and some have shower-rooms not bathrooms, but they compensate with their charm, particularly those under the eaves, and all the little personal touches – books, magazines, bottled water, biscuits – which the thoughtful staff never forget. Dinners, served in a restful pink dining-room overlooking the garden, are both satisfying and imaginative. Sometimes they're themed.

~

NEARBY Bosworth battlefield; Arbury Hall; Tamworth Castle; Coventry Cathedral; Lichfield Cathedral.
LOCATION beside church in NE corner of market square; with ample car parking
MEALS breakfast, dinner; lunch by arrangement
PRICE ££
ROOMS 14; 9 double and twin, 5 single, 5 with bath, 9 with shower; all rooms have phone, TV
FACILITIES sitting-room, conservatory, dining-room, garden
CREDIT CARDS AE, D, MC, V **CHILDREN** accepted
DISABLED access possible to public rooms only
PETS not accepted **CLOSED** Christmas Day, Boxing Day; restaurant Sun (open for lunch once a month), Bank hol Mon **PROPRIETOR** David Arnold

MIDLANDS

BASLOW, DERBYSHIRE

THE CAVENDISH
~ COUNTRY HOUSE HOTEL ~

Baslow, Derbyshire DE45 1SP
TEL (01246) 582311 **FAX** (01246) 582312 **E-MAIL** info@cavendish-hotel.net
WEBSITE www.cavendish-hotel.net

THE CAVENDISH DOESN'T SOUND LIKE a personal small hotel. But the smart name is not mere snobbery – it is the family name of the Duke of Devonshire, on whose glorious Chatsworth Estate the hotel sits (and over which the bedrooms look). And neither the hotel's size nor its equipment interferes with its essential appeal as a polished but informal and enthusiastically run hotel – strictly speaking, an inn, as Eric Marsh is careful to point out, but for practical purposes a country house.

Outside, the solid stone building is plain and unassuming. Inside, all is grace and good taste: the welcoming entrance hall sets the tone – striped sofas before an open fire, elegant antique tables standing on a brick-tile floor, while the walls act as a gallery for Eric Marsh's eclectic collection of more than 300 pictures. The whole ground floor has recently been remodelled, and a café-style conservatory added. Bedrooms are consistently attractive and comfortable, but vary in size and character – older ones are more spacious.

The elegant restaurant claims to have a 'controversial' menu. It is certainly ambitious and highly priced, but it met the approval of recent guests who described the food as 'unsurpassed – we were spoilt to death!' The Garden Room is less formal.

~

NEARBY Chatsworth; Haddon Hall; Peak District.
LOCATION 10 miles (16 km) W of Chesterfield on A619; with ample car parking
MEALS breakfast, lunch, dinner
PRICE £££
ROOMS 23 double with bath; all rooms have phone, TV, minibar, hairdrier
FACILITIES sitting-room, dining-room, bar, garden-room, garden; putting green, fishing **CREDIT CARDS** AE, DC, MC, V **CHILDREN** welcome
DISABLED access difficult
PETS not accepted **CLOSED** never
PROPRIETOR Eric Marsh

MIDLANDS

BLOCKLEY, GLOUCESTERSHIRE

LOWER BROOK HOUSE

~ VILLAGE GUEST-HOUSE ~

Lower Street, Blockley, Moreton-in-Marsh, Gloucestershire GL56 9DS
TEL & FAX (01386) 700286
E-MAIL Lowerbrookhouse@compuserve.com

FOR SOME 300 YEARS, Lower Brook House had been sitting quietly in Blockley between the church and the stream from which it takes its name. Recently though, things have livened up: specifically, Marie Mosedale-Cooper has arrived. With her have come glass, china and silver. Not to mention the bric-a-brac, *objets d'art* or the antique furniture. Or the rugs. Or even the paintings. Somehow it has all fitted in. What she has also brought is her own highly individual, welcoming and inclusive style. The house itself is pure Cotswold, built from the local stone and with its beams, flagstone floors and fireplaces (there is a vast inglenook in the drawing-room) still very much intact and in use. The bedrooms are not large, but you can console yourself by bundling into your robe, eating the chocolates (and then probably some fruit from the bowl to salve your conscience) while you sit and admire the fresh flowers. The soft-red beamed restaurant is cosy but not cramped. The *cuisine* is modern British, with short, pleasing menus, often using vegetables from the garden, teamed with an excellent wine list. Coffee *ad lib* follows in the drawing-room. Lower Brook House is child friendly (babysitting and baby listening are available), and an early children's supper is provided to bring on a bit of peace. All the bedrooms are non-smoking.

~

NEARBY Hidcote Manor Garden; Snowshill Manor; Broadway; Stratford-upon-Avon; Evesham; Cheltenham.
LOCATION on right as you enter village from Moreton-in-Marsh, 4 miles (6.5 km) NW of Moreton-in-Marsh; with car parking
MEALS breakfast, dinner
PRICE ££
ROOMS 5 double and twin with bath or shower; all rooms have TV, hairdrier
FACILITIES sitting-rooms, dining-room, bar, garden **CREDIT CARDS** MC, V
CHILDREN accepted **PETS** not accepted **DISABLED** not suitable **CLOSED** never
PROPRIETOR Marie Mosedale-Cooper

MIDLANDS

BLOCKLEY, GLOUCESTERSHIRE

THE OLD BAKERY
~ VILLAGE GUEST-HOUSE ~

High Street, Blockley, Moreton-in-Marsh, Gloucestershire GL56 9EU
TEL & FAX (01386) 700408

PART OF BLOCKLEY LOOKS as if it was built simply to prove that one *could* build on slopes that steep. Part of the way along the downhill side of Blockley High Street (a narrow road to nowhere), cling four rose-covered Victorian cottages now joined to form The Old Bakery. Linda Helme and John Benson are so enthusiastic about cookery, and warm in their welcome, that you feel they might even relish the challenge of a desert island. As it is, they scour the region for the best of the season and your route to one of their three splendid bedrooms is to visit their red and rose dining-room – and appreciate the four-course dinner that results from their careful and creative preparation of the fruits of their search. The wine list has been selected with care and the wines are offered at prices that can leave room only for very modest margins.

The bedrooms are unfussy but by no means austere: all are a good size and if you can remember a colour (green, yellow or blue), then you'll know which is yours. Each has the kind of bathroom you wish you could take home with you. There is no smoking anywhere in the hotel.

NEARBY Hidcote Manor Garden; Snowshill Manor; Broadway; Stratford-upon-Avon; Evesham; Cheltenham
LOCATION in centre of village, 4 miles (6.5 km) NW of Moreton-in-Marsh; with limited car parking or on street
MEALS breakfast, dinner
PRICE £
ROOMS 3 double and twin with bath; all rooms have TV
FACILITIES sitting-room, dining-room, bar, garden
CREDIT CARDS AE, MC, V
CHILDREN accepted over 12
DISABLED not suitable **PETS** not accepted
CLOSED mid-Dec to mid-Jan, 2 weeks in Jun
PROPRIETORS Linda Helme and John Benson

MIDLANDS

BROAD CAMPDEN, GLOUCESTERSHIRE

MALT HOUSE

~ COUNTRY GUEST-HOUSE ~

Broad Campden, Chipping Campden, Gloucestershire GL55 6UU
TEL (01386) 840295 **FAX** (01386) 841334
E-MAIL Nick@the-malt-house.freeserve.co.uk

I T IS EASY TO MISS THIS 17thC Cotswold house (in fact a conversion of three cottages) in a tiny picture-postcard hamlet comprising little more than a cluster of thatched, wistaria-covered cottages, a church and a pub. Once found, the Malt House is delightful – with low beamed ceilings, antique furniture and leaded windows overlooking a dream garden, where the family cats potter contentedly about. 'Very pleasing, comfortable and quiet,' comments our latest reporter.

The bedrooms, most of which overlook the gardens and paddocks and orchard beyond, are individually decorated in vibrant colours with fine antique furniture and include a room with a four-poster bed. Public rooms are comfortable, but small, with displays of fresh flowers and log fires in winter. The accommodation includes a pleasantly laid out garden suite with a private sitting-room and an entrance to the garden. Guests breakfast and dine in the beamed dining-room, complete with inglenook fireplace.

The Browns' son Julian, who is an experienced chef, cooks inspired three-course evening meals using ingredients that are fresh from the kitchen gardens.

~

NEARBY Batsford Park Arboretum; Sezincote Garden; Snowshill Manor; Stratford-upon-Avon; Cotswold villages; Cheltenham.
LOCATION 1 mile (1.5 km) SE of Chipping Campden just outside village; with ample car parking
MEALS breakfast, dinner
PRICE ££
ROOMS 9; 7 double and twin, 1 single, 1 suite/family, all with bath or shower; all rooms have TV, hairdrier
FACILITIES 2 sitting-rooms, dining-room; croquet **CREDIT CARDS** AE, DC, MC, V
CHILDREN welcome if well-behaved **DISABLED** access difficult **PETS** accepted
CLOSED Christmas **PROPRIETORS** Nick and Jean Brown

MIDLANDS

BROADWAY, WORCESTERSHIRE

COLLIN HOUSE
~ COUNTRY HOTEL ~

Collin Lane, Broadway, Worcestershire WR1 7PB
TEL (01386) 858354 **FAX** (01386) 858697 **E-MAIL** collin.house@virgin.net
WEBSITE www.broadway-cotswolds.co.uk/collin.html

TUCKED WELL AWAY from commercialized Broadway in two acres of orchards and country gardens, this 16thC stone manor house is a haven of peace. The bar is a warm, agreeable place in which to sit, with oak beams, gleaming copper and comfortable armchairs grouped around an imposing inglenook fireplace, where log fires blaze on cool evenings. Another sitting-room features a fine old stone fireplace and ancient mullion window overlooking the gardens.

Keith and Tricia Ferguson took over in 1998 and set about upgrading the bathrooms and bedrooms. Two rooms have four-poster beds, and all are prettily furnished in traditional style, and like the rest of the house, full of interesting items. The extensive gardens come into their own in fine weather. Appetizing 'Cotswold Suppers' can be taken in the bar area, while the candlelit dining-room serves more formal three-course dinners.

Collin House is warmly praised: 'It far exceeded our needs and expectations'; 'Service was outstanding and unobtrusive'; 'Our favourite small hotel'; 'Graceful service with smiles all round. . .this was our first weekend without the children – just what we were looking for,' write several appreciative visitors.

~

NEARBY Snowshill Manor; Batsford Park Arboretum; Sudeley Castle.
LOCATION 1 mile (1.5 km) NW of Broadway, off A44; with ample private car parking
MEALS breakfast, lunch, dinner
PRICE ££
ROOMS 7; 6 double and twin, 1 single, all with bath or shower; all rooms have TV, hairdrier
FACILITIES sitting-room, dining-room, bar, garden; croquet
CREDIT CARDS MC, V **CHILDREN** welcome
DISABLED no special facilities
PETS not accepted **CLOSED** Christmas
PROPRIETOR Keith and Tricia Ferguson

MIDLANDS

BURFORD, OXFORDSHIRE

BURFORD HOUSE
~ TOWNHOUSE HOTEL ~

High Street, Burford, Oxfordshire OX18 4QA
TEL (01993) 823151 **FAX** (01993) 823240
E-MAIL stay@burfordhouse.co.uk/

WITHOUT DISTURBING its historical integrity, Simon and Jane Henty have smuggled comforts from the 21stC into their 15thC Cotswold stone and black-and-white timbered house in the heart of Burford. The whole place positively gleams with personal care and attention, with fresh flowers, books and magazines in the smartly decorated, dark-beamed bedrooms, and their own belongings, including family photos, dotted amongst the public furniture. There are two comfortable and contrasting sitting-rooms downstairs, one of which gives on to a walled and paved garden as does the ground-floor bedroom. There is also that welcome reviver of the thirsty traveller – an honesty bar – and the welcome reviver of the wet walker: a drying-room.

Upstairs there are six more bedrooms, four with four-posters and one of these also has a huge free-standing bath in it. Each thoughtfully organized room is full of character, and each has an immaculate bathroom. Breakfast (included in the price of the room) is an excellent production, taken in the dining-room looking out on to the High Street. Dinner is not available in the hotel, but there are plenty of restaurants and pubs within easy walking distance.

~

NEARBY Cotswold Wildlife Park; Blenheim Palace; Broadway.
LOCATION middle of Burford High Street; parking in street or free car park nearby
MEALS breakfast, light lunch
PRICE ££
ROOMS 7 double with bath; all rooms have phone, TV, fax/modem point, hairdrier
FACILITIES sitting-room, breakfast-room, courtyard garden
CREDIT CARDS AE, MC, V
CHILDREN welcome
DISABLED 1 ground-floor room
PETS not accepted **CLOSED** 2 weeks in Feb
PROPRIETORS Jane and Simon Henty

MIDLANDS

BURFORD, OXFORDSHIRE

THE LAMB
~ TOWN INN ~

Sheep Street, Burford, Oxfordshire OX18 4LR
TEL (01993) 823155 **FAX** (01993) 822228

IF YOU WANT SOME RESPITE from Burford's summer throng, you won't do better than The Lamb, only a few yards behind the High Street, but a veritable haven of tranquillity – particularly in the pretty walled garden; a view endorsed by a recent inspection.

Inside the creeper-clad stone cottages, you won't be surprised to find traditional pub trappings (after all, The Lamb has been an inn since the 15th century), but you may be surprised to discover 15 spacious beamed bedrooms, decorated with floral fabrics and antiques. All are different – 'Shepherds', for example, has a vast antique four-poster bed and a little attic-like bathroom, 'Malt' (in what was once the neighbouring brewery) has a smart brass bed and large stone mullion windows.

The hotel is run by Caroline and Richard De Wolf, with the help of Caroline's mother Bunty. It's very much a family enterprise, although they employ four chefs (one French) to produce the impressive-sounding, daily-changing meals. These are served in the dining-room, looking on to the geranium-filled patio. Coffee can be taken in here, or in the sitting-room or TV-room, both of which have comfortable chairs and sofas grouped around open fires. The Lamb manages to combine the convivial atmosphere of a pub with that of a comfortable hotel.

~

NEARBY Minster Lovell Hall; Cotswold villages; Blenheim Palace.
LOCATION in village; with car parking for 6 cars in courtyard
MEALS breakfast, lunch, dinner
PRICE ££
ROOMS 15 double and twin with bath or shower; all rooms have phone, TV, hairdrier
FACILITIES 3 sitting-rooms, dining-room, bar, garden
CREDIT CARDS MC, V **CHILDREN** welcome **DISABLED** 3 ground-floor bedrooms
PETS dogs in room by prior arrangement **CLOSED** Christmas Day, Boxing Day
PROPRIETORS Richard and Caroline De Wolf

MIDLANDS

CHIPPING CAMPDEN, GLOUCESTERSHIRE

COTSWOLD HOUSE

〜 TOWN HOTEL 〜

The Square, Chipping Campden, Gloucestershire GL55 6AN
TEL (01386) 840330 **FAX** (01386) 840310
E-MAIL reception@Cotswold-house.demon.co.uk

'THE PLACE TO STAY IN POPULAR Chipping Camden: beautiful house, lovely garden, plenty of personality, not expensive, but highly polished and clean as a pin...' – one of the many enthusiastic reports that we've had about Cotswold House. Set in a fine street, the building, dating to 1650, was meticulously renovated in the late 1980s with great attention to detail. However, in September 1999, the hotel changed hands. New owners, Ian and Christa Taylor, have considerable experience in hotel-keeping and, in taking over Cotswold House, have realized their ambition to own a hotel. They have already accomplished something of a coup in attracting Michelin-starred chef Alan Dann, who has raised the cooking here from the good to the exceptional. His food is served in two dining-rooms: one, a brasserie (with courtyard), is also used for afternoon cream teas, and the grander Garden Room Restaurant (marble pillars, classy fabrics, French windows overlooking the garden and often a piano accompaniment). The Regency-style sitting-rooms are large, airy and filled with collector's items.

Each of the bedrooms has a different theme – military, Indian, Colonial American – carried through to the last detail. Our latest inspector noted that 'some of the rooms are looking a bit tired', but the energetic Taylors already have plans to upgrade them. Reports please.

〜

NEARBY Broadway; Stratford-upon-Avon.
LOCATION in main street of town; parking for 12 cars
MEALS breakfast, lunch, dinner
PRICE £££
ROOMS 15; 12 double, 3 single, all with bath; all rooms have phone, TV, hairdrier
FACILITIES 2 sitting-rooms, bar; croquet
CREDIT CARDS AE, DC, MC, V **CHILDREN** accepted over 6
DISABLED access difficult **PETS** not accepted
CLOSED Christmas **PROPRIETORS** Ian and Christa Taylor

MIDLANDS

CORSE LAWN, GLOUCESTERSHIRE

CORSE LAWN HOUSE
~ COUNTRY HOTEL ~

Corse Lawn, Gloucestershire GL19 4LZ
TEL (01452) 780771 **FAX** (01452) 780840 **E-MAIL** hotel@corselawnhouse.u-net.com
WEBSITE www.corselawnhouse.co.uk

THIS TALL, RED-BRICK Queen Anne house, set back across common land from what is now a minor road, must have been one of the most refined coaching inns of its day. Should you arrive in traditional style, you could still drive your coach-and-four down the slipway into the large pond in front of the house, to cool the horses and wash the carriage.

The Hines have been here since the late 1970s, first running the house purely as a restaurant, later opening up four rooms and in recent years adding various extensions (carefully designed to blend with the original building) to provide more and more bedrooms as well as more space for drinking, eating and sitting. The Falstaffian Denis Hine – a member of the famous French Cognac family – and son Giles extend a warm welcome to guests, while Baba Hine cooks. Her repertoire is an eclectic mix of English and French, modern and provincial dishes, all carefully prepared and served in substantial portions; there are fixed-price menus (with a vegetarian alternative) at both lunch and dinner as well as a *carte*, all notably good value.

Bedrooms are large, with a mixture of antique and modern furnishings and the atmosphere of the house is calm and relaxing. Breakfasts are a home-made feast. A recent visitor was enchanted.

~

NEARBY Tewkesbury Abbey; Malvern Hills.
LOCATION 5 miles (8 km) W of Tewkesbury on B4211; with ample car parking
MEALS breakfast, lunch, dinner
PRICE ££
ROOMS 19; 17 double and twin, 2 suites, all with bath; all rooms have phone, TV,
hairdrier **FACILITIES** 3 sitting-rooms, bar, restaurant, 2 meeting-rooms, garden;
croquet, tennis, swimming-pool **CREDIT CARDS** AE, DC, MC, V
CHILDREN accepted if well-behaved **DISABLED** 5 ground-floor bedrooms
PETS accepted in bedrooms **CLOSED** 24-26 Dec
PROPRIETORS Denis, Baba and Giles Hine

MIDLANDS

DIDDLEBURY, SHROPSHIRE

DELBURY HALL

~ COUNTRY GUEST-HOUSE ~

Diddlebury, Craven Arms, Shropshire SY7 9DH
TEL (01584) 841267 **FAX** (01584) 841441 **E-MAIL** wrigley@delbury.demon.co.uk
WEBSITE www.delbury.com

THIS PART OF SHROPSHIRE used to be a dangerous place to live: Offa's Dyke serves as a reminder of how hard it was to keep the Welsh away, and a string of castles runs the length of the Marches. Luckily, things had settled down by the middle of the 18th century when Delbury was built in Corvedale, and this rural Georgian gem was quite obviously designed to let in the wonderful view rather than keep out projectiles. Once past the lodge, you've still got about a mile to go through an 80-acre park before you reach the satisfyingly crunchy gravel between the house and the first lake (of no less than three).

Lucinda and Patrick Wrigley have set this house to rights in every department, inside and out. Their walled garden produces vegetables for the kitchen, their hens lay eggs for breakfast, they cure their own ham, smoke salmon and even churn their own butter. Inside are a stunning double-height hall, with galleries on three sides, a grand drawing-room, dining-room, cosy morning-room, pets and children. Antiques (and ancestors) abound, even in the bedrooms, and you'll get your own bathroom but it will *not* have been hacked out of a corner of your gracefully proportioned room. Patrick is cook and cellar master: he'll give you a chance to vote on what's for dinner and an excellent choice on what to drink with it.

~

NEARBY Ludlow; Stokesay Castle; Much Wenlock.
LOCATION in village 5 miles (8 km) NE of Craven Arms; with ample car parking
MEALS breakfast, dinner
PRICE ££
ROOMS 3 double and twin with bath; all rooms have phone, TV, hairdrier
FACILITIES 2 sitting-rooms, games-room, dining-room, garden **CREDIT CARDS** MC, V
CHILDREN accepted
DISABLED not suitable **PETS** not accepted **CLOSED** Christmas
PROPRIETORS Patrick and Lucinda Wrigley

MIDLANDS

GREAT RISSINGTON, GLOUCESTERSHIRE

LAMB INN

~ COUNTRY INN ~

Great Rissington, Gloucestershire GL54 2LP
TEL (01451) 820388 **FAX** (01451) 820724

IF YOU FOLLOW THE RIVER WINDRUSH as it rises westwards from Burford, and then roughly follow its curve from the north (where it has given Bourton-on-the-Water its name), you will arrive in Great Rissington, deep in the Cotswolds. Overlooking gently rolling farmland and built from the local stone, the original elements of this inn are 300 years old. Taken over 20 years ago by Richard and Kate Cleverly, The Lamb is still very much a pub, indeed it is enough of a pub to merit a recommendation in a national guide to good beer. But it also now has two elements that many other inns lack – good board and lodging. Board comes in the shape of a surprisingly large – and comfortingly busy – restaurant. In its smoking and non-smoking sections, it does a roaring trade in traditional dishes freshly prepared from the best of local produce, often with a modern twist: the most popular of these is a half shoulder of lamb. The wine list is wide-ranging (but, Richard decrees, *no* French wines for the duration of their ban on British beef). The bedrooms are bright and fresh, individually designed by Kate, and more than half have space for sitting as well as for sleeping.

~

NEARBY The Slaughters; Stow-on-the-Wold; Burford; Sudeley Castle.
LOCATION 4 miles (6.5 km) SE of Bourton-on-the-Water, 3 miles (5 km) N of A40; with ample car parking
MEALS breakfast, light (or packed) lunch, dinner
PRICE ££
ROOMS 14; 7 double, 1 twin and 6 suites, all with bath or shower; suites have TV
FACILITIES sitting-room, bar, garden
CREDIT CARDS AE, MC, V
CHILDREN welcome, but not in bar
DISABLED not suitable
PETS accepted in bedrooms by arrangement **CLOSED** Christmas Day, Boxing Day
PROPRIETORS Richard and Kate Cleverly

MIDLANDS

HAMBLETON, RUTLAND

HAMBLETON HALL

~ COUNTRY HOUSE HOTEL ~

Hambleton, Oakham, Rutland LE15 8TH
TEL (01572) 756991 **FAX** (01572) 724721 **E-MAIL** hotel@hambletonhall.com
WEBSITE www.hambletonhall.com

IF YOU'RE PLANNING a second honeymoon, a break from work or a weekend away from the kids, this Victorian former shooting lodge in the grand hotel tradition is a sybaritic paradise, from which only your wallet and your waistline will suffer. The location is unrivalled, standing in stately grandeur on a wooded hillock, surrounded by manicured lawns, surveying the expanse of Rutland Water. The interior is sumptuous. In her design of the rooms, Stefa Hart uses rich, heavy fabrics, combining stripes and chintzes in some of the bedrooms, and showing a preference for delicate colours. The rooms still have their original mouldings and fireplaces, and are furnished with fine antiques and paintings. Bedrooms with a view over the water are the most sought-after and expensive, though one reporter was happy in her smaller, cheaper room overlooking lawns and cedars. A record is kept of the pet likes and hates of regular guests.

Many people are drawn here by the wizardry of Michelin-starred chef, Aaron Patterson. He works his magic on only the freshest of ingredients, whether Angus beef, sea bass or veal sweetbreads. One of the joys of staying here is that you can blow the cobwebs away with an exhilarating walk from the front door of the hotel as far as you want around Rutland Water, birdwatching as you go.

~

NEARBY Burghley House; Rockingham Castle; Stamford.
LOCATION 2 miles (3 km) E of Oakham on peninsula jutting into Rutland Water; with ample car parking
MEALS breakfast, lunch, dinner
PRICE ££££
ROOMS 15 double and twin with bath; all rooms have phone, TV, hairdrier
FACILITIES sitting-rooms, 3 dining-rooms, bar, lift, garden; swimming-pool, tennis, fishing, helipad **CREDIT CARDS** AE, DC, MC, V **CHILDREN** accepted
DISABLED access possible **PETS** by arrangement **CLOSED** never
PROPRIETORS Tim and Stefa Hart

MIDLANDS

HOPESAY, SHROPSHIRE

THE OLD RECTORY
~ COUNTRY GUEST-HOUSE ~

Hopesay, Craven Arms, Shropshire SY7 8HD
TEL (01588) 660245 **FAX** (01588) 660502

IF YOU'D RATHER STAY with friends than go to a hotel, then this elegant 17thC rectory, home to Roma and Michael Villar, might well be the amiable compromise that you've always been looking for. In gentle hills, and surrounded by mature trees, the setting is English countryside at its best. Built when the vicar was second only to the squire in the local pecking-order (and lived in the sort of property that proved it), you can see before you even go in that this is not a house where any corners have been cut. Inside you have the run of the drawing-room (which has an Adam fireplace) and the dining-room with its large oak refectory table. In suitable weather you can step through a floor-level Georgian sash window in the drawing-room to a raised terrace paved with York stone. The whole house has been decorated with a discerning eye, comfortably in keeping with the architecture, and setting off the many excellent pieces of furniture that you are trusted with. Unless it's late enough for a drink (help yourself), you'll be given tea when you arrive. Dinner is a treat. It is taken at eight at the single table, and comes with style but without fanfares from Roma's kitchen; breakfast, ditto, but with Michael in charge. The comfortable bedrooms (and the beds themselves) are good-sized, with bathrooms to match.

~

NEARBY Ludlow; Offa's Dyke; Stokesay Castle; Stretton Hills; Stiperstones.
LOCATION in village beside church, 3.5 miles (5.5 km) NE of Craven Arms; with car parking
MEALS breakfast, lunch on request, dinner
PRICE ££
ROOMS 3 double and twin with bath; all rooms have TV, hairdrier
FACILITIES sitting-room, dining-room, terrace, garden
CREDIT CARDS not accepted **CHILDREN** accepted over 12
DISABLED not suitable **PETS** not accepted **CLOSED** Christmas to Mar
PROPRIETORS Michael and Roma Villar

MIDLANDS

KEMERTON, GLOUCESTERSHIRE

UPPER COURT

~ COUNTRY HOUSE HOTEL ~

Kemerton, near Tewkesbury, Gloucestershire GL20 7HY
TEL (01386) 725351 FAX (01386) 725472 E-MAIL uppercourt@compuserve.com
WEBSITE www.travel-uk.net/uppercourt

KEMERTON IS A PRETTY VILLAGE on Bredon Hill, an outcrop of the Cotswolds, and on the edge of the Vale of Evesham. Its stunning Georgian manor house acts as a home, a shop and a hotel for its friendly owners, Bill and Diane Herford, and their children. The interior is filled with fine furniture and *objets d'art*, some of it stock from their antiques business, and some of it for sale.

Bedrooms are in the grand country house style, three with romantic four-posters. In the lovely, rather wild 15-acre grounds (open under the National Gardens Scheme) can be found the ruins of a thousand-year-old watermill and a huge lake (complete with two islands) on which guests may row and fly-fish for trout in season. As for food, dinner (by prior arrangement) is served in the gracious candlelit dining-room around a communal table; their own or locally grown vegetables feature on the four-course menu.

As well as the bedrooms in the main house, more accommodation is available in the adjoining cottages and the coach house in the courtyards, which are self-catering and can also have meals delivered to them.

NEARBY Cotswold villages; Malvern Hills; Tewkesbury Abbey.
LOCATION 4 miles (6.5 km) NE of M5, exit 9, 1 mile (1.5 km) E of Bredon; from Bredon turn right at war memorial in Kemerton; house is behind parish church; with ample car parking
MEALS breakfast, dinner by arrangement
PRICE ££
ROOMS 5; 3 double, 2 twin, all with bath; all rooms have TV, hairdrier
FACILITIES drawing-room, smoking-room, dining-room, billiards-room, garden; lake, swimming-pool, tennis court
CREDIT CARDS MC, V CHILDREN welcome
DISABLED 2 ground-floor bedrooms PETS accepted by arrangement
CLOSED Christmas PROPRIETORS Bill, Diana and Hamish Herford

MIDLANDS

KINGTON, HEREFORDSHIRE

PENRHOS COURT

~ COUNTRY HOTEL ~

Kington, Herefordshire HR5 3LH
TEL (01544) 230720 **FAX** (01544) 230754
E-MAIL martin@penrhos.co.uk **WEBSITE** www.penrhos.co.uk

PENRHOS COURT IS MORE a way of life than a hotel. In 1971 it was in such a parlous state that it was due for demolition. Martin Griffiths and Daphne Lambert have spent the last 30 years rolling the clock back, but perhaps not as far as 1280, when it was probably built. Now, as well as being a faithfully restored example of medieval architecture, it is an organic farm and (unusually) a certified organic restaurant; Daphne, a professional nutritionist and chef of the restaurant for better than two decades, buys from other organic producers what she doesn't grow herself in her own kitchen garden, and runs organic cookery courses for those who want to become initiates. Menus change through the year to bring to the table the best of whatever is in season. It would be a misnomer to describe the place where you eat as 'the dining-room', because it is self-evidently a large beamed and galleried hall set with oak tables and lit through stained glass windows.

The handsomely decorated and furnished bedrooms are all on the same scale, varying from the merely large to enormous. This is a relaxing, peaceful spot in unspoiled Border countryside and if you want to get back to nature without travelling too far, try the farm pond: there is a perpetual mini-wildlife programme running.

~

NEARBY Offa's Dyke Path; Hergest Croft Garden.
LOCATION 1 mile (1.5 km) E of Kington on A44; in 6-acre grounds with ample car parking
MEALS breakfast, lunch (by arrangement), dinner
PRICE ££
ROOMS 15; 12 double and twin, 3 family rooms, all with bath; all rooms have phone, TV, hairdrier; fax/modem lead by arrangement
FACILITIES 2 sitting-rooms, 3 dining-rooms, bar, garden
CREDIT CARDS AE, DC, MC, V **CHILDREN** welcome **DISABLED** access easy
PETS not accepted **CLOSED** never **PROPRIETORS** Martin Griffiths and Daphne Lambert

MIDLANDS

LANGAR, NOTTINGHAMSHIRE

◆ EDITORS' CHOICE ◆

LANGAR HALL

~ COUNTRY HOUSE HOTEL ~

Langar, Nottinghamshire NG13 9HG
TEL (01949) 860559 **FAX** (01949) 861045
E-MAIL langarhall-hotel@ndirect.co.uk

AFTER THE DEATH of Imogen Skirving's father, a pre-war captain of Nottinghamshire County Cricket Club and the last owner of Langar Hall, she couldn't bear the thought of losing the house, nor could she afford to keep it on, except on the basis of sharing it with guests. Thus was born the concept of Langar Hall as a hotel and, despite burgeoning success, people who stay here feel more like guests in a beautiful Georgian stuccoed country house rather than customers in a hotel. The library appears to be totally unchanged, with hundreds of books available to leaf through with a drink or two before dinner. The food is superb and the wine list well judged.

The best bedrooms are light and airy, with furniture appropriate to the house which Imogen wanted to save, and enjoy glorious views of the Vale of Belvoir. For exercise, you can play croquet or stroll round the village church just behind the house. Best of all is the friendliness of the hostess and her staff. Imogen wanders around the dining-room, pausing at tables of single, bored businessmen and exchanging any sort of gossip, while nothing is too much trouble for the chef or staff. When our inspector realized, at 1 am, after an excellent dinner, that he had forgotten his sponge bag, an assortment of toothbrushes, toothpaste and razors was put at his disposal.

~

NEARBY Belton House; Chatsworth; Sherwood Forest; Lincoln Cathedral.
LOCATION in village behind church; with ample car parking
MEALS breakfast, lunch, dinner
PRICE ££
ROOMS 10; 9 double and twin, 1 suite, all with bath; all rooms have phone, TV, hairdrier **FACILITIES** sitting-rooms, dining-rooms, garden; croquet, fishing, helipad
CREDIT CARDS AE, DC, MC, V **CHILDREN** welcome
DISABLED 1 ground-floor bedroom **PETS** accepted by arrangement **CLOSED** never
PROPRIETOR Imogen Skirving

MIDLANDS

LEAMINGTON SPA, WARWICKSHIRE

THE LANSDOWNE
~ TOWN HOTEL ~

Clarendon Street, Leamington Spa, Warwickshire CV32 4PF
TEL (01926) 450505 **FAX** (01926) 421313

A CREEPER-COVERED Regency house in the heart of Leamington Spa – "just as well there is double-glazing," says our reporter, who liked it not for its location but its food. David Allen (a Swiss-trained chef) and his wife Gillian concentrate on quality and value

On a menu that changes each evening, dishes might include new season's Cornish lamb's kidneys, *lardons* of bacon and caramelized red onions in a red wine cream sauce, marinated herring fillets with apples, celery and walnuts in sour cream, and prime barbary duck breast, oven-roasted and served with a blueberry and cassis *jus*.

The Allens have combined home with hotel. The public rooms are elegantly decorated in vibrant colours; the bedrooms, comfortable and cosy with pine furniture and pretty fabrics. Readers comment on the friendly, relaxed atmosphere, and our reporter thought the Allens charming hosts.

Leamington's heyday as a popular spa town might be over, but the Royal Pump Rooms were reopened to visitors in 1999 as a cultural complex, and there is still much to see in the neighbourhood. The Lansdowne makes an ideal base from which to explore.

~

NEARBY Warwick Castle; Upton House; Stratford-upon-Avon; Kenilworth Castle.
LOCATION in middle of town, near A425 Warwick road; with car parking
MEALS breakfast, dinner, snacks
PRICE ££
ROOMS 9 double, 4 single, 1 family room, all with bath or shower; all rooms have phone, TV, hairdrier
FACILITIES sitting-room, dining-room, bar; discount tickets for Warwick Castle
CREDIT CARDS MC, V
CHILDREN welcome over 5 **DISABLED** 2 ground-floor bedrooms
PETS by arrangement **CLOSED** never
PROPRIETORS David and Gillian Allen

MIDLANDS

LEONARD STANLEY, GLOUCESTERSHIRE

GREY COTTAGE

~ VILLAGE GUEST-HOUSE ~

Leonard Stanley, Stonehouse, Gloucestershire GL10 3LU
TEL & FAX (01453) 822515

THIS STONE-BUILT COTTAGE, owned by Andrew and Rosemary Reeves, dates from 1824 and is spotless and pleasingly furnished. During renovation, original stonework and a tessellated hall floor were laid bare. Theirs is a very private guest-house with a cosy, cottagey atmosphere; there is no roadside advertisement and advance bookings only are accepted.

Generous home cooking includes such dishes as stewed *paupiettes* of plaice with smoked salmon and lime and cumin sauce, followed by prune and coffee mousse. The Reeves often join their guests for after-dinner coffee. An evidently discriminating New York couple give Grey Cottage a rave review: 'Even more than your guide promised. Beautiful garden with a 100-foot Wellingtonia, planted almost 150 years ago. Furnished with appropriate and interesting pieces. . .yet they have made changes that increase visitors' comfort: firm beds, reliable hot water, heated towel rails and fresh fruit.

'The food is fresh, of high quality, and abundant. The Reeves are capable, charming and dedicated – but not intrusive. Unfortunately, most tourists are preoccupied with location, and end up paying more for accommodation nearer the principal sights hereabouts – but actually getting far less.'

~

NEARBY Cotswold villages; Owlpen Manor; Gloucester; Tetbury.
LOCATION 4 miles (6.5 km) SW of Stroud, 1 mile (1.5 km) off A419 between Leonard Stanley and King Stanley; with ample car parking
MEALS breakfast, dinner by arrangement
PRICE £
ROOMS 1 double, 1 twin, 1 single, all with bath or shower; all rooms have TV, hairdrier **FACILITIES** sitting-room, garden-room, dining-room, garden
CREDIT CARDS not accepted **CHILDREN** by arrangement
DISABLED not suitable **PETS** not accepted **CLOSED** occasional holidays
PROPRIETORS Andrew and Rosemary Reeves

MIDLANDS

LINCOLN

D'ISNEY PLACE

~ TOWN GUEST-HOUSE ~

Eastgate, Lincoln, Lincolnshire LN2 4AA
TEL (01522) 538881 **FAX** (01522) 511321 **E-MAIL** info@disney-place.freespace.co.uk
WEBSITE www.disney-place.freespace.co.uk

SINCE MOVING TO this delightful red-brick Georgian house, on a bustling street a few yards from Lincoln Cathedral, David and Judy Payne (he a property developer, she an ex-antique dealer) have been continually improving and adding to it. A few years ago they converted the former billiard-room into a family suite; now they have a fully-equipped cottage for longer-staying guests.

For the purposes of this guide, D'Isney Place, named after its 15thC founder John D'Isney, is on the large side. And unfortunately it has no public rooms or restaurant – though there are plenty of respectable ones within walking distance. But we continue to recommend it because of the comfortable, stylish bedrooms, the well co-ordinated decorations and fabrics, the breakfast (cooked to order, served on bone china and delivered to the rooms along with the morning newspaper) and, last but certainly not least, the impressive walled garden which incorporates a 700-year old tower from the old cathedral close wall.

~

NEARBY Cathedral; Bishop's Palace; Usher Gallery.
LOCATION in middle of city, just E of cathedral; with adequate car parking
MEALS breakfast, snacks at night; no licence
PRICE ££
ROOMS 16 double and twin, all with bath or shower (3 with spa bath), 1 single, with bath; family rooms available; all rooms have phone, TV; some rooms have hairdrier
FACILITIES walled garden
CREDIT CARDS AE, DC, MC, V
CHILDREN welcome
DISABLED ground-floor bedrooms
PETS welcome
CLOSED never
PROPRIETORS David and Judy Payne

MIDLANDS

LITTLE MALVERN, WORCESTERSHIRE

HOLDFAST COTTAGE

∼ COUNTRY HOTEL ∼

Little Malvern, near Malvern, Worcestershire WR13 6NA
TEL (01684) 310288 **FAX** (01684) 311117

'COTTAGE' SEEMS TO BE stretching things somewhat – and yet, despite its size, this Victorian farmhouse does have the cosy intimacy of a cottage, and Stephen and Jane Knowles certainly create an atmosphere of friendly informality.

Inside, low oak beams and a polished flagstone floor in the hall conform to cottage requirement; beyond, headroom improves – though flowery decoration emphasizes the cottage status. Bedrooms are light and airy, with carefully co-ordinated fabrics and papers; some bathrooms are small. Outside, the veranda with its wistaria keeps the scale of the house relatively intimate. The garden – scarcely cottage-style – adds enormously to the overall appeal of the place, with its lawns, shrubberies, fruit trees and delightful 'wilderness'. Beyond is open farmland with spectacular views of the Malvern Hills.

The daily-changing *carte* is based on continental as well as traditional English dishes, employing the best local produce, and might feature chilled beetroot and apple soup, served with natural yogurt and chives, monkfish in smoky bacon jackets with creamy parmesan dressing, or salmon and thyme parcels with tomato butter.

∼

NEARBY Eastnor Castle; Worcester; Hereford; Gloucester.
LOCATION 4 miles (6.5 km) S of Great Malvern on A4104; with ample car parking
MEALS breakfast, dinner
PRICE ££
ROOMS 8; 7 double with bath, 1 single with shower; all rooms have phone, TV, hairdrier
FACILITIES sitting-room, bar, dining-room, conservatory; croquet
CREDIT CARDS MC, V **CHILDREN** welcome
DISABLED access difficult
PETS accepted **CLOSED** first 2-3 weeks in Jan
PROPRIETORS Stephen and Jane Knowles

MIDLANDS

LUDLOW, SHROPSHIRE

NUMBER TWENTY EIGHT

~ TOWN BED-AND-BREAKFAST ~

28 Lower Broad Street, Ludlow, Shropshire SY8 1PQ
TEL (01584) 876996 **FAX** (01584) 876860 **E-MAIL** ross.no28@btinternet.com
WEBSITE www.numbertwentyeight.co.uk

WHETHER IT'S HOUSES or horses that brought you to Ludlow, you'll find plenty of both – all thoroughbreds. The entire centre of Ludlow is listed Grade II (a bit too late for the castle, which is a ruin), and the race-track brings people from far and wide. Number Twenty Eight is (in its most recent incarnation) a Georgian house at the foot of Lower Broad Street which lies below the 13thC arch of Broadgate itself. Strictly speaking, there should be three numbers in its name because, as well as the principal house, there are a merged pair of Tudor mews cottages and a Victorian terrace house, both in the same street, which operate as satellites. Each house has a pair of comfortably furnished double bedrooms where you'll find everything you forgot to bring with you – from razors to sticking plaster – a cosy sitting-room and a garden. But No. 28 is the real headquarters and this is where you will collect a warm welcome from Patricia and Philip Ross, and Daisy their black Labrador will check you out as walking material. Here too is where you need to come if you want an (excellent) cooked breakfast – you can have a simpler one in your room if you prefer. For lunch or dinner take advice from either Ross – they'll tell you which of the three Michelin-starred restaurants is on song at the moment.

~

NEARBY Ludlow Castle; Stokesay Castle; Berrington Hall; Ironbridge; Stiperstones; Stretton Hills.
LOCATION in town centre near River Teme; car parking in street
MEALS breakfast
PRICE ££
ROOMS 6 double and twin with bath or shower; all rooms have phone, TV, hairdrier
FACILITIES sitting-rooms, breakfast-room, gardens **CREDIT CARDS** MC, V
CHILDREN accepted **DISABLED** not suitable **PETS** accepted in Mews rooms
CLOSED never
PROPRIETORS Patricia and Philip Ross

MIDLANDS

MALVERN WELLS, WORCESTERSHIRE

THE COTTAGE IN THE WOOD
~ COUNTRY HOTEL ~

Holywell Road, Malvern Wells, Worcestershire WR14 4LG
TEL (01684) 575859 **FAX** (01684) 560662 **E-MAIL** manager@cottageinthewood.co.uk
WEBSITE www.cottageinthewood.co.uk

THREE BUILDINGS AND a family form this glossy little hotel perched, very privately, in seven wooded acres, high above the Severn valley and with a superb vista across to the Cotswolds thirty-something miles away (binoculars provided). There are bedrooms in all three buildings, taking the hotel over our usual size for this guide; but the smartly furnished Georgian dower house at its heart is so intimate, calm and comfortable that we decided to relent.

A short stroll away is the soon-to-be-rebuilt Coach House, where rooms are smaller but have the best views, and Beech Cottage with four cottage-style bedrooms. The family consists of John and Sue Pattin, their daughters Maria and Rebecca, son Dominic (head chef) and *his* wife Romy. Apart from its food, the restaurant (modern English *cuisine*) has two other substantial qualities: windows that let you see the view and a wine list that lets you roam the world. Walkers can get straight out on to a good stretch of the Malvern Hills and for tourers the Pattins provide leaflets giving concise notes on everything that's worth visiting for 50 miles (80 km) around. For the rest of us, there's a very well-stocked bar and a free video library.

~

NEARBY Malvern Hills; Eastnor Castle; Worcester Cathedral.
LOCATION 2 miles (3 km) S of Great Malvern off A449; with ample car parking
MEALS breakfast, lunch, dinner
PRICE ££
ROOMS 20 double and twin with bath or shower; all rooms have phone, TV, hairdrier; 1 has air-conditioning
FACILITIES sitting-room, dining-room, bar, garden
CREDIT CARDS AE, MC, V **CHILDREN** welcome
DISABLED ground-floor rooms in annexe **PETS** accepted in some rooms
CLOSED never
PROPRIETORS John and Sue Pattin

MIDLANDS

MATLOCK, DERBYSHIRE

RIBER HALL
∽ MANOR HOUSE HOTEL ∽

Matlock, Derbyshire, DE4 5JU
TEL (01629) 582795 **FAX** (01629) 580475
E-MAIL info@riber-hall.co.uk

NEARLY THREE DECADES AGO, Alex Biggin rescued this peaceful, sturdy Elizabethan manor from the verge of dereliction, furnished it sympathetically, and opened it as a restaurant to the applause of local gourmets, who are not spoilt for choice of ambitious and competent French cooking. The bedrooms came later – created in outbuildings across an open courtyard and ranging from the merely charming and comfortable to the huge and delightful, with deep armchairs. Exposed timbers, stone walling, and antique four-posters are the norm. All the thoughtful trimmings you could wish for are on hand. There are no twin beds; five rooms have exotic whirlpool baths.

The spacious, new main dining-room, The Garden Room, has mullioned windows and is furnished with antiques. Wedgwood bone china, and exclusively designed cut glass adorn the dining table. Breakfast is taken in the traditional old dining-room and the recent addition of a new sitting-room has increased the area available for relaxation in the public rooms.

A romantic and cosy pastime at Riber is simply to sit by an open fire on a stormy winter evening – umbrellas are provided for crossing the courtyard. In the morning you can enjoy the delicious seclusion of the luxuriant walled garden and orchard.

∽

NEARBY Chatsworth House; Haddon Hall; Calke Abbey; Carsington Water.
LOCATION 2 miles (3 km) SE of Matlock by A615 (20 minutes from exit 28, M1); take minor road S at Tansley; with car parking in courtyard
MEALS breakfast, lunch, dinner
PRICE £££
ROOMS 11 double with bath; all rooms have TV, minibar, hairdrier
FACILITIES sitting-room with bar service, conservatory; dining-room; tennis court, tennis trainer ball machine **CREDIT CARDS** AE, DC, MC, V **CHILDREN** accepted over 10
DISABLED not suitable **CLOSED** never
PROPRIETOR Alex Biggin

MIDLANDS

MOULSFORD-ON-THAMES, OXFORDSHIRE

BEETLE AND WEDGE
∼ RIVERSIDE INN ∼

Ferry Lane, Moulsford-on-Thames, Oxfordshire OX10 9JF
TEL (01491) 651381 **FAX** (01491) 651376

THE BEST THING ABOUT this large Victorian inn, where Jerome K. Jerome wrote his classic *Three Men in a Boat*, is its superb position on the banks of the Thames. Almost an entire wall of huge windows and glazed doors, overlooking a pretty garden and the river beyond with its colourful boats and barges, makes the most of the setting. For meals, guests can choose between the Dining Room, where Richard Smith's *cuisine* matches the sophistication of the decoration, and the Boathouse, a brasserie-style restaurant with exposed rafters and brickwork, a cosy feel and an *à la carte* menu, featuring delicious chargrilled dishes. But most delightful of all, on fine summer days lunch is served in the Watergarden.

The spacious bedrooms have been individually and tastefully decorated by Richard and Kate Smith; the bathrooms – some of which are large enough to contain a dressing table – have wonderful huge cast-iron baths. The best rooms have a river view.

The Beetle and Wedge has always been enthusiastically endorsed by our readers' letters, though recently there have been one or two dissenting voices, mainly expressing reservations about the 'sky-high prices'. More reports please. It is a no-smoking hotel.

∼

NEARBY Abingdon; Oxford; Thames Valley.
LOCATION 2 miles (3 km) N of Goring on A329; with car parking
MEALS breakfast, lunch, dinner
PRICE £££
ROOMS 10; 9 double, 1 suite, all with bath; all rooms have phone, TV, hairdrier
FACILITIES 2 restaurants, sitting-room, garden
CREDIT CARDS AE, DC, MC, V
CHILDREN accepted
DISABLED ground-floor rooms and adapted WC
PETS accepted by arrangement **CLOSED** never; restaurant Sun eve, Mon
PROPRIETORS Richard and Kate Smith

MIDLANDS

OXFORD

OLD BANK
~ TOWN HOTEL ~

92-94 High Street, Oxford, Oxfordshire OX1 4BN
TEL (01865) 799599 **FAX** (01865) 799598 **E-MAIL** info@oldbank-hotel.co.uk
WEBSITE www.oxford-hotels-restaurants.co.uk

ALL CHANGE IN OXFORD: metropolitan chic has brazenly asserted itself amongst the dreaming spires with the opening, in December 1999, of the Old Bank Hotel. Hardly a quintessential charming small hotel, but we include it for the breath of fresh air it has created in central Oxford. What was, until recently, a venerable bank with a fine Georgian façade and an Elizabethan core, has become a cool, sophisticated hotel with a buzzing brasserie as its centrepiece.

The building has much to recommend it. The best bedrooms are graced with floor-length windows or, in the Tudor part, beams and deep window seats under lattice windows. All the rooms – and the bathrooms – are impeccably decorated in the understated chic-rustic style of the day (think taupe, think beige, think cream). They feel elegant and luxurious, and, because they are new, pristine and unsullied.

As well as a hotel, the Old Bank has become the 'in' place to eat in Oxford. The Quod Bar and Grill stretches across the former banking hall ("weird to think that I used to cash my cheques and see the bank manager here", says one guest, a touch wistfully), and while hotel guests may yearn for a relaxing sitting-room of their own, most will enjoy the buzz and bonhomie that emanates from this always packed, Italian-influenced new meeting place.

~

NEARBY Oxford colleges; Botanical Gardens; Sheldonian Theatre.
LOCATION in city centre, with ample car parking
MEALS breakfast, lunch, dinner; room service
PRICE £££-££££
ROOMS 44; 43 double and twin, 1 suite; all rooms have phone, TV, CD player, fax/modem point, air-conditioning, safe, hairdrier
FACILITIES restaurant, bar, courtyard, lift **CREDIT CARDS** AE, DC, MC, V
CHILDREN accepted **DISABLED** 3 rooms specially adapted **PETS** not accepted
CLOSED Christmas **PROPRIETOR** Jeremy Mogford

MIDLANDS

OXFORD

OLD PARSONAGE

~ TOWN HOTEL ~

1 Banbury Road, Oxford, Oxfordshire OX2 6NN
TEL (01865) 310210 **FAX** (01865) 311262 **E-MAIL** oldparsonage@dial.pipex.com
WEBSITE www.oxford-hotels-restaurants.co.uk

TALK ABOUT CONTRAST. Jeremy Mogford now owns the two best hotels in Oxford, the recently opened Old Bank (see page 191), and this one, much more typical of our guide, occupying a characterful, wistaria-clad house that has been owned by University College since 1320. Compared to its sleek, hip, younger sibling, it seems at first quaint and old-fashioned, yet there is no themed 'olde worlde' charm here, despite the great age of the building. The place has panache: the staff are young and charming, the atmosphere informal, and the laid-back bar/brasserie (part sitting-room, part dining-room) has a clubby, cosmopolitan feel. Here drinks and a varied menu – salmon fish cakes, wild mushroom tart, *tarte tatin* – are served all day long. In fine weather, large white parasols adorn the front terrace (the heavy, studded front door, by the way, is three centuries old), making a delightful place to eat lunch, and there is a roof garden for residents' use in summer too.

Bedrooms – which tend to be on the small side – are pretty and traditional in feel, with pale panelling and unfussy chintz, and marble bathrooms (with telephone). However, changes may be afoot: we've heard that Gladys Wagner, the interior designer of the Old Bank, was set to begin work here too.

~

NEARBY Oxford colleges; Botanical Gardens; Sheldonian Theatre.
LOCATION 5 minutes' walk from city centre, at W end of St Giles, close to junction of Woodstock and Banbury Roads; limited car parking
MEALS breakfast, lunch, dinner; room service
PRICE £££
ROOMS 30; 25 double and twin, 1 single, 4 suites, all with bath; all rooms have phone, TV, hairdrier
FACILITIES sitting-room, dining-room, bar, terrace, roof garden **CREDIT CARDS** AE, DC, MC, V **CHILDREN** accepted **DISABLED** access difficult **PETS** not accepted
CLOSED Christmas **PROPRIETOR** Jeremy Mogford

MIDLANDS

PAINSWICK, GLOUCESTERSHIRE

♦ EDITORS' CHOICE ♦

CARDYNHAM HOUSE
〜 VILLAGE BED-AND-BREAKFAST 〜

The Cross, Painswick, Gloucestershire GL6 6XX
TEL (01452) 814006 **FAX** (01452) 812321 **E-MAIL** info@cardynham.co.uk
WEBSITE www.cardynham.co.uk

Bᵁᴵᴸᵀ ᵂᴵᵀᴴ ᴹᴼᴺᴱʸ ᶠᴿᴼᴹ ᵂᴼᴼᴸ and from pale gold stone out of a local quarry, Painswick is a classic Cotswold town perched rather precariously on (and over the brink of) a steep hillside. If you're not paying attention you might quite easily walk past Cardynham House – a discreet sign above the venerable front door of this Grade II-listed flower-hung building, right on the street, is hardly enough to focus your attention when everything else around is so worth looking at. The real fun starts once you get inside. A cavernous open fireplace, flanked by a bread oven, warms a cosy drawing-room which seems to metamorphose at some point into a conservatory.

Somehow, nine totally unique bedrooms have been created in this apparently modest-sized house, and each one is a triumphal exercise of imagination. Dotted with antiques and murals, each is decorated to a different theme and, even side by side in the same building, they all work unusually well. The most eccentric of all, air-conditioned because it hasn't a window to its name, has been got up like a desert pavilion. Another has its own private patio largely taken up with a covered plunge pool (heated, and with a powered current to swim against). Breakfast is taken in the restaurant which, in the evenings that it's open, serves Thai food.

〜

NEARBY Cheltenham; Chedworth Roman Villa; Cirencester.
LOCATION in village, 3 miles (5 km) N of Stroud; car parking on street
MEALS breakfast
PRICE ££
ROOMS 9; 6 double, 3 family, all with bath or shower; all rooms have phone, TV
FACILITIES sitting-room, breakfast-room
CREDIT CARDS MC, V **CHILDREN** accepted
PETS not accepted
DISABLED not suitable **CLOSED** Christmas; restaurant Sun eve, Mon eve
PROPRIETORS John and Sharon Paterson

MIDLANDS

PAINSWICK, GLOUCESTERSHIRE

PAINSWICK HOTEL

～ COUNTRY HOUSE HOTEL ～

Kemps Lane, Painswick, Gloucestershire GL6 6YB
TEL (01452) 812160 **FAX** (01452) 814059 **E-MAIL** reservations@painswickhotel.com
WEBSITE www.painswickhotel.com

THIS DISTINCTLY UPMARKET Georgian rectory is tucked away in the back lanes of prosperous Painswick. The graceful proportions of the rooms – beautifully and expensively furnished with an elegant mix of classy reproductions, antiques and well chosen objects – the serenity of the gardens, and the fine views of the westerly Cotswold scarp, all contribute to the effect.

Our latest inspection revealed that Painswick manages, despite its class, to retain the feel of a friendly, family-run establishment. It is in a beautiful Cotswold village, and some of the better rooms had the best views of any our inspector had experienced in several weeks on the road. The panelled dining-room is 'elegant rather than cosy', and the food very acceptable, making good use of Gloucestershire produce, including locally reared lamb and home-smoked salmon. A sea water fish tank provides fresh seafood and the cheeseboard includes local farmhouse cheeses, some really unusual.

Painswick was taken over by new owners, Gareth and Helen Pugh, in 1998. We would welcome reports.

～

NEARBY Cotswold villages; Gloucester.
LOCATION near middle of village, 3 miles (5 km) N of Stroud on A46; with car parking in front of hotel
MEALS breakfast, dinner, Sun lunch
PRICE ££
ROOMS 19; 14 double and twin, all with bath, 2 single, 1 with bath, 1 with shower, 3 family rooms, all with bath; all rooms have phone, TV
FACILITIES sitting-room, 2 dining-rooms, bar; croquet **CREDIT CARDS** AE, MC, V
CHILDREN welcome **DISABLED** access difficult
CLOSED never
PETS by arrangement
PROPRIETORS Gareth and Helen Pugh

MIDLANDS

SHIPTON-UNDER-WYCHWOOD, OXFORDSHIRE

LAMB INN
~ VILLAGE INN ~

Upper High Street, Shipton-under-Wychwood OX7 6DQ
TEL (01993) 830465 **FAX** (01993) 832025

NORTH OF BURFORD and skirted by the River Evenlode, Shipton-under-Wychwood is a Cotswold village built in the pale gold native stone. Safely off the main road up a quiet *cul-de-sac*, the early 17thC Lamb Inn was originally three houses, now combined to make a higgledy-piggledy interior full of nooks, crannies and steps. Run by Mrs Angela Hide for The Old English Company, the beamed ceilings are hung with hops and punctuated with horse brasses, while the walls are bare stone and the floors are polished wood. As well as being a working pub, it has a large dining-room where fresh and well-prepared dishes, with seafood and local game strongly represented, are on offer, together with a very reasonable range of wines. Lunchtime buffets in the bar are something of a speciality and a range of dishes (from which you can construct a very appetizing three-course meal) are also available in the evenings for those who prefer to eat where they drink, rather than the other way round. Residents have the use of a cosy sitting-room where a fire burns in winter. None of the bedrooms, reached by a steep and narrow staircase, are particularly large but they are thoughtfully equipped and well decorated - two have four-posters. Bathrooms are most definitely younger than the inn.

~

NEARBY North Leigh Roman Villa; Bruern Abbey; Blenheim Palace; Oxford; Bourton-on-the-Water.
LOCATION at edge of village, 4 miles (6.5 km) N of Burford; with car parking
MEALS breakfast, lunch, dinner
PRICE ££
ROOMS 5 double and twin with bath; all rooms have phone, TV, hairdrier
FACILITIES bar, restaurant, garden
CREDIT CARDS AE, MC, V **CHILDREN** accepted
DISABLED not suitable **PETS** not accepted
CLOSED never; restaurant Sun eve, Mon eve
MANAGER Mrs Angela Hide

MIDLANDS

THE SHAVEN CROWN

~ COUNTRY HOUSE HOTEL ~

Shipton-under-Wychwood, Oxfordshire OX7 6BA
TEL (01993) 830330 **FAX** (01993) 832136

THE SHAVEN CROWN, as its name suggests, has monastic origins; it was built in 1384 as a hospice to nearby Bruern Abbey, and many of the original features remain intact – most impressively the medieval hall, with its beautiful double-collar braced roof and stone walls decorated with tapestries and wrought ironwork. The hall forms one side of the courtyard garden, which is decked with flowers and parasols, and on a sunny day is a lovely place in which to enjoy wholesome pub lunches. Some of the bedrooms overlook the courtyard, others are at the front of the house and suffer from road noise – though this is unlikely to be a problem at night.

Robert and Jane Burpitt, who moved south to take over The Shaven Crown after running a hotel in Dumfriesshire for ten years, have been refurbishing as they promised. Rooms are decorated sympathetically, leaving the low ceilings, uneven floorboards, exposed beams and open fireplaces intact, and are furnished with antiques and Jacobean furniture.

Dinner is taken in the oak-beamed dining-room which leads off the hall. The menu offers plenty of choice and changes with the seasons – it is not elaborate, but the food is interesting and competently cooked. And if you still have the energy after four or five courses, you can join the locals in the narrow chapel-like bar, or adjourn to the hall, which doubles as a sitting-room.

~

NEARBY North Leigh Roman Villa; Breurn Abbey; Blenheim Palace.
LOCATION in middle of village; with ample car parking
MEALS breakfast, lunch, dinner
PRICE ££
ROOMS 9; 7 double and twin, 1 single, 1 family, all with bath; all rooms have TV
FACILITIES restaurant, bar, medieval hall, courtyard garden; bowling green
CREDIT CARDS AE, MC, V **CHILDREN** welcome **DISABLED** 1 ground-floor bedroom
PETS accepted in bedrooms only **CLOSED** never
PROPRIETORS Robert and Jane Burpitt

MIDLANDS

STRATFORD-UPON-AVON, WARWICKSHIRE

CATERHAM HOUSE

~ TOWN BED-AND-BREAKFAST ~

58-59 Rother Street, Stratford-upon-Avon, Warwickshire CV37 6LT
TEL (01789) 267309 **FAX** (01789) 414836

TWO GEORGIAN HOUSES have been knocked together to form this friendly B&B which, despite its central location – just a ten-minute walk from the Royal Shakespeare Theatre – has a surprisingly peaceful ambience. There is a small conservatory-style sitting-room with an eclectic assortment of furniture, where generous teas are served each afternoon. Although there are no gardens, the sitting-room opens out to a colourful terrace. You couldn't call the bedrooms huge, but all are spacious enough to accommodate a comfy chair. Each one is individually decorated with antique furniture (there are even antiques in the pristine, modern bathrooms). Beds are luxuriously downy and many are in French country style, revealing the roots of the owner Dominique Maury. This charming, chatty, Shakespeare-loving Frenchman has owned and run the hotel with his wife Olive since the late 1970s. Without being intrusive, he is always willing to talk, especially about the latest Shakespeare productions.

Apart from tea, breakfast is the only meal served, but guests rate it very highly. One writes, 'I would go back for the breakfasts if for no other reason.' He praised a dried fruit mixture in cinnamon-flavoured juice, the home-made jam, 'served in full jars, not little dishes', and the 'deliciously creamy' scrambled eggs. He also thought that his bill was 'a snip'.

~

NEARBY Royal Shakespeare Theatre; Shakespeare's Birthplace.
LOCATION in centre of town; with car parking
MEALS breakfast
PRICE ££
ROOMS 14; 13 double and twin, 1 family, all with bath or shower; all rooms have TV
FACILITIES sitting-room, breakfast-room, bar
CREDIT CARDS MC, V **CHILDREN** accepted
DISABLED not suitable **PETS** accepted in bedrooms by arrangement
CLOSED Christmas Day
PROPRIETORS Dominique and Olive Maury

MIDLANDS

TETBURY, GLOUCESTERSHIRE

CALCOT MANOR

~ COUNTRY HOUSE HOTEL ~

near Tetbury, Gloucestershire GL8 8YJ
TEL (01666) 890391 **FAX** (01666) 890394 **E-MAIL** reception@calcotmanor.com
WEBSITE www.calcotmanor.co.uk

THIS 15THC COTSWOLD FARMHOUSE has been functioning as a hotel since 1984. Richard Ball took over Calcot Manor from his parents when they retired, and, with a team of dedicated staff, continues to provide the highest standards of comfort and service while preserving a calm and relaxed atmosphere. The lovely old house itself was a sound choice – its rooms are spacious and elegant without being grand – and the setting amid lawns and old barns, surrounded by rolling countryside, is all you could ask for.

Furnishings and decorations are carefully harmonious, with rich fabrics and pastel colours throughout. A converted cottage provides nine family suites, designed specifically for parents travelling with young children. For their entertainment, there's an indoor playroom.

Michael Croft is head chef of both the Conservatory Restaurant and the adjoining Gumstool Inn, which is more informal and moderately priced. In the restaurant, you might dine on asparagus, herb and lemon risotto, followed by seared sea bass served on parmesan mash with a spinach sauce, while in the inn, you could choose baked mature cheddar cheese soufflé and Gloucestershire Old Spot pork sausages with sage and red wine sauce.

~

NEARBY Chavenage; Owlpen Manor; Westonbirt Arboretum.
LOCATION 3 miles (5 km) W of Tetbury on A4135; with ample car parking
MEALS breakfast, lunch, dinner
PRICE £££
ROOMS 21; 16 double, 5 family suites, all with bath or shower; all rooms have phone, TV, hairdrier **FACILITIES** 2 sitting-rooms, dining-room, garden, playroom; swimming-pool, croquet, 2 all-weather tennis courts; **CREDIT CARDS** AE, DC, MC, V
CHILDREN welcome **DISABLED** 4 ground-floor bedrooms **PETS** not accepted
CLOSED never **PROPRIETOR** Richard Ball

MIDLANDS

ULEY, GLOUCESTERSHIRE

OWLPEN MANOR
~ COUNTRY HOUSE COTTAGES ~

Owlpen, near Uley, Gloucestershire GL11 5BZ
TEL (01453) 860261 **FAX** (01453) 860816 **E-MAIL** sales@owlpen.demon.co.uk
WEBSITE www.owlpen.com

NICHOLAS AND KARIN MANDER have converted a clutch of cottages, barns, farmhouses and a mill to provide luxurious 'serviced' self-catering accommodation in their own idyllic Cotswold valley. At the heart of the enterprise is their Grade I-listed Tudor manor, where huge bedrooms, some with four-posters, are also available to guests. The manor dates from the 15th and 16th centuries, when it was home to the de Olepenne family, but after standing empty for more than 100 years, it was restored in 1926 in Arts and Crafts style as many of the furnishings bear witness. Other material relics of the past include the magnificent Tudor Great Hall and a Jacobean wing; and then there is Margaret of Anjou's ghost, which has been glimpsed from time to time.

Owlpen has nine self-contained cottages, ranging in size from Tithe Barn, a split-level studio with massive oak beams and abundant rustic charm, to the 18thC Grist Mill, which sleeps nine and still sports its gigantic waterwheel and mill machinery. All are well furnished and equipped, and have their own private terrace or garden. In the Cyder House Restaurant at the centre of the hamlet, Karin Mander's menu features seasonal produce from the estate: specialities are pheasant, venison and fish dishes from her native Sweden, seasoned with herbs from the Elizabethan herb garden.

~

NEARBY Cirencester; Bath; Cheltenham.
LOCATION 0.5 mile (1 km) E of Uley off B4066; with ample car parking
MEALS breakfast, lunch, dinner
PRICE ££
ROOMS 9 cottages sleeping 2-9 people; all cottages have phone, TV, hairdrier, kitchen **FACILITIES** restaurant, garden **CREDIT CARDS** AE, DC, MC, V **CHILDREN** accepted
DISABLED not suitable **PETS** not accepted
CLOSED never; restaurant Mon and at other times, reservations recommended
PROPRIETORS Nicholas and Karin Mander

MIDLANDS

WATERHOUSES, STAFFORDSHIRE

OLD BEAMS
~ RESTAURANT-WITH-ROOMS ~

Leek Road, Waterhouses, Staffordshire ST10 3HW
TEL (01538) 308254 **FAX** (01538) 308157

THE KITCHEN IS the heart of Old Beams. Chef and owner Nigel Wallis describes his food as 'modern English with a French classic lean' and stresses presentation and freshness – bread is baked twice a day. On the *à la carte* menu you might find dishes such as warm *soufflé* of lobster and scallop, and stuffed leg and saddle of rabbit with tarragon *jus*. He also offers a first-rate, yet reasonably priced wine list. Nigel's effort and skill have been rewarded with a Michelin star. His lively wife Ann and their son, Simon, preside over the restaurant – choose between the oak-panelled dining-room in the 18thC main house and the conservatory extension, with its fantasy murals.

Most of the compact but stylish bedrooms are in a modern building, 'Les Chambres', across the road; each is named after a local pottery company – Royal Stafford, Wedgwood, Royal Doulton – complete with the appropriate china, of course. These rooms have recently been redecorated in sunny colours with bright floral fabrics and a host of personal touches: piles of magazines, chocolates, bowls of fruit, fresh flowers and heaps of large fluffy towels in the swish bathrooms. This is a non-smoking hotel.

~

NEARBY Ashbourne; Biddulph Grange Garden; Sudbury Hall.
LOCATION in middle of village, on A523, 7 miles (11 km) NW of Ashbourne; with parking for 25 cars
MEALS breakfast, lunch, dinner; restaurant licence
PRICE ££
ROOMS 5 double with bath; all rooms have phone, TV
FACILITIES dining-room, conservatory, bar area, garden; fishing
CREDIT CARDS AE, DC, MC, V
CHILDREN accepted
DISABLED ground-floor rooms
PETS not accepted **CLOSED** Jan; restaurant Sun eve, Mon, Sat lunch, Tue lunch
PROPRIETORS Nigel and Ann Wallis

MIDLANDS

WOODSTOCK, OXFORDSHIRE

FEATHERS
~ TOWN HOTEL ~

Market Street, Woodstock, Oxfordshire OX20 1SX
TEL (01993) 812291 **FAX** (01993) 813158 **E-MAIL** enquiries@feathers.co.uk
WEBSITE www.feathers.co.uk

AN AMALGAM OF FOUR tall 17thC townhouses of mellow red brick, now an exceptionally civilized town hotel. One visitor was full of praise for the way the staff managed to make a weekend 'entirely relaxing, without intruding in the way that hotel staff so often do'.

'The upstairs drawing-room (with library and open fire) has the relaxed atmosphere of a well-kept English country home rather than a hotel, with antiques, fine fabrics, an abundance of fresh flowers and a refreshing absence of the ubiquitous 'Olde Worlde'. There is also a cosy study for reading the papers or drinking tea. If you want fresh air, there is a pleasant courtyard garden and bar. Bedrooms are spacious (on the whole) and beautifully decorated, comfortable yet still with the understated elegance that pervades the whole hotel. Five further bedrooms are to be found in the building next door, renovated a few years ago. The elegant panelled dining-room serves excellent food from Mark Treasure's interesting contemporary menu. Recent visitors have been impressed by both the food and service in the 'lively' restaurant.

Technically, this has all the trappings of a smart business hotel – but don't be put off by that because it has character and a very home-like atmosphere.

~

NEARBY Blenheim Palace; Oxford.
LOCATION in middle of town; with limited car parking
MEALS breakfast, lunch, dinner
PRICE £££-££££
ROOMS 22; 17 double with bath, 4 suites with bath, 1 single with shower; all rooms have phone, TV
FACILITIES 2 sitting-rooms, conservatory, bar, dining-room, restaurant
CREDIT CARDS AE, DC, V **CHILDREN** welcome
DISABLED access difficult **PETS** accepted by arrangement **CLOSED** never
MANAGER Martin Godward

MIDLANDS

WORFIELD, SHROPSHIRE

OLD VICARAGE

~ COUNTRY HOUSE HOTEL ~

Worfield, near Bridgnorth, Shropshire WV15 5JZ
TEL (01746) 716497 **FAX** (01746) 716552
E-MAIL admin@the-old-vicarage.demon.co.uk **WEBSITE** www.oldvicarageworfield.com

WHEN PETER ILES and his wife, Christine, decided to convert this sub-stantial red-brick vicarage, which stands in two acres of mature grounds, into a small hotel in 1981, they made every effort to retain the Edwardian character of the place – restoring original wood-block floors, discreetly adding bathrooms to bedrooms, furnishing the rooms with handsome Victorian and Edwardian pieces, carefully converting the coach house to four 'luxury' bedrooms (one of which, 'Leighton', has been spe-cially designed for disabled guests). Readers have praised the large, com-fortable bedrooms, named after Shropshire villages and decorated in sub-tle colours, with matching bathrobes and soaps.

Attention to detail extends to the sitting-rooms (one is the conservato-ry, with glorious views of the Worfe Valley) and the three dining-rooms. The award-winning food (a daily-changing menu with several choices and impressive cheeseboard) is English-based, ambitious and not cheap, served at polished tables by cheerful staff. Peter has a reasonably exten-sive wine cellar. The dining-room is strictly non-smoking, as are the bed-rooms.

~

NEARBY Ludlow; Severn Valley Railway; Ironbridge Gorge Museum.
LOCATION in village, 8 miles (12 km) W of Wolverhampton, 1 mile (1.5 km) off A454, 8 miles (12 km) S of junction 4 of M54; with ample car parking
MEALS breakfast, lunch, dinner
PRICE ££
ROOMS 14 double, 1 family room, 13 with bath, 2 with shower; all rooms have phone, TV, minibar, hairdrier
FACILITIES 2 sitting-rooms, 3 dining-rooms, 1 with bar
CREDIT CARDS AE, DC, MC, V **CHILDREN** welcome
DISABLED 1 specially adapted bedroom
PETS accepted in bedrooms **CLOSED** Christmas
PROPRIETORS Peter and Christine Iles

EAST ANGLIA AND REGION

BEYTON, SUFFOLK

MANORHOUSE

~ COUNTRY BED-AND-BREAKFAST ~

The Green, Beyton, Bury St Edmunds, Suffolk IP30 9AF
TEL (01359) 270960 **FAX** (01359) 271425 **E-MAIL** manorhouse@beyton
WEBSITE www.beyton.com

THIS B&B IN A BEAUTIFUL 15thC Suffolk longhouse is run full-time by husband and wife Mark and Kay Dewsbury, and overlooks the village green. It's an elegant but down-to-earth place – the half-timbered rooms in the main house have been colourwashed and are filled with antiques, but outside, chickens have the run of the gravelled yard, garden and sometimes the vegetable garden too. All of them lay, and between them provide most of the eggs served for breakfast.

There's a great deal of space in which to spread out. The Yellow Room in the main house is suite-sized with its own sitting area, and there are two more rooms – the Garden Room and the Dairy in a converted barn at right angles to the house. The decoration is comfortably rustic: the Dairy has exposed brick and flint walls, the traditional building materials of the area, bright and cheerful furnishings and a walk-in power shower in the large bathroom. French windows open from the Garden Room on to a tiny paved area for sitting out in summer and contemplating the venerable old lichen-covered trees. The Dewsburys are excellent hosts – laid-back and unflummoxed. Their only rule is that it is a non-smoking house. For guests who fancy a stroll, there are a couple of pleasant pubs in the village.

~

NEARBY Bury St Edmunds; Lavenham.
LOCATION 4 miles (6.5 km) E of Bury St Edmunds, signposted off A14; with ample car parking
MEALS breakfast, dinner on request
PRICES £
ROOMS 4 double with bath or shower; all rooms have TV, hairdrier
FACILITIES sitting-room, dining-room, garden
CREDIT CARDS not accepted **CHILDREN** accepted over 5
DISABLED access possible to garden rooms **PETS** not accepted
CLOSED never
PROPRIETORS Mark and Kay Dewsbury

EAST ANGLIA AND REGION

BURNHAM MARKET, NORFOLK

HOSTE ARMS
~ VILLAGE INN ~

Burnham Market, Norfolk, PE31 8HD
TEL (01328) 738777 **FAX** (01328) 730103 **E-MAIL** TheHosteArms@compuserve.com
WEBSITE www.hostearms.co.uk

OVERLOOKING THE GREEN in a village whose main claim to fame is that it was Admiral Nelson's birthplace, this handsome, yellow-and-white 17thC inn has won a clutch of awards for its bedrooms, bar and restaurant. Downstairs, it positively buzzes with life in the evenings, when locals come here to drink and eat – in that order. On Friday nights between October and March a pianist plays jazz in the restaurant, where the brasserie-style menu includes British, European and Oriental-inspired dishes.

The man responsible for its lively reputation, Paul Whittome, bought the Hoste Arms in 1989. Despite being deaf, he is a chatty, affable proprietor, whose wife Jeanne is responsible for the rustic-chic decoration. She clearly has a penchant for dramatic colour schemes, painting walls downstairs deep red, and using colourful plaids and eye-catching striped fabrics in the bedrooms. These vary in style and size; some have been criticized for being poky, so book carefully. Several are on the ground floor, three with small patios that lead on to the pretty walled garden, which provides a welcome refuge when the bar becomes too crowded. Changing art exhibitions mean that the walls are always packed with pictures.

NEARBY Houghton Hall; Holkham Hall; Sandringham House; Titchwell, Holme, Holkham and Cley Nature Reserves.
LOCATION in centre of village; with ample car parking
MEALS breakfast, lunch, dinner
PRICE ££
ROOMS 28; 18 double and twin, 4 single, 4 suites, all with bath; all rooms have phone, TV, hairdrier
FACILITIES 2 sitting-rooms, conservatory, dining-room, bar, garden
CREDIT CARDS MC, V **CHILDREN** accepted
DISABLED ground-floor bedrooms
PETS not accepted **CLOSED** never
PROPRIETORS Paul and Jeanne Whittome

East Anglia and Region

Bury St Edmunds, Suffolk

Ounce House
~ Town hotel ~

Northgate Street, Bury St Edmunds, Suffolk IP33 1HP
Tel (01284) 761779 **Fax** (01284) 768315 **E-mail** pott@globalnet.co.uk
Website www.uk.aol.com/channels/travel/ghg

OUNCE HOUSE IS A RED-BRICK, gable-ended, three-storey house set back from the road, a five-minute walk from the Abbey and pedestrianized shopping streets in the centre of Bury St Edmunds.

The interiors are formal but homely with drawing-room and dining-room decorated in calm colours; these are 'statement' swagged and draped curtains, plenty of lamps, *objets d'art* and interesting pictures. Most of the bedrooms are large and one of the most attractive has pale yellow walls, a crown arrangement over the bedhead, two chintzy armchairs and a decorative chimney piece.

A set menu is offered at dinner and everyone eats around the large, highly polished oval table – the owners, warm and open hosts, are good at putting people at their ease. If you don't want to eat in, there are several restaurants within walking distance. Guests also have the use of the library, which is more like a den, with a large leather wing armchair, smaller easy chairs, an upright piano, shelves packed with books and an honesty bar. It is somewhere to go with a friend for a long conversation, or watch TV, and is one of the few places in the house where you can smoke, though this is tolerated rather than encouraged (you have to burn a scented candle if you indulge).

~

Nearby Cathedral; Abbey; Gershom-Parkington Collection.
Location close to town centre; with ample car parking
Meals breakfast, dinner by arrangement
Price ££
Rooms 3 double and twin with bath; all rooms have phone, TV, hairdrier
Facilities 2 sitting-rooms, library/TV-room, dining-room, garden
Credit cards AE, DC, MC, V
Children welcome **Disabled** access difficult
Pets not accepted **Closed** never
Proprietors Simon and Jenny Pott

EAST ANGLIA AND REGION

TWELVE ANGEL HILL
~ TOWN HOTEL ~

12 Angel Hill, Bury St Edmunds, Suffolk IP33 1UZ
TEL (01284) 704088 **FAX** (01284) 725549

"GETS AWAY WITH TROUSER-PRESSES without being boring," says one of our highly satisfied inspectors. Twelve Angel Hill occupies a house in a mellow brick terrace, close to Bury St Edmund's cathedral. It is Georgian to the front but Tudor behind, and opened as a hotel in 1988 after being thoroughly renovated. The large bedrooms are light, generously proportioned with a special sitting area, in superb condition and beautifully furnished, with antiques and sympathetic reproductions, and have bold floral decoration and fabrics.

The Clarkes have made the most of the original features of the house, and have evidently thought carefully about the comfort of their guests: witness the charming window seat scattered with cushions overlooking the Italian walled garden; a fine four-poster bed with canopy; an intimate oak-panelled bar; and the light, pleasant drawing-room overlooking Angel Hill (not noisy, since it's double-glazed). It all has the feel of a private house, yet manages to include all the bedroom comforts of a hotel. Breakfast is, by all accounts, well above the average.

Totally no-smoking. Dinner can be arranged at one of the many local restaurants. The Clarkes are charming hosts and our inspector saw plenty of evidence that guests are highly impressed.

NEARBY Cathedral; museums; Abbey gardens.
LOCATION on Angel Hill, 100 m from cathedral; with car parking
MEALS breakfast
PRICE ££
ROOMS 6; 5 double, 1 single, all with bath or shower; all rooms have phone, TV, hairdrier
FACILITIES sitting-room, dining-room, bar, patio-room, patio garden
CREDIT CARDS AE, DC, MC, V **CHILDREN** not accepted
DISABLED access difficult **PETS** not accepted **CLOSED** Jan
PROPRIETORS Bernie and John Clarke

EAST ANGLIA AND REGION

CLEY-NEXT-THE-SEA, NORFOLK

CLEY MILL

~ CONVERTED WINDMILL ~

Cley-next-the-Sea, Holt, Norfolk NR25 7RP
TEL & **FAX** (01263) 740209
WEBSITE www.smoothhound.co.uk/hotels/cleymill.html

IMAGINE STAYING IN A 'REAL' WINDMILL. That is the sense of adventure that Cley Mill can induce even in the most world-weary. Memories of *Swallows and Amazons* or the *Famous Five* crowd in as you climb higher and higher in the mill, finally mounting the ladder to the look-out room on the fourth floor. Superb views can be enjoyed over the Cley Marshes, a Mecca for birdwatchers.

The sitting-room on the ground floor of the Mill is exceptionally welcoming – it feels well used and lived-in, with plenty of books and magazines, comfortable sofas, TV and an open fire. Bedrooms in the Mill feel rather like log cabins – there is much wood in the furniture and fittings. They are pretty rooms, with white lace bedspreads, and bathrooms ingeniously fitted in to the most challenging nooks and crannies that the old building provides.

Jeremy Bolam took over the running of the Mill several years ago. He used to run his own restaurant in Battersea, so greater emphasis is put on food and dining in, now, but he won't mind a bit if you simply take B&B.

A recent reporter stayed in The Boathouse, which is usually self-catering, and which takes the overflow from the Mill. She found it 'basic and not very comfortable,' so it's worth holding out for a room in the mill, even though they are sought-after. Try to book well in advance. See also our other windmill (page 38).

~

NEARBY Sheringham Hall; Cromer Lighthouse.
LOCATION 7 miles (11 km) W of Sheringham on A149, on N edge of village; with ample car parking
MEALS breakfast, dinner on request
PRICE ££
ROOMS 7 double, 1 single, 6 with bath, 1 with shower **FACILITIES** sitting-room, dining-room, garden **CREDIT CARDS** MC, V **CHILDREN** welcome
DISABLED access difficult **PETS** accepted **CLOSED** never **MANAGER** Jeremy Bolam

EAST ANGLIA AND REGION

HARTEST, SUFFOLK

THE HATCH

~ COUNTRY BED-AND-BREAKFAST ~

Pilgrims Lane, Cross Green, Hartest, Suffolk IP29 4ED
TEL (01284) 830226 **FAX** (01284) 830226

NARROW LANES RUNNING past fields where horses graze, and even the odd pig crossing the road, bring you to this thatched, timber-framed hall house. It was built in the late 14th century on the old pilgrim's way (now a dead-end lane) to the shrine of St Edmund at Bury. The interior with its appealingly crooked floors and walls is well furnished with antiques, a grandfather clock and a host of personal touches. The Hatch is ideal for families (though toddlers and children under nine are not accepted): the upper double bedroom interconnects with a smaller room making it suitable for parents with a child, and the downstairs bedroom has its own small kitchen with cooker and washing machine.

The Oatens ran a B&B in Kent for many years, so are well-practised in the art and a number of guests are regulars. They are sociable and will chat in their own large kitchen overlooking fields and woods or withdraw discreetly into the background if they think visitors want to be left alone. Guests have their own breakfast-room and sitting-room, where afternoon tea (on the house) is served. The speciality teas and home-made scones, cakes and jam are welcome after a day's exploring. It is non-smoking.

~

NEARBY Ickworth House; Bury St Edmunds; Melford Hall; Lavenham.
LOCATION off B1066, on sharp left turn signposted Cross Green, just before Hartest from Bury St Edmunds; with car parking
MEALS breakfast
PRICE £
ROOMS 3; 2 double, 1 single, 1 with bath, 2 share bath; all rooms have TV, hairdrier
FACILITIES sitting-room, dining-room, garden **CREDIT CARDS** not accepted
CHILDREN babes-in-arms and children over 9 accepted
DISABLED access possible to ground-floor room
PETS accepted in ground-floor room **CLOSED** Christmas Day, Boxing Day
PROPRIETORS Bridget and Robin Oaten

EAST ANGLIA AND REGION

KING'S LYNN, NORFOLK

CONGHAM HALL

COUNTRY HOUSE HOTEL

Grimston, King's Lynn, Norfolk PE32 1AH
TEL (01485) 600250 **FAX** (01485) 601191
E-MAIL reception@conghamhallhotel.demon.co.uk

'QUINTESSENTIALLY ENGLISH' is how some guests describe their stay here. Practically everything about this white 18thC Georgian house, set in 40 acres of lawns, orchards and parkland, is impressive. The spacious bedrooms and public areas are luxuriously furnished and, despite a change of ownership in October 1999, our reporter found the service to be as solicitous and efficient and the staff as helpful and welcoming as ever. Cooking (in the modern British style) is adventurous and excellent, making much use of home-grown herbs. The restaurant is a spacious, airy delight, built to look like an orangerie, with full-length windows overlooking the wide lawns of the parkland, where the herb gardens are an attraction in their own right. Visitors stop to admire the array of 600 herb varieties and to buy samples, from angelica to sorrel. The restaurant doors open on to the terraces for pre-dinner drinks and herb garden strolls. Dressing for dinner is requested.

Personal attention is thoughtful. For walkers and cyclists, the hotel will arrange to collect luggage from guests' previous destinations and deliver it onwards, too. It also keeps a book of special walks, devised by the previous owners, the Forecasts, and can arrange tuition at the Sandringham Shooting School.

NEARBY Sandringham; Ely; Norwich.
LOCATION 6 miles (9.5 km) NE of King's Lynn near A148; with parking for 50 cars
MEALS breakfast, lunch (except Sat)
PRICE ££
ROOMS 14; 11 double, 2 suites, all with bath, 1 single with shower; all rooms have phone, TV
FACILITIES 2 sitting-rooms, bar, dining-room, garden; spa bath, swimming-pool, tennis, croquet, putting **CREDIT CARDS** AE, DC, MC, V
CHILDREN welcome over 12 **DISABLED** easy access to restaurant
PETS not accepted **CLOSED** never **MANAGER** Andrew Chanterell

EAST ANGLIA AND REGION

LAVENHAM, SUFFOLK

THE GREAT HOUSE

~ RESTAURANT-WITH-ROOMS ~

Market Place, Lavenham, Suffolk CO10 9QZ
TEL (01787) 247431 **FAX** (01787) 248007 **E-MAIL** greathouse@clara.co.uk
WEBSITE www.s-h-systems.co.uk/hotels/greathse.html

THE OLD TIMBER-FRAMED houses, the fine Perpendicular 'Wool Church' and the high street full of antiques and galleries make Lavenham a high point of any visitor's itinerary of the pretty villages of East Anglia.

The Great House in the market place was built in the heyday of the wool trade but was extensively renovated in the 18th century and looks more Georgian than Tudor – at least from the outside. It was a private house (lived in by Stephen Spender in the 1930s) until John Spice, a Texan with family roots in Suffolk, had the bright idea of turning it into a restaurant-with-rooms. It is now owned by chef, Régis Crépy, and the food (predominantly French) is the best for miles – 'stunningly good' enthuses one visitor (a fellow hotelier). If you can secure one of its four bedrooms it is also a delightful place to stay. All are different, but they are all light, spacious and full of old-world charm, with beams and antiques. Each has its own fireplace and sitting area, with sofa or upholstered chairs. The dining-room is dominated by an inglenook fireplace which formed part of the original house. In winter, log fires blaze; in summer, French doors open on to a pretty stone-paved courtyard for drinks, lunch or dinner.

NEARBY Little Hall, Guildhall Priory (Lavenham); Melford Hall; Gainsborough's House, Sudbury.
LOCATION 16 miles (26 km) NW of Colchester, in middle of village; with car parking
MEALS breakfast, lunch, dinner
PRICE ££
ROOMS 4 family-size suites with bath; all rooms have phone, TV
FACILITIES sitting-room/bar, dining-room, patio, garden
CREDIT CARDS AE, MC, V
CHILDREN welcome **DISABLED** access difficult **PETS** welcome **CLOSED** 3 weeks in Jan
PROPRIETOR Régis Crépy

EAST ANGLIA AND REGION

LAVENHAM, SUFFOLK

◆ EDITORS' CHOICE ◆

LAVENHAM PRIORY

~ VILLAGE BED-AND-BREAKFAST ~

Water Street, Lavenham, Suffolk CO10 9RW
TEL (01787) 247404 **FAX** (01787) 248472
E-MAIL tim.pitt@btinternet.com **WEBSITE** www.btinternet.com/~lavpriory

GILLI PITT RUNS LAVENHAM PRIORY with great flair, and the term B&B doesn't do it justice. It is a very special place: the beautiful Grade I-listed house dates from the 13th century when it was home to Benedictine monks, and has been restored in keeping with its later life as home to an Elizabethan merchant, complete with original wallpaintings, huge Tudor fireplace and sofas covered in cushions and throws. More important, however, is the warmth of the welcome from Gilli and her husband Tim, which stems from an enjoyment of sharing the main part of their home.

This is a place to enjoy whatever the season. In summer the courtyard garden is fragrant with herbs but in winter it's just as appealing to drink a hot toddy by the fire. The house is large, and as well as the Great Hall sitting-room there's a smaller room (where shelves are stacked with board games) so more than one party can use the public rooms without feeling crowded. Each of the bedrooms has a superb bed, including a four-poster in the Painted Chamber and a solid cherrywood sleigh in the Gallery Chamber: worth a journey in their own right. Breakfast in the Merchants Hall is a feast, with fresh, stewed and candied fruits as well as the full English fry up. There's a no-smoking rule.

~

NEARBY Guildhall; 'Wool Church' of St Peter and St Paul.
LOCATION in centre of village beside Swan; with ample parking
MEALS breakfast
PRICE ££
ROOMS 5 double, 4 with bath, 1 with shower; all rooms have TV, hairdrier
FACILITIES 2 sitting-rooms, dining-room, garden
CREDIT CARDS MC, V
CHILDREN accepted over 10
DISABLED not suitable
PETS not accepted **CLOSED** Christmas and New Year
PROPRIETORS Tim and Gilli Pitt

EAST ANGLIA AND REGION

THE BLACK LION
~ COUNTRY HOTEL ~

The Green, Long Melford, Suffolk CO10 9DN
TEL (01787) 312356 **FAX** (01787) 374557

LONG MELFORD IS A FAMOUSLY attractive Suffolk village, and The Black Lion is at the heart of it, overlooking the green. It is an elegant early 19thC building, decorated and furnished with great sympathy, taste and lightness of touch. The hotel changed hands in December 1999, and the new owner, Craig Jarvis, has reinstated its original name (the previous owners, the Erringtons, had renamed it, 'The Countrymen'). The two dining-rooms, one principally for private functions, offer 'modern *cuisine* with a strong classical influence' and a wide-ranging wine list.

Our latest reporter was also delighted with the accommodation. Bedrooms are comfortable and 'non slick: nothing much matches in a charming sort of way'. She noticed the half-open trunk on a landing, spilling out hats and costumes; an antique typewriter on a desk; and bookcases groaning with old books, in the wine bar. Craig Jarvis plans to update the rooms – we hope that they lose none of their character and charm in the process.

The Erringtons used to organize numerous events, from wine tastings or live jazz in the bar to murder dinners and midsummer balls. These will continue, though 'there may not be quite so many'. We hope that the lively atmosphere and sense of fun will survive the change of ownership. Reports would be welcome.

~

NEARBY Long Melford church; Melford Hall; Kentwell Hall.
LOCATION in village 3 miles (5 km) N of Sudbury, overlooking village green; with car parking
MEALS breakfast, lunch, dinner
PRICE ££
ROOMS 9; 7 double, 1 suite, 1 family room, all with bath; all have phone, TV
FACILITIES sitting-room, 2 dining-rooms, bar
CREDIT CARDS AE, MC, V **CHILDREN** welcome **DISABLED** no special facilities
PETS accepted in bedrooms **CLOSED** Jan **PROPRIETOR** Craig Jarvis

EAST ANGLIA AND REGION

MELBOURN, HERTFORDSHIRE

MELBOURN BURY

~ COUNTRY GUEST-HOUSE ~

Melbourn, near Royston, Hertfordshire SG8 6DE
TEL (01763) 261151 **FAX** (01763) 262375
E-MAIL mazecare@aol.com

THIS GRACIOUS MANOR HOUSE, dating mainly from Victorian times although of much earlier origin, offers an intimate retreat only 20 minutes' drive from Cambridge. The whitewashed and crenellated house, with roses round the door, has a delightful setting in mature parkland with its own lake and gardens.

All the public rooms are furnished with antiques, but have just the right degree of informality to make the house feel like a lived-in home and not a museum – not surprising, when you learn that Sylvia Hopkinson's family have been here for 150 years. As well as an elegant drawing-room, there is a splendid Victorian billiards-room (full-size table) incorporating a book-lined library, and a sun-trap conservatory. The three bedrooms are spacious and comfortably furnished in harmony with the house; particularly delightful is the 'pink room' which looks out over the lake and the garden; it is a profusion of Sanderson prints and antiques, and has a large bathroom.

The Hopkinsons' dinner-party food (by prior arrangement) is home-made, down to the ice-creams and sorbets and served dinner-party style around a large mahogany table in the dining-room.

~

NEARBY Cambridge colleges and Fitzwilliam Museum; Duxford Air Museum; Wimpole Hall; Audley End.
LOCATION 10 miles (16 km) SW of Cambridge, on S side of village off A10; with ample car parking
MEALS breakfast, dinner
PRICE ££
ROOMS 3; 2 double, 1 single, all with bath or shower; all rooms have TV
FACILITIES 2 sitting-rooms, conservatory, dining-room, billiards-room, garden
CREDIT CARDS AE, MC, V
CHILDREN welcome over 8 **DISABLED** not suitable **PETS** not accepted
CLOSED Christmas, New Year, Easter **PROPRIETORS** Anthony and Sylvia Hopkinson

EAST ANGLIA AND REGION

MORSTON, NORFOLK

MORSTON HALL
~ COUNTRY HOTEL ~

Morston, Holt, Norfolk NR25 7AA
TEL (01263) 741041 **FAX** (01263) 740419
E-MAIL reception@morstonhall.demon.co.uk **WEBSITE** www.morstonhall.demon.co.uk

DON'T BE PUT OFF BY the rather severe-looking flint exterior of this solid Jacobean house on the North Norfolk coast. Inside, the rooms are unexpectedly bright and airy, painted in summery colours and overlooking a sweet garden, where a fountain plays in a lily pond and roses flourish. The *raison d'être* of Morston Hall is its dining-room, the responsibility of Galton Blackiston, who shot to fame as a finalist in ITV's 'Chef of the Year'. He has since won huge acclaim for his outstanding modern European *cuisine* and, the icing on the cake, a Michelin star in 1999. His set four-course menu changes daily and might feature: *confit* of leg of duck on sautéed Lyonnaise potatoes with thyme-infused *jus,* or grilled fillet of sea bass served on fennel *duxelle* with *sauce vierge.* The carefully-stocked wine cellar offers a comprehensive selection of – not overpriced – wines from all over the world. Galton and his wife, Tracy, also organize wine-tasting dinners and cookery lessons. He gives a number of half-day cookery demonstrations and runs two three-day residential courses each year. Most of the large bedrooms are decked out in chintz fabrics, with armchairs and all the little extras, such as bottled water, bathrobes and large, warm, fluffy towels.

~

NEARBY Sandringham; Felbrigg Hall; Holkham Hall; Brickling.
LOCATION 2 miles (3 km) W of Blakeney on A149; with ample car parking
MEALS breakfast, Sun lunch, dinner
PRICE £££
ROOMS 6; 5 double and twin, 1 suite, all with bath, 1 with shower; all rooms have phone, TV, video, CD player, hairdrier
FACILITIES 2 sitting-rooms, conservatory, dining-room, garden; croquet
CREDIT CARDS AE, DC, MC, V
CHILDREN welcome **DISABLED** access to public rooms only
PETS accepted in bedrooms **CLOSED** New Year's Eve, 3 weeks in Jan
PROPRIETORS Galton and Tracy Blackiston

EAST ANGLIA AND REGION

NEEDHAM MARKET, SUFFOLK

PIPPS FORD

~ MANOR HOUSE HOTEL ~

Needham Market, near Ipswich, Suffolk IP6 8LJ
TEL (01449) 760208 **FAX** (01449) 760561

THIS BLACK-AND-WHITE, half-timbered manor house was built in 1540 for Richard Hakluyt, a commissioner of maps who opened up much of the globe to explorers. It's fitting that the tide has now turned and visitors come here from all over world for New Zealander Raewyn Hackett-Jones' relaxed, thoughtful hospitality. When Raewyn and her husband bought the house in 1974, the main water supply came from the well by the front door. Now, despite every up-to-date fitting and the fact that it's next to the A14, the house still feels slightly other-worldly, with the River Gipping meandering through the garden, where old-fashioned roses run rampant, and the rooms named after cottage garden plants. There are more rooms in a stable annexe and all guests have the run of the sitting-rooms, the main one with grand piano and log fire.

There are no televisions in rooms, as Raewyn likes people to stay and chat after dinner. The atmosphere encourages sociability, with one large dining table if you want to eat with other guests, or smaller ones if you prefer to dine *à deux*. Food is excellent, with home-made bread, jams and honey from the hives in the garden, game and pork from nearby suppliers and locally smoked fish.

~

NEARBY Blakenham Woodland Gardens.
LOCATION 1 mile (1.5 km) E of Needham Market, off roundabout where A140 meets A14; with car parking
MEALS breakfast, dinner Mon-Sat
PRICE £
ROOMS 9; 5 double, 3 twin, 1 single, all with bath or shower; all rooms have TV, hairdrier
FACILITIES 3 sitting-rooms, dining-room, conservatory, garden; tennis court
CREDIT CARDS not accepted **CHILDREN** accepted over 5
DISABLED not suitable **PETS** not accepted **CLOSED** Christmas to mid-Jan
PROPRIETOR Raewyn Hackett-Jones

EAST ANGLIA AND REGION

NORWICH

BY APPOINTMENT

~ RESTAURANT-WITH-ROOMS ~

25-29 St Georges Street, Norwich, Norfolk NR3 1AB
TEL & FAX (01603) 630730

THERE IS SO MUCH to see in Norwich and if you want to be in the thick of things, then this quirky establishment, in a 15thC merchant's house owned by Timothy Brown and Robert Culyer, might be the place for you. It is in St Georges Street, which runs parallel to Elm Hill, gloriously cobbled and lined with historic houses, and is ideally placed for seeing the sights.

As you enter through the kitchen, you are struck by the friendly atmosphere, which also pervades the five rooms that comprise the restaurant. They have somewhat theatrical furnishings – heavy swagged curtains, rich night-time colours, crystal and silver glittering on impeccably laid tables. In this setting, you choose dishes from the large *carte*, such as fillet of beef, filled with a *duxelle* of tomatoes and mushrooms, wrapped in puff pastry, with a fresh garden mint and mustard sauce. Don't overdo it: otherwise you won't manage the magnificent cooked feast that goes by the name of breakfast the next morning.

The layout of the building seems more like a warren than a house. Appropriately, reception rooms and bedrooms, all with exotic and colourful decoration, are crammed with Victoriana and *objets trouvés*. It may not suit everybody, but it is thoroughly original and, as far as we're concerned, a breath of fresh air.

~

NEARBY Cathedral; Castle; Guildhall; Bridewell Museum.
LOCATION in city centre; with car parking
MEALS breakfast, dinner
PRICE ££
ROOMS 4; 3 double, 1 single, all with bath; all rooms have phone, TV, hairdrier
FACILITIES sitting-room, dining-rooms
CREDIT CARDS MC, V
CHILDREN accepted over 12 **DISABLED** not suitable **PETS** not accepted
CLOSED Christmas Day; restaurant Sun, Mon
PROPRIETORS Timothy Brown and Robert Culyer

EAST ANGLIA AND REGION

NORWICH

OLD CATTON HALL

~ COUNTRY HOUSE HOTEL ~

Lodge Lane, Old Catton, Norwich, Norfolk NR6 7HG
TEL (01603) 419379 **FAX** (01603)400339
E-MAIL enquiries@catton-hall.co.uk **WEBSITE** www.catton-hall.co.uk

AN IMPRESSIVE 17THC gentleman's residence, built from reclaimed Caen stone, local flint and oak timbers, has been transformed with great success into this genteel family-run hotel. Though located in an unprepossessing suburb of Norwich, it has the twin advantages of being within easy reach of the city centre, yet away from the bustle. With its mullioned windows, beamed ceilings, inglenook fireplaces, polished antiques and warm colour schemes, the interior feels intimate and inviting. Owners Anthea and Roger Cawdron are on hand to welcome guests and pamper them during their stay, placing books and glossy magazines by their beds, and a tantalizing array of soaps, bubble baths, lotions and potions in the bathrooms. Named after former inhabitants of the house, the bedrooms have been decorated boldly and with dash in country house style by Anthea, and the beds, some of which are four-posters, are made up with delicious Egyptian cotton sheets.

Anthea's talents also extend to the kitchen, where she prepares interesting dishes, using local produce and herbs from the garden, according to – among others – old family recipes. There is a thoughtfully chosen and not-too-exorbitant wine list.

~

NEARBY Cathedral; Castle; The Broads.
LOCATION 2.5 miles (4 km) NE of Norwich, off B1150; with ample car parking
MEALS breakfast, lunch, dinner
PRICE ££
ROOMS 7 double, twin and family with bath; all rooms have phone, TV, hairdrier
FACILITIES sitting-room, dining-room, garden
CREDIT CARDS AE, D, MC, V
CHILDREN accepted over 12
DISABLED not suitable
PETS not accepted **CLOSED** never; restaurant Sun eve
PROPRIETORS Roger and Anthea Cawdron

EAST ANGLIA AND REGION

SNAPE, SUFFOLK

CROWN INN

~ VILLAGE INN ~

Snape, Suffolk, IP17 1SL
TEL (01728) 688324

SNAPE IS THE TINY VILLAGE close to the estuary of the River Alde, a tidal river which meanders its way through salt marshes to the sea. In the centre of the village is the Crown Inn, boasting the menu and accomplished cooking of a restaurant combined with the liveliness of a local pub. The three small bedrooms are located up a steep spiral staircase off the lounge bar. They are simply decorated with half-timbered walls, sprigged-flower fabrics and stripped pine furniture. They have basic bathrooms and worn carpets, but are well heated and comfortable enough for a night or two's stay.

The heart of the inn is the bar and restaurant downstairs, where both do a brisk trade at weekends. Two polished-wood, high-backed Suffolk settles around the fire make a kind of seating well, or you can sit at tables in the brick-floored dining-room. The wide choice of dishes often includes goose, quail, crayfish, sea bass and steak, with polenta, rocket and wild mushrooms also on the menu. Adnams beers and a 60-strong list of wines are reasons why you might choose to stay rather than drive home. But the Crown is also ideally located for the Aldeburgh Festival (which is not held in Aldeburgh, but just up the road at Snape Maltings). You can book for a pre- or a post-concert dinner and then stay the night.

~

NEARBY Aldeburgh; Orford; Dunwich; Minsmere RSPB Reserve.
LOCATION in village centre, on B1069; Snape is well signposted from A12; with ample car parking
MEALS breakfast, lunch, dinner
PRICE £
ROOMS 3; 2 double, 1 twin, all with bath
FACILITIES dining-room, bar, garden
CREDIT CARDS MC, V **CHILDREN** accepted over 14
DISABLED not suitable **PETS** not accepted **CLOSED** Christmas Day, Boxing Day
PROPRIETOR Diane Maylott

EAST ANGLIA AND REGION

SOUTHWOLD, SUFFOLK

THE SWAN
~ TOWN HOTEL ~

High Street, Southwold, Suffolk IP18 6EG
TEL (01502) 722186 **FAX** (01502) 724800
E-MAIL hotels@adnams.co.uk

ONE OF THE MOST WELCOMING rooms in The Swan is the drawing-room, with its carved wood chimney pieces and architraves, Murano glass chandeliers, chintzy sofas and armchairs, and relaxed atmosphere. On Sunday mornings the place is full of newspapers and chat, with guests and non-residents ordering coffee and shortbread, and, on a fine day, the sun pours in through the windows from the market square. The Swan is ideal for a long stay – the bedrooms at the front are largest, though all, including the standard rooms, are inviting and well decorated in smart, strong colours and with interesting prints on the walls. Many have a view of the sea, lighthouse or square. There are also modern garden rooms, grouped around a former bowling green, with large picture windows which mean that, though you can see out, everyone else can see in.

Staff are professional and helpful and ensure that the hotel operates on a human scale. It made us wish that there were more places like this. Adnams Brewery owns The Swan and its sister hotel, The Crown, down the road, plus a simpler hotel, The Cricketers at Reydon. If you eat at The Crown, a cross billing system operates – just remember to tell reception before you go.

~

NEARBY 'Cathedral of the Marshes'; Dunwich Heath; Minsmere Nature Reserve.
LOCATION next to market square; with car parking
MEALS breakfast, lunch, dinner
PRICE ££-£££
ROOMS 43 double, 26 in main hotel and 17 garden rooms, 40 with bath or shower; all rooms have phone, TV, hairdrier
FACILITIES sitting-rooms, dining-room, bar, lift, garden; croquet
CREDIT CARDS AE, DC, MC, V
CHILDREN welcome **DISABLED** access possible
PETS accepted in garden rooms by arrangement **CLOSED** never
MANAGER Carole Ladd

EAST ANGLIA AND REGION

STOKE-BY-NAYLAND, SUFFOLK

ANGEL INN

~ VILLAGE INN ~

Stoke-by-Nayland, Suffolk, CO6 4SA
TEL (01206) 263245 **FAX** (01206) 263373

A PROPER INN RATHER THAN A PUB, with spick-and-span bedrooms off a long gallery landing upstairs, the Angel Inn has been in business since the 16th century. There are plenty of nooks and crannies in the bar and a variety of seating in the series of interconnecting public rooms. You'll find sofas and chairs grouped together in a corner next to the fire and grandfather clock; and a dining-room with its ceiling open to the rafters, rough brick-and-timber-studded walls and a fern-lined well-shaft 52 feet (16 m) deep. The bedrooms are a fair size, individually and unfussily decorated and are ideal for a one- or two-night stop on a tour of Suffolk.

The public rooms downstairs have great character, with interesting pictures and low lighting, and are filled with the hum and buzz of contented lunch and dinner conversation. The food is excellent, with local produce used where possible, including fresh fish and shellfish from nearby ports, and game from local estates. Dishes might include griddled hake with red onion dressing, or stir-fried duckling with fine leaf salad, Cumberland sauce and new potatoes. Service is informal, friendly and helpful. Children are not allowed in the bar, and though flexible, there are rules about young children eating in the dining-room; it is advisable to check when booking.

~

NEARBY Guildhall; Dedham Vale; Flatford Mill; East Bergholt.
LOCATION in village centre, on B1068 between Sudbury and Ipswich; some car parking on street nearby
MEALS breakfast, lunch, dinner
PRICE £
ROOMS 7; 6 double, 1 twin, all with bath; all rooms have phone, TV, hairdrier
FACILITIES sitting-room, dining-rooms, bar, garden **CREDIT CARDS** AE, MC, DC, V
CHILDREN accepted **DISABLED** not suitable **PETS** not accepted
CLOSED Christmas Day, Boxing Day, New Year's Day
PROPRIETORS Peter Smith, Richard Wright and Mark Johnson

East Anglia and Region

SWAFFHAM, NORFOLK

STRATTONS
~ COUNTRY HOTEL ~

Ash Close, Swaffham, Norfolk PE37 7NH
TEL (01760) 723845 **FAX** (01760) 720458
WEBSITE www.strattons-hotel.co.uk

STRATTONS EPITOMIZES everything we are looking for in this guide. Perhaps it's because Les and Vanessa Scott are such natural hosts who love entertaining; perhaps it's because of their artistic flair (they met as art students); or perhaps it's because they had a very clear vision of what they wanted to create when they bought this elegant listed villa in 1990. A reader writes: '20 out of 20 for staff attitude, value for money, quality of accommodation…An absolute delight.'

Bedrooms, several of which are being upgraded, are positively luxurious. Plump cushions and pillows jostle for space on antique beds, books and magazines fill the shelves, and the same co-ordinated decoration continues into smart bathrooms – one resembling a bedouin's tent. The two beautifully furnished sitting-rooms, *trompe l'oeil* hallway and murals painted recently by a local artist are equally impressive. Yet it is emphatically a family home and you share it with the Scott cats and children. The food is special, too. Vanessa, a cookery writer, continues to gain awards for her cooking. There are fresh eggs every day from their own chickens, and the daily-changing menu is inventive and beautifully presented. It is cheerfully served by Les in the cosy basement restaurant. There is a no-smoking rule.

~

NEARBY Norwich; North Norfolk coast.
LOCATION down narrow lane between shops on main street; with ample car parking
MEALS breakfast, lunch, dinner
PRICE ££
ROOMS 7; 6 double, 1 suite, all with bath or shower; all rooms have phone, TV, hairdrier
FACILITIES 2 sitting-rooms, dining-room, bar
CREDIT CARDS MC, V **CHILDREN** welcome
DISABLED access difficult **PETS** welcome **CLOSED** Christmas
PROPRIETORS Vanessa and Les Scott

EAST ANGLIA AND REGION

WOODBRIDGE, SUFFOLK

RAMSHOLT ARMS

~ COUNTRY PUB-WITH-ROOMS ~

Dock Road, Ramsholt, Woodbridge, Suffolk IP12 3AB
TEL (01394) 411229 **FAX** (01394) 411818

THE RAMSHOLT ARMS is one of only a few buildings visible for miles around on the shores of the Deben Estuary. It lies at the end of a long flat road which cuts through the Suffolk Breckland, a lonely expanse of heath. The pub is right on the water, and at low tide waders walk the silvery, mirror-like surface of the mud. The interior is decorated with artful simplicity, with brown sailcloth blinds lashed to a wooden mast curtain rail at the huge picture windows, and seagrass on the floor. It's well kept and attractive, but the kind of place where nobody frowns at people wearing Wellington boots or sailing clothes, or bringing wet dogs into the bar.

Bedrooms have been refurbished in unfussy style in cool blue or white, with prints on the walls and country furniture. Although all have their own bathrooms, they are not en suite. Some will be made so this year, but meanwhile owner James Adeane promises plenty of hot water to compensate for having to cross the corridor. In the rooms with wide views of the river, guests wake up to the call of curlews or the slapping of halyards against masts.

The food is wonderful: glistening, fresh shell-on-prawns; Orkney herrings; fishcakes; and main courses with chips – perfect for eating after sailing, birdwatching or riverside treks.

~

NEARBY Felixstowe; Orford; Aldeburgh
LOCATION off B1083, follow signs for Bawdsey out of Woodbridge and take right turn to Ramsholt Dock; with ample parking
MEALS breakfast, lunch, dinner
PRICE ££
ROOMS 4 double, all with bath; rooms have TV, hairdrier on request; self-catering house for 8 available to rent.
FACILITIES dining-room, bar, garden **CREDIT CARDS** AE, MC, V
CHILDREN welcome **DISABLED** not suitable **PETS** accepted
CLOSED Jan-Feb; restaurant Mon, Tues **PROPRIETOR** James Adeane

CENTRAL ENGLAND, EAST ANGLIA AND WALES

ALSO RECOMMENDED

HOLYWELL, CAMBRIDGESHIRE

Old Ferry Boat Inn

Holywell, St Ives, Huntingdon, Cambridgeshire PE17 3TG
TEL (01480) 463227 **PRICE ££**

Venerable thatched inn on the picturesque banks of the Great Ouse
with log fires, oak beams and an interesting range of bar food and also
real ales.

LAVENHAM, SUFFOLK

The Angel

Market Place, Lavenham, Sudbury, Suffolk CO10 9QZ
TEL (01787) 247388 **FAX** (01787) 248344 **E-MAIL** angellav@aol.com **PRICE ££**

Renowned for its superb cooking, a restaurant with a cosy bar and eight
simple but comfortable rooms, in Lavenham's lovely old Market Place.

LLANBERIS, GWYNEDD

Pen-y-Gwryd

Nant Gwynant, Gwynedd LL55 4NT
TEL (01286) 870211 **PRICE £**

Small, charmingly old-fashioned coaching inn, high in the desolate
heart of Snowdonia – a place of pilgrimage for mountaineers.

LLANDDEINIOLEN, GWYNEDD

Ty'n Rhos

Seion, Llanddeiniolen, near Caenarfon, Gwynedd LL55 3AE
TEL (01248) 670489 **FAX** (01248) 670079 **E-mail** enquiries@tynrhos.co.uk
WEBSITE www.tynrhos.co.uk **PRICE ££**

Excellent food – home-grown veg, local meat and fish from Cardigan
Bay – in a prettily-decorated traditional Welsh farmhouse.

NORTON, SHROPSHIRE

Hundred House

Norton, near Shifnal, Shropshire TF11 9EE
TEL (01952) 730353 **FAX** (01952) 730355
E-MAIL hphundredhouse@compuserve.com **PRICE £££**

Georgian inn with offbeat decoration – a profusion of patchwork quilts,
cushions, even carpets, gold-painted ceilings and swings in some bedrooms. Welcoming owners and glorious herb and flower gardens.

SHURDINGTON, GLOUCESTERSHIRE

The Greenway

Shurdington, near Cheltenham, Gloucestershire GL51 5UG
TEL (01242) 862352 **FAX** (01242) 862780
E-MAIL relax@greenway-hotel.demon.co.uk **PRICE ££££**

Glossy hotel in a small Elizabethan manor just outside Cheltenham with
a lovely garden, extravagant cuisine and smartly decorated rooms.

THE NORTH-WEST

BASSENTHWAITE LAKE, CUMBRIA

THE PHEASANT
~ COUNTRY INN ~

Bassenthwaite Lake, near Cockermouth, Cumbria CA13 9YE
TEL (01768) 776234 **FAX** (01768) 776002

"A VERY SPECIAL PLACE," says our most recent inspector. Tucked away behind trees just off the A66, The Pheasant was originally an old coaching inn, and there are many reminders of this within, particularly in the little old oak bar, which is full of dark nooks and crannies – a real piece of history, little changed from its earliest days. The building is a long, low barn-like structure that has been exceptionally well maintained. There is a small but well-kept garden to the rear and grounds which extend to 60 acres.

One of the great attractions is the generous sitting space. There are two residents' sitting-rooms to the front, both low ceilinged with small windows and plenty of small prints on the walls. A third, with easy chairs before an open log fire, has the advantage of its own serving hatch to the bar. A grand refurbishment scheme was undertaken in early 2000 by new management, converting the 20 old bedrooms into 16 larger, lighter, more modern rooms with attractive individual decoration and swanky new bathrooms. The dining-room has been organized to make the best of its slightly uncomfortable shape, and an *à la carte* menu introduced. The service is still outstandingly friendly.

~

NEARBY Bassenthwaite Lake; Keswick.
LOCATION 5 miles (8 km) E of Cockermouth, just off A66; with ample car parking
MEALS breakfast, lunch, dinner, bar snacks
PRICE ££
ROOMS 16 double and twin with bath; all rooms have hairdrier; rooms have phone, TV on request·
FACILITIES sitting-rooms, dining-room, bar, garden **CREDIT CARDS** MC, V
CHILDREN welcome, but not in main bar
DISABLED access possible to public rooms and 1 room in bungalow annexe
PETS accepted in public rooms only **CLOSED** Christmas Day
MANAGER Matthew Wylie

THE NORTH-WEST

BLAWITH, CUMBRIA

APPLETREE HOLME
~ FARM GUEST-HOUSE ~

Blawith, near Ulverston, Cumbria LA12 8EL
TEL (01229) 885618

T HE CARLSENS CAME HERE in 1979 after years of running a much bigger and glossier (and in its way very successful) hotel on the shores of Ullswater – because they wanted, in Roy's words, "to go back to looking after people again".

The farm enjoys a lovely and totally secluded setting on the fringe of Lakeland, with nothing but fells in view. The low, stone-built house has been lovingly restored and sympathetically furnished with antiques; pictures and books abound, and open fires on stone hearths supplement the central heating. Two of the equally welcoming bedrooms have the unusual luxury of double-size whirlpool baths.

Roy believes in tailoring his menus (whether for breakfast or dinner) to suit guests' tastes and the local fruits of the land – home-grown vegetables, meat, poultry and dairy produce from neighbouring farms. Sadly, Pooch the sheepdog is not around now to keep you company, but anyone whose appetite needs a lift can take his favourite walk over the fells to Beacon Tarn (map provided).

In the interests of their guests, the Carlsens discourage casual callers, so do phone ahead if you want to look around.

~

NEARBY Rusland Hall; Coniston Water; Lake Windermere.
LOCATION 6 miles (9.5 km) S of Coniston off A5084, in open countryside; with ample car parking
MEALS breakfast, picnic lunch on request, dinner
PRICE ££
ROOMS 3 double with bath; all rooms have phone, TV
FACILITIES 2 sitting-rooms, dining-room, garden
CREDIT CARDS AE, MC, V
CHILDREN not suitable
DISABLED access difficult **PETS** not accepted **CLOSED** never
PROPRIETORS Roy and Shirley Carlsen

THE NORTH-WEST

BORROWDALE, CUMBRIA

THE LEATHES HEAD

~ COUNTRY HOTEL ~

Borrowdale, Keswick, Cumbria CA12 5UY
TEL (01768) 777247 **FAX** (01768) 777363 **E-MAIL** enq@leatheshead.co.uk
WEBSITE www.leatheshead.co.uk

ROY AND JANICE SMITH have recently taken over The Leathes Head in the beautiful Borrowdale Valley. Originally built for a Liverpool shipowner, it is a Lakeland stone Edwardian house perched in its own wooded grounds near Derwent Water. Many of its period features, the plasterwork, the stained glass and a wood-panelled ceiling in the hall, are still there. It is informal enough to attract the walkers and climbers who return to the area year after year (even if it means carrying the newest additions to their families on their backs). Children of all sizes are welcome (the hotel has all the necessary cots and high chairs) and can have a high tea in the evenings to give their parents the chance of a quiet dinner by themselves. All the rooms are comfortably furnished (the largest being at the front) and most can squeeze in an extra bed. The three-acre grounds include lawns big enough and level enough to play *boules* or croquet – and flat areas are few and far between in this region. The real challenges are, of course, the fells beyond the gate and the hotel can help here too, with its extensive collection of walking guides.

NEARBY Derwent Water; Buttermere; Castlerigg Stone Circle.
LOCATION 3.5 miles (5.5 km) S of Keswick, off B5289 to Borrowdale; in garden with ample car parking
MEALS breakfast, dinner; half-board obligatory at weekends
PRICE ££
ROOMS 11 double and twin, 6 with bath, 5 with shower; all rooms have phone, TV, hairdrier
FACILITIES 3 sitting-rooms, dining-room, bar, garden; croquet, boules
CREDIT CARDS MC, V
CHILDREN accepted
DISABLED 2 ground-floor rooms
PETS accepted **CLOSED** never
PROPRIETORS Roy and Janice Smith

THE NORTH-WEST

BOWNESS-ON-WINDERMERE, CUMBRIA

LINDETH FELL

~ COUNTRY HOUSE HOTEL ~

Bowness-on-Windermere, Cumbria LA23 3JP
TEL (01539) 443286 **FAX** (01539) 447455 **E-MAIL** kennedy@lindethfell.co.uk
WEBSITE www.lindethfell.co.uk

To stay at LINDETH FELL is like visiting a well-heeled old friend who enjoys making his visitors as comfortable as possible, who enjoys his food (but likes to be able to identify what's put in front of him), is unreasonably fond of good puddings, has a rather fine wine cellar – and is justifiably proud of the view from his house. Pat and Diana Kennedy's establishment hits this mark (they are always there to see that it does), and, not unsurprisingly, their approach and warm courteous welcome have been duly rewarded with a faithful following.

Approached through trees, and set in large mature gardens glowing with azaleas and rhododendrons in spring, Lindeth Fell's wood-panelled hall leads to a pair of comfortable and attractive sitting-rooms and a restaurant where large windows let in the tremendous view. Weather permitting, drinks and tea can be taken on the terrace, and the same warm weather might even allow for a game of tennis or croquet. Upstairs, the rooms vary in size and outlook. Both qualities are reflected in their price but, as a general rule, the further up the house you go, the smaller the room but the better the view. All the rooms are comfortably furnished and pleasingly decorated.

~

NEARBY Windermere Steamboat Museum; Lake Windermere.
LOCATION 1 mile (1.5 km) S of Bowness off A5074; with ample parking
MEALS breakfast, lunch, dinner
PRICE ££
ROOMS 14; 12 double and twin, 2 single, 12 with bath, 2 with shower; all rooms have phone, TV, hairdrier
FACILITIES sitting-rooms, dining-room, bar, garden, lake; croquet, tennis
CREDIT CARDS MC, V
CHILDREN accepted **DISABLED** access possible to ground-floor bedroom
PETS not accepted **CLOSED** Jan to early Feb
PROPRIETORS Pat and Diana Kennedy

THE NORTH-WEST

BOWNESS-ON-WINDERMERE, CUMBRIA

LINTHWAITE HOUSE

~ COUNTRY HOUSE HOTEL ~

Crook Road, Bowness-on-Windermere, Cumbria LA23 3JA
TEL (01539) 488600 **FAX** (01539) 488601 **E-MAIL** admin@linthwaite.com
WEBSITE www.linthwaite.com

Y<small>OU COULD SAY OF</small> Mike Bevans that he liked the view so much that he bought the best place to see it from. It is our good luck that he and his wife have also created in this Edwardian country house a very profession-ally-run hotel with a unique style. The reception rooms are filled with palms, wicker furniture and old curios as well as antiques. Painted decoys, well-travelled cabin trunks and oriental vases help to evoke days of leisure and service in the far reaches of the Empire. Service here manages to be crisp and amiable at the same time: you are made to feel that you are on holiday and not on parade. Whether you eat in the richly coloured dining-room or the new Mirror Room, the food has come from Ian Bravey's kitchen – well-thought-out menus, beautifully presented. Bad luck, though, if you're under seven: it's an early tea for you, without the option.

Of the bedrooms, the best look directly towards Windermere, some are in a modern annexe, and there is quite a variation in size. They all have style, though, with thoughtful use of fabrics and furnishings, and bath-rooms that are attractive rather than utilitarian. Beyond the terraces out-side are 14 acres of lawn, shrubs, woods and a small lake.

~

NEARBY Windermere Steamboat Museum; Lake Windermere.
LOCATION 1 mile (1.5 km) S of Bowness off the A5074; with ample care parking
MEALS breakfast, lunch, dinner
PRICE ££
ROOMS 26 double and twin with bath; all rooms have phone, TV, hairdrier; some have fax/modem points
FACILITIES sitting-rooms, conservatory, dining-rooms, bar, terrace, garden
CREDIT CARDS AE, MC, V
CHILDREN accepted
DISABLED 1 specially adapted room
PETS not accepted **CLOSED** never
PROPRIETOR Mike Bevans

THE NORTH-WEST

BRAMPTON, CUMBRIA

FARLAM HALL
～ COUNTRY HOUSE HOTEL ～

Brampton, Cumbria CA8 2NG
TEL (01697) 746234 FAX (01697) 746683 E-MAIL farlamhall@dial.pipex.com
WEBSITE www.farlamhall.co.uk

"EXCEPTIONAL," SAYS AN INSPECTOR – "perfect in every way." For over 20 years now the Quinion and Stevenson families have assiduously improved their solid but elegant Border country house. It has its roots in Elizabethan times, but what you see today is essentially a large Victorian family home, extended for a big family and frequent entertaining – the Thompsons, wealthy local industrialists – presided over its heyday. No coincidence that it makes such a good hotel.

"Absolutely beautiful, very large country house set in stunning grounds," continued our inspector. "Beautifully furnished throughout in wonderful taste, many fine pieces of furniture. All the bedrooms are luxurious and charmingly done out. The dining-room and public rooms are discreet and the atmosphere is one of traditional English service and comfort. The family is most welcoming."

Another reporter could find no flaw: 'charming family, quiet surroundings, excellent food, tastefully furnished bedroom'. Bedrooms vary widely and some are decidedly large and swish.

Barry Quinion's dinners range from plain country dishes to mild extravagances, and there is a notable cheeseboard.

Farlam Hall is well placed for the Lakes, Dales and Northumberland Coast as well as Hadrian's Wall.

NEARBY Naworth Castle; Hadrian's Wall.
LOCATION 3 miles (5 km) SE of Brampton on A689, NE of (not in) Farlam village; with ample car parking
MEALS breakfast, dinner; light lunches on request
PRICE ££££
ROOMS 12 double with bath; all rooms have phone, TV, hairdrier
FACILITIES 2 sitting-rooms, dining-room, garden; croquet CREDIT CARDS MC, V
CHILDREN accepted over 5 DISABLED 2 ground-floor bedrooms
PETS welcome in some rooms CLOSED Christmas week
PROPRIETORS Quinion and Stevenson families

THE NORTH-WEST

CARLISLE

NUMBER THIRTY ONE

~ TOWN GUEST-HOUSE ~

31 Howard Place, Carlisle, Cumbria CA1 1HR
TEL & FAX (01228) 597080 **E-MAIL** bestpep@aol.com
WEBSITE www.smoothhound.co.uk/hotels/31.html

SINCE EXPERIENCED HOTELIERS Philip and Judith Parker opened their Victorian town house in the mid-1990s, they have scooped some prestigious awards, including the English Tourism Council's Best B&B in England in 1999. In fact it's not just a B&B, and Philip's superb dinners (he produces a no-choice three-course menu every evening) might be one of the reasons for the place's immediate popularity. The menu is based on what is freshest and best that day, and emphasis is placed on as much as possible being home-made. Philip bakes his own bread, makes jam and marmalade, and even has a 'smokee' where he smokes the results of successful fishing expeditions.

There are just three bedrooms, all decorated with flair and taste: Blue is the largest, with a walk-in wardrobe; Yellow has a half-tester bed and a Mediterranean bathroom; and the smallest, but most dramatic, Green, is done out in Oriental style with a black-and-gold dragon breathing fire behind the pillows. Downstairs, the sitting-room is charmingly cluttered with objects and mementoes, which lend it a suitably Victorian flavour, and there's a pretty patio garden. With Number Thirty One, the Parkers have achieved that rare thing – a winning combination of hospitality and hands-on professionalism. They have a no-smoking policy.

~

NEARBY Cathedral; Castle; Tullie House; Hadrian's Wall.
LOCATION in city centre; with free on-street car parking for guests
MEALS breakfast, dinner
PRICE ££
ROOMS 3 double and twin with bath; all rooms have TV, hairdrier
FACILITIES sitting-room, dining-room, patio garden **CREDIT CARDS** AE, MC, V
CHILDREN accepted over 16
DISABLED not suitable
PETS not accepted **CLOSED** Dec-Mar
PROPRIETORS Philip and Judith Parker

THE NORTH-WEST

CROSTHWAITE, CUMBRIA

CROSTHWAITE HOUSE
~ COUNTRY GUEST-HOUSE ~

Crosthwaite, near Kendal, Cumbria LA8 8BP
TEL & FAX (01539) 568264
E-MAIL crosthwaite.house@kencomp.net

WHITE WITH DAMSON BLOSSOM in the spring, Lyth Valley is a gentle land-scape with distant fells to remind you of where you are. Crosthwaite House is an attractive Georgian building with classic proportions and fine, tall rooms. Robin and Marnie Dawson are the relaxed owners who make their guests very welcome. There is an open fire in the comfortable sitting-room and a varied collection of books and games. You get the feeling that no one would think you at all odd if, after a long walk and a hot shower, you just dozed off in front of the television until supper time.

Good hearty breakfasts are always there in the mornings in the wooden-floored dining-room, but evening meals tend to be more movable feasts: if there aren't enough takers, you might be encouraged to take a short pre-dinner stroll to the Punch Bowl Inn and eat there. Luckily, it doesn't really matter where you eat – you'll get an excellent meal either way. There are six bright and simply furnished bedrooms, each with their own shower-room (although these can be something of a snug fit). Side windows are being let into the rooms at the rear of the house so that they can share the view with those at the front.

~

NEARBY Lake Windermere; Hill Top; Sizergh Castle.
LOCATION in countryside just off A5074, 5 miles (8 km) W of Kendal; with ample car parking
MEALS breakfast, dinner
PRICE £
ROOMS 6; 5 double and twin, 1 single, all with shower; all rooms have TV
FACILITIES sitting-room, dining-room, garden
CREDIT CARDS not accepted
CHILDREN welcome
DISABLED access difficult
PETS accepted **CLOSED** late Nov to Feb
PROPRIETORS Robin and Marnie Dawson

THE NORTH-WEST

GRASMERE, CUMBRIA

WHITE MOSS HOUSE

~ COUNTRY HOUSE HOTEL ~

Rydal Water, Grasmere, Cumbria LA22 9SE
Tel (01539) 435295 **Fax** (01539) 435516 **E-mail** dixon@whitemoss.com
Website www.whitemoss.com

LIKE MANY MODERN PARENTS, Wordsworth probably had to resort to bribery to persuade his son to fly the nest. Whether true or not, Wordsworth certainly bought him White Moss House and visited here often. Built of grey Lakeland stone, now creeper-clad, and set in a pretty, rose-rich garden above the road from Grasmere to Ambleside, Sue and Peter Dixon's small hotel has a disproportionately large (but richly deserved) reputation for the quality of its food and the scope of its cellar. There is a firm timetable for the superb five-course dinners (no choice until you reach dessert) which are served in the snug dining-room and which always end with a selection of the best of British cheeses. Not surprisingly, the breakfasts are also masterpieces, so it's just as well that there are walks to suit all ages which start from the front door.

The whole house seems to have comfort as its watchword. None of the pretty bedrooms are vast, but all are filled with a host of little touches ranging from fresh flowers to bath salts. If taken together, the two largest bedrooms get exclusive use of a sitting-room (bridge players take note), and there are two bedrooms removed from the main house in a cottage a little further up the hill, which have the best views.

~

Nearby Rydal Mount; Dove Cottage.
Location 1 mile (1.5 km) S of Grasmere on A591; with ample car parking
Meals breakfast, dinner (half-board obligatory except Sun)
Price £££
Rooms 9; 7 double, 6 with bath, 1 with shower, 2-bedroom 'cottage suite'; all rooms have phone, TV, hairdrier
Facilities sitting-room, dining-room, bar, garden; fishing
Credit cards AE, MC, V **Children** older children welcome
Disabled access difficult **Pets** accepted in cottage suite only
Closed Dec-Feb
Proprietors Sue and Peter Dixon

THE NORTH-WEST

GREAT LANGDALE, CUMBRIA

OLD DUNGEON GHYLL
∽ COUNTRY HOTEL ∽

Great Langdale, Ambleside, Cumbria LA22 9JY
TEL & **FAX** (01539) 437272

LANGDALE IS A MAGNIFICENT VALLEY in the centre of the Lake District, dominated by the Langdale Pikes. Walkers and climbers flock here to hike and scale some of the highest mountains in England (including the Scafell range). In 1885 the Old Dungeon Ghyll Hotel (then known as Middlefell) was run by John Bennett, a well-known guide for tourists. The historian G. M. Trevelyan bought it in the early 1900s and gave it to the National Trust. The horse-drawn 'charas' bringing visitors from Little Langdale over Blea Tarn Pass would stop at the top and blow their horn, a signal to get lunch or tea ready – the number of blasts matching the number of passengers. As an unofficial home for most of Britain's climbing clubs, the visitors' book was like a roll-call of the leading British climbers.

Neil and Jane Walmsley have been the proprietors since 1983 and have continued to improve and develop this popular family hotel retaining as many old features as possible. The climbers were a pretty uncritical bunch (any kind of a roof was a luxury), but there is now a comfortable residents' sitting-room with an open fire, a warm busy bar (open to the public) and a snug dining-room offering wholesome uncomplicated food. There are fewer bathrooms than bedrooms, although four of the rooms have their own showers.

∽

NEARBY Lake Windermere; Grasmere; Kendal.
LOCATION 7 miles (11 km) NE of Ambleside off B5343; in countryside with limited car parking
MEALS breakfast, packed lunch, dinner, bar meals
PRICE ££
ROOMS 17; 14 double, twin and family, 4 with shower, 3 single
FACILITIES sitting-room, dining-room, 2 bars, garden
CREDIT CARDS AE, MC, V
CHILDREN welcome **DISABLED** access difficult **PETS** welcome **CLOSED** 24-26 Dec
PROPRIETORS Neil and Jane Walmsley

THE NORTH-WEST

HAWKSHEAD, CUMBRIA

◆ EDITORS' CHOICE ◆

EES WYKE

~ COUNTRY HOUSE HOTEL ~

Near Sawrey, Hawkshead, Ambleside, Cumbria LA22 0JZ
TEL & FAX (01539) 436393

ESTHWAITE WATER, to the east of Windermere, has been kept safely in private hands, so has escaped the development that has ravaged some of the other Lakes. Ees Wyke, a gem of a white-painted Georgian mansion, is perched above park-like meadows that roll gently down to the reed banks on the shore, punctuated here and there by sheep and mature trees. As well as unmarred views, Margaret and John Williams have happily discovered the secret of making people feel instantly at home. No one could be more relaxed than Ruff the dog, whose speciality is imitating the famous immovable object.

This is a well-kept house, with everything just so, even down to a plentiful supply of games and books for those inclement days. In the dining-room are beautiful large windows to show off the view (these are new since Beatrix Potter stayed here for her holidays), Windsor chairs and crisp white tablecloths. The dinners (John's department) run to five generous and unhurried courses and the price/quality ratio of the wine list is definitely tipped in your favour. The bedrooms are attractive and generously proportioned, most with small but well-equipped bathrooms, and comfortable enough to allow you to build up the strength you need to tackle the truly heroic breakfast.

~

NEARBY Hill Top; Lake Windermere; Grasmere.
LOCATION in hamlet on B5285, 2 miles (3 km) SE of Hawkshead; with car parking
MEALS breakfast, dinner
PRICE ££
ROOMS 8 double and twin, 3 with bath, 5 with shower; all rooms have TV, hairdrier
FACILITIES 2 sitting-rooms, dining-room, garden
CREDIT CARDS AE **CHILDREN** accepted over 8
DISABLED 1 ground-floor room
PETS accepted in bedrooms **CLOSED** Jan-Feb
PROPRIETORS John and Margaret Williams

THE NORTH-WEST

KIRKBY LONSDALE, CUMBRIA

◆ EDITORS CHOICE ◆

HIPPING HALL
~ COUNTRY HOTEL ~

Cowan Bridge, Kirkby Lonsdale, Cumbria LA6 2JJ
TEL (01524) 271187 **FAX** (01524) 272452 **E-MAIL** hippinghall@aol.com
WEBSITE www.dedicate.co.uk/hipping-hall

'MORE LIKE STAYING WITH FRIENDS than in a hotel' is the typical reaction to a weekend at Hipping Hall. When we last visited we were much impressed – it was fairly priced, too. But a change of ownership was announced as we went to press, so we wait to hear whether Ian and Jos Bryant's laid-back style has been adopted by the Skeltons.

The Bryants were very experienced, and knew exactly what they were doing. They adopted the house-party approach – you expected to make friends with strangers: helped yourself to drinks from the sideboard, and dinner was eaten at one table under the minstrel's gallery in the spectacular beamed Great Hall. Jo's daily five-course feast (no choice, but preferences taken account of) used home-grown and local produce. 'The food was excellent as was the way it was presented,' is a recent commentator's verdict.

Parts of the Hall date back to the 15th century when a hamlet grew up around the 'hipping' or stepping stones across the beck. After a strenuous day on the fells, you can sink into sofas in front of a wood-burning stove at the other end of the Great Hall. Bedrooms (no smoking allowed) are spacious, comfortable and furnished with period pieces. More reports would be welcome.

~

NEARBY Yorkshire Dales; Lake District; Settle to Carlisle railway.
LOCATION on A65, 2.5 miles (4 km) SE of Kirkby Lonsdale; in 3-acre walled gardens with ample car parking
MEALS breakfast, dinner
PRICE ££ **ROOMS** 7; 5 double, 4 with bath, 1 with shower; 2 suites with bath; all rooms have phone, TV, hairdrier **FACILITIES** sitting-room, dining-room, breakfast-room, conservatory with bar, garden; croquet, boules **CREDIT CARDS** AE, MC, V
CHILDREN welcome over 12 **DISABLED** not suitable
PETS accepted in bedrooms by arrangement
CLOSED Nov to mid-Mar, except for private weekend parties
PROPRIETORS Mr and Mrs Skelton

THE NORTH-WEST

LOW LORTON, CUMBRIA

WINDER HALL
~ COUNTRY GUEST-HOUSE ~

Low Lorton, near Cockermouth, Cumbria CA13 9UP
TEL & FAX (01900) 85107 **E-MAIL** winderhall@lowlorton.freeserve.co.uk **WEBSITE**
www.winderhall.freeserve.co.uk

IF YOU TAKE THE BEAUTIFUL road from Keswick by the Whinlatter Pass, you will drop down towards Low Lorton into the prettiest countryside you could wish for. Winder Hall is a Grade II-listed Tudor manor, spruced up in the 17th century by the addition of an imposing façade, and more recently by Mary and Derek Denman. Nothing about their meticulous restoration and decoration of this house jars with its historical character, and above all it offers the luxury of *real* space to move around in. In doubtful weather the spotless pink and cream drawing-room is the scene for afternoon tea – taken outside if it's warm enough. It is also the home of the honesty bar. The original hall is now the oak-panelled dining-room, where you can have a set four-course dinner (with wine from a short but comprehensive list and at distinctly non-predatory prices).

The six bedrooms (some big and the rest bigger still) are punctiliously decorated and furnished, two of them complete with four-posters. Only one has a vast fireplace and priest's hole, but they all greet you with fresh flowers and hand-made chocolates. At the foot of the garden the River Cocker flows past, and you can look along it to the mellow stone arches of Low Lorton Bridge.

~

NEARBY Derwent Water; Keswick; Loweswater.
LOCATION 3 miles (5 km) S of Cockermouth, off B5289; with car parking
MEALS breakfast, dinner
PRICE ££
ROOMS 6; 5 double and 1 twin, 3 with bath, 3 with shower; all rooms have TV, hairdrier
FACILITIES sitting-room, dining-room, garden
CREDIT CARDS MC, V
CHILDREN accepted over 8
DISABLED not suitable **PETS** not accepted **CLOSED** Christmas
PROPRIETORS Mary and Derek Denman

THE NORTH-WEST

MUNGRISDALE, CUMBRIA

THE MILL
~ COUNTRY HOTEL ~

Mungrisdale, Penrith, Cumbria CA11 0XR
TEL (01768) 779659

THIS FORMER 17THC mill cottage below Skiddaw still has the mill race running past it and is in very open, very unspoiled countryside. Like Mungrisdale itself (which you can pass through in three minutes), it is by no means large, but manages to maintain a big reputation for its welcome, its food and its thoroughly professional management. High season must test its capacity a little, but it has a substantial fan-club who come back year after year. The snug dining-room, where crazy stacks of candle stubs and their accumulated drips, look like small-scale models of spectacular limestone caverns, and where strangers actually talk to one another, is the scene both for first-rate breakfasts and Eleanor Quinlan's excellent five-course dinners. How she manages to find time to bake the bread as well is a mystery to one and all.

Wall space everywhere is almost entirely given over to the results of 30 years' worth of oil and watercolour collecting by the Quinlans. Some bedrooms are quite small, but if you need more space there are two bedrooms in the picturesque old mill which share a sizeable old sitting-room. "Popular with bridge players," says John Quinlan. All around are excellent walks for people of all ages and any abilities. Don't mistake this hotel for the neighbouring Mill Inn.

~

NEARBY Derwent Water; Ullswater; Hadrian's Wall.
LOCATION 9.5 miles (15 km) W of Penrith close to A66, in village; with parking for 15 cars
MEALS breakfast, dinner
PRICE ££
ROOMS 7 double and twin with bath; all rooms have TV
FACILITIES sitting-room, TV-room, games-room, dining-room, garden
CREDIT CARDS not accepted **CHILDREN** welcome **DISABLED** access difficult
PETS accepted in bedrooms by arrangement **CLOSED** Nov-Mar
PROPRIETORS Richard and Eleanor Quinlan

THE NORTH-WEST

NEWLANDS, CUMBRIA

SWINSIDE LODGE
~ COUNTRY HOTEL ~

Grange Road, Newlands, Keswick, Cumbria CA12 5UE
TEL & FAX (01768) 772948

THIS ATTRACTIVE VICTORIAN Lakeland house occupies a picture-postcard setting by Derwent Water, far removed from the fleshpots of Keswick. There's no wine to be had and for dinner you eat what you're given (until pudding, anyway). So why do people queue up in droves to stay here? Visit it once and the answer becomes crystal clear: if you want wine, then take your own (as Graham Taylor does not even charge corkage, it will certainly be the best value you could find anywhere), and the excellent four-course dinners, with a choice of freshly-baked breads, are exactly what you'd cook for yourself if you had the imagination to think them up, knew how and had the time to do it. As for the hotel itself, it is decorated with flair (*not* overdone) and you are trusted with good carpets and even better furniture. Everything that should be clean is clean, and everything else has been polished. The comfortable bedrooms are no different. The hotel's prime assets, though, are outside. Lying at the foot of Cat Bells as it does, there are walks of every description through genuinely unspoiled territory – and if you haven't the energy, you can always sit and look at it. All in all a relaxed, friendly, keenly priced (no-smoking) hotel.

NEARBY Derwent Water; Bassenthwaite Lake.
LOCATION 3 miles (5 km) SW of Keswick, 2 miles (3 km) S of A66; with garden and parking for 10 cars
MEALS breakfast, dinner; no licence
PRICE ££
ROOMS 7; 5 double, 2 twin, 6 with bath, 1 with shower; all have TV, hairdrier
FACILITIES 2 sitting-rooms, dining-room, garden
CREDIT CARDS AE, MC, V
CHILDREN accepted over 10
DISABLED not suitable
PETS not accepted **CLOSED** Dec, Jan
PROPRIETOR Graham Taylor

THE NORTH-WEST

SEATOLLER, CUMBRIA

SEATOLLER HOUSE
~ COUNTRY GUEST-HOUSE ~

Seatoller, Borrowdale, Keswick, Cumbria CA12 5XN
TEL & **FAX** (01768) 777218
E-MAIL seatollerhouse@bt.connect.com

IT SHOULD BE SAID at the outset that a stay at Seatoller House is something quite different from the run-of-the-mill hotel experience. You eat communally at set times, and to get the best out of the place you should take part in the social life of the house. If you do, the 'country house party' effect, much vaunted elsewhere, really does come about.

Seatoller House is over 300 years old and has been run as a guest-house for more than 100 years; the first entry in the visitors' book reads 23 April 1886. The long, low house, built in traditional Lakeland style and looking like a row of cottages, is in the tiny village of Seatoller, at the head of Borrowdale and the foot of Honister Pass. Bedrooms are simple and comfortable, and all now have their own bathrooms (although some are physically separate from the bedrooms). The dining-room is in a country-kitchen style, with a delightfully informal atmosphere – one that spills over into the two sections of the low-ceilinged sitting-room. Food is excellent; and if you are thirsty, just wander to the fridge, take what you like and sign for it in the book provided.

Several times a year the house is taken over by members of the Lakes Hunt, who enjoy running up and down the surrounding fells in pursuit not of foxes (the traditional quarry), but of one another. A change of management a couple of years ago; so reports please.

~

NEARBY Derwent Water; Buttermere; Keswick.
LOCATION 8 miles (13 km) S of Keswick on B5289; parking for 12 cars
MEALS breakfast, packed lunch, dinner (not Tue)
PRICE £
ROOMS 9; 5 double, 4 family, all with bath
FACILITIES sitting-room, library, dining-room, tea-room, garden
CREDIT CARDS MC, V **CHILDREN** by arrangement
DISABLED 2 ground-floor bedrooms **PETS** welcome in bedrooms
CLOSED Dec to Feb **PROPRIETORS** Morven Sneddon and Jay Anson

THE NORTH-WEST

WASDALE HEAD, CUMBRIA

WASDALE HEAD

~ COUNTRY INN ~

Wasdale Head, Gosforth, Cumbria CA20 1EX
TEL (01946) 726229 **FAX** (01946) 726334 **E-MAIL** wasdaleheadinn@msn.com
WEBSITE www.wasdale.com

THE WASDALE HEAD is in a site unrivalled even in the consistently spectacular Lake District. It stands on the flat valley bottom between three major peaks – Pillar, Great Gable and Scafell Pike (England's highest) – and only a little way above Wastwater, England's deepest and perhaps most dramatic lake.

Over the last decade and a half, the old inn has been carefully and thoughtfully modernized, adding facilities but retaining the characteristics of a traditional mountain inn. The main sitting-room of the hotel is comfortable and welcoming, with plenty of personal touches. The pine-panelled bedrooms are not notably spacious but they are adequate, with fixtures and fittings all in good condition. There are also six self-catering apartments in a converted barn, and three hotel apartments. The dining-room is heavily panelled, and decorated with willow-pattern china and a pewter jug collection. Children under eight are not allowed in here after 8 pm. Food is solid English fare, served by young, friendly staff. There are two bars. The one for residents has some magnificent wooden furniture, while tasty bar meals are served in the congenial surroundings of the public bar, much frequented by walkers and climbers.

~

NEARBY Hardknott Castle Roman Fort; Ravenglass and Eskdale Railway; Wastwater; Scafell.
LOCATION 9 miles (14.5 km) NE of Gosforth at head of Wasdale; with ample car parking
MEALS breakfast, bar and packed lunches, dinner
PRICE ££ **ROOMS** 13; 7 double and twin, 3 single, 3 suites, 11 with bath, 2 with shower; all rooms have phone; also 6 self-catering apartments and 3 hotel apartments **FACILITIES** sitting-room, dining-room, 2 bars, garden
CREDIT CARDS AE, MC, V **CHILDREN** welcome
DISABLED access possible to ground floor only **PETS** not accepted in public areas
CLOSED never **MANAGER** Howard Christie

THE NORTH-WEST

WATERMILLOCK, CUMBRIA

OLD CHURCH

~ COUNTRY HOTEL ~

Watermillock, Penrith, Cumbria CA11 0JN
TEL (01768) 486204 **FAX** (01768) 486368 **E-MAIL** info@oldchurch.co.uk
WEBSITE www.oldchurch.co.uk

THERE ARE MANY HOTELS with spectacular settings in the Lakes, but for our money there are few to match that of this whitewashed 18thC house on the very shore of Ullswater.

Since their arrival in the late 1970s, Kevin and Maureen Whitemore have developed the hotel carefully and stylishly. The three sitting-rooms, one of which is formed by the entrance hall, are all very well furnished with clever touches in their decorations that give some hint of Maureen's interior design training. They also have the natural advantage of excellent views across the lake. The bedrooms are all different in decoration, but they too show a confident and a harmonious use of colour. Most have lake views and are pleasantly free of modern gadgetry.

Ex-accountant Kevin does more than keep the books in order: his daily-changing dinners are both enterprising and expertly prepared, with a reasonable choice at each course.

"Everything one expects of a charming small hotel," says one completely satisfied visitor, "with not a single jarring note."

NEARBY Dalemain; Penrith Castle; Brougham Castle; Ullswater.
LOCATION 5.5 miles (9 km) S of Penrith on A592; on lakeshore with ample car parking
MEALS breakfast, dinner
PRICE ££
ROOMS 10 double with bath; all rooms have phone, TV, hairdrier
FACILITIES 2 sitting-rooms, dining-room, bar, garden; boat, fishing
CREDIT CARDS AE, MC, V
CHILDREN welcome
DISABLED access difficult
PETS not accepted
CLOSED Nov-Mar; restaurant Sun eve
PROPRIETORS Kevin and Maureen Whitemore

THE NORTH-WEST

WHITEWELL, LANCASHIRE

THE INN AT WHITEWELL
~ COUNTRY INN ~

Whitewell, Forest of Bowland, near Clitheroe, Lancashire BB7 3AT
TEL (01200) 448222 **FAX** (01200) 448298

PAST AND PRESENT COME TOGETHER with great effect at this welcoming inn with a glorious situation, on a riverbank plumb in the middle of the Forest of Bowland. In the 14th century, it was a small manor house where the Keeper of the Forest lived. Today, some of the original architecture survives and rooms are furnished with antiques, but modern comfort is the order of the day, with, for example, videos and hi-tech stereo systems in all the bedrooms. Most of these are spacious and attractive with warm lighting and prints clustered on the walls; many contain an extra sofa bed; a couple have four-posters. To keep romance alive, you can book one of the rooms with a fireplace and snuggle up to a cosy peat fire while your favourite CD plays on the Bang and Olufsen.

Food is an important consideration here. English dishes feature predominately on the menu – seasonal roast game or grilled fish, followed by wicked home-made puddings and a selection of farmhouse cheeses. Alternatively, bar meals are on offer at lunchtime and in the evening. A recent visitor reports that standards in the kitchen have dropped while prices have soared. More reports please.

~

NEARBY Browsholme Hall; Clitheroe Castle; Blackpool.
LOCATION 6 miles (9.5 km) NW of Clitheroe; with ample car parking
MEALS breakfast, picnic lunch on request, dinner, bar meals
PRICE ££
ROOMS 15; 14 double and twin, 1 suite, all with bath; all rooms have phone, TV, CD; some have minibar, hairdrier, peat fire
FACILITIES dining-rooms, bar, garden; fishing
CREDIT CARDS AE, D, MC, V
CHILDREN welcome
DISABLED 2 ground-floor bedrooms
PETS welcome **CLOSED** Feb
PROPRIETOR Richard Bowman

The North-West

Windermere, Cumbria

Gilpin Lodge
~ Country House Hotel ~

Crook Road, near Windermere, Cumbria LA23 3NE
Tel (01539) 488818 **Fax** (01539) 488058 **E-mail** hotel@gilpin-lodge.co.uk
Website www.gilpin-lodge.co.uk

JUST OCCASIONALLY, whether by luck or judgement, you can arrive some-where that tells you to congratulate yourself on your choice of hotel before you even step in through the door: Gilpin Lodge is one of these happy places. John Cunliffe's grandmother lived in this Edwardian house for 40 years, and when he and his wife Christine came back 25 years later, it had become a rather ordinary B&B. Now, with manicured grounds and gleaming paint, quite substantially and wholly sympathetically enlarged, and set on a peaceful hillside with moor beyond the boundary, you are to some extent prepared for the warm welcome and deep-pile comfort wait-ing for you inside. This is a highly professional and well-staffed operation, yet still driven by the enthusiasm of owners whose unmistakeable priority is the happiness of their guests.

If your tastes run to good pictures, fine furniture and immaculate ser-vice you will be happy; if they include excellent and imaginatively present-ed food with more than the occasional touch of outright luxury (when did you last have a strawberry sorbet with pink champagne for breakfast?) you will be happier still; and if you want a large, thoughtfully decorated room, probably with its own sitting area, and a bathroom to talk about when you get home, then you're in luck. If you have the energy, there is free access to the nearby country club.

~

Nearby Windermere Steamboat Museum; Holker Hall; Sizergh Castle; Kendal; Grasmere.
Location on B5284 Kendal to Bowness road, 2 miles (3 km) SE of Windermere; with ample car parking
Meals breakfast, lunch, dinner
Price £££ **Rooms** 14 double and twin with bath; all rooms have phone, TV, minibar, hairdrier **Facilities** 2 sitting-rooms, 3 dining-rooms, garden
Credit cards AE, DC, MC, V **Children** accepted over 7 **Disabled** access possible to ground-floor rooms **Pets** not accepted **Closed** never
Proprietors John and Christine Cunliffe

THE NORTH-WEST

WINDERMERE, CUMBRIA

HOLBECK GHYLL

COUNTRY HOUSE HOTEL

Holbeck Lane, Windermere, Cumbria LA23 1LU
TEL (01539) 432375 FAX (01539) 434743
E-MAIL accommodation@holbeck-ghyll.co.uk WEBSITE www.holbeck-ghyll.com

AN AWARD-WINNING HOTEL in a classic Victorian Lakeland house, ivy-clad with steep slate roofs and mullioned windows – plus oak panelling and Art Nouveau stained glass. Our latest reporter had a 'friendly welcome' and was impressed by its superb set-back position providing both privacy from the bustle of Windermere and grand lake views from the immaculate gardens; also indeed by the two comfortable sitting-rooms, both home-like and beautifully furnished with plenty of contrasting harmonious fabrics.

The Nicholsons, professional hoteliers both, took over in 1988 and have refurbished to very high standards in a traditional, slightly formal style – though proprietors and staff alike are friendly and relaxed. Bedrooms and bathrooms are beautifully and individually decorated, very spacious, some with their own sitting-room. At the top of the house is a 'very special' four-poster room. In the Lodge nearby are six further rooms (four are self-catering), with breathtaking views. The food is a clear attraction: pre-dinner canapés are served while you select from the inventive daily- changing menu designed by chef Stephen Smith, recent winner of a Michelin star. No smoking in the dining-rooms. The grounds are being developed, and there is now a jogging trail, from which you can spot deer and red squirrels, as well as a tennis court, croquet and putting.

NEARBY Lake Windermere.
LOCATION 3 miles (5 km) N of Windermere, E of A591; with ample car parking
MEALS breakfast, light lunch, dinner
PRICE ££££
ROOMS 13 double and twin, 1 family room, all with bath; all have phone, TV, hairdrier
FACILITIES 2 sitting-rooms, 2 dining-rooms, garden; health spa, tennis, croquet, putting CREDIT CARDS AE, DC, MC, V CHILDREN welcome
DISABLED access difficult PETS accepted in bedrooms only CLOSED never
PROPRIETORS David and Patricia Nicholson

THE NORTH-WEST

WINDERMERE, CUMBRIA

STORRS HALL

~ COUNTRY HOUSE HOTEL ~

Windermere, Cumbria LA23 3LG
TEL (01539) 447111 **FAX** (01539) 447555 **E-MAIL** reception@storrshall.co.uk
WEBSITE www.storrshall.co.uk

A CHANGE OF OWNERSHIP at Storrs Hall has given a new and opulent lease of life to a hotel that had become sadly dilapidated. In 1997 Blackpool antiques dealer, Richard Livstock, and Northern businessman, Les Hindle, bought this Georgian pile, built to look like an Italian lakeside villa and spectacularly positioned on a promontory jutting out into Lake Windermere. They have given the place a no-expense-spared facelift, filling the beautifully proportioned rooms with superb pieces of antique furniture, statues, paintings, rare books, and Richard Livstock's own collection of model ships. The ships are particularly apposite since it was a maritime fortune that financed the building of the house. As well as the handsome drawing-room with its 1910 Steinway grand, guests can retreat to the library or writing-room or, if feeling more sociable, to the cheerful bar decorated with hunting and fishing trophies. On chilly days, log fires blaze in the reception-rooms.

A recent report praises 'the large bedrooms', most of which have uninterrupted views of the glittering lake, and contains plaudits for the food: 'The cooking is sophisticated and assured, the service delightful – go before word gets round.'

~

NEARBY Windermere Steamboat Museum; Lake Windermere.
LOCATION 2 miles (3 km) S of Bowness off A592; with ample car parking
MEALS breakfast, lunch, dinner
PRICE ££££
ROOMS 18; 14 double and twin, 4 suites, all with bath; all rooms have phone, TV, hairdrier
FACILITIES sitting-rooms, dining-rooms, bar, garden; fishing
CREDIT CARDS AE, MC, V
CHILDREN accepted over 12 **DISABLED** no special facilities
PETS accepted in bedrooms by arrangement **CLOSED** late Dec to early Feb
MANAGER Nigel Lawrence

THE NORTH-WEST

WITHERSLACK, CUMBRIA

OLD VICARAGE
~ COUNTRY HOTEL ~

Church Road, Witherslack, near Grange-over-Sands, Cumbria LA11 6RS
TEL (01539) 552381 **FAX** (01539) 552373 **E-MAIL** hotel@old-vic.demon.co.uk
WEBSITE www.oldvicarage.com

REVISITING A COUPLE OF YEARS AGO, our happy impressions of the Old Vicarage were reconfirmed. The key to the charm is its peace and seclusion, with large, mainly wooded grounds, at the edge of a tiny, half-asleep Lakes village – yet some of the area's major tourist sights and thoroughfares are only minutes away by car. There are views out to some low fells.

The building is no more, nor less, than a Georgian vicarage: some of the reception rooms are smallish, but it's all pleasantly but unexceptionally furnished, with some interesting touches here and there, to create a relaxing atmosphere. The bedrooms are not swanky, but comfortable, and usually prettily done; the priciest, especially in the annexe, are spacious and well equipped with CD players and verandas. And here's more charm: the prices are certainly fair, if not good value.

The owners are relaxed and welcoming. The food is impressive, with the recent introduction of an *à la carte* menu, prepared on the premises using fresh ingredients: which is more than can be said of some reputable Lakes hotels, where dinner is delivered to the back door by caterer's van. The wine list is unusually well chosen and explained.

~

NEARBY Levens Hall and Topiary Garden; Sizergh Castle; Holker Hall.
LOCATION 5 miles (8 km) NE of Grange off A590; with ample car parking
MEALS breakfast, dinner, Sun lunch
PRICE £££
ROOMS 14 double and twin, 10 with bath, 4 with shower; all rooms have phone, TV, hairdrier
FACILITIES 2 sitting-rooms, breakfast-room, dining-room, garden; tennis court
CREDIT CARDS MC, V
CHILDREN welcome **DISABLED** not suitable
PETS accepted by arrangement **CLOSED** never
PROPRIETORS Jill and Roger Burrington-Brown, Irene and Stanley Reeve

THE NORTH-EAST

ARNCLIFFE, NORTH YORKSHIRE

AMERDALE HOUSE
~ COUNTRY HOTEL ~

Arncliffe, Littondale, Skipton, North Yorkshire BD23 5QE
TEL & FAX (01756) 770250

SINCE THEY TOOK IT OVER in 1987, the Crappers (ex-restaurateurs) have gradually transformed this hotel and the bedrooms have all been refurbished over the last few years. The setting is one of the most seductive in all the Dales: on the fringe of a pretty village in a lonely valley, wide meadows in front, high hills behind.

We visited a few years ago and were smitten with the location ('total peace and serenity'); the comfortable and beautifully decorated bedrooms and bathrooms – the top-floor four-poster bedroom is particularly charming and romantic with stunning views; and the exceptional welcome given by Nigel Crapper, who is also the chef. A more recent inspector endorsed this praise. Its food, in the modern English style, is, to quote a visitor, 'unbelievably good'. Dishes singled out by our inspector include local lamb with minted couscous and a port and redcurrant *jus*; pan-roast fillet of sea bass with baked cherry tomatoes and a warm pesto dressing; avocado pear salad with a lightly curried mayonnaise; and a terrine of oranges in Campari and orange jelly. Nigel's imaginative menus change frequently and the food often gets ecstatic press reviews. Amerdale House is usefully situated for a number of Dales sights – and is well priced, too.

~

NEARBY Wharfedale; Grassington; Pennine Way.
LOCATION in a rural setting, 7 miles (10 km) NW of Grassington, 3 miles (5 km) off B6160; with ample car parking
MEALS breakfast, dinner
PRICE ££
ROOMS 11; 8 double with bath, 3 twin with shower; all rooms have phone, TV, fax/modem point, hairdrier
FACILITIES sitting-rooms, bar, dining-room, garden **CREDIT CARDS** MC, V
CHILDREN welcome **DISABLED** 1 ground-floor room **PETS** not accepted
CLOSED Nov to mid-Mar
PROPRIETORS Nigel and Paula Crapper

THE NORTH-EAST

BOLTON ABBEY, NORTH YORKSHIRE

DEVONSHIRE ARMS

~ COUNTRY HOUSE HOTEL ~

Bolton Abbey, Skipton, North Yorkshire BD23 6AJ
TEL (01756) 710441 **FAX** (01756) 710564
E-MAIL dev.arms@legend.co.uk

A S YOUR HELICOPTER WHIRLS towards its helipad, you can see that the moorland of the Dales proper comes to within a mile or so of the 17thC Devonshire Arms. Follow the path down the bank of the Wharfe, which gives the valley its name, for the half mile from Bolton Abbey village to the stone bridge and you're there. Owned by the Duke and Duchess of Devonshire, the hotel is doubly graced since it contains antiques and paintings from Chatsworth, the family seat; the Duchess has masterminded their placement and the design of the interior. This is a hotel in two parts, old and new. The elegant old wears its years well and has happily grown out of exact right angles. The new extension, which has brought with it an indoor swimming-pool, gym and beauty salon, still has its sharp corners, but is settling in well. The dining alternatives cover a similar spectrum. On the one hand is the quiet comfort of the classical Burlington Restaurant, and on the other a buzzy blue and yellow brasserie with dishes to suit most moods and a snappy wine list to go with them. The bedrooms also come in old and new varieties: the older win on character and the newer score better with their views.

~

NEARBY Castle Howard; Skipton Castle; Brontë Parsonage; Harewood House.
LOCATION on B6160 just N of junction with A59; in grounds with ample car parking
MEALS breakfast, lunch, dinner
PRICE £££-££££
ROOMS 41; 38 double and twin, 1 family, 2 suites, all with bath; all rooms have phone, TV, hairdrier; some have fax, video
FACILITIES 3 sitting-rooms, conservatory, 2 dining-rooms, 2 bars, gym, sauna, indoor swimming-pool, garden; tennis, croquet, putting, helipad, fishing
CREDIT CARDS AE, DC, MC, V
CHILDREN accepted **DISABLED** 1 specially adapted room
PETS accepted **CLOSED** never
MANAGER Jeremy Rata

THE NORTH-EAST

CROOKHAM, NORTHUMBERLAND

THE COACH HOUSE

~ COUNTRY GUEST-HOUSE ~

Crookham, Cornhill-on-Tweed, Northumberland TD12 4TD
TEL (01890) 820293 **FAX** (01890) 820284
WEBSITE www.secretkingdom.com/coach/house.htm

LYNNE ANDERSON IS a charming hostess, whose energy and enthusiasm have not dimmed in more than 20 years of looking after guests in this group of converted 17thC farm buildings. Some bedrooms are in outbuildings, grouped around a sunny courtyard, while others are in a separate stone house. They are generally large, furnished simply but attractively, with crisp white linen on the beds and cheered by vases of fresh flowers, an attention to detail that is typical of Lynne, whose devoted guests often return year after year.

There's an honesty bar in the pleasant beamed sitting-room, where guests are served afternoon tea, with delicious home-baked cakes, and congregate for pre-dinner drinks. Great Gothic windows look out to a damson orchard, where sheep can often be spotted grazing under the trees – a perfect rural scene. The four-course dinners are wholesome affairs employing much local produce – border beef and lamb, Tweed salmon and vegetables from the garden. You may feel you should restrain yourself at breakfast: there's a choice of fresh fruit, home-made cereals and porridge, bacon and eggs, devilled kidneys and kedgeree.

NEARBY Northumberland National Park; Holy Island.
LOCATION 4 miles (6.5 km) E of Cornhill-on-Tweed on A697; with ample car parking
MEALS breakfast, dinner
PRICE ££
ROOMS 9; 7 double and twin, 2 single, 7 with bath; all rooms have phone, TV; 7 have fridge
FACILITIES 2 sitting-rooms, dining-room, terrace, garden
CREDIT CARDS MC, V **CHILDREN** welcome
DISABLED 3 specially adapted rooms
PETS accepted
CLOSED Nov to Easter
PROPRIETOR Lynne Anderson

THE NORTH-EAST

GAINFORD, COUNTY DURHAM

HEADLAM HALL
~ MANOR HOUSE HOTEL ~

Gainford, Darlington, County Durham DL2 3HA
TEL (01325) 730238 **FAX** (01325) 730790 **E-MAIL** admin@headlamhall.co.uk
WEBSITE www.headlamhall.co.uk

'EXTRAORDINARY HOUSE, fine grounds, reasonable rates,' was the message from one of our scouts about this mansion in a peaceful hamlet just north of the Tees. And so it is: a grand Jacobean house on three floors, its mellow stone all but hidden by creepers, with substantial Georgian additions – standing in four acres of beautiful formal gardens, with mellow stone walls, massive hedges and a canalized stream. As for the rates – although they have crept up (no doubt partly because of all the leisure facilities), they are still reasonable. But it is equally true that Headlam is not among the best-furnished country hotels in the land – and therein lies part of its appeal, for us at least. Although there are abundant antiques alongside the reproductions (the Robinsons furnished the place from scratch after they took it over in the late 1970s) there is a comfortable ordinariness about the place which is refreshing, and though larger than most of the hotels featured in this guide, it is very friendly. What impressed our most recent inspector was that, despite the hotel's emphasis on modern facilities, the staff were among the most courteous and helpful that he'd come across. He also reported that standards in the restaurant are improving.

NEARBY Barnard Castle; Yorkshire Dales.
LOCATION 7 miles (11 km) W of Darlington, off A67; with ample car parking
MEALS breakfast, lunch, dinner
PRICE ££
ROOMS 36 double with bath; all rooms have phone, TV, hairdrier; some have fax/modem point **FACILITIES** sitting-room, bar, dining-room, restaurant, snooker-room, indoor swimming-pool, sauna, gym, garden; croquet, tennis, fishing
CREDIT CARDS AE, DC, MC, V **CHILDREN** welcome **DISABLED** 3 ground-floor bedrooms
PETS welcome in public rooms **CLOSED** Christmas Eve, Christmas Day
PROPRIETOR John Robinson

THE NORTH-EAST

GOLCAR, WEST YORKSHIRE

WEAVERS SHED
~ RESTAURANT-WITH-ROOMS ~

Knowl Road, Golcar, Huddersfield, West Yorkshire HD7 4AN
TEL (01484) 654284 **FAX** (01484) 650980 **E-MAIL** info@weavers-shed.demon.co.uk
WEBSITE www.weavers-shed.demon.co.uk

AT FIRST ACQUAINTANCE GOLCAR would probably be dropped from just about anybody's list of places of outstanding natural beauty. But it has a fine secret – and the secret is the Weavers Shed. High on a hill, away from Huddersfield, in what started life in the 18th century as a cloth finishing mill and still has a fine flagged floor, is an excellent restaurant – and, what's more, you can sleep very comfortably indeed where you have just eaten. Owner (and chef) Stephen Jackson and his collaborators in the kitchen are also keen market gardeners and have a plot which supplies many of their needs for fresh herbs, fruit and vegetables. Other elements of the menu are equally carefully chosen, with pork, for example, from traditional breeds and fish only featuring if the market is offering something worthwhile on the day. The style is modern British which, because of its simplicity, offers no hiding place for second-rate ingredients. Not surprisingly, the same sort of care has been taken with the wine list.

The bedrooms are in the house next door. Built originally for the owner of the mill, it is a substantial building with light airy rooms, filled with a pleasing mixture of ancient and modern furniture and good-quality but unfussy fabrics. You won't forget breakfast.

~

NEARBY Peak District National Park; Pennine Way.
LOCATION 3 miles (5 km) W of Huddersfield on A62 and B6111; with ample car parking
MEALS breakfast, lunch, dinner
PRICE ££
ROOMS 5 double and twin with bath; all rooms have phone, TV, fax/modem point, hairdrier
FACILITIES 2 restaurants, bar, garden **CREDIT CARDS** AE, DC, MC, V **CHILDREN** accepted
DISABLED access possible **PETS** not accepted **CLOSED** Christmas Day, Boxing Day, New Year's Eve, New Year's Day; restaurant Sun, Mon, Sat lunch
PROPRIETORS Stephen and Tracy Jackson

THE NORTH-EAST

ASHFIELD HOUSE

~ COUNTRY GUEST-HOUSE ~

Summers Fold, Grassington, near Skipton, North Yorkshire BD23 5AE
TEL & FAX (01756) 752584 **E-MAIL** info@ashfieldhouse.co.uk
WEBSITE www.ashfieldhouse.co.uk

EVEN IN LATE SEASON, Wharfedale in general, and Grassington in particular, still exercise a magnetic attraction for visitors. Linda and Keith Harrison's small private stone and slate hotel is a peaceful sanctuary at the end of its own yard, just off the picture-postcard main square. What's more, and unlike anywhere else in Grassington, you can park your car there. When you arrive, a log fire will be burning if there's any excuse at all, and tea will be on the table. Oak and pine furniture, bare beams and stone walls are combined with fresh flowers and neat new furnishings to make this very much a home from home. An excellent dinner is served in the pretty dining-room at seven each evening except Saturday, with a choice of starter and pudding. Wines are carefully chosen and good value. The bedrooms are modestly sized and most have their own shower-rooms (one has its own bathroom just outside the door).

Beyond the house, insulated from the bustle of the town, is a quiet walled garden with a table and chairs where you can simply sit and enjoy the sunshine if the prospect of a walk along the river seems too testing. Breakfasts are hearty and varied. This is a non-smoking hotel.

~

NEARBY Skipton Castle; Gordale Scar; Janet's Foss; Ripon.
LOCATION in Grassington, just NW of main square; with ample car parking
MEALS breakfast, dinner
PRICE ££
ROOMS 7 double and twin with bath or shower; all rooms have TV, hairdrier
FACILITIES 2 sitting-rooms, 1 with bar, dining-room, garden
CREDIT CARDS MC, V
CHILDREN welcome over 5
DISABLED not suitable
PETS not accepted
CLOSED Jan to mid-Feb
PROPRIETORS Keith and Linda Harrison

THE NORTH-EAST

HAWES, NORTH YORKSHIRE

SIMONSTONE HALL

~ COUNTRY HOUSE HOTEL ~

Hawes, North Yorkshire DL8 3LY
TEL (01969) 667255 **FAX** (01969) 667741
E-MAIL simonstonehall@demon.co.uk

THERE WERE MAJOR CHANGES at Simonstone Hall a few years ago following a change of ownership. Outside, it is the same dignified, slightly forbidding, large Dales country house; but as you enter you will probably hear the lively chatter coming from the extensive new bar area which is intended to recreate the hotel as a place that will attract local non-residents as well as overnight guests. To have this popular country pub within an essentially dignified old country hotel is something of a novelty – and not unpleasant. The pub is handsomely done out; bar meals and the range of wines by the glass are imaginative; waiters in black tie and apron, French bistro-style, bustle about. It gives the place an injection of life, but if you've come here for peace, or as a romantic twosome, just cross the hall and slump in the stylish drawing-room. Beyond is the panelled Game Tavern, serving Sunday lunch and an excellent three-course dinner for only £22.50.

There are three different styles of bedroom: small, standard and superior – the latter are handsomely done out in country house style, some with sleigh beds, others with four-posters. Prices have risen in all three categories so they're not the bargains they were. Since our last visit the management has changed again. We'd welcome further reports.

~

NEARBY Pennine Way; Wharfedale; Ribblesdale.
LOCATION 1.5 miles (2.5 km) N of Hawes on Muker road; with ample car parking
MEALS breakfast, bar lunch, Sun lunch, dinner
PRICE £££
ROOMS 18 double and twin with bath and shower; all rooms have phone, TV
FACILITIES bar, 2 sitting-rooms, garden-room, garden **CREDIT CARDS** AE, DC, MC, V
CHILDREN welcome
DISABLED access possible to ground floor only
PETS welcome **CLOSED** never
MANAGER Mrs Jill Peterson

THE NORTH-EAST

HAWNBY, NORTH YORKSHIRE

THE HAWNBY HOTEL

⁓ COUNTRY HOTEL ⁓

Hawnby, near Helmsley, York, North Yorkshire Y06 5QS
TEL (01439) 798202 **FAX** (01439) 798344

AFTER A SPECTACULAR DRIVE through rolling valleys and the unspoiled stone village of Hawnby, this hotel may come as something of a let-down. It is not until you are ushered into the elegant sitting-room that you realize how deceptive first appearances can be.

The 'village pub' façade hides an exquisite small hotel which was decorated with obvious flair by the Countess of Mexborough. The hotel used to be part of the 13,000-acre Mexborough Estate and Lady Mexborough gave it much personal attention, refurbishing the six bedrooms which are named after colour schemes (Cowslip, Coral, Jade and so on), choosing Laura Ashley wallpaper and fabrics throughout the cosy rooms and immaculate bathrooms.

The hotel does suffer slightly from a lack of space. The sitting-room is at one end of the dining-room, and although it does not feel cramped and can be curtained off at guests' request, it might be noisy and crowded at peak times. The hotel caters for shooting parties, and is popular with walkers. Reports continue to heap praise on The Hawnby: 'Having visited the hotel on three occasions, my wife and I have found the hotel's high standards … remain consistent.' 'This charming country hotel … is an ideal base for touring North Yorkshire'; a 'gem' with 'fabulous views' 'home cooking' and 'friendly service'. Dave and Kathryn Young are the new owners.

⁓

NEARBY Rievaulx Abbey; Jervaulx Abbey; North Yorkshire Moors National Park.
LOCATION at top of hill in village 7 miles (11 km) NE of Helmsley; with car parking
MEALS breakfast, dinner, bar snacks
PRICE £ **ROOMS** 6 double and twin with bath; 2-bedroom self-catering cottage for 4 available; all rooms have phone, TV, hairdrier
FACILITIES sitting-room/dining-room, bar **CREDIT CARDS** MC, V
CHILDREN accepted **DISABLED** access difficult **PETS** not accepted **CLOSED** Feb
PROPRIETORS Dave and Kathryn Young

THE NORTH-EAST

HUNMANBY, NORTH YORKSHIRE

WRANGHAM HOUSE
~ COUNTRY HOTEL ~

Stonegate, Hunmanby, North Yorkshire YO14 0NS
TEL (01723) 891333 **FAX** (01723) 892973 **E-MAIL** wrangham@mywebpage.net
WEBSITE: www.mywebpage.net/wrangham

WRANGHAM HOUSE is a well-preserved and elegant Georgian former vicarage set in an acre of wooded garden. The main part of the house was built in the second half of the 18th century. The eponymous Francis Wrangham added a wing, now housing the dining-room, in 1803. Mervyn Poulter and his wife Margaret, both recently returned from the British Virgin Islands, offer a warm reception and comfortable accommodation. Downstairs there is a light panelled sitting-room with a handsome tiled fireplace, a snug and well-stocked bar and a fair-sized dining-room looking out over the garden. Dinners here are a blend of contemporary and bourgeois (the latter signifying that the use of cream and the art of sauce-making is, thankfully, alive and well). Lunch is only served on Sundays, but Sunday lunch *it* is with roast sirloin and all the trimmings.

The bedrooms are individually furnished and decorated. Four are in the Coach House and one of these (on the ground floor) is equipped for guests with disabilities. Parking is a little scarce in Hunmanby but Wrangham House has plenty of its own. Almost uniquely, Hunmanby has a railway station that survived the sweeping cuts in the 1960s – if you want to let the train take the strain you can arrange to be picked up at the station.

~

NEARBY Scarborough Castle; North Yorkshire Moors National Park.
LOCATION behind church in village, 1 mile (1.5 km) SW of Filey; with ample car parking
MEALS breakfast, dinner; Sun lunch
PRICE ££ ROOMS 12; 11 double and twin, 1 single, 7 with bath, 5 with shower; all have phone, TV, hairdrier
FACILITIES sitting-room, dining-room, bar, garden **CREDIT CARDS** AE, MC, V
CHILDREN accepted over 12
DISABLED 1 specially adapted room
PETS by arrangement **CLOSED** never
PROPRIETORS Mervyn and Margaret Poulter, and Diane Norvick

THE NORTH-EAST

LASTINGHAM, NORTH YORKSHIRE

LASTINGHAM GRANGE

~ COUNTRY HOUSE HOTEL ~

Lastingham, North Yorkshire Y06 6TH
TEL (01751) 417345/417402 **FAX** (01751) 417358
E-MAIL reservations@lastinghamgrange.com **WEBSITE** www.lastinghamgrange.com

LASTINGHAM GRANGE – a wistaria-clad former farmhouse – nestles peacefully in a delightful village on the edge of the North Yorkshire Moors National Park. Unlike many country house hotels, it manages to combine a certain sophistication – smartly decorated public rooms, friendly unobtrusive service, elegantly laid gardens – with a large dash of informality, which puts you immediately at ease. From the moment you enter, you feel as if you are staying with friends. Recently, we had this reaction from an inspector: 'Family feeling; very child-friendly; charming rooms; however, dining-room a little dour.'

The main attraction is the garden. You can enjoy it from a distance – from the windows of the large L-shaped sitting-room (complete with carefully grouped sofas, antiques and a grand piano) – or, like most guests, by exploring. There is a beautifully laid rose garden, enticing bordered lawns and an extensive adventure playground for children.

In comparison, bedrooms are more ordinary. They are perfectly comfortable, with well-equipped bathrooms, but some people may find the decoration unsophisticated in places. Jane cooks straightforward English meals.

~

NEARBY North Yorkshire Moors National Park; Scarborough; Rievaulx Abbey.
LOCATION at top of village, 6 miles (9.5 km) NW of Pickering; with ample car parking
MEALS breakfast, lunch on request, dinner
PRICE £££
ROOMS 12; 10 double, 2 single, all with bath; all rooms have phone, TV, hairdrier
FACILITIES sitting-room, dining-room, terrace, garden
CREDIT CARDS not accepted **CHILDREN** welcome
DISABLED access difficult **PETS** accepted in bedrooms by arrangement
CLOSED Dec to mid-Mar
PROPRIETORS Dennis and Jane Wood

THE NORTH-EAST

LEEDS

42 THE CALLS
~ TOWN HOTEL ~

42 The Calls, Leeds, West Yorkshire LS2 7EW
TEL (0113) 244 0099 **FAX** (0113) 234 4100 **E-MAIL** hotel@42thecalls.co.uk
WEBSITE www.42thecalls.co.uk

EXPECT THE UNEXPECTED at 42 The Calls. Through a small glass-porched entrance and revolving doors, the sight of massive beams, girders, ducts and grain chutes are, one supposes, in keeping for an old corn-mill-turned-hotel. The real surprises are the airy split-level foyer with light wooden floors and mirrored doors, the ultra-modern bar with a stylish display of decanters, a cosy sitting area and a quirky collection of modern chairs and amusing glass and wood tables. Jonathan Wix, who converted the mill in 1992, relishes this mix of old and new.

In the bedrooms, fabrics and furniture are traditional; some feature cleverly designed desk lamps that are black ceramic shelves in the shape of the number 42. A two-way serving hatch means that breakfast can be placed straight into the room, or shoes and laundry collected, without disturbance. Every comfort has been considered – a coffee machine, iron and ironing board, CD player and radio with a switchable extension to the bathroom; hot water bottles are available and some rooms overlooking the river have fishing rods. Suites are full of character, with vast sitting-rooms.

Formal frock coats belie the friendliness of the staff, and although somewhat larger than our usual choice of entry, its delightful idiosyncracy makes 42 The Calls one of *the* places to stay in Leeds.

~

NEARBY Corn Exchange; Tetley's Brewery; museums; galleries; West Yorkshire Playhouse.
LOCATION Exchange quarter, overlooking river Aire in central Leeds; with inexpensive valet parking
MEALS breakfast, snacks
PRICE £££ **ROOMS** 41; 31 double, 7 single, 3 suites, all with bath; all rooms have phone, TV, fax/modem point, CD player, minibar, hairdrier **FACILITIES** sitting-room, breakfast-room, bar, lift **CREDIT CARDS** AE, DC, MC, V **CHILDREN** welcome
DISABLED 1 specially adapted room **PETS** by arrangement
CLOSED Christmas **PROPRIETOR** Jonathan Wix

THE NORTH-EAST

NEWTON-LE-WILLOWS, NORTH YORKSHIRE

THE HALL

~ COUNTRY GUEST-HOUSE ~

Newton-le-Willows, Bedale, North Yorkshire DL8 1SW
TEL (01677) 450210 **FAX** (01677)450014

AS WELL AS BEING VERY BEAUTIFUL, Bedale is in the heart of horse country. The Middleham Moors, where the racehorses are ridden out each morning, are only a few minutes' drive away.

Some of the places in this guide are only welcoming because of their hosts; and some can make you feel welcome all by themselves: The Hall belongs firmly in the latter category and, when Oriella Featherstone adds her hospitality, the two make an irresistible combination. The stable block and paddock beside the two-acre garden are not for show either – visiting horses can be put up as well. The Georgian house is filled with antiques and oddments from other places and other times, but is very much for living in rather than just admiring: the drawing-room may be grand, but you also get the impression that you can put your feet up if you want. Tea, coffee and fruit cake are perpetually available in the kitchen as a virtuous alternative to the honesty bar. Dinner, if you ask for it, is home-cooked, traditional, and taken at the single table; breakfast is as generous as you could want. There are fresh flowers in the bedrooms which are large, light and well furnished and are not let down by their bathrooms.

Walkers will be pleased by what opens up for them right outside the front door; and there's a drying-room.

~

NEARBY Middleham; Jervaulx Abbey; Bolton Abbey; Thorp Perrow; Fountains Abbey; Newby Hall.
LOCATION 4 miles (6.5 km) W of Bedale; with ample car parking
MEALS breakfast, lunch, dinner
PRICE ££
ROOMS 5; 3 double, 1 twin, 1 suite, all with bath or shower
FACILITIES 2 sitting-rooms, breakfast-room, dining-room, garden
CREDIT CARDS not accepted
CHILDREN accepted **DISABLED** not suitable **PETS** accepted **CLOSED** never
PROPRIETOR Oriella Featherstone

THE NORTH-EAST

NUNNINGTON, NORTH YORKSHIRE

RYEDALE COUNTRY LODGE
~ RESTAURANT-WITH-ROOMS ~

Nunnington, near Helmsley, York, North Yorkshire YO6 25XR
TEL (01439) 748246 **FAX** (01439) 748346

NUNNINGTON IS IN GENTLER farming country than the high Dales, and Peter and Gerd Handley's small country hotel is a welcome sight. Not long here (but by no means new to the business or the area), the Handleys are developing a keen following for their food, and systematically uprating the quality of the bedrooms.

Once past the urns full of flowers and stone dogs that guard the front door, you find yourself in the sitting-room with its rich assortment of flowers and plants, comfortable sofas, restful blue-and-pink colouring and pleasing tapestries. There's a wonderful collection of furniture, comprising some highly individual pieces, and these are interspersed with curios and quirky confections assembled by Gerd.

The dining-room and conservatory look out over farmland – pleasant enough, but your main enjoyment will be the imaginative food, well cooked and well executed, and well presented by friendly staff. There's plenty of it, and a wine list to match. And it won't be spolt by the bill. Prices here are low enough to make you look twice. Excellent value.

~

NEARBY Nunnington Hall; Rievaulx Abbey; Castle Howard.
LOCATION 4 miles (6.5 km) SE of Helmsley off B1257, 1 mile (1.5 km) W of village; in open country with ample car parking
MEALS breakfast, dinner
PRICE ££
ROOMS 7; 5 double, 2 twin, all with bath; all rooms have phone, TV, hairdrier
FACILITIES sitting-room, conservatory/dining-room, garden; fishing
CREDIT CARDS MC, V
CHILDREN accepted by arrangement
DISABLED 1 ground-floor room
PETS accepted by arrangement
CLOSED never
PROPRIETORS Peter and Gerd Handley

THE NORTH-EAST

PATELEY BRIDGE, NORTH YORKSHIRE

SPORTSMAN'S ARMS

~ COUNTRY HOTEL ~

Wath-in-Nidderdale, Pateley Bridge, near Harrogate, North Yorkshire HG3 5PP
TEL (01423) 711306 **FAX** (01423) 712524

OUR LATEST INSPECTION confirms that the Sportsman's Arms is going from strength to strength. The long, rather rambling building dates from the 17th century, and the setting is as enchanting as the village name sounds; the River Nidd flows across the field in front; Gouthwaite reservoir, a birdwatchers' haunt, is just behind; glorious Dales country spreads all around.

Jane and Ray Carter have been running the Sportman's Arms, with the help of a young enthusiastic team, for over 20 years now, and continue to make improvements. Bedrooms (two with four-posters) have been redecorated and are light and fresh, with brand new bathrooms. Six more rooms, four with views across open countryside, have been created in the barn and stable block. All the public rooms have recently been refurbished as well.

And then there is the food. The Sportsman's Arms is first and foremost a restaurant, and the large dining-room is the inn's focal point, sparkling with silver cutlery and crystal table lights. The lively menu embraces sound, traditional local fare, as well as fresh fish and seafood brought in daily from Whitby. To back it up, there is a superb wine list – and an extremely reasonable bill.

~

NEARBY Wharfedale; Wensleydale; Fountains Abbey; Bolton Abbey.
LOCATION 2 miles (3 km) NW of Pateley Bridge, in hamlet; with ample car parking
MEALS breakfast, bar lunch, dinner
PRICE ££
ROOMS 13 double and twin with bath or shower; all rooms have TV
FACILITIES 3 sitting-rooms, bar, dining-room; fishing **CREDIT CARDS** MC, V
CHILDREN welcome
DISABLED easy access to public rooms **PETS** welcome by arrangement
CLOSED Christmas Day, Boxing Day, New Year's Day
PROPRIETORS Jane and Ray Carter

THE NORTH-EAST

YORKE ARMS
VILLAGE INN

Ramsgill-in-Nidderdale, near Harrogate, North Yorkshire HG3 5RL
TEL (01423) 755243 **FAX** (01423) 755330 **E-MAIL** enquiries@yorke-arms.co.uk
WEBSITE www.yorke-arms.co.uk

O N THE GREEN IN A PRETTY Nidderdale village, the creeper-clad Yorke Arms has been a fully-functioning pub for the past 150 years. It's a traditional 'no-frills' village inn, the ideal setting for owners Frances and Gerald Atkins to accomplish their aim of providing good food and a warm welcome. You are greeted as you enter by flagged floors, beams and (in winter) open fires. There is also a reassuring feeling of order: what should have been polished has been polished, and what should have been swept has been.

In the restaurant, wooden tables and a wooden floor strewn with rugs keep the techno-age at bay and serve as a showcase for Frances Atkins' daily-changing menu: traditional and modern English dishes are her starting-point, but she also draws on other *cuisines* from all over the world. Old favourites such as Yorkshire hot pot and halibut cheesy mash usually make an appearance. The wine list is comprehensive and sympathetically priced. Simpler meals are available in the brasserie or in the lounge.

The bedrooms are unpretentious, but freshly decorated and comfortably furnished, and range in size (and price) from cosy to a modest suite, 'Gouthwaite', which boasts a sofa and armchairs. Bathrooms are outdated, but are gradually being renewed.

NEARBY Harewood House; Newby Hall; Fountains Abbey; Ripon Cathedral.
LOCATION in centre of village; take Low Wath Road from Pateley Bridge bordering Gouthwaite Reservoir; with parking
MEALS breakfast, lunch, dinner; room service
PRICE ££
ROOMS 13; 11 double and twin, 2 suites, all with bath; all rooms have phone, TV, hairdrier; some have minibar
FACILITIES sitting-room, games-room, dining-rooms, bars, garden
CREDIT CARDS AE, D, MC, V **DISABLED** not suitable **PETS** accepted in some public rooms **CLOSED** never **PROPRIETORS** Frances and Gerald Atkins

THE NORTH-EAST

REETH, NORTH YORKSHIRE

BURGOYNE HOTEL

~ VILLAGE HOTEL ~

On the Green, Reeth, Richmond, North Yorkshire DL11 6SN
TEL & **FAX** (01748) 884292

THE BURGOYNE HOTEL stretches its late-Georgian length along the top of the sloping green in Reeth. If you turn round and look the other way, you'll see why: the Swale Valley is extremely pretty, and with only the green in front of it, the Burgoyne has an uninterrupted view. Inside, time, money and taste have conspired to produce something of a masterpiece to which has been added the magic ingredient of a warm welcome. There are two elegant and richly furnished sitting-rooms on the ground floor with Medieval touches here and there: stone coats of arms on the fireplaces and 'Gothic' oak doors. The restaurant, where the snowy napkins, the crystal and the silver stand out against the cool blues of the decoration, is a kind of inner sanctum where Peter Carwardine's culinary art joins Derek Hickson's scientific (certainly encyclopaedic) understanding of wines.

The bedrooms, most of which face the valley, are beautifully appointed and deeply comfortable. Window seats offer pleasant perches for people who just want to sit and enjoy the view. Rather than hack space for bathrooms out of the well-proportioned rooms, one or two bathrooms are across the corridor – voluminous robes and slippers are provided for the short journey.

~

NEARBY Richmond Castle; Middleham Castle.
LOCATION 10 miles (16 km) W of Richmond on B6270; with car parking
MEALS breakfast, packed lunch on request, dinner; room service
PRICE ££
ROOMS 8 double and twin with bath; all rooms have phone, TV, hairdrier
FACILITIES sitting-room, dining-room, garden; fishing
CREDIT CARDS MC, V
DISABLED access possible to ground-floor room
PETS accepted by arrangement
CLOSED early Jan to mid-Feb
PROPRIETORS Derek Hickson and Peter Carwardine

THE NORTH-EAST

RIPLEY, NORTH YORKSHIRE

BOAR'S HEAD
~ COUNTRY HOUSE HOTEL ~

Ripley, Harrogate, North Yorkshire HG3 3AY
TEL (01423) 771888 **FAX** (01423) 771509 **E-MAIL** boarshead@ripleycastle.co.uk
WEBSITE www.ripleycastle.co.uk

ANYONE WITH A SPARE INN and enough paintings and antique furniture to furnish it could do worse than emulate Sir Thomas and Lady Ingilby's successful renovation of the Boar's Head in Ripley. It is a thriving establishment with helpful, pleasant staff who do not leave your comfort to chance. There are bedrooms in the inn itself, lighter more contemporary ones in its cobbled courtyard, and across the road, in the peace and quiet of Birchwood House, are four of their six best rooms. All have fresh flowers, pristine modern bathrooms and thoughtful decoration.

The public rooms are warm and welcoming, filled with period furniture; seascapes and ancestors share the walls. There is a choice for dinner: you can either go to the relaxed bar/bistro (packed when we visited) or the richer candlelit comfort of the restaurant to agonize over a choice that includes crisp sea bass with squid ink noodles, or supreme of guinea fowl on a sweet pea purée. Fresh vegetables and game make seasonal appearances from the Ingilby Estate, presided over by their castle.

~

NEARBY York; Fountains Abbey; Studley Royal Water Gardens
LOCATION in village centre, 3 miles (5 km) N of Harrogate on A61; with ample parking
MEALS breakfast, lunch, dinner
PRICE ££
ROOMS 25 double and twin with bath; all rooms have phone, TV, fax/modem point, hairdrier; minibar on request
FACILITIES sitting-room, dining-rooms, 2 bars, garden; tennis, fishing
CREDIT CARDS AE, MC, DC, V
CHILDREN accepted
DISABLED 1 specially adapted room, 8 ground-floor rooms
PETS accepted in some rooms only
CLOSED never
PROPRIETORS Sir Thomas and Lady Ingilby

THE NORTH-EAST

ROMALDKIRK, COUNTY DURHAM

ROSE AND CROWN
∽ COUNTRY INN ∽

Romaldkirk, Barnard Castle, County. Durham DL12 9EB
Tel (01833) 650213 **Fax** (01833) 650828 **E-mail** hotel@rose-and-crown.co.uk
Website www.rose-and-crown.co.uk

THE ROSE AND CROWN was built in 1733 in this very pretty light stone village. It owes its original layout to the Saxons and its name to the patron saint of the church next door. Thoroughly renovated by Christopher and Alison Davy some ten years ago, the Rose and Crown has gone from strength to strength. It is set in the centre of the three-green village – (each green has its own set of stocks, and sometimes its own small group of cows). The bars are comfortingly traditional: real ales, natural stone walls, log fires, old photographs, copper and brass knick-knacks. Excellent pub food with 'blackboard specials' is served in the bistro-style 'Crown Room'. More traditional four-course dinners, English but imaginatively so, are served on white linen in the wood-panelled dining-room and, when in season, often feature moorland game, fresh fish from the East Coast, and locally grown vegetables. Fresh bread is baked on the premises every day.

There are seven comfortable bedrooms, attractively decorated and furnished with antiques, in the main building. Five more have been added round the courtyard at the back, and open directly on to it. All come with vases of fresh flowers.

∽

Nearby Barnard Castle; Egglestone Abbey; High Force.
Location in centre of village, on B6277, 6 miles (9.5 km) NW of Barnard Castle; with ample car parking
Meals breakfast, dinner, Sun lunch
Price ££
Rooms 12; 11 double and twin, 1 family, 9 with bath, 3 with shower; all rooms have phone, TV, hairdrier
Facilities sitting-room, dining-room, bar **Credit cards** MC, V **Children** welcome
Disabled 1 ground-floor bedroom **Pets** accepted in bedrooms
Closed Christmas Day, Boxing Day; restaurant Sun eve
Proprietors Christopher and Alison Davy

THE NORTH-EAST

WALKINGTON, HUMBERSIDE

THE MANOR HOUSE

 COUNTRY HOUSE HOTEL

Northlands, Walkington, Humberside HU17 8RT
TEL (01482) 881645 **FAX** (01482) 866501

THIS LATE-VICTORIAN HOUSE may not be what most people expect of a manor house, but that can be forgiven. Under the practised eye of chef-patron Derek Baugh and his wife, it has made an exceptionally civilized hotel. The furnishings are opulent, with a sprinkling of antiques and plenty of rich fabrics in carefully harmonized colours. The drawing-room is spacious, dividing naturally into several different sitting areas, but still manages to have a human scale. On sunny days, there is plenty of light from a tall bow window, and the whole room is drawn together by a pale carpet with a geometric pattern. The original conservatory serves as a dining-room – a particularly pleasant place in which to eat on a summer evening.

When our inspector revisited, she particularly liked the 'perfect, tranquil location just outside the village'. She thought the bedrooms (great views) a little modern given the character of the house – but comfortable and smart. Bathrooms are equipped with very large towels and an 'amazing' range of extras, such as body lotions. A bungalow housing two double bedrooms, a bathroom and shower is ideal for families.

The food is elaborate and modern; the wine list, reflecting Derek's abiding interest in wine, is long, interesting and mainly European.

NEARBY Beverley Minster; Skidby Windmill Museum.
LOCATION on the Newbald road NW of Walkington, 4 miles (6.5 km) SW of Beverley; with ample car parking
MEALS breakfast, lunch by arrangement, dinner; 24-hour room service
PRICE ££
ROOMS 7; 5 double, 1 twin, 1 family, all with bath; all have phone, TV, minibar
FACILITIES sitting-room, conservatory, dining-room
CREDIT CARDS MC, V **CHILDREN** accepted
DISABLED no special facilities **PETS** by arrangement **CLOSED** never
PROPRIETORS Derek and Lee Baugh

THE NORTH-EAST

WINTERINGHAM FIELDS

~ MANOR HOUSE HOTEL ~

Winteringham, Lincolnshire DN15 9PF
TEL (01724) 733096 **FAX** (01724) 733898

HALFWAY BETWEEN SCUNTHORPE and the Humber Bridge is one of Britain's gastronomic hot spots. Furthermore, you can sleep in great comfort no more than a few paces from the table. The hotel is in the middle of Winteringham, a quiet country village on the south bank of the Humber Estuary. Swiss chef Germain Schwab and his wife Annie are crusaders for high standards in the preparation and, above all, appreciation of good food – witness their second Michelin star.

The rambling 16thC house is full of nooks and crannies and still has many original features such as exposed timbers, period fireplaces and oak panelling. These are set off by the warm colours of walls and fabrics and the antique furniture.

The bedrooms are all uniquely decorated and sympathetically furnished. There are four in the main house (with not a single right-angle between them), three in the courtyard, which is the preserve of a large (friendly) boxer and an even larger (friendly) Great Dane, and one in a cottage round the corner. Two more rooms have just been made from a dovecote a couple of minutes away. All are named after former residents of the house or local dignitaries.

~

NEARBY Normanby Hall; Thornton Abbey; Lincoln.
LOCATION in centre of village on S bank of Humber, 4 miles (6.5 km) W from Humber Bridge on A1077; with ample car parking
MEALS breakfast, lunch, dinner; room service
PRICE ££ **ROOMS** 10; 8 double, 2 suites, all with bath; all rooms have phone, TV, hairdrier **FACILITIES** sitting-room, 2 dining-rooms, conservatory, garden; helipad
CREDIT CARDS AE, MC, V **CHILDREN** babes-in-arms and children over 8 accepted
DISABLED access difficult **PETS** accepted by arrangement
CLOSED one week in Aug, 2 weeks at Christmas; restaurant Sun, Mon, Bank hols, last week in Mar
PROPRIETORS Germain and Annie Schwab

SOUTHERN SCOTLAND

CANONBIE, DUMFRIES AND GALLOWAY

RIVERSIDE INN

~ VILLAGE INN ~

Canonbie, Dumfries and Galloway DG14 0UX
TEL (01387) 371512

FOR MORE THAN 25 years the Phillipses have been at the helm of this country-house-turned-inn, which you could view as a pub, a restaurant or a hotel. We guess that motorists travelling between England and Scotland remain the mainstay of trade, despite the fact that the A7 from Carlisle to Edinburgh has been shifted westwards to bypass Canonbie. For those who do pause there, Canonbie and the Riverside are, not surprisingly, more attractive now that little traffic separates the hotel from the public park it faces, and from the River Esk, which it overlooks 50 yards away.

Inside, the atmosphere is warm and friendly. The comfortable bar and the cosy sitting-rooms have the occasional beam and are furnished in traditional, chintzy style, while the dining-room is brighter, with candlelit wooden tables. You can eat either in the bar or in the restaurant; wherever, the food is good, using fresh local produce, such as salmon from the Esk, and home grown vegetables.

Bedrooms at the Riverside are comfortable but worn at the edges; bathrooms definitely need updating. Thoughtful extras include electric blankets and a basket of fruit in each.

~

NEARBY Hadrian's Wall and the Borders.
LOCATION 11 miles (18 km) N of M6 on A7, in village by river; with garden and ample car parking
MEALS breakfast, lunch, dinner
PRICE ££
ROOMS 7 double, 4 with bath, 3 with shower; all rooms have TV
FACILITIES 2 sitting-rooms, bar, dining-room; fishing, tennis, bowls
CREDIT CARDS MC, V **CHILDREN** welcome
DISABLED 1 ground-floor bedroom **PETS** accepted by arrangement
CLOSED Christmas, New Year, 2 weeks in Feb and Nov
PROPRIETORS Robert and Susan Phillips

SOUTHERN SCOTLAND

THE HOWARD

～ TOWNHOUSE HOTEL ～

34 Great King Street, Edinburgh EH3 6QH
TEL (0131) 557 3500 **FAX** (0131) 557 6515 **E-MAIL** reserve@thehoward.com
WEBSITE www.thehoward.com

THE ONLY INDICATION THAT 34 Great King Street is a hotel is the simple brass plate to the right of the front door. The location, a cobbled street in Edinburgh's New Town (new in the early 1800s, that is), could hardly be bettered, within walking distance of Princes Street and the Castle, but almost free of traffic noise.

The 1820s building, comprising three terraced townhouses, displays all the elegance and sense of proportion one associates with the Georgian era. Push open the door, and willing service is immediately on hand, including directions to the hotel's own private car park. After checking in, the charming reception staff will ask if you'd like some tea and shortbread, thus reinforcing the sense of being a guest in a friend's house.

Public rooms are elegant and captivating, although the drawing-room could do with better lighting. The breakfast-room is graced by delightful Italianate murals, uncovered during restoration. Only the starkly modern '36' restaurant, with its reputable food, strikes a different note. Bedrooms are supremely comfortable.

～

NEARBY Edinburgh Castle; Holyrood Palace; Princes Street.
LOCATION in New Town, E of Dundas St; car parking
MEALS breakfast, lunch, dinner; room service
PRICE ££££
ROOMS 16; 12 double and twin, 2 single, 2 suites; all rooms have phone, TV, fax/modem point, hairdrier
FACILITIES drawing-room, bar, breakfast-room, restaurant, lift
CREDIT CARDS AE, DC, MC, V
CHILDREN welcome
DISABLED access possible
PETS accepted by arrangement
CLOSED Christmas
PROPRIETOR Peter Taylor

SOUTHERN SCOTLAND

EDINBURGH

SIBBET HOUSE

~ TOWNHOUSE BED-AND-BREAKFAST ~

26 Northumberland Street, Edinburgh EH3 6LS
TEL (0131) 556 1078 **FAX** (0131) 557 9445 **E-MAIL** sibbet.house@zetnet.co.uk
WEBSITE www.sibbet-house.co.uk

A FIRST CLASS BED-AND-BREAKFAST establishment in the heart of
Edinburgh's New Town district – definitely a cut above the norm.
Privately owned by the Sibbet family (Jim Sibbet has now retired and the
house is run by Jens and Anita Steffen), it is an elegant and comfortable
Georgian family home, lavishly decorated with antiques and pretty fabrics.
On the ground floor is the vermillion breakfast-room, with white cornices,
antique furniture and some Russell Flint prints on the walls. A splendid
wooden hanging staircase, dominated by a cupola, leads to the bedrooms
and to the charming drawing-room. The bedrooms, which are on two
floors, could belong to a four-star hotel: they are large, beautifully
furnished and thoughtfully equipped, including a decanter of sherry. In
the basement is the suite, which includes a modern kitchen, conservatory
dining-room, patio garden and the use of a garage and washing machine.

Breakfasts at Sibbet House are feasts, with home-made breads, jams
and marmalades, as well as a tempting selection of cooked dishes such as
French toast, *frittatas* and omelettes.

Finally – and we don't think this is a threat – Jim Sibbet will play his
bagpipes on request.

~

NEARBY Edinburgh Castle; Holyrood Palace; Princes Street.
LOCATION in New Town, N of Princes Street; car parking
MEALS breakfast
PRICE ££
ROOMS 5; 4 double and twin, 1 suite; all rooms have phone, TV, hairdrier
FACILITIES sitting-room, breakfast-room, bar
CREDIT CARDS MC, V
CHILDREN accepted over 8 **DISABLED** access difficult
PETS accepted by arrangement
CLOSED Christmas
PROPRIETOR Jim Sibbet

SOUTHERN SCOTLAND

GLASGOW

ONE DEVONSHIRE GARDENS

~ TOWNHOUSE HOTEL ~

1 Devonshire Gardens, Glasgow G12 0UX
TEL (0141) 339 2001 **FAX** (0141) 337 1663 **E-MAIL** markcalpin@btconnect.com
WEBSITE www.one-devonshire-gardens.co.uk

THERE ARE A FAIR NUMBER of apparently unselfish people who, without a qualm, and certainly not for reasons of economy, would postpone their plans to visit Glasgow if they discovered that there was not a room to be had at One Devonshire Gardens. Ken McCulloch's hotel (actually three terraced houses in a row on the western side of the city) has that effect on many of its *habitués*. Where else would a baker get up at four every morning to make sure your shortbread was fresh? The entire hotel has an air of restrained luxury: in the public rooms ancestors gaze down from richly covered walls towards good antiques and plump upholstery. A pre-dinner drink by the drawing-room fire should already have put you in a good mood before Andrew Fairlie's offerings in the smart restaurant make you feel better still – and show why Michelin have accorded him a star. It is almost superfluous to add that the wine list – and the advice if you want it – are of matching quality. The bedrooms are opulent: soft lighting, deep colours and heavyweight fabrics in some, pale and light-handed in others; all with fine furniture and sumptuous bathrooms. Fresh fruit and flowers, your own CD player and up-to-date magazines complete the picture. Staff are polite, discreet and attentive.

~

NEARBY city centre; Cathedral; Hunterian Musueum and other sights.
LOCATION 2 miles (3 km) from centre at junction of Great Western and Hyndland roads; with car parking
MEALS breakfast, lunch, dinner
PRICE ££££
ROOMS 27 double and twin, 24 with bath, 3 with shower; all rooms have phone, TV, minibar, hairdrier
FACILITIES 2 sitting-rooms, study, dining-room, bar, patio garden
CREDIT CARDS AE, DC, MC, V
CHILDREN welcome **DISABLED** not suitable **PETS** accepted in bedrooms
CLOSED late Dec to early Jan **PROPRIETOR** Ken McCulloch

SOUTHERN SCOTLAND

GULLANE, EAST LOTHIAN

GREYWALLS

~ COUNTRY HOUSE HOTEL ~

Muirfield, Gullane, East Lothian EH31 2EG
TEL (01620) 842144 **FAX** (01620) 842241 **E-MAIL** sue@greywalls.co.uk
WEBSITE www.greywalls.co.uk

GREYWALLS IS A SLICK, expensive country house hotel, with – by our standards – quite a large number of bedrooms, but despite this we cannot resist including such a distinctive place. It is a classic turn-of-the-century house by Sir Edwin Lutyens, with gardens laid out by Gertrude Jekyll, and – more to the point for golf enthusiasts – it overlooks the tenth green of the famous Muirfield championship course.

The feel of Greywalls is very much one of a gracious private house, little changed in atmosphere since the days when King Edward VII was a guest. Furnished largely with period pieces, public rooms include an Edwardian tea-room, a little bar well stocked with whiskies, and a particularly appealing panelled library. This is a delightful room – with no sense of a hotel about it – in which to curl up on one of the sofas either side of the fire, and leaf through one of the many books from the shelves. Dinner, served in a room overlooking the golf course, is elegantly presented and imaginative. Bedrooms are attractive, comfortable and well equipped, particularly those in the original house rather than the new wing.

~

NEARBY golf courses; beaches; castles; Edinburgh.
LOCATION in village, 17 miles (27 km) E of Edinburgh off A198 to North Berwick; ample car parking
MEALS breakfast, lunch, dinner; room service
PRICE ££££
ROOMS 23; 19 double and twin, 4 single, all with bath; all rooms have phone, TV, hairdrier
FACILITIES 2 sitting-rooms, library, bar, dining-room, conservatory, garden; tennis, croquet
CREDIT CARDS AE, DC, MC, V
CHILDREN welcome
DISABLED bedrooms on ground floor **PETS** accepted, but not in public rooms
CLOSED Nov to Mar **PROPRIETORS** Giles and Ros Weaver

SOUTHERN SCOTLAND

PORTPATRICK, DUMFRIES & GALLOWAY

KNOCKINAAM LODGE

~ COUNTRY HOTEL ~

Portpatrick, Dumfries & Galloway DG9 9AD
Tel (01776) 810471·**Fax** (01776) 810435

GALLOWAY IS VERY MUCH an area for escaping the hurly-burly, and Knockinaam Lodge complements it perfectly (as well as being the ideal staging post for anyone bound for the ferry at Stranraer to Northern Ireland). Succeeding proprietors of the Lodge have had a reputation for fine food and warm hospitality, and the tradition is still maintained with the help of an enthusiastic staff and the present owners, Michael Bricker and Pauline Ashworth.

The house, a low Victorian villa, was built as a hunting lodge in 1869 and extended at the turn of the century. It was used by Sir Winston Churchill as a secret location in which to meet General Eisenhower during the Second World War. The rooms are cosy in scale and furnishings, the bedrooms varying from the stylishly simple to the quietly elegant. A key part of the appeal of the place is its complete seclusion – down a wooded glen, with lawned garden running down to a sandy beach. Children are welcome, and well catered for, with special high teas.

We would welcome reports on whether the prices here still represent value for money. Dinner, on our last inspection, was adventurous and competently cooked, but there were a few frayed edges about the place.

~

Nearby Logan, Ardwell and Glenwhan Gardens; Castle Kennedy.
Location 3 miles (5 km) SE of Portpatrick, off A77, in large grounds; ample car parking
Meals breakfast, lunch, dinner; room service
Price £££-££££ **Rooms** 10; 9 double with bath, 1 single with shower; all rooms have phone, TV, video, hairdrier
Facilities 2 sitting-rooms, bar, dining-room, garden; croquet, helipad
Credit Cards AE, DC, MC, V **Children** welcome
Disabled access easy, but no ground-floor bedrooms
Pets accepted, but not in public rooms **Closed** never
Proprietors Michael Bricker and Pauline Ashworth

SOUTHERN SCOTLAND

TARBERT, ARGYLL

SKIPNESS CASTLE

~ COUNTRY HOUSE GUEST-HOUSE ~

Skipness, by Tarbert, Argyll PA29 6XU
TEL (01880) 760207 **FAX** (01880) 760208
E-MAIL sophie@skipness.freeserve.co.uk

THE 'CASTLE' REFERS TO THE very fine 13thC Scottish Norman keep and St Brendan's chapel which stand beside the James family home, with magical views across Kilbrannan Sound to the Isle of Arran beyond. The estate has been owned by Libby James' family since the 1930s; in 1969 the original Victorian mansion was severely damaged by fire, and a smaller version was built in its place using old materials and much of the old stone. There are three comfortable bedrooms available for guests, as well as the striking first-floor drawing-room, with a self-service bar for drinks. The house is beautifully furnished with antiques and family portraits. Members of the extended family are liable to appear for dinner, prepared by Libby James and often including vegetables from the garden and game from the estate. Breakfast includes porridge cooked overnight in the Aga.

For lunch or afternoon tea, you can head for the James' popular Seafood Cabin, serving delicious seafood platters as well as salmon rolls and an excellent chocolate cake. The only non-brick structure to be licensed in Scotland, it attracts customers from all over Argyll. Outside, chickens, ducks and peacocks compete for the crumbs. Sophie James, who runs the estate and the cabin, is a mine of information about the area.

NEARBY Mull of Kintyre; Isle of Arran; Tarbert; Loch Fyne.
LOCATION from A83 to Campbeltown, pass Kennacraig ferry terminal and take B8001 signposted Skipness; also reached via ferry from Isle of Arran to Cloanaig, 2 miles (3 km) from Skipness; ample car parking
MEALS breakfast, dinner
PRICE ££
ROOMS 3 double or twin, all with bath
FACILITIES sitting-room, dining-room **CREDIT CARDS** not accepted
CHILDREN accepted
DISABLED access difficult **PETS** accepted **CLOSED** Oct to mid-March
PROPRIETORS Libby and Nick James

Southern Scotland

ALSO RECOMMENDED

DUNS, BERWICKSHIRE

Wellfield House

Preston Road, Duns, Berwickshire TD11 3DZ

TEL & FAX (01361) 883189 E-MAIL john.bimson@virgin.net PRICE ££

A reader's letter drew our attention to this beautifully run guest-house, a Georgian mansion, in Border country close to excellent fishing and golf.

EDINBURGH

Drummond House

17 Drummond Place, Edinburgh EH3 6PL

TEL & FAX (0131) 557 9189 E-MAIL drummondhouse@cableinet.co.uk PRICE ££

Georgian townhouse bed-and-breakfast with a beautifully proportioned interior and homely rather than grand furnishings.

MAYBOLE, AYRSHIRE

Culzean Castle

Maybole, Ayrshire KA19 8LE

TEL (01655) 884455 FAX (01655) 884503 E-MAIL culzean@nts.org.uk PRICE ££££

The top floor of Robert Adam's last masterpiece was given as a gift for his lifetime to President Eisenhower, and is now an unusual small hotel.

SKIRLING, LANARKSHIRE

Skirling House

Skirling, by Biggar, Lanarkshire ML12 6HD

TEL (01899) 860274 FAX (01899) 860255

E-MAIL skirlinghouse@dial.pipex.com PRICE ££

Built in 1908, this fascinating Arts and Crafts house with a 16thC Florentine drawing-room ceiling makes a beautifully run guest-house.

HIGHLANDS AND ISLANDS

ACHILTIBUIE, ROSS-SHIRE

SUMMER ISLES

~ COUNTRY HOTEL ~

Achiltibuie, by Ullapool, Ross-shire IV26 2YG
Tel (01854) 622282 **Fax** (01854) 622251

'THERE IS A MARVELLOUS amount of nothing to do' at Summer Isles. The emphasis is on eating well, sleeping well and relaxing in beautiful surroundings. "Take your Wellingtons, your sunglasses, your dog, walking shoes, insect repellant, camera, paint boxes, binoculars and comfy clothes," advise Mark and Geraldine Irvine, whose family have owned this remote, cottagey, civilized hotel since the late 1960s.

The views across Loch Broom and the Summer Isles are riveting, and the hotel's public rooms make the most of them with large picture windows. The decorations and furnishings are simple and cosy, with a touch of sophistication. There is a wood-burning stove in the sitting-room to keep you warm, and modern art and photographs on the walls in the dining-room. The food is a major attraction – the Irvines must be the holders of one of the furthest-flung Michelin stars in the British Isles, gained for the delicious and health-conscious cooking of Chris Firth-Bernard, featuring freshly-caught fish and shellfish and home-grown fruit and vegetables. Bedrooms are comfortable; best is the galleried Boathouse suite, which is stylish and spacious, with a spiral staircase leading up to the bedroom.

~

Nearby Ullapool; Inverewe Gardens; beaches.
Location 10 miles (16 km) N of Ullapool, turn left on to single track road for 15 miles (24 km) to Achiltibuie; hotel is close to village post office; with ample car parking
Meals breakfast, lunch, dinner
Price ££-£££
Rooms 13; 11 double and twin, 2 suites, all with bath; all rooms have phone, hairdrier; suites have TV **Facilities** dining-room, sitting-room, 2 bars, sun-room; fishing **Credit Cards** MC, V **Children** welcome over 6
Disabled access difficult **Pets** dogs allowed in bedrooms, but not public rooms
Closed mid-Oct to Easter **Proprietors** Mark and Geraldine Irvine

HIGHLANDS AND ISLANDS

ARISAIG, INVERNESS-SHIRE

ARISAIG HOUSE

~ COUNTRY HOUSE HOTEL ~

Beasdale, by Arisaig, Inverness-shire PH39 4NR
TEL (01687) 450622 **FAX** (01687) 4506626
E-MAIL ArisaiGHse@aol.com **WEBSITE** www.relaischateaux.fr/arisaig

IT IS WITH SOME RELIEF that one leaves tacky Fort William behind, and takes the Road to the Isles. The scenery becomes wilder, the road narrower and for most of the journey you travel alongside lochs. Arisaig House appears a few miles before the village of the same name and is a haven of quiet luxury where everything appears to run effortlessly, along pre-ordained lines. The food, fittingly, is superb, the wine list excellent without being exorbitantly priced, and the atmosphere extremely relaxing.

The stone manor house is outwardly rather austere, but natural light floods the house, reflecting off polished furniture; with an abundance of fresh flowers in every room and a light touch in the decoration, the impression is one of tranquillity. At the rear of the house, beautiful gardens and terraces are planted with roses, azaleas and rhododendrons; beyond the gardens, wooded walks lead down to Loch nan Uamh and the Sound of Arisaig. The view from some of the bedrooms (Sheil was our favourite) towards the Isles is stupendous, particularly as the sun sets.

Arisaig House is not cheap, but in our view not overpriced either. More reports, please.

~

NEARBY ferry to Eigg, Rhum and Canna from Arisaig harbour.
LOCATION on A830, 3 miles (5 km) E of Arisaig; in 20 acres of grounds with ample car parking
MEALS breakfast, lunch, dinner; room service
PRICE ££££
ROOMS 12; 10 double and twin, 2 suites, all with bath; all rooms have phone, TV, hairdrier
FACILITIES sitting-room, drawing-room, bar, billiards-room, dining-room, terrace, garden; croquet, helipad **CREDIT CARDS** MC V
CHILDREN not accepted
DISABLED access difficult **PETS** not accepted **CLOSED** Nov to Easter
PROPRIETOR Smithers family

HIGHLANDS AND ISLANDS

BALQUHIDDER, PERTHSHIRE

MONACHYLE MHOR

~ FARMHOUSE HOTEL ~

Balquhidder, Lochearnhead, Perthshire FK19 8PQ
TEL (01877) 384622 **FAX** (01877) 384305
E-MAIL MonachyleMhorHotel@Balquhidder.freeserve.co.uk

A SMALL, FAMILY-RUN FARMHOUSE with a charm all its own. The setting is both serene and romantic – as well it might be: this was the family home of Rob Roy MacGregor, approached along the Braes of Balquhidder (described in *Kidnapped*) and set beside Lochs Doine and Voil.

Jean Lewis came here 16 years ago from her native Monmouth and, together with her two sons Tom and Rob, first farmed the 2,000-acre estate and then opened the building as a hotel as well. Tom Lewis is the highly-praised chef, and the hotel's restaurant – situated in a light and airy conservatory overlooking the two lochs – is popular with locals and guests alike. Much of the produce comes from the farm, including lamb, beef and organic vegetables.

Bedrooms are simple and homely. Some have loch views and those converted from the old farmstead across a courtyard are particularly spacious and furnished in a suitably rustic style.

For a relaxing, inexpensive country break in magnificent scenery and with memorable food, Monachyle Mhor would be hard to beat.

~

NEARBY in the heart of Rob Roy country.
LOCATION on private estate; turn off A84, 11 miles (17.5 km) N of Callander at Kingshouse Hotel, then follow single-track lane for 6 miles (9.5 km); well-signposted; ample car parking
MEALS breakfast, lunch, dinner
PRICE ££
ROOMS 13; 10 double and twin, 3 suites, all with bath; all rooms have phone, TV, hairdrier
FACILITIES sitting-room, bar, restaurant, terrace, garden; fishing, stalking
CREDIT CARDS DC, MC, V
CHILDREN accepted over 12 **DISABLED** access difficult at present – plans afoot
PETS not accepted
CLOSED never **PROPRIETORS** Jean, Tom and Rob Lewis

HIGHLANDS AND ISLANDS

BUNESSAN, ISLE OF MULL

ASSAPOL HOUSE

~ LOCHSIDE GUEST-HOUSE ~

Bunessan, Isle of Mull PA67 6DW
TEL (01681) 700258 **FAX** (01681) 700445
E-MAIL alex@assapolhouse.demon.co.uk **WEBSITE** www.assapolhouse.demon.co.uk

A NIGH-ON PERFECT EXAMPLE of a family-run guest-house, and an especially useful address for people wanting to take a day-trip to Iona, burial-place of the ancient kings of Scotland. The spick-and-span, gleaming white-painted former manse stands on an inland loch, where you can fish for brown trout, surrounded by open countryside. It is the home of Thomas (a retired ship's captain) and Onny Robinson, and their son Alex. All three pitch in to create a welcoming and comfortable retreat.

There are two sitting-rooms in which to relax: one homely and civilized, the other more masculine, with plenty of books to browse through and CDs to play. The terracotta-painted dining-room has well-spaced separate tables; dinner is served at 7.45 pm and guests congregate in the sitting-room beforehand for pre-dinner drinks. The food is a joint family effort, and much enjoyed. The four-course menu begins with home-made soup, followed by a salmon terrine, perhaps, or smoked duck salad. Main courses feature local beef, venison and lamb, and there are two puddings to choose from, one cooked by Onny, the other by Alex.

Bedrooms are pretty and straightforward, with attention to detail, including fresh flowers and up-to-date magazines.

~

NEARBY ferry to Iona, Staffa and Fingal's cave; beaches.
LOCATION from Craignure take A849 to Fionnphort; approaching Bunessan school on right, take signposted road on left to hotel; ample car parking
MEALS breakfast, packed lunch, dinner
PRICE ££
ROOMS 5; 4 double and twin, 1 single, all with bath; all rooms have phone, TV, hairdrier
FACILITIES 2 sitting-rooms, dining-room, garden; fishing
CREDIT CARDS MC, V
CHILDREN accepted over 10 **DISABLED** access difficult **PETS** not accepted
CLOSED Nov to Mar **PROPRIETORS** Robertson family

HIGHLANDS AND ISLANDS

COLBOST, ISLE OF SKYE

THREE CHIMNEYS
∼ SEASIDE RESTAURANT-WITH-ROOMS ∼

Colbost, Dunvegan, Isle of Skye IV55 8ZT
TEL (01470) 511258 **FAX** (01470) 511358 **E-MAIL** eatandstay@threechimneys.co.uk
WEBSITE www.threechimneys.co.uk

FOR MANY YEARS CHEF Shirley Spear and her husband Eddie have run Three Chimneys as an award-winning seafood restaurant in an idyllic seaside location in the far north-western corner of Skye. The good news is that you can now, having enjoyed yourself at dinner, stay the night - in style. The six suites created in a new building called the House Over-By, are luxurious, highly original – if understated - rooms designed to blend with the seascape and the changing light. Each contemporary, spacious and high-ceilinged room (some are on two levels) has direct access to the beach; bathrooms are heavenly. The view looks west to the Minch and sometimes to the misty islands of the Outer Hebrides on the horizon. Breakfast is served in a room overlooking the seashore and the islands in Loch Dunvegan.

Three Chimneys itself is a simple former crofter's cottage in which stone walls and exposed beams are mixed with modern furniture and fittings. As you would expect, the menu is a mainly fishy one – in the mornings you can watch the fishing boats set off to catch your dinner – but Highland beef, lamb and game are also a feature, and the puddings are just as good.

∼

NEARBY Dunvegan Castle; The Cuillins.
LOCATION from Dunvegan take the single-track B884 toward Glendale for 5 miles (8 km); car parking
MEALS breakfast, lunch, dinner
PRICE £££
ROOMS 6 suites, all with bath; all rooms have phone, TV, video, CD player, minibar, hairdrier
FACILITIES breakfast-room, 2 dining-rooms, bar, children's play area; yacht mooring **CREDIT CARDS** AE, MC, V
CHILDREN welcome **DISABLED** 1 room specially adapted **PETS** not accepted
CLOSED never **PROPRIETORS** Shirley and Eddie Spear

HIGHLANDS AND ISLANDS

ROYAL HOTEL
∼ TOWN INN ∼

Melville Square, Comrie, Perthshire PH6 2DN
TEL (01764) 679200 **FAX** (01764) 679219 **E-MAIL** reception@royalhotel.co.uk
WEBSITE www.royalhotel.co.uk

ALL TOO OFTEN, town hotels, surviving on a diet of passing trade, show a distinct lack of enthusiasm and a rather blank face to the world; it's only occasionally that we find a new one which excites our interest. Comrie's Royal Hotel is such a one: from the moment you step inside, it feels right. Situated in the centre of this attractive little Highland town, and dating from 1765, it began life as a coaching inn, and earned its grand title after a visit by – who else? – Queen Victoria, accompanied by her servant, John Brown.

The atmosphere is homely, yet at the same time elegant and stylish, with log fires in the public rooms as well as squashy sofas, comfortable armchairs, antiques and oil paintings. There is a Brasserie for informal dining, as well as the main restaurant. The staff are naturally friendly, with a nice sense of humour. While our inspector was being shown one of the bedrooms, the maid, who was cleaning the fireplace, commented wryly "...and this one comes complete with Cinderella".

All eleven of the well-appointed bedrooms have been individually planned and furnished with an eye for detail and design and a touch of luxury (bathrobes and so on). The hotel's modish makeover is the brainchild of Edward Gibbons, son of its owners.

∼

NEARBY Loch Earn; Glenturret Distillery; Drummond Castle.
LOCATION in centre of Comrie, on A85, about 25 miles (40 km) W of Perth; limited car parking
MEALS breakfast, lunch, dinner; room service
PRICE £££
ROOMS 11; 10 double and twin, 1 suite, all with bath; all rooms have phone, TV, fax/modem point, hairdrier, safe
FACILITIES sitting-room, library, 2 dining-rooms **CREDIT CARDS** AE, MC, V
CHILDREN accepted **DISABLED** access difficult
PETS accepted **CLOSED** never **PROPRIETOR** Edward Gibbons

HIGHLANDS AND ISLANDS

DUNKELD, PERTHSHIRE

KINNAIRD

~ COUNTRY HOUSE HOTEL ~

Kinnaird Estate, by Dunkeld, Perthshire PH8 0LB
TEL (01796) 482440 **FAX** (01796) 482289
E-MAIL enquiry@kinnairdestate.demon.co.uk **WEBSITE** www.kinnairdestate.com

THE WORD 'RAVE' is hardly appropriate for this supremely genteel and gracious establishment, but a rave review was what our latest inspector gave it: 'We rate it as one of the finest places to stay anywhere in Europe' was his verdict. Nothing could be faulted, but it was the staff – welcoming without being obsequious, attentive without being irritating, whom they felt transformed an expensive hotel into something that felt like value for money.

Parts of Kinnaird date back to the 1770s, but today it exudes an air of Edwardian grandeur, softened by the use of sophisticated pale coloured fabrics and masses of fresh flowers. Fine antique furniture, pictures and porcelain abound; the large drawing-room has a huge open log fire and deep armchairs and sofas into which to sink. Leading off it is a billiard-room with views down to the River Tay. Bedrooms are luxurious yet welcoming, with books, gas log fires and king-size beds fitted with electric blankets. The food is delicious, the wine list well-chosen and the candlelit dining-room exquisitely decorated with yellow drapes and hand-painted Italianesque frescoes.

~

NEARBY Pitlochry; Blairgowrie; Crieff; Loch Tay; Tay Forest.
LOCATION private 9000-acre estate NE of Dunkeld; from A9 turn W on to B898 for 4.5 miles (7 km); ample car parking
MEALS breakfast, lunch, dinner; room service
PRICE ££££
ROOMS 9; 8 double and twin, 1 suite, all with bath; all rooms have phone, TV, video, fax/modem point, CD player, hairdrier
FACILITIES drawing-room, morning-room, study, billiard-room, 2 dining-rooms, lift, garden; bowling, tennis, croquet, shooting, fishing
CREDIT CARDS MC, V **CHILDREN** accepted over 12
DISABLED 1 room specially adapted **PETS** accepted by arrangement
CLOSED Mon, Tue, Wed in Jan and Feb **PROPRIETOR** Constance Ward

HIGHLANDS AND ISLANDS

FORT WILLIAM, INVERNESS-SHIRE

THE GRANGE

~ EDGE-OF-TOWN BED-AND-BREAKFAST ~

Grange Road, Fort William, Inverness-shire PH33 6JF
TEL (01397) 705516 **FAX** (01397) 701595

WE WERE DELIGHTED TO discover this outstanding bed-and-breakfast establishment on the outskirts of Fort William, run with great flair by Joan and John Campbell. A ten-minute walk from the fairly charmless town centre brings you to this late Victorian house, set in pretty terraced grounds overlooking Loch Linnhe.

A feminine touch is distinctly in evidence in the immaculate interior, which is decorated with admirable taste and a flair for matching fabrics with furnishings and fittings. First glimpsed, you might expect a stand-offish 'don't touch' approach from the owners, but nothing could be further from the truth at The Grange. Joan Campbell, responsible for the decoration, is naturally easy-going with a great sense of hospitality.

All four bedrooms are superbly, and individually, decorated and furnished, their bathrooms lavish and luxurious – it all comes as rather a surprise. The Rob Roy room was the one chosen by Jessica Lange, who stayed here during the filming of *Rob Roy*, while the Terrace Room has, as its name suggests, its own terrace leading on to the gardens. Two of the bedrooms have Louis XV-style king-size beds; all four overlook the garden and Loch Linnhe. A delightful place.

~

NEARBY Ben Nevis; 'Road to the Isles'; Loch Ness.
LOCATION on outskirts; from town centre take A82 towards Glasgow, then turn left into Ashburn Rd; hotel is at top on left; limited car parking
MEALS breakfast
PRICE ££
ROOMS 4 double and twin, all with bath; all rooms have TV, hairdrier
FACILITIES breakfast-room, sitting-room, garden, sea loch close by
CREDIT CARDS not accepted
CHILDREN not accepted **DISABLED** access difficult **PETS** not accepted
CLOSED mid-Nov to Easter
PROPRIETOR Joan and John Campbell

HIGHLANDS AND ISLANDS

GLENLIVET, BANFFSHIRE

MINMORE HOUSE

~ COUNTRY HOUSE HOTEL ~

Glenlivet, Banffshire AB37 9DB
TEL (01807) 590378 **FAX** (01807) 590472

WE HAVE ALWAYS BEEN impressed by the friendly, relaxed atmosphere at Minmore House, which continues to be generated by its new owners, Brett and Christine Holmes.

It is a solid mid-Victorian family home set in four-and-a-half acres of landscaped gardens. It stands adjacent to the famous Glenlivet whisky distillery, and was the home of George Smith, the distillery's founder. Not surprisingly, whisky plays its part in the hotel, and the fine oak-panelled bar displays an impressive range of single malts. From the hotel, enthusiasts can follow the signposted Whisky Trail, visiting renowned Speyside whisky distilleries.

'Proper' Scottish breakfasts, with kippers and smoked haddock, are on offer, as well as complimentary afternoon tea. In the award-winning restaurant, the five-course set dinners (with vegetarian options) have a Scottish bias. The hotel has a tranquil, relaxed atmosphere, with open fires in all the public rooms. With the exception of the two single rooms, the bedrooms and bathrooms are spacious. The Holmes are happy to arrange all manner of activities – golf, shooting, stalking, salmon and trout fishing, walking, and castle and distillery visits.

A recent visit revealed that all was in good order here.

~

NEARBY Glenlivet Distillery; Ballindalloch Castle.
LOCATION on the B9008, next to the Glenlivet Distillery, in 4.5-acre gardens; with ample parking
MEALS breakfast, picnic lunch on request, dinner
PRICE ££
ROOMS 10; 8 double and twin, 2 single, all with bath; all rooms have phone
FACILITIES 2 sitting-rooms, bar, dining-room, garden; croquet lawn, tennis court, swimming-pool **CREDIT CARDS** MC, V **CHILDREN** welcome
DISABLED access difficult **PETS** accepted **CLOSED** mid-Oct to Easter
PROPRIETORS Brett and Christine Holmes

HIGHLANDS AND ISLANDS

ISLE OF ERISKA, ARGYLL

ISLE OF ERISKA HOTEL

～ ISLAND MANSION ～

Isle of Eriska, Ledaig, Oban, Argyll PA37 1SD
TEL (01631) 720371 **FAX** (01631) 720531 **E-MAIL** office@eriska-hotel.co.uk
WEBSITE www.eriska-hotel.co.uk

A SPLENDID HOTEL WHICH has the twin advantages of seclusion, since it
is set on its own remote island, and accessibility: it is connected to the
mainland by a short road bridge. And for those who like to keep
themselves occupied during their stay, its leisure centre, which includes
a magnificent 17-metre heated swimming-pool, and its sporting
opportunities, will appeal.

Built in 1884 in grey granite and warmer red sandstone, in Scottish
Baronial style, the Buchanan-Smith's hotel is a reminder of a more
expansive and confident era. If it reminds you in feel, if not in appearance,
of Balmoral, you will not be surprised to learn that the original wallpaper
on the first-floor landing is also found in the royal castle. In fact the
experience of staying here is very much like being in an old-fashioned
grand private house, comfortable rather than stylish, with a panelled great
hall, and roaring log fires and chintz fabrics much in evidence. In the
library-cum-bar you can browse through the books with a malt whisky in
hand, while excellent six-course dinners are served in the stately dining-
room. The handsome bedrooms vary in size and outlook.

～

NEARBY Oban; Isle of Mull; Inverary Castle; Glencoe.
LOCATION on private island connected by road bridge; from Connel take A828
toward Fort William for 4 miles (6.5 km) to N of Benderloch village, then follow
signs; ample car parking
MEALS breakfast, dinner
PRICE ££££
ROOMS 17; 12 double and twin, 2 single, 3 family rooms, all with bath; all rooms
have phone, hairdrier **FACILITIES** 3 drawing-rooms, bar/library, dining-room, indoor
swimming-pool, gym, sauna, garden; 9-hole golf course, tennis court, croquet,
clay pigeon shooting, water sports **CREDIT CARDS** AE, MC, V **CHILDREN** welcome
DISABLED access possible **PETS** accepted **CLOSED** Jan
PROPRIETORS Buchanan-Smith family

HIGHLANDS AND ISLANDS

ISLEORNSAY, ISLE OF SKYE

EILEAN IARMAIN

~ SEAFRONT HOTEL ~

Isleornsay, Sleat, Isle of Skye IV43 8QR
TEL (01471) 833332 **FAX** (01471) 833275 **E-MAIL** hotel@eileaniarmain.co.uk

HEARING THE SOFT LILT OF THE voices of the staff is one of the pleasures of a stay at this traditional Skye hotel, and a sure sign that you are in the Western Isles. This is a bilingual establishment, and the friendly and welcoming staff are fluent in both Gaelic and English; they wear tags which give their names in both languages.

The hotel is part of an estate belonging to Sir Iain and Lady Noble. Its three buildings are beautifully situated right on the water's edge, on the small rocky bay of Isleornsay, looking across the Sound of Sleat to the mainland Knoydart Hills beyond. If you are lucky, you may see otters on the shore.

The hotel's core is a white-painted Victorian inn which comprises the reception area, two appealing dining-rooms and six bedrooms. A further six bedrooms are in a building opposite, while the latest addition, opened in 1999, houses four split-level suites. All the rooms are traditional in character, hospitable and homely, with modern fittings and smart bathrooms. In each is a complimentary miniature bottle of whisky supplied from Sir Iain's distillery.

The restaurant specializes in local fish, shellfish and game, and enjoys a local reputation.

~

NEARBY Clan Donald Centre; Aros Heritage Centre; Dunvegan Castle.
LOCATION on water's edge, on estate between Broadford and Armadale in the S of the island, 20 minutes' drive from Skye Bridge or Mallaig ferry point; ample car parking
MEALS breakfast, lunch, dinner
PRICE ££-£££
ROOMS 16; 12 double, twin or triple, 4 suites, all with bath; all rooms have phone, TV, hairdrier **FACILITIES** sitting-room, 2 dining-rooms; anchorage for yachts **CREDIT CARDS** AE, MC, V **CHILDREN** welcome **DISABLED** access possible to suites **PETS** accepted **CLOSED** never **PROPRIETOR** Sir Iain Noble

HIGHLANDS AND ISLANDS

KENTALLEN OF APPIN, ARGYLL

ARDSHEAL HOUSE

~ COUNTRY HOUSE HOTEL ~

Kentallen of Appin, Argyll PA38 4BX
TEL (01631) 740227 **FAX** (01631) 740342 **E-MAIL** info@ardsheal.co.uk
WEBSITE www.ardsheal.co.uk

ARDSHEAL HOUSE IS THE family home of Neil and Philippa Sutherland, charming hosts who succeed in making their guests entirely at home.

The feeling of well-being begins as soon as you turn off the main road and take a two-mile (3-km) single-track private lane that leads to the house on the banks of Loch Linnhe. It was originally built in the early 16th century, but, having been destroyed by fire in the 1745 uprising, was rebuilt in 1760 and extended over the intervening years. The natural woodland, one of the oldest in Scotland, and lovely garden which surrounds it, provide a wonderful setting with many mature trees, shrubs, lawns and flower gardens.

Public rooms are elegant, with antique furniture, paintings, comfortable chairs and sofas, and log fires in most rooms. The dining-room is a light, sunny conservatory and, in Scottish country house tradition, there is a billiard-room with full-size table. Bedrooms, full of family antiques and pictures, do not disappoint. Amazingly, the owners plan to reduce the present number of bedrooms and make the existing ones larger. Philippa is an excellent cook, and prepares a daily-changing no-choice menu. In all, a lovely, relaxing place to stay, with superlative views.

~

NEARBY Glencoe; Ben Nevis; Oban; Isle of Mull; Isle of Skye.
LOCATION 17 miles (27 km) SW of Fort William off the A828, in private estate; ample car parking
MEALS breakfast, lunch, dinner
PRICE ££
ROOMS 6 double and twin, 5 with bath, 1 with shower; all rooms have phone, hairdrier
FACILITIES 2 sitting-rooms, billiards-room, garden; pebble beach
CREDIT CARDS MC, V **CHILDREN** not accepted
DISABLED 1 room on ground floor **PETS** accepted **CLOSED** mid-Dec to mid-Jan
PROPRIETORS Neil and Philippa Sutherland

HIGHLANDS AND ISLANDS

◆ EDITORS' CHOICE ◆

TAYCHREGGAN
～ LOCHSIDE INN ～

Kilchrenan, by Taynuilt, Argyll PA35 1HQ
TEL (01866) 833211 **FAX** (01866) 833244 **E-MAIL** taychreggan@btinternet.com
WEBSITE www.scotlands-commended.co.uk/taych.htm

APPROACHED BY A six-mile (9.5-km) single-track road, this former drovers' inn, much modernized, is an isolated, utterly peaceful haven, surrounded by 25 acres of garden and natural woodland, and lapped by the waters of Loch Awe, with spectacular views. A great place in which to unwind, especially for fishermen: the hotel has its own fishing rights, boats and ghillie and a well-equipped rod-room. Riding, deer stalking, rough shooting, water sports and golf can also be arranged.

The core of the hotel is the old stone house, with exposed stone walls inside, and its pretty cobbled courtyard where, on sunny days, you can relax with a drink (an impressive range of malt whiskies is available). The fairly formal, two-part dining-room is distinguished by huge arched picture windows which unite the room with the lovely view beyond, and makes a memorable setting for dinner. Food is taken seriously, and is very good: inventive and sophisticated, using fresh local produce, with a fine wine list to match.

Bedrooms are all different, contemporary in feel, with some antique pieces. Ask for a loch view, even though you will pay more. The staff here are exemplary.

～

NEARBY Inverary; Loch Lomond; Kilchurn Castle; Western Isles.
LOCATION 1 mile (1.5 km) E of Taynuilt on A85, take the B845 and follow signs; ample car parking
MEALS breakfast, lunch, dinner
PRICE ££
ROOMS 19; 18 double and twin, 1 suite, all with bath; all rooms have phone, hairdrier
FACILITIES 2 sitting-rooms, TV lounge, bar, restaurant, snooker-room, courtyard, garden; fishing, water sports **CREDIT CARDS** AE, MC, V
CHILDREN accepted over 12 **DISABLED** access difficult **PETS** accepted **CLOSED** never
PROPRIETOR Annie Paul

HIGHLANDS AND ISLANDS

KILLIECRANKIE, PERTHSHIRE

KILLIECRANKIE HOTEL

~ COUNTRY HOTEL ~

Killiecrankie, by Pitlochry, Perthshire PH16 5LG
TEL (01796) 473220 **FAX** (01796) 472451 **E-MAIL** killiecrankie.hotel@btinternet.com
WEBSITE www.btinternet.com/~killiecrankie.hotel

A SENSIBLE, REASSURING SORT of establishment in a delightful setting which somehow encapsulates the modest Scottish country hotel. Built as a manse for a local clergyman in 1840, it stands at the foot of the Pass of Killiecrankie, formed by the River Garry slicing through the surrounding granite hills, and in its own attractive grounds – a lovely place in which to relax and watch out for wildlife, including red squirrels and roe deer.

The ten straightforward yet comfortable bedrooms are done out in mainly striped or plaid fabrics, and custom-made furniture and fittings finished in natural pine, lending them a somewhat Scandinavian air. An unexpected touch: beds are turned down each evening. The mahogany-panelled bar is a cosy, convivial place in which to gather for drinks, and a bright conservatory section is set for light lunches and imaginative bar snacks, including a selection of *tapas*. This is also where guests eat breakfast, overlooking the garden. In the main restaurant, the dinner menu changes daily and may include dishes such as smoked haddock omelette with a warm plum tomato and basil salad, or medallions of Scotch beef set on *rösti* potato with caramelized shallots and red wine sauce.

~

NEARBY Pitlochry; Pass of Killiecrankie; Blair Atholl; Glamis.
LOCATION in 4 acres, 3 miles (5 km) N of Pitlochry, just off A9 on the B8079; ample car parking
MEALS breakfast, lunch, dinner
PRICE ££
ROOMS 10; 7 double and twin, 2 single, 1 suite, all with bath; all rooms have phone, TV, hairdrier
FACILITIES sitting-room, 2 dining-rooms, bar, conservatory, garden
CREDIT CARDS MC, V
CHILDREN accepted **DISABLED** no special facilities **PETS** accepted
CLOSED Jan **PROPRIETORS** Colin and Carole Anderson

HIGHLANDS AND ISLANDS

KINGUSSIE, INVERNESS-SHIRE

THE CROSS

~ RESTAURANT-WITH-ROOMS ~

Tweed Mill Brae, Kingussie, Inverness-shire PH21 1TC
TEL (01540) 661166 **FAX** (01540) 661080
E-MAIL relax@TheCross.co.uk

RUTH HADLEY'S INSPIRED COOKING has long made her and husband Tony's well-established, award-winning restaurant-with-rooms a must for gourmets. In a secluded four-acre waterside setting, down a private drive, The Cross is a modest, former 19thC tweed mill which houses nine fresh and simple bedrooms, as well as the restaurant and a residents' sitting-room. A strict no-smoking policy operates in the dining-room and in the bedrooms.

Bedrooms are individually furnished, and include canopied, twin and king-size beds. One has a balcony overlooking the Gynack, which flows alongside the mill, and where you may sometimes see salmon swimming and herons fishing.

Tony Hadley has received praise from his guests for the atmosphere he creates and told our inspector that "nothing is too much" for them. This did not, however, extend to being able to supply our famished inspector with a snack on a wet Sunday lunchtime, despite the fact that he had driven miles to visit. He could, as a result, be accused of being biased, but although the hotel has been in our guide for many years, he felt that it lacked both charm and facilities.

~

NEARBY Aviemore; Loch Insh; Highland Folk Museum.
LOCATION from the traffic lights in Kingussie town centre, take Ardbroilach Rd for 200 m, then turn left down Tweed Mill Brae; ample car parking
MEALS breakfast, dinner; room service
PRICE ££
ROOMS 9 double and twin, all with bath; all rooms have phone, TV on request, airdrier
FACILITIES sitting-room, restaurant, garden; fishing
CREDIT CARDS MC, V **CHILDREN** not accepted
DISABLED no special facilities **PETS** not accepted **CLOSED** Dec to Mar
PROPRIETORS Tony and Ruth Hadley

HIGHLANDS AND ISLANDS

MUIR OF ORD, ROSS-SHIRE

THE DOWER HOUSE
~ COUNTRY HOUSE HOTEL ~

Highfield, Muir of Ord, Ross-shire IV6 7XN
TEL (01463) 870090 **FAX** (01463) 870090 **E-MAIL** thedowerhouse@compuserve.com
WEBSITE www.thedowerhouse.co.uk

THIS FORMER DOWER HOUSE of a baronial home, which burnt down in the 1940s, was converted from thatched farmhouse to charming residence in the Georgian cottage *ornée* style in about 1800. It became a hotel, run by Robyn and Mena Aitchison as if it were a private house receiving paying guests, in 1989. Something of an oasis in the rugged landscape between the rivers Beauly and Conon, it is set in beautifully maintained mature gardens and grounds.

The elegant, red-walled dining-room, with its highly polished mahogany tables, makes a stunning setting for evening meals, and Robyn's self-taught cooking does not disappoint. Herbs and vegetables are from the garden, eggs from their hens, and meat, game and seafood are all local. The menu offers no choice, though it changes every day. The sitting-room has comfortable chairs, flowery fabrics, plenty of books, an open fire and a bar concealed in a cupboard.

The five bedrooms vary in size and furnishings and are fairly simple. The largest is the most luxurious, with an enormous bed and spacious bathroom, while the suite looks on to the pretty garden. All the baths are traditional cast iron, with period fittings.

~

NEARBY Inverness; Culloden; beaches.
LOCATION 1 mile (1.5 km) N of Muir of Ord, 14 miles (22 km) NW of Inverness on the A862 to Dingwall; car parking
MEALS breakfast, dinner
PRICE ££-£££
ROOMS 5; 4 double and twin, 1 suite, all with bath; all rooms have phone, TV
FACILITIES sitting-room, dining-room, garden
CREDIT CARDS MC, V
CHILDREN accepted by arrangement
DISABLED no special facilities **PETS** accepted by arrangement
CLOSED never **PROPRIETORS** Robyn and Mena Aitchison

HIGHLANDS AND ISLANDS

NAIRN, NAIRNSHIRE

CLIFTON HOUSE
~ TOWN HOTEL ~

Nairn, Nairnshire IV12 4HW
TEL (01667) 453119 **FAX** (01667) 452836
E-MAIL macintyre@clara.net

IT IS NOT UNUSUAL TO COME upon small hotels with a theatrical touch, but the Clifton is in a different league: it actually is a theatre, staging plays and recitals in the dining-room during the winter months, to the delight of all. Gordon Macintyre has lived here all his life, more than 40 of those years as a hotelkeeper, and his act is thoroughly polished.

The Victorian house is richly furnished to ensure not only the comfort but also the amusement of guests; paintings fill the walls, flowers fill antique vases, books fill shelves, knick-knacks fill every other nook and cranny. Whatever your mood, one of the public rooms should suit – the drawing-room has stunning red, gold and black wallpaper with pomegranate motif, originally designed by Pugin for the Robing Room in the Palace of Westminster. Bedrooms are individually decorated and furnished in what Gordon (with characteristic modesty and humour) calls "a mixture of good antiques and painted junk". The bathrooms, however, are in need of upgrading.

The cooking imposes French provincial techniques on the best local produce – particularly seafood, upon which lunch in the smaller Green Room is largely based – and there is a fine, long wine list. Typically, breakfast is served without time limit.

~

NEARBY Cawdor Castle; Brodie Castle; Culloden.
LOCATION on the seafront in middle of town, close to A96; ample car parking
MEALS breakfast, lunch, dinner
PRICE ££
ROOMS 12; 8 double, 4 single, all with bath
FACILITIES 2 sitting-rooms, TV-room, 2 dining-rooms
CREDIT CARDS AE, DC, MC, V
CHILDREN welcome **DISABLED** no special facilities
PETS accepted
CLOSED mid-Dec to late Jan **PROPRIETOR** J. Gordon Macintyre

HIGHLANDS AND ISLANDS

PITLOCHRY, PERTHSHIRE

KNOCKENDARROCH HOUSE

~ TOWN MANSION ~

Higher Oakfield, Pitlochry, Perthshire PH16 5HT
TEL (01796) 473473 **FAX** (01796) 474068 **E-MAIL** info@knockendarroch.co.uk
WEBSITE www.knockendarroch.co.uk

PITLOCHRY IS A PARTICULARLY agreeable Highland town, and Knockendarroch House is the place to stay. Built in 1880 for an Aberdeen advocate, it displays more château-esque elegance than Scottish Baronial pomp. It stands on a plateau above the town, surrounded by mature oaks (its Gaelic name means Hill of Oaks).

Furnished in careful good taste, the house feels gracious and welcoming. There are two interconnecting sitting-rooms in which to relax, with green ceilings, white cornices and pastel green curtains and carpets - all very soothing. The dining-room is light and spacious, with many windows and some attractive furniture. The cooking draws praise, but we would like reports, please. Hosts Tony and Jane Ross, who are professional hoteliers, offer a glass of complimentary sherry to guests as they choose their evening meal.

All the bedrooms have views; those from the second floor are spectacular. They are all well furnished and two have small balconies.

Guests attending the famous Pitlochry Festival Theatre (which began here at Knockendarroch House) are served an early dinner, and a courtesy bus is laid on to take them to and from the town.

~

NEARBY Blair Castle; Killiecrankie Pass; Loch Tummel.
LOCATION close to town centre, 26 miles (41 km) N of Perth on A9; car parking
MEALS breakfast, dinner
PRICE ££
ROOMS 12 double and twin, all with bath; all rooms have phone, TV, hairdrier
FACILITIES 2 sitting-rooms, dining-room, garden
CREDIT CARDS MC, V
CHILDREN accepted over 12
DISABLED access possible to 1 room **PETS** not accepted
CLOSED mid-Oct to Feb
PROPRIETORS Tony and Jane Ross

HIGHLANDS AND ISLANDS

PORT APPIN, ARGYLL

AIRDS HOTEL
~ FERRY INN ~

Port Appin, Argyll PA38 4DF
TEL (01631) 730236 **FAX** (01631) 730535 **E-MAIL** airds@airds-hotel.com
WEBSITE www.relaischateaux.fr/airds

THE OWNERS OF THIS OLD FERRY INN on the shores of Loch Linnhe have very sensibly taken every advantage of its superb location: the dining-room, the conservatory and many bedrooms face the loch. To capitalize further, they have also created, across the road, an attractive lawn and rose garden, in which guests can sit and admire the view across the loch to the island of Lismore. The sunsets here are stunning.

Despite its fairly ordinary exterior, Airds Hotel, a member of the Relais & Châteaux group, is a smart and decorous establishment, impeccably run and maintained. The interior is elegant, with two sitting-rooms prettily furnished with comfortable chairs, deep-pile carpets and open fires. Rooms are full of flowers and books, and paintings are in abundance. Each of the bedrooms is individually decorated and carefully furnished, with very comfortable bathrooms. Each day the dinner menu and wine list is left in your room, so that you can consult it at leisure, give your orders by late afternoon, and relax before dinner with an aperitif, confident that there will be no unnecessary delays. The dining-room is somewhat formal and hushed, but the food, cooked by Betty Allen, is highly praised and often features such local delicacies as Lismore oysters, smoked salmon or venison.

~

NEARBY Oban; Glencoe; 'Road to the Isles'; Ben Nevis.
LOCATION between Ballachulish and Connel, 2 miles (3 km) off A828; car parking
MEALS breakfast, light lunch, dinner; room service
PRICE £££
ROOMS 12; 11 double and twin, 1 suite, all with bath; all rooms have phone, TV, hairdrier
FACILITIES 2 sitting-rooms, conservatory, dining-room, garden; shingle beach
CREDIT CARDS MC, V **CHILDREN** accepted **DISABLED** no special facilities
PETS not accepted **CLOSED** mid to end-Dec; last 3 weeks in Jan
PROPRIETORS Allen family

HIGHLANDS AND ISLANDS

PORTREE, ISLE OF SKYE

VIEWFIELD HOUSE
~ COUNTRY GUEST-HOUSE ~

Portree, Isle of Skye, IV51 9EU
TEL (01478) 612217 **FAX** (01478) 613517

'IT WON'T SUIT EVERYONE,' writes our reporter about Viewfield House, 'but for those seeking an age gone by, the experience would be memorable.'

This is an imposing Victorian country mansion, which, as the name suggests, has some fine views from its elevated position. The need for costly repairs to the roof prompted Evelyn Macdonald, Hugh's grandmother, to open Viewfield House to guests. The delight of it is that the distinctive character of the house was preserved; and though you will not lack for comfort or service, a stay here is likely to be a novel experience. The house is full of colonial memorabilia: stuffed animals, and birds; priceless museum relics; and a magnificent collection of oil paintings and prints.

The rooms are original, right down to the wallpaper in one instance (though all but a couple now have en suite bathrooms in the former dressing-rooms); there is a classic Victorian parlour and a grand dining-room with two huge wooden tables. Guests are entertained house-party style, although separate tables can be arranged if they prefer not to dine communally – we admire this flexibility. There is a five-course fixed menu, but individual needs can be met. The food, cooked by Linda Macdonald, is hearty, traditional and plentiful.

~

NEARBY Trotternish Peninsula.
LOCATION on outskirts of town, 10 minutes walk S of centre; from A87 towards Broadford, turn right just after BP garage on left; with car parking
MEALS breakfast, packed lunch, dinner
PRICE ££ **ROOMS** 9 double, 7 with bath, 2 single, 1 with bath, 1 family room
FACILITIES sitting-room, dining-room, TV-room
CREDIT CARDS MC, V **CHILDREN** welcome **DISABLED** 1 specially adapted room on ground floor **PETS** accepted, but not in public rooms **CLOSED** mid-Oct to mid-Apr
PROPRIETORS Hugh and Linda Macdonald

HIGHLANDS AND ISLANDS

SCARISTA, ISLE OF HARRIS

SCARISTA HOUSE

~ ISLAND GUEST-HOUSE ~

Scarista, Isle of Harris, Western Isles HS3 3HX
TEL (01859) 550238 **FAX** (01859) 550277 **E-MAIL** ian@scaristahouse.demon.co.uk
WEBSITE www.scaristahouse.demon.co.uk

HARRIS HAS LITTLE IN THE way of hotels, but Scarista would stand out even among the country houses of the Cotswolds.

The converted Georgian manse stands alone on a windswept slope overlooking a wide stretch of tidal sands on the island's western shore. The decoration is elegant and quite formal, with many antiques, but the atmosphere is relaxed and, by the open peat fires, conversation replaces television. The bedrooms, all with private bathrooms, have selected teas and fresh coffee, as well as home-made biscuits. Most of them are in a new single-storey building; the one in the house itself is non-smoking.

The Callaghans quit banking and antiques to take over at the beginning of 1990, and have since refurbished the public areas and most of the bedrooms. They aim to be welcoming and efficient, but never intrusive, and to preserve that precious private home atmosphere.

One of Scarista's greatest attractions, particularly rewarding after a long walk over the sands, is the meals. The imaginatively prepared fresh, local and garden produce, and an impressive wine list, ensure a memorable dinner in the candlelit dining-room.

NEARBY beaches; golf; boat trips.
LOCATION 15 miles (24 km) SW of Tarbert on A859, over-looking sea; in 2-acre garden, with ample car parking
MEALS breakfast, packed/snack lunch, dinner
PRICE £££
ROOMS 5 double, all with bath; all rooms have phone, hairdrier
FACILITIES library, 2 sitting-rooms, dining-room
CREDIT CARDS MC, V
CHILDREN welcome over 8
DISABLED no special facilities **PETS** accepted in annexe but not house
CLOSED Oct to April
PROPRIETORS Ian and Jane Callaghan

HIGHLANDS AND ISLANDS

SLEAT, ISLE OF SKYE

KINLOCH LODGE
∽ COUNTRY HOTEL ∽

Sleat, Isle of Skye, Highland IV43 8QY
TEL 01471) 833214 **FAX** (01471) 833277 **E-MAIL** kinloch@dialpipex.com
WEBSITE www.kinloch-lodge.co.uk

THIS WHITE-PAINTED STONE house, in an isolated position with uninterrupted sea views, at the southern extremity of the Isle of Skye, was built as a farmhouse around 1700 and later became a shooting lodge. But it escaped the baronial treatment handed out to many such houses – "thank goodness," says Lady Macdonald, whose style is modern interior-designer rather than dark panelling and tartan. The house has that easy-going private-house air. The guests' sitting-rooms are comfortably done out in stylishly muted colours; there are open fires, and family oil paintings grace the walls. The dining-room is more formal, with sparkling crystal and silver on polished tables. All but three of the bedrooms are undeniably on the small side. Since our last visit, the Macdonalds have built the New House with accommodation for themselves and five more double rooms for guests. New House is quite remarkable as it looks, both inside and out, as old as the Lodge, and includes a magnificent stone spiral staircase, as well as a wealth of books, portraits and *objets d'art*.

The food at Kinloch Lodge is renowned – Lady Macdonald has written cookery books and gives cookery demonstrations. We would welcome reports on the food.

∽

NEARBY Clan Donald Centre.
LOCATION in 60-acre grounds, 6 miles (9.5 km) S of Broadford, 1 mile (1.5 km) off A851; ample car parking
MEALS breakfast, lunch by arrangement, dinner
PRICE ££
ROOMS 15 double, 13 with bath; all rooms have radio, hairdrier
FACILITIES 2 sitting-rooms, bar, dining-room; fishing
CREDIT CARDS MC, V
CHILDREN accepted **DISABLED** access reasonable – 1 ground-floor bedroom
PETS accepted by arrangement, but not in public rooms **CLOSED** Christmas week
PROPRIETORS Lord and Lady Macdonald

HIGHLANDS AND ISLANDS

CORRIEGOUR LODGE
~ LOCHSIDE HOTEL ~

Loch Lochy, by Spean Bridge, Inverness-shire PH34 4EB
TEL (01397) 712685 **FAX** (01397) 712696 **E-MAIL** info@corriegour-lodge-hotel.com
WEBSITE www.corriegour-lodge-hotel.com

A FORMER VICTORIAN HUNTING LODGE commanding outstanding views over Loch Lochy and set in six acres of mature woodland and garden within the 'Great Glen'. With its own attractive private beach and jetty on the loch, as well as a fishing boat and the services of a private fishing school at its disposal, this is an obvious choice for keen anglers, as well as walkers and climbers, pony trekkers and sailors.

The reception hall at Corriegour Lodge is somewhat gloomy, but negative first impressions are quickly dispelled when the proprietor, Christian Drew, comes on the scene. Her friendliness and enthusiasm for the hotel she runs with her son, Ian, are infectious. The decoration throughout the rest of the hotel is cosy and pleasant, with a log fire in the sitting-room and magical views over the loch from the large picture windows in the restaurant. Many of the comfortable bedrooms have the same view.

Food is an important element here, using local meat, fish and game. For pudding you could have cloutie dumpling with rum custard. The staff are genuinely friendly and willing to help.

More reports please.

~

NEARBY Cawdor Castle; Urquhart Castle; Loch Ness; Glencoe.
LOCATION between Spean Bridge and Invergarry, in own grounds, 17 miles (27 km) N of Fort William on A82; ample car parking
MEALS breakfast, dinner
PRICE ££
ROOMS 9; 7 double and twin, 2 single, all with bath; all rooms have TV, hairdrier on request **FACILITIES** sitting-room, bar, dining-room, terrace; private beach and jetty, fishing **CREDIT CARDS** AE, DC, MC, V **CHILDREN** accepted over 8
DISABLED no special facilities **PETS** not accepted
CLOSED Nov-Apr(open some weekends in Feb, Mar)
PROPRIETORS Ian and Christian Drew

HIGHLANDS AND ISLANDS

STRACHUR, ARGYLL

CREGGANS INN
~ LOCHSIDE INN ~

Strachur, Argyll PA27 8BX
TEL (01369) 860279 **FAX** (01369) 860637 **E-MAIL** info@creggans-inn.co.uk
WEBSITE www.creggans-inn.co.uk

OVERLOOKING LOCH FYNE, this former hunting lodge of the 3000-acre Strachur Estate was first opened as an inn some 40 years ago by Sir Fitzroy Maclean. His son, Sir Charles Maclean, has set out to transform a fairly simple establishment into something rather more sophisticated, with high standards of modern comfort. A recent visitor felt that he wasn't quite there yet, but to be fair, the continuing programme of refurbishment is still underway.

A major natural advantage is the position of the inn. The views over Loch Fyne and across the Mull of Kintyre to the Western Isles are breathtaking. Many parts of the Strachur Estate, including the private flower garden, are open to guests and a wealth of country activities is available.

The comfortable bedrooms are best described as homely rather than elegant and finding your way around the maze of corridors can be tricky after a glass or two. The condition of some of the public rooms needs attention. Reports on the cooking are excellent: drawing heavily on local products such as scallops and langoustines from Loch Fyne, it is light, inventive and delicious. The wine list is unusually good and well priced.

~

NEARBY Inverary town and castle; Loch Fyne; Loch Lomond.
LOCATION on E shore of Loch Fyne; from Glasgow via Loch Lomond and the A83, or from Gourock by car ferry across the Clyde to Dunoon and the A815; ample car parking
MEALS breakfast, lunch, dinner
PRICE ££
ROOMS 17; 15 double and twin, 1 single, 1 suite, all with bath; all rooms have phone, TV, hairdrier **FACILITIES** 2 sitting-rooms, 2 bars, restaurant, small shop, garden; country sports **CREDIT CARDS** AE, DC, MC, V **CHILDREN** welcome
DISABLED 2 rooms on ground floor **PETS** accepted **CLOSED** never
PROPRIETOR Sir Charles Maclean

HIGHLANDS AND ISLANDS

STRONTIAN, ARGYLL

KILCAMB LODGE

~ LOCHSIDE HOTEL ~

Strontian, Argyll PH36 4HY
TEL (01967) 402257 **FAX** (01967) 402041

THERE IS A SENSE OF ADVENTURE in travelling to a hotel by ferry, particularly when it then involves a ten-mile journey, first alongside a loch and then over a pass through a steep-sided glen. Drop down through the glen, pass through the small village of Strontian, and there, in a romantic setting on the shores of Loch Sunart, is Kilcamb Lodge.

Originally built in the early 18th century, with Victorian additions, Kilcamb is a beautifully restored country house with ten bedrooms, each with a loch view. Set amidst lawns and woodland, filled in spring with the colours of rhododendrons, azaleas and many wild flowers, it is a romantic and calming bolt-hole, the perfect choice for nature lovers: sea otters, seals, pine martens, red and roe deer, and golden eagles can all be seen.

The ground-floor public rooms are pleasantly furnished with light and attractive pastel fabrics. There is a wonderful Victorian wrought-iron staircase and a large stained glass window. All the bedrooms are individually decorated and have triple lined curtains (it stays light very late in summer). To cap it all, the cooking is admirable, with an excellent wine list.

~

NEARBY ferry to Isle of Mull and Skye; Castle Tioram; Glencoe.
LOCATION Corran ferry to Ardgour from the A82 near Ballachulish, then follow A861 to Strontian; in 28 acres with ample car parking
MEALS breakfast, light lunch, dinner
PRICE ££
ROOMS 11; 10 double and twin, 1 single, all with bath; all rooms have TV, hairdrier
FACILITIES 2 sitting-rooms, bar, restaurant, garden; private beach, fishing, mountain bikes
CREDIT CARDS MC, V
CHILDREN welcome **DISABLED** no special facilities
PETS accepted by arrangement **CLOSED** Jan, Feb
PROPRIETORS Peter and Anne Blakewa

HIGHLANDS AND ISLANDS

◆ EDITORS' CHOICE ◆

ALTNAHARRIE
〜 LOCHSIDE INN 〜

Ullapool, Ross-shire IV26 2SS
TEL (01854) 633230

BRITAIN HAS GOOD HOTELS IN MANY unlikely-sounding places, but this one takes first prize. Ullapool itself is pretty remote, but to get to Altnaharrie you have to make a ten-minute crossing of Loch Broom by the inn's private ferry – or tackle it from Little Loch Broom and hike 2 miles over the mountains.

Such complete seclusion has a powerful appeal in itself, but the really remarkable thing about staying here is that it involves no compromises whatever. The lochside inn, though simple, is as welcoming a house as you will find anywhere; what is more, the food is widely acknowledged to be stunningly good. Gunn does the cooking, and brings to it the same originality she employs in painting and weaving. Fresh local ingredients form the basis of her set menus, which defy classification but have achieved wide acclaim. There are no better restaurants in the Highlands, and few in the whole of Britain – witness the many awards, including Scotland's only two Michelin stars.

The centuries-old white-painted stone house, only a pebble's throw from the loch, is warmly and prettily decorated with woven wall hangings, Middle Eastern rugs and a sprinkling of antiques. Note, however, that prices are among the highest in these pages.

〜

NEARBY Loch Broom Highland Museum; Ullapool; Inverewe Gardens.
LOCATION SW of Ullapool across Loch Broom – reached by private launch; private car park in Ullapool
MEALS breakfast, light lunch, dinner; room service
PRICE ££££
ROOMS 8 double, all with bath **FACILITIES** 2 sitting-rooms, dining-room
CREDIT CARDS MC, V **CHILDREN** welcome if well-behaved, but not suitable for small children **DISABLED** access difficult **PETS** dogs may be accepted by prior arrangement **CLOSED** Nov to Easter
PROPRIETORS Fred Brown and Gunn Eriksen

HIGHLANDS AND ISLANDS

WALLS, SHETLAND ISLANDS

BURRASTOW HOUSE

~ SEAFRONT GUEST-HOUSE ~

Walls, Shetland Islands, ZE2 9PD
TEL (01595) 809307 **FAX** (01595) 809213 **E-MAIL** burr.hs.hotel@zetnet.co.uk
WEBSITE www.users.zetnet.co.uk/burrastow-house-hotel

ON THE REMOTE WEST SIDE of Shetland, at the end of the single-track road, on a rocky promontory overlooking Vaila Sound and the Island of Vaila, stands this calm, solid 18thC stone house. It has been a guest-house since 1980, and for the last 12 years has been run with enthusiasm by Bo Simmons, along with her husband, Henry Anderton. In 1995 an extension was built to accommodate three more en suite bedrooms. Peace, quiet, a love of nature and total informality are the keynotes here.

The original bedrooms in the compact main house are the ones to go for if you can. Both are large, and one has a second bedroom which is perfect for children. There are splendid beds in each: a four-poster in one and a half-tester, draped in blue silk, in the other. The newer bedrooms have less character, but they're comfortable. In the public rooms there are peat fires, books, an eclectic mix of furnishings and wonderful views from the windows, you may spy seals and otters. Bo has made her mark with her natural, homely cooking, and has written a cook book, *A Taste of Burrastow*. Dinners, which feature four courses with a choice of dishes, are served in the cosy panelled dining-room at a communal table – be prepared to mix.

~

NEARBY Vaila Sound; Walls.
LOCATION on seafront, 2 miles (3 km) W of Walls; ample car parking
MEALS breakfast, light/packed lunch, dinner
PRICE ££
ROOMS 5; 4 double and twin, 1 family suite, 3 with bath, 2 with shower; TV, hairdrier on request
FACILITIES dining-room, 2 sitting-rooms; dinghy
CREDIT CARDS AE, MC, V
CHILDREN welcome **DISABLED** access possible; 1 room specially adapted
PETS accepted by arrangement **CLOSED** Jan, Feb
PROPRIETOR Bo Simmons

HIGHLANDS AND ISLANDS

WHITEBRIDGE, INVERNESS-SHIRE

KNOCKIE LODGE
~ COUNTRY HOUSE HOTEL ~

Whitebridge, Inverness-shire IV1 2UP
TEL (01456) 486276 **FAX** (01456) 486389 **E-MAIL** info@knockielodge.co.uk
WEBSITE www.knockielodge.co.uk

SET HIGH ON THE HEATHER-COVERED hills above Loch Ness, this country house hotel, built as a hunting lodge for Lord Lovat in 1789, is a perfect place to enjoy a Highland holiday: salmon fishing, deer stalking, sailing, pony trekking, climbing and hill walking are all on offer. What sets Knockie Lodge apart is a sense of vitality so often absent in these generally somnulent and sedate types of hotel. The reason: the enthusiasm of the young proprietors, Louise Dawson and Nicholas Bean, and their staff.

The welcome begins in the entrance hall, graced with fresh flowers and antiques. The theme is carried through to the attractive, individually decorated bedrooms (without TVs to spoil the peace), some with exceptional views over Loch nan Lann and the mountain Beinn a Bhacaidh. A covered terrace shares the same view, and you can walk from here down to Loch Ness.

In a hotel where the nearest alternative to dining in is a half-hour drive away, the food must satisfy, and it does. Head chef Mark Dexter was trained at The Savoy and The Dorchester and it shows. Guests have consistently praised the meals here. They dine at the same time, albeit at separate tables.

~

NEARBY Inverness; Fort Augustus; Loch Ness; Culloden.
LOCATION follow sign off B862 along S side of Loch Ness; the hotel is 2 miles (3 km) along a single-track road in grounds; ample car parking
MEALS breakfast, light lunch on request, dinner
PRICE £££
ROOMS 10; 8 double and twin, 2 single, all with bath; all rooms have phone, hairdrier **FACILITIES** 3 sitting-rooms, snooker-room, dining-room, terrace, garden
CREDIT CARDS DC, MC, V **CHILDREN** accepted over 10 **DISABLED** access difficult
PETS accepted by arrangement **CLOSED** Nov to May
PROPRIETORS Louise Dawson and Nicholas Bean

HIGHLANDS AND ISLANDS

ALSO RECOMMENDED

BANFF, ABERDEENSHIRE

Eden House

by Banff, Aberdeenshire AB45 3NT
TEL (01261) 821282 FAX (01261) 821283 PRICE ££

An elegant Grade II-listed private house with a fine portico and sweeping views from the huge bay windows. Communal dining; friendly owners.

DRUMNADROCHIT, INVERNESS-SHIRE

Polmaily House

Drumnadrochit, Inverness-shire IV3 6XT
TEL (01456) 450343 FAX (01456) 450813
E-MAIL polmailyhousehotel@btinternet.com PRICE ££

Every conceivable activity to keep children happy is on offer at this family hotel, from pet-cuddling to video games, a tree-house to pony riding.

BUNCHREW, INVERNESS-SHIRE

Bunchrew House

Bunchrew, Inverness-shire IV3 8TA
TEL (01463) 234917 FAX (01463) 710620 ££

A pink sandstone turreted mansion with large, comfortable bedrooms (try for one with a sea view) and a rather formal dining-room.

INVERNESS

Glenmoriston Town House

20 Ness Bank, Inverness, Inverness-shire IV2 4SF
TEL (01463) 223777 FAX (01463) 712378 E-MAIL glenmoriston@cali.co.uk
WEBSITE www.glenmoriston.com PRICE ££

Useful new address in an area not blessed with stylish hotels. An old hotel has been given a modern makeover and snazzy food.

UIG, ISLE OF LEWIS

Baile-na-Cille

Timsgarry, Uig, Isle of Lewis, Western Isles HS2 9JD
TEL (01851) 672242 FAX (01851) 672241 E-MAIL randjgollin@compuserve.com
PRICE ££

Stunningly set, lovingly restored 18thC manse run as a relaxed guest-house by the Gollins'; good food is served around a communal table.

ULLAPOOL, ROSS-SHIRE

Ceilidh Place

West Argyll Street, Ullapool, Ross-shire IV26 2TY
TEL (01854) 612103 FAX (01854) 612886
E-MAIL reception@ceilidh.demon.co.uk PRICE ££

A lively, friendly combination of arts centre, coffee shop, bakery, bookshop, restaurant and guest-house with simple accommodation.

NORTHERN IRELAND

BELFAST

GREENWOOD HOUSE

~ TOWN GUEST-HOUSE ~

25 Park Road, Belfast, Co. Antrim BT7 2FW
TEL (028) 9020 2525 **FAX** (028) 9020 2530
E-MAIL greenwood.house@virgin.net

JUST OFF THE (infamous) Ormeau Road, on a quiet tree-lined residential street, this is a double-fronted, red-brick Victorian house in a small garden behind a privet hedge. Until three years ago it was a retirement home, but a transformation has been brought about by the delightful young present owners, Jason and Mary Harris. 'What a welcome change from dark colours, frills and fussiness,' observed our inspector. Downstairs, the old maplewood floors and original cornicing remain, but the decoration is Habitat-style, contemporary and fresh, with bright fabrics in primary colours and much wrought-ironwork. The dining-room – at the front – has wrought-iron tables and chairs made by local craftsmen, wrought-iron curtain rails, red and yellow curtains, a handsome old fireplace and modern prints on the walls. Jason makes breakfast; the menu is written up on a blackboard. The same bright theme continues upstairs: wrought-iron bedsteads, a navy-blue and green colour scheme, mirrors in smart black frames, light wood tables with black trim, 'open' wardrobes (or an iron frame enclosed by fabric). Bathrooms are very white. Some rooms are quite large; those at the front look out over a park. The house style is informal and cheerful.

~

NEARBY city centre.
LOCATION in residential area, 1 mile (1.5 km) S of city centre; with car parking
MEALS breakfast, dinner on request
PRICE £
ROOMS 7; 5 double, 2 twin, 3 with bath, 2 with shower, 2 single with shower; all rooms have TV; hairdrier on request
FACILITIES sitting-room, dining-room, garden
CREDIT CARDS AE, MC, V
CHILDREN welcome **DISABLED** 1 ground-floor bedroom
PETS not accepted **CLOSED** Christmas week
PROPRIETORS Jason and Mary Harris

NORTHERN IRELAND

PORTAFERRY, CO. DOWN

THE NARROWS
~ SEASIDE GUEST-HOUSE ~

8 Shore Road, Portaferry, Co. Down BT22 1JY
TEL (028) 4272 8148 **FAX** (028) 4272 8105
E-MAIL reservations@narrows.co.uk

THIS IS AN ARCHITECTURAL treat. Not only that: its seafront position in a pretty fishing village on the tip of the beautiful Ards Peninsula; its sunny, bright rooms with views over the water; and its prices, which take some beating, all make this a gem. Around an 18thC courtyard, owner-brothers Will and James Brown have restored and extended their father's family house with the help of architect, Rachel Bevan. The result is an exciting, airy, pleasing combination of old and new. The 13 bedrooms, all named after islands in Strangford Lough, have windows looking over boats and the new yacht pontoon. Decoration is simple, with white walls, coconut matting, natural wood floors, pine furniture and white-tiled bathrooms. Rooms in the older building have aged timber beams; all have good beds and power showers. The ground-floor restaurant is a bright, functional room, with wood floors, sponged terracotta-coloured walls and bare wood tables, serving delicious Modern Irish food, with local seafood, such as Portaferry mussels, smoked salmon, and sea bass. Organic vegetables and herbs come from the garden. The odd well-placed colourful piece of hand-weaving, painting or photograph hangs on the walls. Moorings available.

~

NEARBY Exploris Aquarium; Mount Stewart (National Trust); golf.
LOCATION on seafront in centre of town; with parking for 4-5 cars
MEALS breakfast, lunch, dinner
PRICE ££
ROOMS 13; 12 double and twin, 1 single, 3 with bath, 10 with shower; all rooms have phone, TV
FACILITIES sitting-room, restaurant, sauna, lift, garden, terrace
CREDIT CARDS AE, MC, V
CHILDREN welcome **DISABLED** 8 accessible rooms **PETS** accepted with own bedding
CLOSED 2 weeks in Feb
PROPRIETORS Will and James Brown

IRISH REPUBLIC

BALLYCORMAC HOUSE
~ CONVERTED FARMHOUSE ~

Aglish, Borrisokane, Co. Tipperary
TEL (067) 21129 **FAX** (067) 21200

SET AMID NORTH TIPPERARY FARMLAND, almost exactly in the middle of Ireland, this is a 300-year-old-farmhouse which has long been well known as a guest-house, but which was taken over from the previous occupants in 1994 by an energetic American couple, Herbert and Christine Quigley. It's ideal for guests who simply wish to relax, or small groups who want to take advantage of their specialist holidays based on riding, fox-hunting, golfing, fishing and shooting. We learned, on going to press, that the Quigleys have left, so readers' reports would be especially welcome.

The Quigleys upgraded the pretty but compact house, creating a warm and cosy retreat. There are log fires in winter, and in summer guests can see the organic herb, fruit and vegetable gardens which provide produce for meals. And this is where the Quigleys' real prowess lay. Herb was a superb baker, and so breakfast might feature traditional Irish soda bread, or his own version of *pain au chocolat*, chocolate cherry soda bread, while dinner at the communal table might be accompanied by anything from home-made Swedish *limpa* to Indian *naan*. Let's hope that the new owners can maintain this quality and individuality.

~

NEARBY Terryglass; Birr.
Location in 2 acres of garden, 0.5 mile (1 km) N of Borrisokane, signposted on right; with ample car parking
MEALS breakfast, picnic lunch on request, dinner
PRICE IR££
ROOMS 5; 3 double, 1 suite, 1 single, all with bath
FACILITIES sitting-room, dining-room, garden
CREDIT CARDS MC, V
CHILDREN welcome over 6 **DISABLED** access difficult **PETS** lodging available
CLOSED never
PROPRIETOR John Lang

IRISH REPUBLIC

ARDARA, CO. DONEGAL

THE GREEN GATE

〜 COTTAGE BED-AND-BREAKFAST 〜

The Green Gate, Ardvally, Ardara, Co. Donegal
TEL (075) 41546

THIS LITTLE PLACE, a tiny farmhouse with stone outbuildings, owned and converted by a Frenchman who came to Donegal 11 years ago to write about "life, love and death", is bursting with charm. The book never got finished, but Paul Chatenoud, who left behind his musical bookshop and flat in Paris for a wilder existence on the top of a hill overlooking the Atlantic, has created what must be the most beautiful small B&B in Ireland. So much love and care has gone into this enterprise; he's done most of it with his own hands, from thatching the cottage roof to plumbing and whitewashing the four guest rooms. Simple they may be, but he thinks of everything: hot water bottles, a map in each room, and a bath in which you can rest your head back and gaze out of the window at the sky and the sea. His garden is filled with primroses, fuchsia and small birds, and he has planted hundreds, if not thousands, of orange montbretia up the lane. Breakfast is taken *chez lui*; in his own cosy kitchen he serves coffee/tea, cornflakes, bacon, eggs, sausage, toast and home-made jam – any time before 2 pm. And you get his delightful company. An English composer came for a night and was still there a week later. 'A treasure' says an entry in the visitors' book.

〜

NEARBY Ardara (for tweed); Glenveagh National Park.
LOCATION 1 mile (1.5 km) from Ardara, up a hill; with car parking
MEALS breakfast
PRICE £
ROOMS 4; 2 double, 2 triple; all with bath and shower
FACILITIES garden, terrace
CREDIT CARDS not accepted
CHILDREN welcome
DISABLED access possible **PETS** welcome in room
CLOSED never
PROPRIETOR Paul Chatenoud

IRISH REPUBLIC

BALLYLICKEY, Co. CORK

SEA VIEW HOUSE
~ COUNTRY HOTEL ~

Ballylickey, Bantry, Co. Cork
TEL (027) 50073 **FAX** (027) 51555

KATHLEEN O'SULLIVAN GREW UP in this white Victorian house, a stone's throw from Ballylickey Bay. In 1978 she turned it into a successful small hotel. Her plan for an extension, to give double the number of rooms, was finally realized in 1990. 'Kathleen is a delightful hostess,' writes a recent reporter, and Sea View really is a 'very nice, quiet comfortable hotel.'

The new bedrooms are all similar in style, beautifully decorated in pastel colours and floral fabrics with stunning antique furniture – especially the bedheads and wardrobes, and matching three-piece suites, collected or inherited from around the Cork area. The rooms in the old part of the house are more irregular and individual. All front rooms have large bay windows and views of the garden and sea (through the trees). The 'Garden Suite' downstairs is especially adapted for wheelchairs.

There are two sitting-rooms – a cosy front room adjoining the bar and a large family room at the back. The dining-room has also been extended (though many regular guests do not believe it). Our reporter thought the food 'excellent and generous'; breakfast was 'wonderful' with a big choice and traditional Irish dishes, such as potato cakes. The menu changes daily, and Kathleen is forever experimenting with new dishes – roast smoked pheasant on the day we visited.

~

NEARBY Bantry; Beira Peninsula; Ring of Kerry.
LOCATION in countryside, just off N71, 3 miles (5 km) N of Bantry; in large grounds with ample car parking
MEALS breakfast, lunch (Sun only), dinner
PRICE IR££
ROOMS 17; 14 double, 13 with bath, 1 with shower, 3 family with bath; all rooms have phone, TV, hairdrier **FACILITIES** 2 dining-rooms, 2 sitting-rooms, TV-room, bar, garden **CREDIT CARDS** AE, MC, V **CHILDREN** welcome **DISABLED** 1 specially adapted room **PETS** accepted in bedrooms only **CLOSED** Nov-Mar
PROPRIETOR Kathleen O'Sullivan

IRISH REPUBLIC

THE ALGIERS INN
~ VILLAGE INN ~

Baltimore, Co. Cork
TEL (028) 20145 **FAX** (028) 21675
E-MAIL jkwalsh@tinet.ie

THIS IS HARD TO BEAT ON PRICE or atmosphere. Baltimore, a fishing village and popular sailing centre, buzzes with life in the summer. Kieron Walsh has rooms which are basic and clean, up a little narrow staircase above his snug, traditional bar and restaurant. His mother, Ellen, is house-keeper, and has more guest rooms next door at The Old Post House. She hangs the inn's sheets and towels out on the washing line in the garden and serves breakfast in her front room, which has hooks for hanging up sides of bacon, left over from the days when the post office sold anything from needles to boots. A steel pillar props up the ceiling; old gas lamps have been converted to electricity. Large windows – with spider plants cascading out of hanging baskets – look on to the street and the over-grown ruins of O'Driscoll's Castle opposite. Over a substantial Irish break-fast, including Clonakilty black and white pudding, Mrs Walsh can tell you about the infamous Sack of Baltimore in 1631, when Algerian pirates came into the harbour, killed two people, and took more than a hundred locals back to North Africa as slaves. On rough nights, you might find sailors coming in for a shower and a bed on dry land; Kieron serves a terrific plate of fresh haddock or whiting, more or less straight off the pier, with chips and salad.

~

NEARBY Skibbereen; Mizen Head; Bantry; Cork.
LOCATION in village centre; parking on street
MEALS breakfast, lunch in season, dinner
PRICE IR£
ROOMS 5; 2 double, 2 twin,1 family (7 rooms next door); hairdrier on request
FACILITIES restaurant, sun terrace, beer garden
CREDIT CARDS MC, V **CHILDREN** welcome
DISABLED not possible **PETS** accepted in kennels by arrangement
CLOSED Christmas week
PROPRIETOR Kieron Walsh

IRISH REPUBLIC

BANTRY, CO. CORK

BANTRY HOUSE

~ HERITAGE HOUSE WITH GUEST ACCOMMODATION ~

Bantry, Co. Cork
TEL (027) 50047 **FAX** (027) 50795

IN A SPECTACULAR SETTING on a hillside overlooking Bantry Bay, this is one of the most beautiful houses in Ireland. It is filled with treasures brought home in the19th century by the 2nd Earl of Bantry from his European travels: a fireplace believed to have come from the Petit Trianon; a tapestry made for Marie Antoinette. He also set out a lovely formal Italian garden and a 'staircase to the sky', a flight of steps that, from the top, gives a view of the sea over the roof of the house. The current owner, Egerton Shelswell-White, was farming in Alabama when he inherited the house (it has belonged to his family since 1739) on his mother's death. It had been sadly neglected and there was a great deal of restoration work to be done. Guests stay in comfortable and snug quarters in a specially-adapted wing of the house; some rooms have sea views, others overlook the Italian garden and stone steps and terracing. Bedrooms have family furniture and bathrooms have lashings of hot water. You are given a key to the front door so you are free to walk in the gardens in the middle of the night and look at the stars over Bantry Bay. There's a billiard-room with drinks tray and a little sitting-room with a fire. Mr Shelswell-White, a music lover, waits at table and is a charming host. A tour of the house comes after breakfast.

NEARBY Bantry; Ring of Kerry; Killarney; Cork.
LOCATION in grounds overlooking Bantry Bay (main entrance in Bantry Town); with car parking
MEALS breakfast, lunch (tea-room), dinner
PRICE IR££
ROOMS 8; 5 double, 2 twin, 1 family, all with bath; all rooms have phone, hairdrier
FACILITIES sitting-room, dining-room, billiard-room, tea-room, shop, garden; tennis
CREDIT CARDS AE, MC, V **CHILDREN** welcome
DISABLED not suitable **PETS** not accepted **CLOSED** Nov to early Mar
PROPRIETORS Egerton and Brigitte Shelswell-White

IRISH REPUBLIC

BUTLERSTOWN, CO. CORK

BUTLERSTOWN HOUSE
~ COUNTRY HOUSE ~

Butlerstown, Bandon, Co. Cork
TEL & FAX (023) 40137
MOBILE (087) 2203672

L IS JONES AND ROGER OWEN are an obviously happy couple who appear to be over the moon with their escape from South Wales to the lovely light and landscape of West Cork, and the elegant spaces of this delightful Georgian house. Their pleasure is infectious and gives the place a special warmth. The airy rooms are filled with fine antiques – Roger is, usefully, a furniture restorer as well as 'butler' – and classic colours enhance the simple lines and architectural details of the house. A smart navy-blue front door leads into the hall with bifurcated staircase; ornate plasterwork in the house takes the shape of scallop shells, flowers, grapes, vine leaves and ribbon tied into bows. Lis's bathrooms are a treat: she likes brass taps, heated towel rails, blue-and-white striped tiles. There's a four-poster in one room and twin French mahogany beds in another. The drawing-room has a hi-fi and view of the bluebell wood where badgers roam at night; the dining-room has a long, polished table and Spode on a Monmouth dresser. Lis's breakfasts have a Celtic flavour with cockles and laver bread; there's local milk, butter, and free-range eggs, as well as smoked salmon and haddock. Some of the best things about living in Butlerstown House, say Roger and Lis, are the fresh air and the stars in the West Cork night sky.

NEARBY Kinsale; Clonakilty; Bandon; Cork.
LOCATION in 10-acre grounds; with car parking
MEALS breakfast, dinner on request for house parties only
PRICE IR££
ROOMS 4; 2 double, 2 twin, 2 with bath, 2 with shower; all rooms have hairdrier; TV on request
FACILITIES sitting-room, dining-room, garden, terrace
CREDIT CARDS MC, V **CHILDREN** accepted over 12 **DISABLED** not possible
PETS accepted by arrangement **CLOSED** Christmas to early Feb
PROPRIETORS Elisabeth Jones and Roger Owen

IRISH REPUBLIC

CASHEL, CO. TIPPERARY

CASHEL PALACE HOTEL

~ CONVERTED BISHOP'S PALACE ~

Main Street, Cashel, Co. Tipperary
TEL (062) 62707 **FAX** (062) 61521
E-MAIL reception@cashel-palace.ie

CHARM AND GRACE oozes out of every pore of this exquisite 18thC former archbishop's palace in the historic market town of Cashel, with its famous and dramatic Rock, one of Ireland's most visited sites. The story is that the Devil, in a hurry to fly on his way, bit a chunk out of the Slieve Bloom Mountains and dropped it here. From right outside the hotel drawing-room you may follow the Bishop's Walk, which leads you through the delightful garden and a grassy meadow to the Rock and its cluster of grey ruins. In the garden are two mulberry trees planted in 1702 for the coronation of Queen Anne, and the descendants of the original hops planted by one of the Guinness family in the mid-18th century (there's plenty of the 'black', velvety stuff in the Guinness Bar, with flagged cellar floor and terracotta walls). We don't have enough room to sing all the praises of this jewel in the heart of racing country that used to be owned by trainer Vincent O'Brien; breakfast is served in the pine-panelled room named after him. There are four-poster beds, fine antiques and pictures, and spacious bathrooms – with towelling gowns – and a magnificent early-Georgian red pine staircase in the entrance hall with 'barley sugar' banisters. You have the choice of two restaurants and there are ten new bedrooms in the old mews and stables. Book early.

~

NEARBY Rock of Cashel; Holycross Abbey; Clonmel.
LOCATION in gardens, set back off road in town centre; with car parking
MEALS breakfast, lunch, dinner
PRICE IR££-£££
ROOMS 23 (13 in house, 10 in mews); 12 double, 7 twin, 4 single, all with bath; all rooms have phone, TV, hairdrier
FACILITIES sitting-room, 2 dining-rooms, lift, garden, terrace
CREDIT CARDS AE, DC, MC, V **CHILDREN** welcome
DISABLED access possible **PETS** not accepted **CLOSED** 24-27 Dec
PROPRIETORS Pat and Susan Murphy

IRISH REPUBLIC

CASTLEGREGORY, CO. KERRY

THE SHORES COUNTRY HOUSE

~ COUNTRY GUEST-HOUSE ~

Cappatigue, Castlegregory, Co. Kerry
TEL & FAX (066) 713 9196
E-MAIL theshores@tinet.ie

WE HEARD GLOWING REPORTS of The Shores – on the north side of the Dingle Peninsula – on our travels, and of farmer's wife Annette O'Mahony's passion for looking after guests. She has recently more or less rebuilt her house to add on three extra rooms so that she can get her hands on some more people to cosset. The setting for the house is fabulous: just over the road in front is the 26-mile long sandy Brandon Bay beach; in five minutes, you can be in the sea. Towering up behind is Mount Brandon, the second highest mountain in Ireland. All rooms have sea views. One has its own balcony; there's a long balcony, too, for general use. And there's a library. Annette takes, as she says, "exceptional pride" in the interior decorating of the house, and there are all kinds of charming details in her rooms, such as writing desks, porcelain dolls, Laura Ashley papers and fabrics, cream and white bedlinen. Her style could loosely be described as Victorian. In her new cherry-wood kitchen she makes porter cake to accompany a welcome cup of tea on arrival, scrambles eggs and pours maple syrup over waffles for breakfast. Milk is from the farm. For dinner, there might well be beef raised on O'Mahony pastures, fresh salmon, prawns in garlic butter. Flasks of coffee and packed lunches hold you over through the day.

~

NEARBY Tralee; Dingle; Killarney; golf at Ballybunion.
LOCATION 1 mile (1.5 km) W of Stradbally on Connor Pass; with car parking
MEALS breakfast, packed lunch, dinner
PRICE IR£
ROOMS 6; 3 double, 2 twin, 1 triple, 3 with bath, 3 with shower; all rooms have hone, TV, hairdrier
FACILITIES sitting-room, garden
CREDIT CARDS AE, DC, MC, V
CHILDREN welcome **DISABLED** ground-floor room available **PETS** not accepted
CLOSED Dec-Feb **PROPRIETOR** Annette O'Mahony

I R I S H   R E P U B L I C

CLIFDEN, CO. GALWAY

ROCK GLEN COUNTRY HOUSE HOTEL

~ COUNTRY HOTEL ~

Clifden, Co. Galway
TEL (095) 21035 **FAX** (095) 21737
E-MAIL rockglen@iol.ie

WITH CLEMATIS AND VIRGINIA CREEPER around the front door, Rock Glen is a proud winner of an award for the Most Romantic Hotel in Ireland and what we found was full of charm. The setting of this former shooting lodge, built in 1815, is glorious: in front of the hotel, a path through a meadow of long grass, wild flowers and yellow iris, leads to the shoreline. A yacht bobs about at anchor in the little bay. In the evenings, Connemara ponies and cattle come down to the water's edge. Rising up behind the hotel are the Twelve Pins Mountains. With miles of sandy beaches nearby and rugged countryside criss-crossed with drystone walls, it's a lovely place to walk, or simply to sit and quietly enjoy watching the ebb and flow of the tide. Hosts John and Evangeline Roche (who was born in Clifden) are veterans who have thought of everything: a glassed-in extension to the bar has sofas in which to install yourself comfortably for the long view; turf fires; soft candlelight in the dining-room. They have taken the unusual step of reducing the number of bedrooms, to improve space and comfort for guests. Some rooms have balconies. The Roches' daughter, Siobhan, has come home to take over the management of this inviting, cosy place.

~

NEARBY Clifden; Connemara National Park; Kylemore Abbey.
LOCATION in own grounds by the sea, 1.5 miles (2 km) S of Clifden on the N59 to Galway; with car parking
MEALS breakfast, bar lunch, dinner
PRICE IR££
ROOMS 26; 23 double and twin, 3 family, all with bath or shower; all rooms have phone, TV, hairdrier
FACILITIES dining-room, sitting-room, TV-room, snooker, garden; croquet, putting, tennis **CREDIT CARDS** AE, DC, MC, V
CHILDREN welcome **DISABLED** ground-floor rooms available **PETS** not accepted
CLOSED mid-Jan to mid-Mar
PROPRIETORS John and Evangeline Roche

IRISH REPUBLIC

SEVEN NORTH MALL

~ TOWNHOUSE BED-AND-BREAKFAST ~

7 North Mall, Cork, Co. Cork
TEL (021) 397191 **FAX** (021) 300811
E-MAIL sevennorthmall@tinet.ie

ALTHOUGH THE LOCATION – in the centre of Cork – might seem hard to find, the one-way system through the city leads, magically, to North Mall, a row of elegant townhouses in a leafy terrace overlooking the River Lee. No. 7 – a tall, mid-18thC listed house – is charming, and perfectly placed for walking to restaurants, art galleries, theatres and the wealth of other attractions this lively city has to offer. (A useful map is provided.) Another major asset is secure parking in the private courtyard through the archway. There is no sign outside the house to spoil the gracious face it presents to the world. The Hegartys found it in a derelict state and have taken great care in the restoration: any original feature that could be kept has been. Angela Hegarty, whose hand is everywhere, likes proper bathrooms with deep baths, windows and fresh air, blankets on beds, wainscotting, stripped wood floors and attention to detail. She squeezes the oranges for fresh juice at breakfast, grinds the Java coffee beans, serves tea in teapots, and comes to the table herself to take orders. Scrambled eggs are cooked precisely as you would like them and are beautifully presented on plates from the East Cork pottery of Stephen Pearce. It is advisable to book ahead in order to avoid disappointment. Not surprisingly, this place has a cult following.

~

NEARBY city centre; university; Cork airport; Cork ferry terminal.
LOCATION riverside townhouse; with car parking
MEALS breakfast
PRICE IR£
ROOMS 7; 5 double, 1 twin, 1 single, 6 with bath, 1 with shower; all rooms have phone, TV, hairdrier
FACILITIES sitting-room, terrace **CREDIT CARDS** MC, V
CHILDREN welcome over 12 **DISABLED** one room possible
PETS not accepted **CLOSED** mid-Dec to early Jan
PROPRIETORS Angela Hegarty

IRISH REPUBLIC

DOYLE'S SEAFOOD RESTAURANT
~ RESTAURANT-WITH-ROOMS ~

John Street, Dingle, Co. Kerry
TEL (066) 51174 **FAX** (066) 51816

"MOST ATTRACTIVE AND UNEXPECTED," says one of our most experienced inspectors. "A charming homey feeling – they give you your own door key." It is in fact a delightful, small hotel in the middle of a quaint fishing village on the Dingle Peninsula. The visitors' book perches on an antique writing-desk in the elegant sitting-room; it drips with superlatives, and rightly so.

Sean and Charlotte Cluskey have recently taken over from the Doyles, who originally gave their name to the place over two decades ago when they moved to this wild and lovely corner of Kerry. Eight spacious bedrooms and a sitting-room were added next door to the restaurant when the neighbouring house came on the market. The bedrooms are all beautifully decorated: the four back rooms have balconies looking over the tiny garden, and the two downstairs rooms (suitable for disabled guests) open on to it. Fresh flowers and potted plants abound throughout.

The restaurant is as popular and cosmopolitan as ever, and it is easy to see why. The menu is mainly, but not exclusively, fishy, and changes with the seasons. By all accounts the food really is superb, and pretty good value, too. We welcome more reports.

~

NEARBY Dingle Peninsula; Ring of Kerry; beaches; historical sites.
LOCATION just off main street; parking on street
MEALS breakfast, lunch, dinner
PRICE IR££
ROOMS 8 double with bath; all rooms have phone, TV, hairdrier
FACILITIES sitting-room, dining-room, garden
CREDIT CARDS DC, MC, V
CHILDREN welcome
DISABLED 2 ground-floor bedrooms
PETS not accepted **CLOSED** mid-Nov to mid-Mar
PROPRIETORS Sean and Charlotte Cluskey

IRISH REPUBLIC

TRINITY LODGE

∾ TOWN GUEST-HOUSE ∾

12 South Frederick Street, Dublin 2
TEL (01) 679 5044/5184 **FAX** (01) 679 5223
E-MAIL trinitylodge@tinet.ie

OWNER PETER MURPHY OPENED this three-storey Georgian house in the heart of Dublin just off Nassau Street opposite Trinity College – in 1997 as an elegant, little guest-house that would not have any of the things he hates about hotels. So, guests are given individual attention from the moment they step in through the blue front door and he places a candle in each room to give a special romantic glow to evenings. This is a handsome, listed building and in order to keep its character and symmetry, Peter chose not to put in a lift, or carve chunks out of rooms for bathrooms. But, he's got almost everything else in the way of comfort and convenience, such as air-conditioning, trouser presses and personal safes. Colours are appropriately Georgian, green, deep red, yellow. There's a little sitting area in the entrance hall, with a window looking on to the street and some comfortable armchairs. Pictures in the house are by the Dublin artist, Graham Knuttel, who lives next door and whose work is very popular with Hollywood stars (he has a commission to paint a portrait for Robert de Niro). They are in bold bright colours and, as one of the staff observes, "have very suspicious-looking people in them, who don't want to look directly at you". You can walk easily to all the local sights from here.

∾

NEARBY National Art Gallery; Temple Bar; Dublin Castle; the Liffey.
LOCATION a short walk from Trinity College; with limited car parking (with charge; booking essential)
MEALS breakfast
PRICE IR££
ROOMS 13; 2 double, 2 single, 6 family (with twin beds), 3 suites with sitting and kitchen area, all with shower; all rooms have phone, TV, air-conditioning, hairdrier, safe
FACILITIES sitting-room
CREDIT CARDS AE, MC, V **CHILDREN** welcome **DISABLED** not possible **PETS** not accepted
CLOSED never **PROPRIETOR** Peter Murphy

IRISH REPUBLIC

GLIN, CO. LIMERICK

GLIN CASTLE
~ HERITAGE HOUSE ~

Glin, Co. Limerick
TEL (068) 34173/34112 **FAX** (068) 34364
E-MAIL knight@iol.ie

ONE OF THE OUTSTANDING private houses of the world, this is the home of the 29th Knight of Glin, who represents Christie's in Ireland, and his wife who bears the charming title of Madam FitzGerald. On the banks of the Shannon, it is dreamy and beautiful, in pale stone and with castellations. As might be imagined with a title that goes back to the 14th century it is filled with family history and lovely family things. Even when the Knight is at the castle, guests have the run of the house and garden. Friendly young staff are endlessly attentive. Glin exudes grace, and manages to be both grand and intimate at the same time. The entrance hall, which may have been used as a ballroom in the past, has Corinthian pillars and a plaster ceiling apparently untouched since the 1780s. In the reception rooms is a unique collection of Irish 18thC mahogany furniture. To go to bed, you take the flying staircase – the only one of its kind in Ireland – to the first floor. Some rooms here have four-poster beds, and all have fabulous bathrooms.

You may tag along behind one of the guided parties to learn all about the place. A cosy little private sitting-room for guests has deep pink sofas round the fire, family photographs and after-dinner coffee. Be sure to make time for a walk to the walled garden.

~

NEARBY Limerick; golf at Ballybunion; Ring of Kerry.
LOCATION on 400-acre estate, on river's edge; with car parking
MEALS breakfast, dinner; room service
PRICE IR£££
ROOMS 15; 14 double, 1 twin, 2 with dressing-rooms, all with bath; all rooms have phone, TV, hairdrier
FACILITIES sitting-room, dining-room, garden; tennis
CREDIT CARDS AE, DC, MC, V **CHILDREN** accepted **DISABLED** not suitable
PETS kennels provided **CLOSED** end Nov to Feb
PROPRIETORS Desmond and Olda FitzGerald

IRISH REPUBLIC

GOREY, CO. WEXFORD

MARLFIELD HOUSE
~ COUNTRY HOUSE HOTEL ~

Gorey, Co. Wexford
TEL (055) 21124 **FAX** (055) 21572
E-MAIL info@marlfieldhouse.ie **WEBSITE** www.marlfieldhouse.ie

A SIGN IN THE DRIVE of this stunning Regency house once owned by the Earls of Courtown and now a Relais & Châteaux hotel (one of the best in Ireland), reads: 'Drive carefully, pheasants crossing'. Not only is this a preserve of all good things for people, but it is pretty comfortable for animals, too. There's a little dog basket for a terrier beside the 18thC marble fireplace in the semi-circular architect-designed hall. Mary Bowe's peacocks, bantams, ducks and geese are cherished and indulged almost as much as her guests. This is a gorgeous, overblown place, a feast for the eyes because of Mary's passion for interior decoration. Her taste is reflected in Waterford crystal chandeliers, little French chairs, gilded taps and a domed conservatory dining-room, with *trompe l'oeil* and trellis. Garlanded with awards – Hostess of the Year, Wine List of the Year, Best Breakfast, One of the World's Most Enchanting Hideaways – the hotel has a tradition of warm hospitality and the Bowes' daughter, Margaret, is now very much at the helm. Bedrooms are sumptuous and charming. Jewels in the crown are the State Rooms, decorated with rich fabrics and fine antique furniture: the French Room, with marble bathroom, overlooks the lake; the Print Room has views of the rose garden. Outstanding food.

~

NEARBY Waterford; Kilkenny; Wexford; Rosslare; beaches.
LOCATION in 35-acre gardens and woodland, 1 mile (1.5 km) out of Gorey on Wexford road; with car parking
MEALS breakfast, lunch, dinner
PRICE IR£££
ROOMS 20; 18 double and twin, 2 single, all with bath; all rooms have phone, TV, airdrier
FACILITIES sitting-room, bar, dining-room, sauna, garden, terraces; tennis, croquet
CREDIT CARDS AE, DC, MC, V **CHILDREN** welcome; no under-10s in dining-room
DISABLED access possible
PETS welcome **CLOSED** mid-Dec to mid-Jan **PROPRIETORS** Bowe family

I R I S H   R E P U B L I C

INNISHANNON, Co. CORK

INNISHANNON HOUSE

~ COUNTRY HOTEL ~

Innishannon, Co. Cork
TEL (021) 775121 **FAX** (021) 775609

CONAL O'SULLIVAN returned to his Irish roots in 1989 when he and his wife Vera moved to this attractive, imposing 18thC house on the banks of the Bandon River. The couple are seasoned hoteliers and travellers, having run hotels all over the world (their last stop the Caribbean) but they are particularly excited at this latest challenge.

The hotel has already become a welcoming haven for visitors, its comfortable, attractive rooms hung with the O'Sullivans' extensive collection of modern art (including two possible Gauguins in the dining-room). Vera has a great eye for interior design, and has decorated all the bedrooms with infinite care and flair – No. 16 is a cosy attic room with an antique bedspread, No. 14 a fascinating circular room with small round windows and a huge curtained bed. Irish hero, Michael Collins' bath is the latest addition to the antiques around the hotel – to join that of Winston Churchill. The enormous suite has a Victorian bathroom.

The O'Sullivans' son, Pearse, does the cooking, with emphasis on seafood, lobster and seasonal produce. Dinner in the lovely pink dining-room is a gastronomic delight. Pre-dinner drinks are served outside in summer, or in the airy lounge, or cosy bar – full of photos of Conal's car rallying days. Innishannon is not the last word in seclusion or intimacy there are facilities for conferences and wedding receptions.

~

NEARBY Kinsale; Cork.
LOCATION on banks of river, near village; with car parking
MEALS breakfast, lunch, dinner
PRICE IR££-£££
ROOMS 13; 7double, 6 twin, all with bath and shower; all rooms have phone, TV, hairdrier **FACILITIES** dining-room, sitting-room, bar, garden, terrace; fishing, boating **CREDIT CARDS** AE, DC, MC, V **CHILDREN** welcome **DISABLED** ground-floor suite available **PETS** accepted in bedrooms **CLOSED** mid-Jan to mid-Mar
PROPRIETORS Conal and Vera O'Sullivan

IRISH REPUBLIC

KANTURK, CO. CORK

ASSOLAS COUNTRY HOUSE

~ COUNTRY HOUSE ~

Kanturk, Co. Cork
TEL (029) 50015 **FAX** (029) 50795
E-MAIL assolas@tinet.ie

THIS HISTORIC, mellow country house, in a fairy-tale setting of award-winning gardens beside a slow-flowing river, has been in the Bourke family since the early years of this century. The familiar story of escalating maintenance costs and dwindling bank balances led to their taking in guests in 1966, and since then they have never looked back. Assolas is still their family home, and the business of sharing it has obviously turned out to be a pleasure. One recent visitor described her stay there as 'stunning, with wonderful, beautifully served food'.

The house was built around 1590, and had unusual circular extensions added at two corners in Queen Anne's time; beyond the expanses of lawn are mature woods, and then hills and farmland. Inside, the public rooms are richly decorated and elegantly furnished, almost entirely with antiques, and immaculately kept. The bedrooms are notably spacious and many have large luxury bathrooms – the 'circular' rooms at the corners of the house are particularly impressive. Three of the rooms are in a renovated stone building in the courtyard. The food, prepared by Hazel Bourke, is in what might be called modern Irish style – country cooking of fresh ingredients (many home-grown).

~

NEARBY Killarney; Ring of Kerry; Limerick; Blarney.
LOCATION 12 miles (19 km) W of Mallow, NE of Kanturk, signposted from N72; with ample car parking
MEALS breakfast, light or packed lunch, dinner
PRICE IR££-£££
ROOMS 9 double/family rooms with bath; all rooms have phone
FACILITIES sitting-room, dining-room, garden; tennis, croquet, fishing, boating
CREDIT CARDS AE, DC, MC, V
CHILDREN welcome **DISABLED** access fair **PETS** welcome in stables
CLOSED Nov-Apr (except by prior arrangement)
PROPRIETORS Bourke family

IRISH REPUBLIC

LEENANE, CO. GALWAY

DELPHI LODGE

~ FISHING LODGE ~

Leenane, Co. Galway
TEL (095) 42222 **FAX** (095) 42296
E-MAIL delfish@iol.ie

THE 2ND MARQUESS OF SLIGO – who had been with Byron in Greece – thought this wild place as beautiful as Delphi, and built himself a fishing lodge here in the mid-1830s. When Peter Mantle, a former financial journalist, came across the house, it was semi-derelict. Falling under the same spell, he restored it with great care and vision, and Delphi is one of the finest and foremost sporting lodges in Ireland. Fishing is its main business, but everyone is made welcome here. Peter, a lively host and raconteur, runs it like a friendly country house. On our visit, on a misty April evening, wood smoke was rising from the chimney, a new delivery of Crozes Hermitage was stacked up in the hall and Mozart was playing in the snug little library overlooking the lake. Among the guests were a couple of bankers in their Jeremy Fisher waterproofs, a novelist finishing a book, and some Americans from Philadelphia. Salmon are weighed and measured in the Rod Room, creating frissons of excitement and stories for the communal dinner table; the ghillies come in during breakfast to discuss prospects for the day ahead. Bedrooms are unfussy but pretty, with pine furniture; larger ones have lake views; bathrooms have piles of fluffy, white towels. Book well ahead. Heaven for walkers.

~

NEARBY Westport; Kylemore Abbey; Clifden; golf.
LOCATION by the lake in wooded grounds on private estate; with car parking
MEALS breakfast, lunch, dinner
PRICE IR£-££
ROOMS 12; 8 double, 4 twin, all with bath; all rooms have phone; hairdrier on request
FACILITIES drawing-room, billiard-room, library, dining-room, garden; lake
CREDIT CARDS AE, MC, V
CHILDREN welcome **DISABLED** 2 ground-floor rooms
PETS not accepted **CLOSED** mid-Dec to mid-Jan
PROPRIETORS Peter and Jane Mantle

IRISH REPUBLIC

MAYNOOTH, CO. KILDARE

MOYGLARE MANOR

~ COUNTRY HOUSE ~

Moyglare, Maynooth, Co. Kildare
TEL (01) 6286351 **FAX** (01) 6285405
E-MAIL moyglaremanor@iol.ie

THIS LOVELY 18THC stone country house in the middle of the stud farm belt is so opulent as to seem fabulously decadent. When we visited, people were having lunch by candlelight in the gorgeous deep pink, chandeliered dining-room, with draped curtains as thick as blankets, blazing fires and potted palms. A sweet aroma of roses comes in from the garden, filled with tall, dignified trees, and clouds of clematis cover the back of the house. Our inspector had never seen quite so many varieties of decorated lampshade: pleated, tasselled, fringed; or so many fabulous arrangements of flowers. It is all very Naughty Nineties, with lashings of Regency stripes, alabaster vases, and rooms crammed with ornate antique furniture, square chairs, round chairs, stuffed and buttoned chairs, and heavy gilt mirrors, put together so artfully by owner Nora Devlin to make a world of its own. It is meant to be fun – and it is. Bedrooms are large and comfortable, some with love seats, four-posters, and lashings of pink, ribbons and bows, drapes and frills. The history of the house is long and fascinating: Bridget, Countess of Tyrconnell, heard of the Flight of the Earls while walking in the garden here in 1607. The award-winning 16-page wine list is also long and fascinating; in the cellar is almost every Château Yquem since 1945.

~

NEARBY Maynooth; horses; Castletown House; National Stud.
LOCATION in countryside, 3 miles (5 km) from Maynooth; with car parking
MEALS breakfast, lunch, dinner
PRICE IR££
ROOMS 16; 14 double and twin, 2 triple, all with bath; all rooms have phone, hairdrier; TV on request
FACILITIES sitting-room/bars, dining-rooms, garden, terraces
CREDIT CARDS AE, DC, MC, V
CHILDREN accepted over 12 **DISABLED** possible **PETS** not accepted **CLOSED** 24-26 Dec
PROPRIETOR Norah Devlin

IRISH REPUBLIC

SHANAGARRY, CO. CORK

BALLYMALOE HOUSE

∼ CONVERTED FARMHOUSE ∼

Shanagarry, Midleton, Co. Cork
TEL (021) 652531 **FAX** (021) 652021

THIRTY BEDROOMS NORMALLY rules out a hotel for this guide, but we cannot resist this amiable, rambling, creeper-clad house – largely Georgian in appearance but incorporating the remains of a 14thC castle keep – set in rolling green countryside. Visitors in 1998 were 'immensely impressed' and found the staff 'as well-drilled as an army, but jolly, with abundant charm'.

The Allens, who have been farming here for over 40 years, opened as a restaurant in 1964 and started offering rooms three years later. Since then they have added more facilities and more rooms – those in the main house now outnumbered by those in extensions and converted outbuildings.

Despite quite elegant and sophisticated furnishings, the Allens have always managed to preserve intact the warmth and naturalness of a much-loved family home. But not all visitors agree: one reporter judged that Ballymaloe was becoming rather commercialized. Even that reporter, however, was impressed by the standard of food. Mrs Allen no longer takes an active role in the cooking. It is now Rory O'Connell who prepares the Classic French and Irish dishes alongside original dishes, all based on home produce and fish fresh from the local quays. (Sunday dinner is always a buffet.) Just as much care is lavished on breakfast, and the famous children's high tea.

∼

NEARBY beaches; cliff walks; fishing; golf.
LOCATION 20 miles (32 km) E of Cork, 2 miles (3 km) E of Cloyne on the Ballycotton road; with ample car parking
MEALS breakfast, lunch, dinner
PRICE IR££-£££ **ROOMS** 33 double and twin, 31 with bath, 2 with shower; all rooms have phone **FACILITIES** 3 sitting-rooms, conference/TV-room, conservatory, library; tennis, golf, swimming-pool **CREDIT CARDS** AE, DC, MC, V **CHILDREN** welcome
DISABLED access easy; some specially adapted rooms **PETS** not accepted
CLOSED Christmas **PROPRIETORS** Allen family

HOTEL NAMES

In this index, hotels are arranged in order of the most distinctive part of their name; other parts of the name are also given, except that very common prefixes, such as 'The' are omitted.

HOTEL NAMES

HOTEL NAMES

HOTEL LOCATIONS

In this index, hotels are arrangd by the name of the city, town or village they are in or near. Where a hotel is located in a very small place, it may be under a larger nearby place

HOTEL LOCATIONS

HOTEL LOCATIONS

COUNTY LOCATIONS

In this index, hotels are arranged under the the name of the county in which they are located. Hotels are organized by the name of the city, town or village they are in or near. Where a hotel is located in a very small place, it may be under a larger nearby place

COUNTY LOCATIONS

County Locations

COUNTY LOCATIONS